Sun Tzu

at

GETTYSBURG

Sun Tzu

★ ★ ★ at ★ ★ ★

GETTYSBURG

Ancient Military Wisdom in the Modern World

Bevin Alexander

W. W. NORTON & COMPANY

NEW YORK / LONDON

For information about permission to reproduce selections from this book,
write to Permissions, W. W. Norton & Company, Inc.,
500 Fifth Avenue, New York, NY 10110

For information about special discounts for bulk purchases, please contact
W. W. Norton Special Sales at specialsales@wwnorton.com or 800-233-4830

Manufacturing by RR Donnelley, Harrisonburg
Book design by Ellen Cipriano
Production manager: Devon Zahn

Library of Congress Cataloging-in-Publication Data

Alexander, Bevin.
Sun Tzu at Gettysburg : ancient military wisdom
in the modern world / Bevin Alexander. — 1st ed.
p. cm.
Includes bibliographical references and index.
ISBN 978-0-393-07813-8 (hardcover)
1. Sunzi, 6th cent. B.C. Sunzi bing fa. 2. Command of troops—Case studies.
3. Military history—Case studies. 4. Tactics—Case studies. 5. Military art and science.
I. Title.
U101.S96A44 2011
355.02—dc22
2011002189

W. W. Norton & Company, Inc.
500 Fifth Avenue, New York, N.Y. 10110
www.wwnorton.com

W. W. Norton & Company Ltd.
Castle House, 75/76 Wells Street, London W1T 3QT

1 2 3 4 5 6 7 8 9 0

CONTENTS

LIST OF MAPS

INTRODUCTION

To Avoid Strength,
Strike Weakness

We have only one masterwork on the conduct of war. It was produced 2,400 years ago by a Chinese sage named Sun Tzu. His small book, *The Art of War*, spells out universal principles that describe the nature of war, and these principles are still valid today.[1] This current volume is designed to show that commanders who unwittingly used Sun Tzu's axioms in important campaigns over the past two centuries were successful, while commanders who did not apply them suffered defeat, sometimes disastrous, war-losing calamities.

Sun Tzu's principles can be applied to any military problem, from the smallest engagement to the largest campaign. Other leaders in other times discovered a number of these principles, but only Sun Tzu put together a comprehensive summary of the essential elements that make warfare succeed. It is this unique contribution to our understanding of armed conflict that led the renowned English strategist Basil H. Liddell Hart to call Sun Tzu's book "the concentrated essence of wisdom on the conduct of war."[2]

Sun Tzu's book has influenced Oriental warfare profoundly for over two thousand years, but it became widely known in the West only in the

1970s. This occurred primarily because both France and the United States encountered guerrilla forces in Vietnam who used Sun Tzu's axioms to defeat their armies. Although the Vietnamese Communists possessed only minuscule military power, they nullified the vastly greater strength of the French and the Americans and drove them out of the country.

Until *The Art of War* became generally recognized in the West, military leaders had to rely on statements and conclusions reached by individual thinkers over the eons. Although some arrived independently at a few of the axioms articulated by Sun Tzu, none produced an all-inclusive theory of warfare. For example, the Bible (2 Samuel 5:23–25) contains an injunction to strike indirect blows against the enemy, but this axiom is buried in a vast narrative of inchoate warfare between the Jews and Philistines. Homer tells a marvelous tale of how the beauty of Helen, the abducted wife of Menelaus, launched a thousand ships against Troy, but he offers very little about how the Trojan War was fought. Herodotus and Thucydides describe fascinating histories of the ancient Greeks but give almost no details about how they won and lost their wars. Xenophon's march of the ten thousand Greeks to the sea is one of the great adventure stories of all time. Though he provides tantalizing hints of how the Greeks surmounted obstacles, like getting through enemy-infested mountains, he provides little information on the theories the Greeks employed to conduct war.

From narratives written long after they died, we can put together a few ideas about how Alexander the Great conquered the Persian Empire and how Hannibal forced Rome to "tremble in her gates." But neither great captain left any account of his theory of war. Three Byzantine treatises, Emperor Maurice's *Strategikon* of 578, Emperor Leo the Wise's *Tactica* of 900, and Nicephorus Phocas's discourse of 980, gave practical instructions on warfare that allowed the Eastern Roman Empire to endure for hundreds of years. Between the time of these ancient warriors and the present, there have been few enough pronouncements by military leaders, and no overall theory of warfare. Robert the Bruce

(1274–1329) left a "testament" urging the Scots to avoid stand-up war with the English and keep their independence by guerrilla-like war in hills and morasses. The French general Pierre-Joseph de Bourcet (1700–1780) proposed a "plan with branches," of dividing an army into several columns and marching them on separate targets—forcing the enemy to divide his strength and allowing concentration on one or more ill-defended objectives. Napoléon Bonaparte (1769–1821) produced no summary of his axioms, but his campaigns reveal that he relied on the offensive, pursued a defeated enemy, trusted on speed to gain time, and concentrated superior strength on the battlefield. The Prussian Carl von Clausewitz (1780–1831) made the important point that war is only a continuation of national policy, not an end in itself. But his emphasis on total war and bloodshed undermined his theory. If war is a continuation of policy, the *goal* is the primary purpose. In emphasizing *victory*, however, Clausewitz looked only to the end of the war, not the subsequent peace. Thomas J. "Stonewall" Jackson (1824–1863) said, "Always mislead, mystify, and surprise the enemy. . . . Never fight against heavy odds."

These examples show that, though military leaders throughout history have occasionally produced incisive thoughts about warfare, none except Sun Tzu has demonstrated an extensive understanding of war in all of its aspects. Accordingly, Sun Tzu provides us the only comprehensive, coherent guide to the way war should be conducted. We can also follow his advice to solve specific problems before we have advanced irretrievably into harm's way, such as assuring that our soldiers can be properly fed, ascertaining the size and nature of the enemy we are about to face, and learning essential facts about the terrain into which we are going to advance.

This book examines a number of decisive operations in the modern age—beginning with the battles of Saratoga in 1777 and Yorktown in

1781 that guaranteed American independence, then the pivotal battles of Waterloo in 1815 and Gettysburg in 1863, and going forward to the Korean War in 1950, when we walked blindly into a terrible, costly, unnecessary conflict with Red China. It shows how these campaigns were actually carried out, and whether the commanders followed the universal principles of *The Art of War.*

Sun Tzu's axioms can be employed in any military context in any war. His most profound principle is that "the way to avoid what is strong is to strike what is weak." He writes this same principle in a different way: as water seeks the easiest path to the sea, so armies should avoid obstacles and seek avenues of least resistance. The general should find a way to achieve his goals indirectly, not by direct confrontation.

A related Sun Tzu admonition is to "strike into vacuities," that is, to move into undefended space, and to "attack objectives the enemy must rescue." One should move *around* the enemy to cut him off from retreat or succor, or to attack some point that he cannot afford to lose. This point might be a railway line that brings supplies, an important city, or a road or a mountain that bars the enemy's line of retreat.

Napoléon Bonaparte understood the requirement for indirection quite well. In most cases, he sought to push his decisive force onto one wing or into one flank of the enemy, seeking to envelop him, drive him from his base, and in this way destroy him. This was how he opened the 1805 campaign, by swinging far to the north, then descending on the rear of the Austrian army along the Danube River. But he inexplicably failed to use this same axiom at Waterloo in 1815, and this led to his defeat. The indirect approach of isolating an enemy or forcing him to scramble to protect some vital point is in contrast to the direct assaults and headlong clashes between opposing armies that have characterized most wars and most generals throughout history.

Sun Tzu's maxims are disarming because, once pointed out, they appear to be the obvious, most sensible thing to do. But all great ideas are simple. The trick is to see them and to act on them.

The West's intense awareness of Sun Tzu came in the wake of a decision by the Chinese Communist leader Mao Zedong to assist the ruling Nationalist Party in China in resisting the aggression of Japan, which finally resulted in open war in 1937. In that year Mao published a small book entitled *Guerrilla Warfare* that was widely distributed in China at ten cents a copy. Mao's book embodied the experience of his guerrilla struggle against the Nationalists, which began in 1927 and came to a temporary halt and a united front with the Nationalists after the "long march" of a few thousand Communists from Jiangxi province in southeastern China to Yan'an in Shaanxi province in north China in 1934–1935. Mao was quick to acknowledge that Sun Tzu gave him practically all the ideas he incorporated into his methods.

Mao's book showed how the Japanese could be stymied by a similar guerrilla war. Such a war did not develop, however. The Nationalist leader Chiang Kai-shek realized that the Communists were much more skilled in this kind of combat than the Nationalists, and any successes would be credited to them. This would undermine the Nationalists and lead to Chiang's ouster. Chiang refused to institute a guerrilla campaign. When the United States came into the war in December 1941, he saw that all he had to do was wait, and the United States would win the war for him.

Mao's book thus failed in its original intent. But it was the first systematic analysis of guerrilla warfare ever written, and it became the basic textbook for waging revolutionary and anticolonial struggles throughout the globe after the end of World War II. Its application was especially evident in the Communist insurgency against the French and later the Americans in Vietnam under Ho Chi Minh and his principal general, Vo Nyugen Giap. By using Mao's methods, the Communists hobbled both nations' modern armies. Vietnam was overwhelming proof that the principles of Sun Tzu put forward in Mao's book were valid.

The primary aim of Mao's system was to direct small groups of soldiers to make modest but frequent attacks against enemy towns, bases, depots, and lines of supply and communication, and then to disappear quickly like "fishes" into the "water" of the surrounding population. The goal was to obligate the enemy to disperse his forces widely to protect his vital points. Even guarded, these positions remained vulnerable, because the enemy could not predict which position Mao's forces would attack next. The effect was to render the enemy insecure and passive, and therefore demoralize him and nullify his strength.

Mao's indebtedness to Sun Tzu was recognized by Samuel B. Griffith, a Marine Corps captain who translated Mao's work into English in 1940. This original translation received little attention, but in 1961 Griffith, a retired brigadier general at the time, reissued the volume with a comprehensive introduction. Two years later he published a highly praised translation of *The Art of War*.[3] These books set in motion a host of new translations of and commentaries on Sun Tzu's work.

Although Sun Tzu is justifiably famous for teaching us how to conduct war, his most important admonition is to urge people to avoid war. "Warfare is the greatest affair of state," he writes, "the basis of life and death, the way to survival or extinction." If wars are unavoidable, he urges nations to conduct swift campaigns and to undertake short conflicts with as little damage as possible. In all history, he emphasizes, "there is no instance of a country having benefited from prolonged warfare."

Sun Tzu

at

GETTYSBURG

O N E

Saratoga, 1777: The Battle That
Transformed the World

By 1775, much had changed in America and in Britain since the first English settlers landed at Jamestown in Virginia in 1607 and at Plymouth in Massachusetts in 1620. These little perch sites on the edge of an unknown continent had grown into thirteen highly prosperous, highly assertive colonies boasting two and a half million people, one-third the population of Great Britain. Britain itself had grown immensely. In 1707 Scotland had joined England in the United Kingdom. In the Seven Years' War of 1756–1763 it had ousted France from Canada and largely from India and had become the earth's major imperial power. Driven by the invention of an efficient steam engine in 1769 and by tools that mechanized cloth making and iron production, Britain was entering the Industrial Revolution and had become the leading manufacturing country in the world.

In 1775, therefore, neither the tremendously successful British establishment nor the comparably successful colonies were willing to compromise on a fundamental difference between them: who had the right to rule? Parliament had gained supremacy in the Glorious Revolution of 1688 and claimed the authority to decide all matters, including taxation. The colonies elected no members of Parliament and asserted that taxation without representation was tyranny. British leaders answered that Britain had created the colonies, and therefore the colonists had no claim to parliamentary seats. The colonists disputed this in principle, but, far more important, they were moving away from any sense of being Britons at all.

As the historian Frederick Jackson Turner wrote, with every step of the colonists away from the coast, they became increasingly aware of the limitless frontier before them, and they became less and less European and "more and more American."[1] A sense of democracy and equality spread from the earliest days of the colonies. The idea of liberty and freedom long predated Thomas Jefferson and the Declaration of Independence.

The essential thrust of the American experience, therefore, was toward a separate American existence. The only chance Britain had to stop this movement was by offering the Americans complete and total equality. The great Scottish philosopher Adam Smith proposed just such a course in his classic work, *The Wealth of Nations*.[2] But even this might not have been enough, and Britain's leaders were unwilling to make any real concessions. They were drawn almost entirely from the aristocratic class, and they saw any grant of rights to the Americans as a loss of privilege and wealth to themselves.

Consequently, British leaders responded with force to the armed resistance of the colonists at Lexington, Concord, and Bunker Hill in Massachusetts in 1775. They rejected any compromise. The result was revolt and, on July 4, 1776, the proclamation of independence in Philadelphia.

The British leaders should not have resorted to war until they had exhausted all other possibilities, or until they had come up with a practical plan to gain victory. That is the first and most fundamental axiom of Sun Tzu.[3] They did neither.

Most astonishingly, British leaders largely disregarded their most powerful weapon, the Royal Navy. They might have won the war with few casualties if they had occupied or blockaded all the major American ports and protected their conquests with the Royal Navy. The Americans depended on exports, mostly agricultural or forest based, and on imports of manufactured goods. Closing the ports might in time have led to a compromise. Such a policy would have been consistent with a fundamental Sun Tzu axiom: that one should advance into the enemy's vacuities, that is, into undefended or indefensible places.[4] The Americans could not have kept any of their ports open against British sea power, as was demonstrated by the ease with which the British seized and held on to New York.[5]

A blockade strategy would have nullified the colonies' great strength—their vast extent. It would also have nullified the Americans' ability to wear down the British army by attrition. There would have been no need for land campaigns. British soldiers would have been required to fortify and garrison some but not all of the major ports. Behind such prepared fortifications, backed by Royal Navy guns, the British would have been invincible.[6]

This was precisely the strategy General Winfield Scott advocated in 1861 to end the American Civil War. Scott told President Abraham Lincoln the North should capture New Orleans, seal up the other Southern ports, and form a large army along with armored gunboats to move down the Mississippi River and cut off the western Southern states. Newspapers named it the "Anaconda Plan," since it called for strangling the South the way an anaconda snake strangles its victims. Scott then wanted to do nothing more, simply hold on. With its ports closed and communication with the rest of the world cut off, the rebellion, Scott said, would die for lack of resources. But Lincoln rejected this plan. He wanted to crush the rebels by military force. Even so, Lincoln adopted a sea blockade and seizure of the Mississippi, devoting a substantial part of the North's resources to these purposes.

The American expert on sea power, Alfred Thayer Mahan, specifically notes the similarity of the Anaconda Plan to Britain's opportunity to seal off the colonies.[7]

The British also could have used the Royal Navy to isolate the colonies and to subdue them one region at a time. Mahan writes that the colonies were so intersected with estuaries, lakes, and navigable rivers that they "were practically reduced to the condition of islands, so far as mutual support went." Chesapeake Bay and the rivers feeding it, for example, offered easy avenues by which boats and ships could penetrate deep into the interior of Virginia, Maryland, and Pennsylvania and cut off huge sections of the country. New England especially could have been sealed off from the other colonies by vessels on the Hudson River and on Lakes George and Champlain.[8]

Sun Tzu admonishes leaders to avoid all campaigns not based on detailed analysis of the options available.[9] The failure to exploit the Royal Navy is astounding, given the English resolve for more than a century prior to the American Revolution to dominate the oceans. It demonstrates that a nation must do more than produce the world's biggest fleet or the most powerful army. Far more important, it must find leaders who know how to use these instruments.

This did not happen. British leaders resolved to win, not by making brilliant strategic moves to close the ports or to isolate regions, but by beating down resistance by main force. Since the colonies extended for a thousand miles north and south and for an average of 150 miles inland, this strategy was extremely problematical, for the British could rule only the ground on which their soldiers stood. There was no possibility of creating an army large enough to dominate all colonial territory.

In the actual conduct of the war, the British leaders largely disregarded the terrain of North America and the experience gained from battles that had been fought in America in years past. They believed they could transfer European battle theories to America with little or no alteration. They brought to America the same highly disciplined mercenary forces that made up European armies. In Europe these armies were trained to withstand repeated musket volleys at short range. When one side became weakened and disorganized by this fire, the issue was generally settled by a bayonet charge directly at the vulnerable enemy force. This usually caused the attacked force to collapse in chaos.

Belief in the bayonet charge was an article of faith in the British army. British officers saw that Americans were unsuited to the extreme discipline that made it possible for mercenaries to endure musket volleys before cracking. Americans were notoriously ill disciplined and individualistic. When stand-up fights developed, Americans scattered as soon as the British launched a bayonet charge.

To the British, this was a fatal flaw, a guarantee that they could win any major collision. They disdained the usual American practice of remaining behind trees or stone fences and picking off British soldiers with their muskets or longer-ranged rifles. They thought little of American reliance on sharpshooters, hastily built field fortifications, surprise sweeps on the enemy flanks and rear, and harassment of enemy vanguards and rear guards.

But the American system of fighting was far more effective than the European system. Unlike the generally open pastoral landscapes of Europe where there was little cover, the terrain in America was largely deep forest with only occasional stretches of cleared ground. There were many places to hide. Americans much preferred cover to the extremely costly European practice of standing in the open and exchanging fire with enemy soldiers also in the open.

Americans had learned much in their collisions with the Indians on the frontier. Indians never attacked settlers head-on. They always tried to sneak up on their enemy, to ambush him, to cut off his retreat, to attack swiftly—and to get away just as swiftly. Americans had been deeply influenced by British General Edward Braddock's disastrous expedition to seize the French bastion of Fort Duquesne (present-day Pittsburgh) in western Pennsylvania in 1755. Indians had ambushed Braddock's force of 2,000 men in the tangled forests along the Monongahela River, killing or wounding 863, with Braddock himself dying.

Americans adapted naturally to this pattern of warfare, and this is how they fought the first engagements of the Revolution, at Lexington and Concord and Bunker Hill. But British leaders refused to profit by the experience of General Braddock, and they refused to examine American methods objectively. Instead, they saw these methods as evidence of weakness. Confidence grew that a British army could overcome any confrontation by a bayonet charge. Once dispersed, so the theory went, the rebels were certain to return meekly to the rule of the mother country.[10]

This attitude violated a basic axiom of Sun Tzu: "One who knows the enemy and knows himself will not be endangered in a hundred engagements. One who does not know the enemy but knows himself will sometimes be victorious, sometimes meet with defeat."[11] British officers knew themselves, but they did not know the American enemy. They never adapted to the American way of war, and their occasional battlefield successes never achieved a resolution of the conflict.

In the fall of 1776, General John Burgoyne returned to England after service in America with an imaginative new plan to end the rebellion. Burgoyne proposed that an army of around 8,000 British regulars and German mercenaries, plus Indians and a few Canadians, be assembled at Montreal and drive southward along Lakes Champlain and George and then along the Hudson River to Albany, New York. This was largely unsettled, near-frontier country. But Burgoyne thought the effort was worth the danger, because he called for an army under General Sir William Howe to move up the Hudson from New York City and meet him at Albany. Howe commanded a large force of British regulars and German mercenaries who had seized New York City in July–September 1776 and were using the port as the main British base in America.

Burgoyne's plan was to isolate New England, which then could be conquered at leisure. Burgoyne believed that the surrender of New England would so demoralize the colonies to the south that they would give up as well.[12]

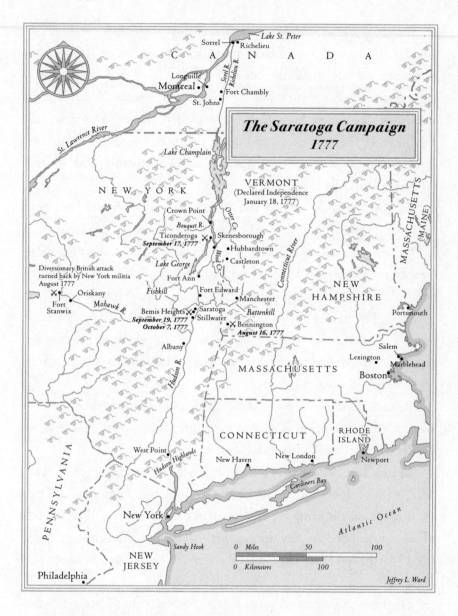

Burgoyne's plan would entail much greater risk than a navy campaign with the identical objective. This was because Burgoyne's supply line would be vulnerable along most of its length. American militiamen could emerge from the wilderness and attack it at many places. Naval vessels, on the other hand, could carry most of their supplies on board, and they could replenish them as needed from other vessels.

. Burgoyne's plan violated one of the most important teachings of Sun Tzu: do not advance into territory where one can be attacked but where one cannot attack the enemy.[13] The forested and largely unsettled terrain on Burgoyne's line of march was eminently suitable for ambushes. The longer his supply line extended, the greater was its vulnerability. If the Americans could cut this line, his soldiers would be isolated, unless General Howe was able to rescue them quickly. If not, Burgoyne would be forced to surrender.

Burgoyne and the rest of the British leadership should have been aware of precisely such a peril, drawn from fairly recent history. In 1708 the Swedish king, Charles XII, led his unsupported army to Poltava, far into southern Russia on a tributary to the Dnieper River. At Poltava, the Swedish army was unable to advance and unable to retreat, its supply line having been severed and the men left starving. There, in June 1709, Peter the Great's Russian army overwhelmed the Swedes, eliminated Sweden as a major power, and turned Russia into the strongest country in eastern Europe.[14]

Poltava should have warned the British not to undertake a similar unsupported expedition deep into the interior of frontier America. But the British disregarded the danger entirely.

In London, Burgoyne presented his idea to Lord George Germain, head of the colonial office, which directed the war. Germain had been cashiered from the army for cowardice in the Seven Years' War and was wholly unqualified to run the colonial office. But the prime minister, Lord North, and King George III disregarded his failures and kept him in office.

Germain soon demonstrated that he had no strategic sense whatsoever and virtually no idea of how to conduct a war. Germain snubbed Burgoyne and took no action on his proposal, but Burgoyne was able to get King George to read the plan. The king liked it and directed Germain to carry it out.

Germain waited until March 26, 1777, to inform Sir Guy Carlton, governor-general of Canada, of the plan's adoption, and gave few details. Howe received a copy of Germain's letter to Carlton but no instructions as to what was expected of him. Germain wrote Howe eight letters between March 3 and April 19, 1777, but he never once referred to the Burgoyne expedition or in what manner Howe was supposed to cooperate.[15] The entire British strategy depended on the union of the two armies at Albany, yet Germain did not spell this out to the commander of one of these armies.

Meanwhile, Howe was developing a completely contradictory plan. He wanted to capture the American capital, Philadelphia. He was convinced the rebellion would evaporate once the site of the Continental Congress was seized. Howe wrote Germain and Carlton to this effect on April 2, 1777. Yet Philadelphia was the main town of only one of the thirteen colonies. America, unlike France and Austria, was not a nation-state. Capture of Philadelphia would little affect the other colonies' administrative, political, and economic structures.

In the letter to Carlton, Howe said he would probably be in Pennsylvania about the time Burgoyne's army approached Albany, and he would have too much on his hands to undertake a movement up the Hudson River. Howe's only hint of some possible help was a vague comment that there might be "a diversion occasionally upon Hudson's River."

Howe repeated in his letter to Germain his repudiation of Burgoyne's campaign. Now an almost inconceivable event occurred: Germain replied on May 18 approving Howe's scheme to capture Philadelphia, a task Howe explained that he intended to accomplish by advancing on the sea, not marching overland.

Demonstrating a complete ignorance of the huge expanse of America, Germain went on to say that whatever Howe elected to do, Germain assumed that "it will be executed in time for you to cooperate with the army ordered to proceed from Canada."[16] He should have known—or found out—that there was not the slightest possibility that Howe could sail from New York, capture Philadelphia, and still have time to rendezvous with Burgoyne.

Germain's plain duty was to veto Howe's plan and order him to assist Burgoyne. His failure to do this was the single greatest reason why Britain lost the American War of Independence. It was a monstrous failure of leadership, and it violated a basic axiom of Sun Tzu: nations should plan their campaigns with extreme care and then follow them with great fidelity. Failure to do this can result in disaster.[17]

Germain didn't send Carlton a copy of his letter to Howe. So Burgoyne did not realize the full extent of Germain's and Howe's irresponsibility—that they had compromised the whole campaign. Burgoyne relied on Howe's ambiguous hint of a "diversion" on "Hudson's River." It was the slenderest of reeds on which to lean.

It is incomprehensible that Germain and Howe did not recognize the danger in which Burgoyne's army would be placed. Any reasonably qualified officer should have seen that Burgoyne—without the pressure of another British army coming on the rear of the Americans—would be isolated in a hostile, alien land.

Burgoyne commenced his march from Montreal on June 1, 1777. He went through rolling country to Lake Champlain. His army of 8,000 comprised about half British regulars and half German mercenaries. With him was a detachment of Canadians, and some hired Indian warriors. Hiring Indians aroused the intense antagonism of the Americans, because the Indians were known for drunkenness and extreme violence against men, women, and children.

At St. Johns (St.-Jean-sur-Richelieu)—where Lake Champlain flows into the Richelieu or Sorel River, which empties into the St. Lawrence River—the army boarded bateaus, flat-bottomed boats, each carrying thirty-five men, that were rowed southward up the lake.

The British proceeded to Crown Point. Ten miles to the south lay Fort Ticonderoga on the western side of the lake and just north of the falls that connect Lake George with Lake Champlain. Fort Ticonderoga (originally Fort Carillon), a star-shaped edifice 530 feet wide, had been built by the French in 1755–1758 out of local bluestone on the southern flank of a peninsula that jutted out into Lake Champlain.

Ticonderoga was held by 2,000 Americans under Major General Arthur St. Clair. Americans believed the fort was impregnable, but it was dilapidated and had been sited by the French facing south to block an advance by the British, not to defend against an attack from the north. In July 1776, an American engineer, John Trumball, decided that Rattlesnake Hill, just across the lake to the south, was a better defensive location because cannons mounted on its crest would have a clear field of fire down the lake to the north and could also cover the fort. The Americans renamed the hill Mount Independence and started fortifying it. Work was incomplete as the British approached, however. Nothing had been done about Sugar Loaf Hill (later called Mount Defiance), a steep elevation six hundred feet high, directly west of Mount Independence and just southwest of the fort. Trumball concluded that guns on this hill could dominate both the fort and Mount Independence. He was ridiculed for his idea, and it remained unoccupied.

When Burgoyne came up on Fort Ticonderoga on July 1, 1777, he and his artillery commander, Major General William Phillips, saw at once that Sugar Loaf Hill was key to the position and ordered cannons atop it. On July 6, seeing British cannons about to bombard the fort, General St. Clair ordered an evacuation and retreated southward. The British occupied the fort without resistance.

The Americans withdrew hastily to Skenesborough, twenty-two miles south of Ticonderoga. They were quickly followed by Burgoyne. He now decided, rather than moving back and advancing along Lake George, to build a road from Skenesborough to Fort Edward, on the Hudson River twenty miles south. After great effort, the British arrived at Fort Edward on July 30.

Meanwhile a diversionary British effort had started at Oswego on Lake Ontario and advanced through western New York to seize Fort Stanwix (now Rome) on the eastward-flowing Mohawk River. Once the fort was captured, the aim was to proceed down the Mohawk to join Burgoyne at Albany, eliminating resistance along the way. This force, poorly led and depending on Indians, collided with militia units. The Indians were interested only in pillage and disappeared when they met determined settler resistance. The British regulars quickly retreated back into Canada, the whole operation having been a dismal failure.

Meanwhile, Burgoyne was at Fort Edward, trying to assemble sufficient food, draft animals, carts, and other supplies to move forward. On August 3, an officer-courier got through the American lines with a letter from General Howe. In it Howe dropped the bombshell: he was going to Pennsylvania, and offered no help to Burgoyne. Howe announced that Sir Henry Clinton would be left in command at New York and would "act as occurrences may direct."[18] But it was clear that Clinton, having been left with few troops, was not about to take on the job that Howe had refused.

Here was the moment of truth for Burgoyne. He was left with two choices: retreat to Canada or attack a vastly larger army behind defensive fortifications that the Americans were certain to set up. Sun Tzu has positive advice in such a situation: retreat. "The small army that acts inflexibly will become the captives of the large enemy," he says.[19] Common sense also called on Burgoyne to withdraw and preserve the army to fight another day. He made the opposite decision.

Meanwhile Burgoyne's shaky supply system was barely able to keep up with the army's day-to-day needs, while most of his Indian allies deserted and took their loot back to their homes. Burgoyne had relied on the Indians as scouts to find out American dispositions. Now he was left blind in the heart of enemy country. Burgoyne abandoned Skenesborough and moved his supplies along Lake George, leaving small garrisons to guard the supply line back to Canada. His main strength was two regiments posted at Fort Ticonderoga.

To help solve the supply problem, Burgoyne sent a small foraging expedition to Bennington, Vermont, thirty-five miles southeast of Fort

Edward. But that force, largely German, was virtually destroyed by Vermont, New Hampshire, and Massachusetts militiamen on August 16, 1777. The Americans boldly swarmed all around the Germans and sent them fleeing, costing Burgoyne almost a thousand men. The Germans were so hard-pressed they had no chance to mount a culminating bayonet charge.

The Bennington operation demonstrates how Burgoyne lacked any real strategic sense. He failed to heed a fundamental rule of war, which is also one of Sun Tzu's primary axioms: keep one's aims secret from the enemy. "Warfare," Sun Tzu says, "is the way of deception."[20] Burgoyne's aims, on the contrary, were quite transparent. His direct path of movement pointed indisputably down the Hudson valley. Hence the American commander, Horatio Gates, was able to entrench directly in his line of march at Bemis Heights, a few miles south of the village of Saratoga on the western bank of the Hudson River and about twenty-five miles south of Fort Edward. Gates fortified these heights and waited on the British.[21]

If, on the other hand, Burgoyne had made a feint toward New England, he could have divided American forces and vastly increased the odds of overcoming a reduced force left at Bemis Heights. The Americans were fearful that Burgoyne's aim was to conquer New England, and a deceptive move eastward would have doubled their concern. If Burgoyne's strike on Bennington had been mounted with half of his army, he would have gained needed supplies and also thoroughly deceived the Americans as to his strategic purpose. This would have drawn off many if not most of the Americans on a wild goose chase. Burgoyne then could have quickly concentrated his army and moved on Bemis Heights.

As it was, the Bennington victory vastly encouraged the Americans. They discovered that they could destroy a British force. Burgoyne now knew the Americans could sever his already tenuous supply line. Since he intended to advance, he had to secure food, wagons, and horses along the way. In this frontier country, there were few enough of these items to begin with, and the patriots tried to move as much as did exist out of British reach.

Meanwhile, on July 23, 1777, General Howe, with 18,000 British and German troops, set sail from New York in 170 topsail vessels and 60 smaller ships. American General George Washington, getting word that the fleet was seen off Sandy Hook, New Jersey, moving toward the open sea, reasoned that Howe was headed for Philadelphia. He left a garrison on the Highlands just north of New York City and set off across New Jersey with the rest of his army for Philadelphia.

Major General Clinton remained in New York with 3,000 British regulars, 1,000 German mercenaries, and 3,000 loyalist Americans.

On July 29, the British ships reached the Delaware Capes and entered the bay with the apparent intention of moving up the Delaware River to Philadelphia. But the ships reversed course, slipped out to sea, sailed through the Virginia Capes, and arrived on August 25 at Head of Elk (Elkton), Maryland, the northernmost port of Chesapeake Bay. The British army went ashore and commenced marching toward Philadelphia.

On September 11, Washington, with about 11,000 men, tried to stop Howe's advance at Brandywine Creek, in Chester County, Pennsylvania, ten miles north of Wilmington, Delaware. But Howe skillfully turned Washington's right, or western, flank, forcing Washington back on Philadelphia, with a loss of 1,000 Americans and 500 British.

On September 21, the British conducted a surprise attack at night using bayonets only and routed the brigade of General Anthony Wayne near Paoli Tavern at Malvern, a few miles west of Philadelphia. Howe occupied Philadelphia on September 26, forcing the Continental Congress to flee to Lancaster and then to York, Pennsylvania.[22]

On October 4, Washington, now with 13,000 men, attempted a complicated movement against Howe's main encampment at Germantown, six miles northwest of Philadelphia. The effort failed, with the loss of 1,100 men.[23] This forced Washington to overwinter his army at Valley Forge under extremely harsh conditions, while the British enjoyed the shelter and comforts of nearby Philadelphia.

Meanwhile, on September 17, 1777, a 500-man American force under Colonel John Brown staged a surprise raid on Fort Ticonderoga, freeing 118 American captives, capturing 155 British soldiers and 119 Canadians, burning stores, driving off cattle and horses, and destroying most of the bateaus on Lakes Champlain and George. Brown and his men then boarded a small schooner and several gunboats and tried to eliminate a small British garrison on Diamond Island, a few miles north of the southern end of Lake George. But they were driven off by British gunboats. Brown's feat was a stunning reminder to Burgoyne that his supply line to Canada had vanished.

Even so, Burgoyne decided to advance. He concluded that despite the odds, the only chance of gaining success was to defeat the American army entrenched at Bemis Heights. On September 19, 1777, Burgoyne collided with this army. It was the biggest battle of the war, involving 9,000 men on the American side and 7,200 on the British side, with heavy fire from cannon and muskets, as well as highly effective patriot sharpshooters who concentrated on picking off British officers.

Fighting ended at nightfall with neither side having made headway or withdrawn. The battle had been a tumultuous melee of hand-to-hand fighting. There had never been the slightest chance for the British to launch their supposedly decisive charge with naked bayonets. Instead there had been a few chaotic short charges and countercharges by individual units on both sides, but nothing significant. The British were astonished at the staying power of the Americans. They lost 600 men, very heavy casualties for so small an army and twice as many as the Americans lost.

That same day, a courier from General Clinton got through to Burgoyne saying that Clinton was at last advancing up the Hudson with 2,000 men, all he could get together. Burgoyne was overjoyed and decided to wait until Clinton arrived before attacking again. But Clinton's expedition was a will-o'-the-wisp. It was far too small, encountered heavy opposition while attempting to seize two forts along the Hudson in the Highlands, and became vulnerable to being surrounded itself. Clinton pulled back to New York.

Skirmishes resumed on Bemis Heights for a number of days. As more American reinforcements arrived nearly every day, the few remaining Indians and the Canadians sensed defeat and began to melt into the forests. Food for the British was running short. Many men got sick. By the first of October, Burgoyne had only 5,000 men fit for combat.

Burgoyne realized his last hope was a bold stroke that might break through the American barrier. In a council of war on October 6, he decided to attack. The effort, however, came too late. Not only were the Americans strongly entrenched, but they now numbered close to 20,000 men. On October 7, Burgoyne advanced, only to be driven back in a series of bitter engagements. Burgoyne withdrew northward, hoping to get away. On October 12, the Americans surrounded the army at Fishkill Creek, only a few miles north. Five days later Burgoyne surrendered.

The British had committed the same blunder that Charles XII had committed at Poltava in 1709. He was blocked from advancing or retreating in the heart of hostile country, with no help of rescue.

The effect of the victory was immediate. The American envoy in Paris, Benjamin Franklin, found the French—once they realized that the Americans might win after all—abandoning their previous indifference and discovering an intense interest in American welfare. In December, the French agreed to a treaty, signed in February 1778, recognizing the United States of America as independent. France actually declared war on June 1, 1778.[24] France wanted to avenge itself against Britain for its losses in the Seven Years' War. In addition, France persuaded Spain to join in an alliance, although Spain refused to recognize American independence and tried to stop any expansion of America west of the Appalachian Mountains.

T W O

The Carolinas, Yorktown, and Independence, 1781

The thrust of the colonies toward a separate existence outside the British Empire had been building for decades prior to the American Revolution. The colonists had long since developed patterns and attitudes at odds with those in Britain. Most especially, they believed they had the inherent right to own land, to move when and where they pleased, and to follow whatever trades or careers they wanted. They resented the tiny minority of aristocrats who ruled Britain and who exerted enormous pressure on the "lower classes" to keep them in "their proper stations."[1] They disdained the fact that the aristocrats owned nearly all the land and exacted huge rents from the "common people" to farm or to live in tenements in the towns.

A sense of equality, democracy, and opportunity had been present almost from the beginning in America. It was constantly reinforced by the realization that beyond the Appalachians, a boundless, bountiful land was waiting for everyone. No aristocracy, however selfish, could deprive them of it. No one had to be subservient to the rich and the privileged. The frontier broke all the bonds. Even those who had no intention of becoming pioneers shared in the freedom, because moving to the frontier was always an option.

Prior to the victory at Saratoga, many colonists had doubts about separation from the mother country. Some clung to residual loyalty. Others could not conceive that a group of colonies with nothing approaching a "real army" could defy the might of Britain. But the victory and the French alliance changed everything. The prospect of success now seemed tangible. A new hope beckoned on the horizon. Americans saw the silhouette of a nation far greater in size, hope, aspirations, and opportunity than anything that existed in Europe.

Accordingly, all tendencies toward compromise and accommodation with Britain collapsed after Saratoga. The efforts that Britain made to make amends were greeted with scorn.

The British government itself was incapable of deep-seated change. What it now offered—everything short of independence—was too little and too late. Any possible chance for a settlement had died at Saratoga. A peace commission headed by the earl of Carlisle got nowhere when it arrived in Philadelphia.

Britain's narrow ruling class was unwilling to give up its claim to rule the colonies, or to offer the colonies equality with Britain, as Adam Smith had proposed in *The Wealth of Nations.* Instead, despite the evidence of Saratoga, they resolved to continue the same policy they had embarked on at the beginning: using British army regulars and hired German mercenaries to stamp out the rebellion with brute force. This policy had not worked so far. The disaster at Saratoga was evidence of its failure.

Leaders of countries and of armies are characteristically unwilling to admit that their plans have miscarried, and they are reluctant to turn to new strategies, especially if their political opponents or competitors proposed them. The inclination of all leaders and all commanders is to keep on adding more force to achieve the same goals when previous efforts have failed.

We have seen abundant cases of this predisposition since the Revolution. Here are two of many examples: In World War I, 1914–1918, leaders sacrificed millions of men for four years by continuing to launch hopeless charges against the machine guns, cannons, and field fortifications of the western front. In the Vietnam War, 1965–1972, American commanders continued to send troops on "search and destroy" missions against Vietnamese Communists, even though these missions nearly always failed and the Reds could withdraw safely into the forests or into the civilian population.

British leaders during the Revolution were especially inept. The government was composed of aristocrats who offered no ideas about how to pursue a war successfully. Lord George Germain, the man in charge of operations, was incompetent. General Sir William Howe, the senior commander in America, was an adequate orthodox soldier, but his insistence on going to Philadelphia instead of helping Burgoyne revealed his total lack of strategic sense. Howe's deputy, Sir Henry Clinton, who replaced Howe in early June 1778, was only marginally more capable than Howe, and he also lacked any vision for a different approach to the war. None of the admirals proposed using the Royal Navy to subdue the colonies. They were all deepwater sailors who focused on defeating enemy fleets on the open sea or seizing enemy merchant ships. It did not occur to any of them to institute a blockade of all the American ports or to divide and conquer by sending flotillas onto the estuaries, lakes, and rivers of the colonies. British leaders disregarded the American strategy, which was to exploit the vast extent of the colonies to absorb and ultimately to overcome the British armies. George Washington and his Continental army would always have great difficulty defeating British forces. But victory in battle was not necessary. The British could control only the ground on which their soldiers stood. Everything else was free.

The British made a fundamental blunder in not understanding and not trying to undermine the American strategy. "The highest realization of warfare is to attack the enemy's plans," Sun Tzu says.[2] One should never ignore enemy strategy. Rather, one should study it to find a counterstrategy to defeat it.

The semi-guerrilla warfare that the Americans developed from the outset remained the standard American method of conducting the war. Washington's direct challenges at Brandywine Creek and Germantown were contradictions of this method, and both failed. But the battle of Bennington, the raid on Fort Ticonderoga, and the deadly blocking action at Saratoga were examples of it, and they succeeded.

Since the occupation of Philadelphia by General Howe had produced no benefits whatsoever, Clinton ordered its evacuation and began moving the British army back to New York City by land.

During the severe winter of 1777–1778 at Valley Forge, General Washington had appointed a Prussian volunteer, Baron Friedrich Wilhelm Augustin von Steuben, to train the Continental army. Steuben had served on the staff of Frederick the Great, and he did much to reorganize and instill discipline in Washington's ragged little force.

Washington, feeling that the Continental army now might meet the British on even terms, decided to challenge Clinton as he retreated across New Jersey. At Monmouth Court House (now Freehold Borough), Washington sent General Charles Lee with 5,000 men to attack Clinton's rear guard on June 28, 1778. But Lee committed his forces piecemeal, and his efforts were disorganized. The rearguard commander, General Charles Cornwallis, 1st Marquess Cornwallis, ordered a counterattack, and Lee's forces promptly disintegrated into chaos. Washington relieved Lee of his command. The engagement was a sobering reminder that the Americans still lacked good leadership and disciplined staying power against a determined British attack.

The British withdrew to Sandy Hook, where Royal Navy ships carried the army across the Lower Bay to the safety of Manhattan.

Monmouth was the last important battle in the northern theater.

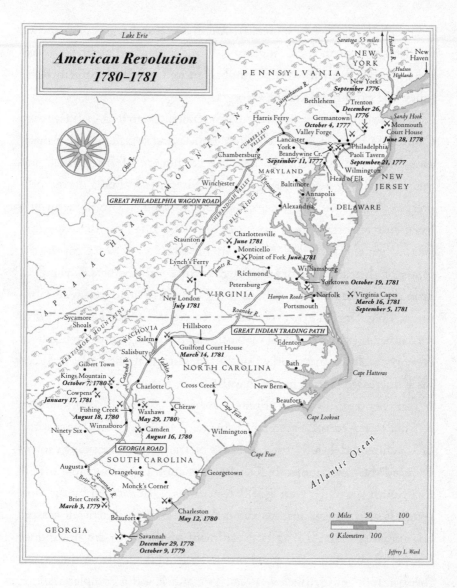

Lord Germain decided to transfer major operations southward. He conceived a new plan: first to conquer Georgia, then the Carolinas, and lastly Virginia, after which he felt the colonies to the north would feel isolated and would surrender.

General Clinton accordingly sent by sea 3,500 men under Lieutenant Colonel Archibald Campbell to Savannah, Georgia. Campbell crushed a 1,000-man militia force and seized Savannah on December

29, 1778. Early in 1779, General Augustine Prevost, in command of the British garrison at St. Augustine, Florida, marched north to Savannah with 3,000 men, while Campbell moved up the Savannah River valley and captured Augusta, Georgia.

An attempt to recapture Augusta failed March 3, 1779, when Campbell's force executed a perfect converging attack on the Americans, mostly militia, camped near the confluence of Brier Creek and the river halfway between Augusta and Savannah. While a decoy force pressed directly on the Americans, holding their attention, a turning force crossed Brier Creek upstream and descended on the American rear. When the surprised Americans mistakenly opened a gap in the center of their line, the British charged with fixed bayonets. The militia promptly broke and ran without firing a shot. A small group of Continental regulars held their position but were surrounded and forced to surrender. This was the kind of battle the British had expected to fight everywhere. It had not worked out often, but the results at Brier Creek vastly increased British hopes that the tide was turning.

In September 1779, French Admiral Comte Charles Henri d'Estaing arrived off Savannah from the West Indies with a squadron of warships and 4,000 French soldiers on transports. D'Estaing's forces besieged the town, joined by General Benjamin Lincoln from Charleston, South Carolina, with 1,300 Americans. Discouraged by the slow progress of the siege, anxious about the arrival of the hurricane season, and impatient after a long bombardment of the town did not induce Prevost to surrender, d'Estaing ordered a frontal assault on the British fortifications on October 9, 1779. The attack was a complete failure. The French and Americans lost 830 men; the British, 150. Refusing to continue the siege, d'Estaing sailed back to France. Lincoln returned to Charleston.

The failure to recapture Savannah and d'Estaing's abandonment of his allies caused American confidence in the French to drop sharply, seriously damaged morale, and greatly raised the hopes of General Clinton and the loyalists.

Seeing a golden opportunity to seize Charleston, Clinton left German General Wilhelm von Knyphausen in command in New York and set out on December 26, 1779, with ninety transports carrying 8,500 men and General Cornwallis as second in command. The flotilla was escorted by fourteen warships under Admiral Marriot Arbuthnot.

General Lincoln's American force totaled 5,400 men; Clinton, with Prevost's troops, had more than twice as many. Instead of abandoning Charleston and keeping his army as a threat in the interior, Lincoln foolishly withdrew into the town on March 29, 1780. Clinton's cannons and Admiral Arbuthnot's guns began a severe bombardment that lasted until May 12, when Lincoln surrendered, the worst American disaster of the war.[3]

With the capture of Charleston and Savannah, the British reached a decisive fork in the road. In one direction lay a continuation of the policy that had failed them so far. In the other direction lay an opportunity for a radical change in strategy and possible victory.

British policy from the outset had been to march over the landscape with the intention of destroying all American forces in their path, frightening the patriots into surrender, and emboldening the loyalists to join the British army. This policy had not worked. The British had lost an army at Saratoga. They had undertaken a massive offensive to capture Philadelphia, winning all of their engagements against Washington and gaining precisely nothing. Even the defeat of the Americans at Monmouth Court House had resulted in no change in American defiance.

But the British seizure of Charleston and Savannah presented unmistakable evidence of success and demonstrated how a new strategy could be effective. The ports' capture largely closed off the commerce of South Carolina and Georgia. There were no other important ports south of Chesapeake Bay. North Carolina's coastline was mostly cloaked by the aptly named barrier islands. Only Wilmington was easily accessible to the sea. It was a small port, however, and of limited use to regions in the interior because of poor roads.

The proper decision of General Clinton, therefore, was to employ the Royal Navy to seize or to blockade the other major ports along the seaboard and thereby close down the foreign commerce of the colonies. The ports of Chesapeake Bay could be sealed by occupying Portsmouth and patrolling the Virginia Capes with a squadron. Likewise, Philadelphia and Wilmington, Delaware, could be shut down by stationing a squadron in the upper Delaware Bay. Only Portsmouth, New Hampshire, and Boston would have to be occupied. Since the British already held Charleston, Savannah, and New York City, the colonies could be deprived of most of their trade with the capture of the two New England ports and the blockade of Chesapeake and Delaware bays.

Newport, Rhode Island, however, would need to be closed by a strong Royal Navy squadron, which could also slow traffic out of New London and other Connecticut ports. A French force of 5,000 troops, along with seven French ships of the line, the standard warships of the time, each with 74 guns, had occupied Newport in July 1780, and it became the headquarters of the French commander in America, Jean Baptiste de Vimeur, comte de Rochambeau. If Newport were closed off, Rochambeau's naval squadron would be neutralized, and the main French fleet—if it appeared in North American waters—would have no safe harbor.

But none of this came about. General Clinton did not conclude that stopping South Carolina's and Georgia's overseas trade would force the people to come to terms. He did not see that the British needed to do no more than hold Charleston and Savannah. He did not see that the occupation or blockade of other ports would achieve the same results. The strategic opportunity was staring him in the face, but he did not see it. Inability to understand that indirect ways can often achieve goals when direct attacks fail is unfortunately quite common.

As the nineteenth-century military historian Theodore Ayrault Dodge wrote, "The maxims of war are but a meaningless page to him who cannot apply them."[4]

Clinton did conclude, however, that the people of South Carolina were so depressed by the loss of their port and their only important city that resistance would collapse throughout the colony.[5] Clinton's assumption would have made sense in Europe, where wars were mainly dynastic clashes, the populace had little patriotic fervor, and the capture of a major provincial city usually settled matters. But this was not the case in America. A large portion of the populace was deeply committed to ousting the British, and an intense desire burst out all across the upcountry to resist the British and to liberate the city.

Clinton, assuming the battle had been won, continued the same British policy of marching armies through the country with the intention of overawing the people. He left Lord Cornwallis in command with 8,500 men, told him to occupy the rest of the colony, and returned to New York in June 1780.

Cornwallis's own behavior and that of his men worsened the situation greatly. He dispatched 2,500 men into the backcountry to subdue the people and establish outposts. His men were high-handed, arrogant, and cruel. During the next three months Cornwallis's severe measures, especially the brutality of Lieutenant Colonel Banastre Tarleton, aroused strong and effective guerrilla opposition, led by Francis Marion, Thomas Sumter, and Andrew Pickens. Francis Marion learned guerrilla warfare while fighting Cherokee Indians, and he applied his knowledge artfully to defeat isolated British parties and to harass their columns.[6] Americans were especially incensed by the massacre of a small force by Tarleton at Waxhaws (present-day Buford), near the North Carolina border, on May 29, 1780. Tarleton's cavalry charged a retreating force of Virginia Continentals under Abraham Buford. Just as the Virginians raised the white flag of surrender, Tarleton's horse was struck by a musket ball and fell. His men, thinking their commander had been shot, stabbed wounded Americans where they lay and gave no quarter to men who were surrendering. The killing frenzy soon stopped, but of the 350 Virginians, 260 were killed or wounded. The massacre aroused intense opposition throughout the backcountry of the Carolinas and Virginia. "Tarleton's quarter!" and "Remember Buford!" became rallying cries for the patriots.

The Continental Congress—without consulting Washington—appointed Horatio Gates, the hero of Saratoga, to replace Lincoln as the southern commander. Gates, an Englishman, had spent most of his life in the British army in North America. He came over to the American side as the first adjutant general and assisted George Washington in organizing American forces.

Gates re-formed the Continental army at Charlotte, North Carolina, in late July 1780 and advanced on the British outpost at the important crossroads of Camden, seventy miles southeast of Charlotte. He had about 3,700 men, 1,500 Continental regulars and the rest militia. Cornwallis came up with a force from Charleston, raising British strength to 2,100 men, 600 loyalist volunteers and the rest British regulars. He also had Tarleton's legion of 250 cavalry and 200 mounted infantry, who were formidable in pursuing broken troops.

On August 16, 1780, Gates formed up his little army in the traditional European manner: his best troops, the Continentals and North Carolina militia, called the Tar Heels, on the right (the post of honor), and his raw and most inexperienced troops, the remaining militia, on the left. Cornwallis also lined up his troops in the traditional manner: his regulars on the right and his loyalists on the left. So the weakest American forces were facing the strongest British forces. As the battle opened, Cornwallis's regulars fired a volley into the militia and launched a charge with bayonets. The militia at once broke and fled, collapsing the entire left flank. The American Continentals and Tar Heels on the right attacked the British left, but the British regulars halted their pursuit of the militia, wheeled left, and launched another bayonet charge into the American flank. The Continentals and the North Carolinians held their ground and fought back fiercely. Cornwallis now ordered

Tarleton's cavalry to charge the rear of the American line. This broke up Gates's army, and it disintegrated.

In one hour of combat, the Americans lost 2,000 men, half of them taken as prisoners. Tarleton pursued the survivors for twenty miles. General Gates, mounted on a swift horse, fled back to Charlotte.

Two days later Tarleton surprised the guerrilla leader Thomas Sumter at Fishing Creek, just north of Great Falls on the Catawba River, forty miles south of Charlotte. He killed 150 Americans and captured 200.

These two devastating blows seemed to prove to Cornwallis and the other British officers that they were correct in their theory that the Americans always broke and ran. They figured the war was as good as won. But things were not as they seemed. Tarleton's surprise at Fishing Creek was a chance event, while Gates's attack at Camden had been a foolish attempt to copy the battle tactics of Europe when he didn't have the army to carry them out.

Cornwallis now figured that he had a clear path to Virginia. In September 1780, he reached Charlotte with his main army and ordered Major Patrick Ferguson, commanding a force of loyalist volunteers, to guard his western flank. Ferguson moved to Gilbert Town in Rutherford County, North Carolina, at the edge of the high mountains about a hundred miles west of Charlotte. There Ferguson sent a paroled rebel deep into the Great Smoky Mountains with the warning that if the rebels did not stop resisting British arms, he would march over the mountains, hang their leaders, and lay the country waste with fire and sword.[7]

This was not the sort of threat likely to frighten the Scotch-Irish settlers, who made up the overwhelming majority of the people in Piedmont and western North Carolina. They were descended from Scottish Presbyterians who, after the English had driven the Irish out of Ulster in the seventeenth century, had created a thriving country based on sheep and woolen and linen cloth manufacture. But as soon as they became successful, the English Parliament prohibited export of their cloth and ousted their Presbyterian pastors, while the English landlords began charging rents far higher than the land could support. The Scotch-Irish left northern Ireland in a great wave of emigration to America beginning in the 1690s and accelerating after 1717. They carried with them a powerful anger against England, as well as their traditional Scottish love of freedom.

Ferguson's message stirred both emotions. Irate Scotch-Irish men gathered their horses, guns, and provisions together, assembled at Sycamore Shoals on the Watauga River (present-day Elizabethton, in eastern Tennessee), formed themselves into companies, and set out for Gilbert Town, picking up other volunteers along the way. When they arrived, Ferguson was gone. They elected their youngest leader, William Campbell, as their commander and started out in search of Ferguson.

At Cowpens (a short distance over the North Carolina line, and a few miles northwest of present-day Gaffney, South Carolina), they were joined by 400 upcountry South Carolinians, also Scotch-Irish, on October 6.

A spy reported that Ferguson was encamped on top of Kings Mountain, an isolated elevation about thirty miles to the east. The settlers wanted to capture Ferguson before he could reach Charlotte and gain protection from Cornwallis. They selected 900 of their best men and horses, who set off and arrived at Kings Mountain on the afternoon of October 7, 1780.

Ferguson had pulled up on the mountain because he felt no enemy could approach without showing himself. The patriots decided to surround the mountain and, using continuous fire, to close in on the top.

The patriots divided into four columns and moved against the loyalists from all sides. Because of their exposed position, Ferguson's men were being picked off by sharpshooters, while their own aim was poor because they were shooting downhill.[8] The patriots gained a foothold on the summit and closed in on the loyalists. Ferguson tried to cut through on a horse but was riddled with bullets. The second in command raised the white flag, but it took a while for the patriots to stop firing—they remembered Tarleton's massacre of the Americans at Waxhaws.

Not a single one of Ferguson's men escaped. Reports showed that 225 loyalists were killed, 163 wounded, and 716 captured, against a loss of 28 patriots killed and 68 wounded.

News of the victory set the countryside ablaze and brought out the militias of North Carolina and Virginia. Cornwallis found himself surrounded by a hostile population (he called Charlotte "a hornet's nest," a name Charlotteans have borne proudly to this day). He abandoned Charlotte and moved ninety miles south to Winnsboro.

Nathanael Greene, the new American commander who replaced Gates, meanwhile split up the small Continental army into guerrilla bands, and Cornwallis followed suit. Cornwallis learned that Daniel Morgan was operating west of Kings Mountain. He detailed Banastre Tarleton with 1,100 men to chase him down and destroy him. Morgan assembled his 1,900 men at the largely open grazing area of Cowpens. His force included Continental regulars and militia from Virginia, the Carolinas, and Georgia.

Morgan, an experienced soldier who had won fame at Saratoga, placed his best troops—Continental regulars and some seasoned militia from Georgia and Virginia—on a hill in the center of the position. The British would be approaching from another hill to the southeast. Morgan drew up two lines in the low ground between the two hills, the first of skirmisher sharpshooters and the second of militia. The sharpshooters and militia would be firing uphill at the British, who would be silhouetted against the morning sunlight and provide easy targets. Morgan told the sharpshooters to delay the advance and then retire, and the militia to fire just two shots and then retreat to the rear. The withdrawal of the sharpshooters and militia would mask the third line. When Tarleton's men reached this line, they would be tired, disorganized, and attacking uphill.

When Tarleton arrived on January 17, 1781, he sent his infantry forward directly on the Americans, leaving 200 cavalry in reserve.

After shooting down fifteen British dragoons, the skirmishers retreated. The British hesitated, but advanced again, this time reaching the militiamen. As ordered, they poured two volleys into the British, who suffered heavy casualties and halted in confusion. The British re-formed, however, and moved forward again. The Americans seemingly broke in confusion and fled to the rear. Tarleton took this withdrawal as a full-blown collapse and advanced headlong into Morgan's final line on the hill. Here the attacking British met the solid fire of Morgan's best troops and recoiled in shock. Just then, Morgan's small cavalry force struck one flank, while the militiamen, who had re-formed in the rear, came back and struck the other flank.

The British force had been stopped in front and enveloped on two sides. Half of the British soldiers fell to the ground in dismay. Tarleton collided with some American cavalrymen but was able to flee from the field. The British lost 772 men, 120 killed and 652 captured, some of them wounded. Patriot losses were about 150. Morgan had fought a masterly battle, soundly defeating the most hated officer in the British army.

The victories of Kings Mountain and Cowpens changed the entire character of the war in the Carolinas. Cornwallis saw no possibility of subduing either colony. He then made a most strange decision: he resolved to continue to pursue the patriots in hopes of defeating them. He was unable to catch Greene, however, as he marched northward through Piedmont North Carolina to Hillsboro (between present-day Burlington and Durham). On March 15, 1781, Greene at last tried to challenge Cornwallis at Guilford Court House (just northwest of present-day Greensboro), but Greene's militiamen panicked and bolted from the field.

Though Cornwallis won this battle, he lost the campaign. His losses were so great and his supplies so scant that he decided to abandon the interior of the Carolinas and march to Wilmington on the coast, 200 miles southeast of Guilford Court House. There he was resupplied by sea. Other than a temporary occupation of Wilmington, the only places still held by the British south of Virginia were Charleston and Savan-nah.[9] The idea that the British could eliminate resistance by marching through the colonies had been proved false.

In a bizarre way, the British were conducting a war that closely resem-bled the methods the U.S. Army used in Vietnam in 1965–1972. The British divided up their forces and attempted wide-ranging "search-and-destroy missions" that played directly into the hands of the Americans, as similar methods played directly into the hands of the Vietnamese Communists. This pattern characterized the campaign in the Carolinas from mid-1780 to early 1781. It was marked by the superb guerrilla operations of Francis Marion, Thomas Sumter, and Andrew Pickens, and by the modest but telling battlefield victories at Kings Mountain and Cowpens, which demonstrated what could happen to British forces if they were isolated.

But the guerrillas were also able to strike swift blows at the edges of the main British army. If pressed, they could withdraw into swamps and forests, where British pursuers could seldom find them. The indi-rect warfare of the guerrilla leaders put the British on the defensive, led to casualties, and denied them successful results. As soon as the British moved on, they lost control of the country they had occupied. There were no permanent conquests. Every gain was ephemeral.

British officers not only failed to see that their European tactics were never going to work in America, but also fell into the trap of try-ing to run down the scattered American forces and defeat them. In the Carolinas and later in Virginia, they chased the Americans over an area of 60,000 square miles (an area larger than England and Wales together) and never did more than kill or capture a few of them, while suffering staggering losses themselves.

No guerrilla war conducted by determined leaders and supported by a substantial portion of the population can be defeated. This was

how the Scots preserved their freedom against England for centuries—
by following the "testament" of Robert the Bruce to avoid pitched
battles and fight only among hills and morasses. Although the Scottish
wars had occurred a long time previously, they were part and parcel of
the British military experience and should have been known to senior
officers. Far more recent and far more representative of what the British faced in the Carolinas was General Edward Braddock's expedition
to Fort Duquesne in 1755, when Braddock lost his life and half of his
army to an Indian ambush.

Once it became clear that British methods were not working in
America—and they had plainly failed by the time of Cowpens on January 17, 1781—then another method was necessary. A far better policy
would have been to attack the enemy's strategy, one of Sun Tzu's tenets.
The British still could have abandoned a land war entirely and blockaded the American ports. But such an epiphany did not occur.

Instead, Lord Cornwallis proposed to Lord Germain on April 18,
1781, that major operations be transferred to Chesapeake Bay, hoping that a successful operation there would induce the Carolinas to
surrender. He was opposed by Clinton, but he got solid backing from
Germain and King George.[10]

Cornwallis and Germain came to this conclusion not only because
of the disappointing results of the Carolinas campaign but also because
the British had little scope for operations out of New York City, their
principal bastion. George Washington's troops blockaded the port on
the land side. It is strange that it took the British until 1781 to realize
that the magnificent harbors of Hampton Roads in the Chesapeake Bay
offered their best chance—next to a blockade of American ports—of
stamping out the rebellion. Chesapeake Bay is the largest estuary in
North America and is fed by most of the rivers of eastern Pennsylvania, Maryland, and Virginia.

If a strong Royal Navy flotilla occupied the bay and set up a naval
and supply base at one of the Hampton Roads harbors, then patrolled
the Virginia Capes, the British could guarantee their supply line back to

Britain. And the rivers could be used as highways to penetrate deep into the interior. Large regions could be isolated and conquered, and the navy could play as large a role as the army. But this was not the thinking of Thomas Graves, the admiral who had replaced Marriot Arbuthnot in command of the British squadron at New York. Graves had no interest in operations in bays and rivers.

On the other hand, Cornwallis wanted to evacuate New York, bring the British army and the Royal Navy squadron to the Chesapeake, and begin conquering Virginia and the other middle colonies. Clinton opposed abandoning New York, and Germain hovered between the two, unable to accept so resolute a plan as Cornwallis's but hoping vaguely to combine the efforts in New York and Hampton Roads.[11]

But combining the two was strategically impossible. British land forces would be separated by hundreds of miles of patriot-held territory. Most critically the limited naval forces had to be either divided between the two locations, leaving both unable to contest a major French challenge, or concentrated at one point, leaving the other unprotected. The choice was clear.[12]

This is why Sun Tzu and all great strategists call for concentrating forces at a single crucial location—because a decision can be made there.[13] Napoléon Bonaparte stated the principle quite succinctly: "It is the same with strategy as with the siege of a fortress: concentrate your fire against a single point, and once the wall is breached, all of the rest becomes worthless and the fortress is captured."[14] Dividing one's aims between two locations halves the forces at both places. There was little chance for a decisive victory at New York, but there was a strong chance for victory in the Chesapeake. Victory there would permit recovery of New York later.

But Germain, Clinton, and Graves were unable to make the choice. They adopted a policy of offense from the Chesapeake but kept the main army and the fleet based at New York, hoping that the ships could rush down to the Virginia Capes if a French fleet threatened. By failing to concentrate their power at the single critical point where the issue had to be decided, the British leaders set up the conditions for disaster.

Concentration was vital because Britain's ships were limited in number on the North Atlantic coast. The Royal Navy, though bigger than any other country's fleet, was inadequate at all times to secure North America and the Atlantic sea lanes, while also protecting Britain against invasion and preventing the French from recovering the lands it lost in the Seven Years' War.[15]

Britain thus adopted in the Chesapeake exactly the policy it had adopted in Burgoyne's 1777 campaign down from Canada: Cornwallis was burdened with a huge task but was given few means—most notably no naval protection—to carry it out. He would be just as isolated as Burgoyne if his sea connection was broken, even for a short time, since all of his supplies and reinforcements had to come by water from New York or England.

At the first of the year 1781, Clinton sent the traitor Benedict Arnold with 1,600 men to the Chesapeake port of Portsmouth. Arnold's treason had occurred on September 21, 1780, when the Americans discovered his plot to transfer to the British the bastion of West Point, a key strategic position on the Hudson River north of New York City. Arnold had been one of George Washington's favorite commanders. He was brave, tenacious, and gifted as a military leader. But he was also egotistical and self-interested. When he did not get the promotions he expected, Arnold hardened his heart against the American cause and offered his services to the British—at a price. In secret correspondence with General Clinton, Arnold promised to deliver West Point, which he commanded, along with the 3,000 American defenders, to the British for £20,000 sterling (about $1 million today). When the plot was aborted, Clinton still gave Arnold £6,000 sterling and appointed him a brigadier general in the British army.

Arnold served George III with the same skill and daring he had shown in the patriot cause. He devastated Richmond, Virginia, forcing the governor, Thomas Jefferson, to flee. He then raided supply depots and torched plantations, villages, and iron foundries before moving back to Portsmouth. In May, hobbled by gout, Arnold returned to New York. Later in Connecticut, he burned ships, warehouses, and much of the town of New London, a major port for patriot privateers. After the war, Arnold was treated with coldness and contempt in Britain. He died as he lived, a man without a country.

To protect Virginia as best he could, Washington sent a French volunteer, Marie-Joseph du Motier, marquis de Lafayette, to command patriot forces in Virginia. He had about 3,500 men. Cornwallis meanwhile moved up from Wilmington and took command of a small British expeditionary force at Petersburg, Virginia, on May 20, 1781. Counting the garrison at Portsmouth, Cornwallis had 8,000 men.

Cornwallis tried without success to bring Lafayette to battle. He destroyed all the stores he could find around Richmond and then moved to Williamsburg to find a base for his army. He soon decided on Yorktown, close to Williamsburg, a few miles upstream from Hampton Roads on the York River.

Meanwhile Cornwallis's cavalry launched raids deep into the Virginia interior. In June 1781, Tarleton struck Charlottesville, where he nearly caught Jefferson, while Lieutenant Colonel John Simcoe seized the Continental army's weapons and ammunition depot at Point of Fork, junction of the Rivanna and James rivers, about fifty miles west of Richmond. In July 1781, Tarleton raided as far as New London in Bedford County, 120 miles west of Richmond.

Neither Clinton nor Germain made any effort to reinforce Cornwallis or to recognize that he might be in peril if a French squadron closed off the Virginia Capes for any length of time. Clinton and Germain were extremely slow in realizing that access to the Chesapeake was mandatory to protect Cornwallis. Yet they had received fair warning. On March 8, 1781, a squadron of eight French ships under Charles

Sochet Destouches tried to seize control of the Chesapeake and land a French troop detachment to reinforce Lafayette. British lookouts spotted Destouches's ships soon after they departed Newport, Rhode Island. Eight British ships at Gardiners Bay on the eastern end of Long Island, went in pursuit. The two squadrons collided just outside the Virginia Capes on March 16. Although the British suffered more damage than the French, Destouches abandoned his attempt and returned to Newport.

Only six days later, on March 22, 1781, a fleet of twenty-six French ships of the line and a large convoy including troop transports sailed from Brest, France, under François-Joseph-Paul, comte de Grasse. Off the Azores, five ships parted company to challenge the English in the East Indies. The remainder made for the West Indies.

On May 8, 1781, the French frigate *Concorde* docked at Boston and the son of Comte Rochambeau, the French commander in America, disembarked along with Jacques-Melchior Saint-Laurent, comte de Barras, new commander of the French naval squadron at Newport. The younger Rochambeau, Donatien-Marie-Joseph de Vimeur, carried the welcome news of de Grasse's expected arrival in the West Indies.

Rochambeau and George Washington quickly met at Wethersfield, Connecticut. Rochambeau had been informed privately by his son that de Grasse would definitely sail north in July or August. Washington already expected him to do so, however, and he wanted de Grasse to strike at New York. Rochambeau preferred to focus on Chesapeake Bay, but he did not say so to Washington.[16] Rochambeau wrote a letter to de Grasse, which was dispatched on the same fast frigate *Concorde* to Cap François (present-day Cap-Haïtien) in Haiti and was waiting for de Grasse when he put into the port on July 16. In it he urged the admiral to sail to Chesapeake Bay, and he asked de Grasse to respond immediately.[17]

When de Grasse received Rochambeau's letter at Cap François, he sent a reply on the *Concorde*. On August 15, 1781, the frigate docked at Boston, and Washington and Rochambeau learned that the French fleet was headed for the Chesapeake with 3,500 French soldiers de Grasse was bringing along to reinforce the forces in Virginia.

Leaving 4,000 troops at West Point to watch Clinton in New York, Washington and Rochambeau set out on August 20 with 2,000 Americans and 4,000 French on the 400-mile march to Virginia. On August 30 they were greeted by cheering crowds at Philadelphia, and on September 6 they reached Head of Elk (Elkton), Maryland, the northernmost port of Chesapeake Bay.

Meanwhile, de Grasse was coming north. He took the longer, little-used Old Bahamas Channel to hide his approach. Pursuing him on the direct route was the British admiral Sir Samuel Hood, with fourteen warships.

Hood had so few ships because of the bad judgment of Sir George Rodney, naval commander in the West Indies. When he received reports that de Grasse's fleet, accompanied by 200 homeward-bound French merchantmen, had left Martinique for Cap François, he assumed that de Grasse would escort the merchant ships back to France and would detach no more than twelve or fourteen warships for action off the American coast. Rodney, therefore, sent only fourteen of his own ships under Admiral Hood to cooperate with Thomas Graves at New York. Rodney figured they would be able to defeat de Grasse.

Returning to England because of bad health, Rodney took the rest of the British fleet and 150 British merchantmen with him. This was a most unfortunate decision because it relied on the enemy making the same judgment that Rodney had made. De Grasse did not do so. He delayed the departure of the French merchantmen and—following the doctrine that fleets should be concentrated, not dispersed—brought his whole fleet north. The British, who had only five serviceable ships at New York, were therefore inferior in numbers off the American coast.

On August 27, de Barras left Newport to rendezvous with de Grasse. He made a wide circuit out to sea to avoid the English. De Barras had eight men-of-war (ships of the line), four frigates, and eighteen transports—carrying all the French siege artillery.

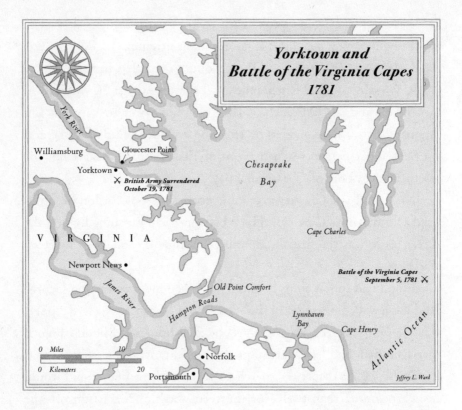

Admiral Hood, coming north, put into Chesapeake Bay the same day. He was hunting for de Grasse but found the bay empty. Hood sailed on to New York, where Admiral Graves told him de Barras had departed Newport, pointing to a junction with de Grasse and a joint move into the Chesapeake. The combined squadron of nineteen ships, with Graves in command as senior officer, set out to beat the French into the bay.

But it was too late. On August 30, de Grasse's fleet dropped anchor in Lynnhaven Bay, just within the Virginia Capes. The 3,500 troops he brought with him joined Lafayette.

Though surprised to find de Grasse already in the Chesapeake when he arrived on September 5, 1781, Graves prepared to attack. But he took so long to form his ships in line of battle (the ships in a row, one behind the other) that de Grasse was able to get into the Atlantic and challenge the British. In a series of running encounters, de Grasse's ships delivered heavier fire than the British, damaging the British rigging and slowing the ships. Now the British were vulnerable to a new attack by the French. But de Grasse adhered to his main task, keeping the British from entering the bay. He avoided another collision and blocked entrance to the capes time after time. Meanwhile de Barras slipped into the Chesapeake with the French siege artillery. When Graves got word of de Barras's arrival, he realized that he was heavily outnumbered, and returned to New York to repair his rigging. Cornwallis was now trapped within the Chesapeake. No supplies or reinforcements could possibly reach him in time to save him.

Once Graves had departed, de Grasse returned to the Chesapeake, brought some of Washington's and Rochambeau's troops down from Head of Elk and nearby locations (other boats brought the remainder), and agreed to remain inside the bay until Yorktown had surrendered.

Cornwallis was heavily outnumbered and outgunned. Washington and Rochambeau assembled every soldier they could find. By September 27 they had 17,000 men, more than twice the number of Cornwallis's. But lack of firepower was the British commander's greatest weakness. His position at Yorktown depended on the guns of British ships to protect him. But there were no ships, and French siege artillery now ranged around his defenses. They began to bombard the ramparts on October 9. On October 14, French and American detachments seized two key redoubts and quickly mounted cannons on them. These guns dominated the entire British position. A desperate attempt to cross the York River and escape through Gloucester Point on the opposite bank during a heavy storm failed.

On October 17, Cornwallis began negotiations to surrender, and on October 19, his force of 8,000 men marched out to a tune titled "The World Turned Upside Down."

With this capitulation, the British gave up any hope of subduing the colonies. Peace negotiations soon began.[18] But the issue had been decided a month before, off the Virginia Capes. The naval engagement was a small affair, but it isolated Cornwallis and guaranteed his defeat.

Today we look back on the American Revolution and we generally conclude that its outcome was predestined, that the American thrust for independence was too great and too powerful to be deflected. Yet people of good will can solve the most intractable of disputes. And there is nothing inevitable about military victory.

In all conflicts, political solutions and military victories occur when leaders can see ways to achieve them. If there are no such leaders, disaster usually results. The necessity for vision is at the heart of the first and most important axiom of Sun Tzu: "Warfare is the greatest affair of state, the basis of life and death, the way to survival or extinction."[19] American independence came because Britain possessed unbelievably bad leaders who were incapable either of accepting a peaceful solution or of conducting a successful war.

Let us imagine for a moment what might have happened if more capable leaders had come along in Britain during the crucial years between 1770 and 1775 when revolt was building. Two options, one peaceful and one military, were possible.

The peaceful solution would have been for Britain to propose a political union with the colonies, either a federal state or dominion status, such as what Britain came to later with Canada, Australia, New Zealand, and South Africa. If Britain had proposed either solution, most of the impetus for revolt would have died because the colonies would in actuality have become independent. Good feelings, cooperation, and mutual aid would have ensued. The resulting commonwealth of English-speaking countries would have become the most powerful force on earth. Its democratic thrust might have deflected into peaceful paths much of the empire-building greed and avarice that caused such immense conflict, dissension, and wars in the century and a half that followed.

If a political settlement could not have been achieved, a military victory could have been attained with an iron blockade of the colonial ports. Even if British leaders had chosen the correct way to win, however, they would soon have realized that the colonies were growing so fast that they would one day surpass Britain in size and strength. A condition of political servitude could not be sustained. The only correct solution in 1775, therefore, was not war but the offer of union or dominion status.

Given the selfishness and short-sightedness of the leaders of Britain, neither a peaceful solution nor a military victory was possible. Thus, the denouement at Yorktown was perhaps inevitable after all.

THREE

Napoléon at
Waterloo, 1815

The American Revolution helped to bring on the French Revolution of 1789 because it inflamed a desire for democracy among the common people of France, and its cost drove the French monarchy into bankruptcy.

King Louis XVI of France, although his country was the most populous and the richest in Europe, was unable to meet its obligations because the aristocracy paid few taxes. They owned the vast majority of the property and possessed all but a fraction of the wealth, but the peasants and the townspeople (the "Third Estate") bore the brunt of taxation.

The situation was unsustainable. It ended with the storming of the Bastille, a royal prison, on July 14, 1789, by a Parisian mob. The attack was inspired by the success of the American Revolution and by the teachings of the French philosopher Jean-Jacques Rousseau, who wrote in 1762, "Man is born free, and everywhere he is in chains."

The revolutionaries ousted the king and set off a prolonged collision with the crowned heads of Europe. The royal army dissolved in the chaos of the revolution, and the people had to build a new army from scratch. The National Convention government based the new army on patriotism and popular wars of expansion. The nation's emotional symbol was Rouget de Lisle's "Marseillaise," the most rousing of war hymns, sung for the first time on April 25, 1792.

The patriotic army that materialized was completely alien to the savagely disciplined mercenary armies of the kings. Given any chance for freedom, most mercenary soldiers deserted. The new French soldiers mostly served willingly and were in general more intelligent than the dregs of society who made up the royal armies. Discipline was much less rigid, and volley firing at close range, the primary element of the professional armies, was largely replaced by aimed fire of individual soldiers—almost a direct copy of the practices of Americans in their revolution.

French armies became immensely more mobile and flexible than the mercenary armies. Commanders were not constantly worried that soldiers would desert. Most of the wagons, draft horses, and other paraphernalia that followed royal armies disappeared. Soldiers largely did without tents, supply columns, and bases of supply in the rear. Occupied cities were forced to pay for food for the soldiers. When this failed, the soldiers plundered the enemy countryside. Armies no longer marched in solid masses. They were divided into divisions that moved on separate roads, but they could combine quickly, if necessary, to fight a battle.

This was the new model army that Napoléon Bonaparte inherited. Bonaparte, a poor member of the minor nobility in Corsica, graduated from a military academy in France, having attended on a scholarship paid by the king. He burst upon the world's consciousness when he posted cannons at the entrance to Toulon harbor in 1793. The British fleet—realizing it could be bottled up and destroyed—immediately abandoned the port, and the British occupiers withdrew. Thus almost without losses, Napoléon completely neutralized a powerful enemy force and eliminated a major threat to France.

Promoted to brigadier general, Bonaparte stopped a royalist attempt to restore the monarchy with a "whiff of grapeshot" from cannons that killed many royalists marching against the National Convention on October 5, 1795. His decisive action got him command of the army in Italy in 1796. In the Italian campaign, which followed, Bonaparte shattered the Austrian and Piedmontese armies and gained much territory for France. On November 9, 1799, he staged a coup d'etat and became dictator.

Napoléon is one of the great examples of the influence of genius on the destiny of nations. As the historian Leonard Krieger writes, "History is always the result of the meeting between a situation and a personality."[1] But it makes all the difference in the world whether this personality is a genius or an ordinary man or woman.

Napoléon dominated warfare from his first campaign in Italy until his defeat at Waterloo in 1815. Throughout this long and decisive period, he encountered no competitor with a trace of his genius, except the English admiral Horatio Nelson. And the arenas in which these men fought were entirely separate.

The appearance of a military genius turns all accepted ways of doing things on their heads. A military genius sees things other people do not see. For example, everyone regarded the narrow entrance to Toulon as a great safety factor, because ships within its enclosed harbor were immune from attacks by enemy ships outside. But when Bonaparte arrived, he at once saw that this same safe harbor could be a prison. All he had to do was seal off its entrance with cannons that could blast any ship that tried to get out.

Seeing things in a broad panorama and being able to take in a situation in a single quick view are marks of military genius. Alexander the Great could observe the dispositions of the enemy as a whole as he approached a field of battle. He saw the enemy's weakest place at once, and that is where he struck with overwhelming force. Napoléon recognized this gift quite clearly. "Success in war depends on *coup d'oeil* [seeing things at a glance], and sensing the psychological moment in battle," he said. "At Austerlitz, had I attacked six hours earlier, I would have been lost."[2]

Napoléon also recognized that success depends on the general. "An army of lions led by a stag will never be an army of lions," he said. He also said, "In war men are nothing; it is the man who is everything. The general is the head, the whole of an army. It was not the Roman army that conquered Gaul, but Caesar; it was not the Carthaginian army that made Rome tremble in her gates, but Hannibal; it was not the Macedonian army that reached the Indus, but Alexander."[3]

The celebrated German military historian Hans Delbrück points out that the secret of the great commander is his blending of boldness and caution.[4] This is also the judgment of Sun Tzu.[5] Napoléon based his campaigns on meticulous study and preparation.[6] Before every operation he meditated about what might happen if one approach was tried, and what might happen if another was tried. But he never began by asking, "What can the enemy do?" He first sought to place his own army in the best position and then asked, "What now can the enemy do?" This gave Napoléon the initiative. When a campaign opened, Napoléon used his cavalry, spies, and seizure of letters in post offices to confirm or eliminate his hypotheses. In this manner he simplified his own plan and uncovered the enemy's plan.[7]

The keys to Napoléon's success were mobility, concentration of force, and surprise. Napoléon said that "the loss of time is irreparable in war. Operations only fail through delays. Space we can recover, lost time never."[8] For the decisive battle, Napoléon cut down all subsidiary operations so as to concentrate the greatest possible numbers at the point of decision. He knew that an inferior force that is correctly assembled will generally defeat a superior force that is not. His surprises were seldom tactical. Nearly all were strategic. At Marengo in 1800, he used the St. Bernard passes in the western Alps to descend unexpectedly on the rear of the Austrian army in northern Italy. In the

1805 campaign, he marched eastward through southern Germany, then turned abruptly south to fall on the rear of an Austrian army at Ulm on the Danube River. In the 1806 Jena campaign, he advanced precipitately, not from the west as expected, but from southern Germany, cutting the Prussian army off from its supplies and bases. Napoléon's very supremacy as a field commander became his downfall. As the historian John A. Lynn writes, "He neither knew what was enough nor when to stop." He thus was doomed to fail sooner or later. In this Napoléon was the exact opposite of Frederick the Great of Prussia. After seizing Silesia, the object of his ambition, Frederick said, "Henceforth I would not attack a cat except to defend myself."[9]

After his victory over the Russians and Austrians at Austerlitz in 1805, Napoléon had the opportunity to impose a peace placing France as the supreme power on the continent. If he had given Austria easy terms and allowed it to expand into the Balkans at the expense of Russia, he would have made Austria an ally and raised it as a bulwark against Russia, the major challenge on land to France. Instead, Napoléon imposed a humiliating peace and annexed huge portions of Austrian territory, leaving it as an enemy bent on revenge.

A settlement with Austria would have left only Prussia, beside Russia, as a competitor on the continent. Napoléon knew that Prussia's army was a fossil unchanged from the old regime of the eighteenth century and was certain to fall, as in fact it did in 1806. But Prussia, as well, could have been kept intact in the east as a shield against Russia.

Thus France could have imposed a peaceful order on the continent, leaving only Britain as an enemy.[10] But here, as well, he could have reached a settlement. Instead of setting up the Continental System to stop British trade with Europe, he could have opened the ports of the continent to Britain. It would have taken Britain only a short time to realize that its economic interests outweighed its fear of Napoléon. But Napoléon was so obsessed with war that he could imagine no political solutions, only battlefield victories.[11] Accordingly, he attacked Russia in 1812 because it withdrew from the Continental System. This was a fatal decision. Russia was too poor to sustain an invading army, and its people burned most of the food supplies that were available. This forced Napoléon to retreat, and led to inevitable defeat and his banishment to the little Italian island of Elba in 1814.

If Napoléon was such a supreme commander, and if he had no rivals, why, then, did he ultimately lose? The answer can be found in his very supremacy as a war leader. Napoléon depended wholly on himself to devise and carry out his campaigns. Part of the reason was that he felt he understood warfare better than anyone else. But more important was his realization that he was an upstart who had seized power by a coup d'etat and who held it as an autocrat. He never felt secure as chief of the French state.

Accordingly, the officers he promoted to become his marshals were not brought up to command but to obey. Napoléon told his chief of staff, Marshal Louis-Alexandre Berthier, "Keep strictly to the orders which I give you; I alone know what I must do." His memorialist, Armand-Augustin-Louis, marquis de Caulaincourt, wrote, "No one, not even the general staff, dared to assume the responsibility of giving the most trifling order."[12]

Personal command had been difficult enough in the eighteenth century when armies were comparatively small. But warfare in the Napoleonic era became ever more intense and complex. Armies grew far too large for a single person to control. Although Napoléon adopted the division system of a force of all arms, and the corps system of several divisions capable of standing alone for some time, he did not give the commanders of these bodies freedom to act on their own.

This failure had two major consequences. It became impossible for Napoléon to control adequately the large armies that came into being from 1807 onward. And the generals Napoléon selected never developed into leaders who could make and carry out independent decisions. This grew into a deadly flaw. The incapacity of subordinate commanders was the principal reason why Waterloo turned out as it did.

Living on Elba was a poor substitute for running the French Empire, and the island was geographically too close to France for Napoléon to resist returning. In March 1815, Napoléon succumbed to the entice-ment, remounted the throne, and challenged the allies to remove him if they could.

The allies, principally the Austrians, Prussians, Russians, and Brit-ish, had twice the forces Napoléon could raise. They resolved to close in on Paris from north and east and crush Napoléon by force of arms. From Belgium, a British-Dutch-German army under Arthur Welles-ley, duke of Wellington, and a Prussian army under Marshal Gebhard Leberecht von Blücher would press south. From Germany an Austrian army under Marshal Karl Philipp, prince of Schwarzenberg would advance west, with the Russians following.[13]

Schwarzenberg, marching through Germany, would be slow. The Russians, coming behind, would be even slower. Napoléon could ignore both for the moment.

A fortuitous opportunity appeared in Belgium. The combined forces of Wellington, with 88,000 men, and Blücher, with 123,000 men, were much greater than the French forces guarding the Belgian frontier, 124,000 men. But the allies were not concentrated. Welling-ton had posted his army in the vicinity of Brussels, and Blücher around Namur, thirty-five miles southeast. Between them lay a large gap. If Napoléon could seize the crossroads of Quatre-Bras (Four Branches) halfway between Brussels and Namur, he would be in the central posi-tion between the British and the Prussian armies. From there he could beat in turn the British and the Prussians, then swing southeast to deal with the Austrians and the Russians.

Napoléon used the central position wherever possible, and it is a basic element in Sun Tzu's axioms.[14] But generals have seldom adopted the strategy. Far from seeing the central position as an opportunity, most generals see it as a peril—fearing their army would be crushed if placed between two enemy forces.

To Napoléon, however, the chance to divide his enemy was not to be missed. He ordered the Army of the North (five corps plus the

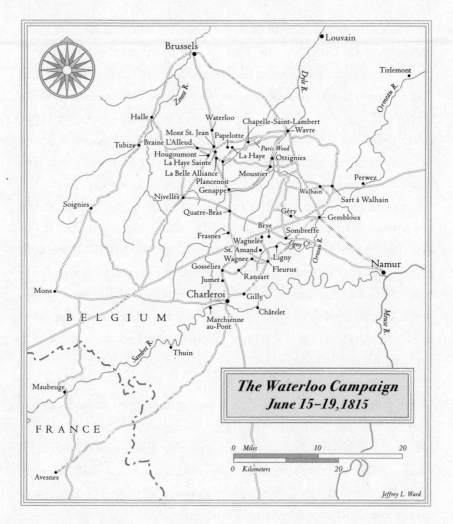

The Waterloo Campaign
June 15–19, 1815

Imperial Guard) to concentrate in the vicinity of Avesnes, France, some thirty miles southwest of Quatre-Bras and twenty-six miles southwest of Charleroi, Belgium. On June 12, he left Paris for Avesnes. The allies only discerned these movements on the night of June 13–14, when Prussian outposts became aware of many bivouac fires along the French-Belgian frontier, which ran in a northwest-southeast direction about thirteen miles northeast of Avesnes and thirteen miles southwest of Charleroi. The sentries were members of the 33,000-man 1st Corps of Hans Ernst von Zieten, whose most advanced elements were almost on the frontier southwest of Charleroi.

Zieten reported the French presence to Marshal Blücher, who ordered the 1st Corps to pull back to Sombreffe, twelve miles northeast of Charleroi, and directed his other three corps to join it there. His 2nd Corps was just east of Sombreffe, and his 3rd Corps was about fifteen miles to the southeast. But Blücher's 4th Corps was near Liège, thirty miles northeast, and it would take two days or longer to arrive. Bringing together only three of his four corps at Sombreffe was irresponsible, especially since Blücher was determined to accept battle.

So Blücher committed the first violation of a Sun Tzu principle: concentration of as many men as possible at the point of decision. The Prussian commander also perpetrated a related violation of the same principle by placing himself within reach of the French with an inferior force.[15] He should have ordered the concentration of his army farther north, so that his 4th Corps could join the other three corps. Napoléon in fact had anticipated that Blücher would move back toward Liège to bring all his forces together.

On the morning of June 15, Napoléon rode up to Charleroi, twelve miles south of Quatre-Bras. There he made two profoundly bad choices. He gave Marshal Michel Ney command of the left wing of his army, the 1st and 2nd Corps and a cavalry division, and he gave his cavalry chief, Marshal Emmanuel de Grouchy, command of his right wing, the 3rd and 4th Corps and two cavalry divisions. Neither commander was adequate for his responsibilities.

Ney, though renowned for his bravery, lacked judgment and had learned little from the many battles he had fought. In 1808 Napoléon had said that Ney was "as ignorant as the last-joined drummer boy." Grouchy was a skilled cavalry commander, but he had never commanded a corps, much less an army wing. Napoléon had refused to take back Joachim Murat, the best cavalry leader in Europe, because Murat had deserted to the allies in January 1814. After Waterloo Napoléon deeply regretted this decision and said that if Murat had been on the scene, he would have won the battle.

Napoléon had left as Paris governor his most able commander,

Louis-Nicolas Davout. With vastly inferior forces, Davout pushed back the main Prussian army at Auerstädt and gained an immense French victory in the Jena campaign of 1806. Napoléon said he could trust no one else to hold the capital. Davout replied, "If you are victor, Paris will be yours, and if you are beaten, neither I nor anyone else can do anything for you."[16]

Napoléon had named two officers who could not make good decisions. These fateful choices were going to determine the outcome of the battle of Waterloo.

Napoléon's instructions to Ney were to sweep the enemy off the Brussels-Charleroi road and to occupy Quatre-Bras that very day. Napoléon ordered Grouchy to push back the Prussians toward Sombreffe. His aim was to separate the British and the Prussian armies so neither could help the other.

Grouchy moved too slowly, and Napoléon went forward himself and speeded up the attack, driving Zieten's corps back to Ligny Creek, four miles southwest of Sombreffe.

Meanwhile, Ney drove a Prussian detachment out of the village of Gossalies, a few miles north of Charleroi, but sent only his cavalry division on to Quatre-Bras, seven miles beyond. There the horsemen encountered the Dutch Nassau Brigade. Unable to overrun it, they withdrew.

Marshal Ney violated a basic Sun Tzu principle on this day. One must know the enemy's plans and the terrain, Sun Tzu says. One must not learn them as one goes along. The failure to do so makes for ill-considered decisions.[17] Ney should have put together a combined force of infantry, artillery, and cavalry to seize Quatre-Bras. More important, he should have commanded this force in person. If he had done so, he would have seen that the crossroads were lightly held, and he could have seized them easily. Napoléon said that an officer who does not know the enemy's dispositions does not know his trade. How ironic that the very person he put in charge of his left wing was just such an officer!

Thus Ney committed the first great strategic blunder of the Water-loo campaign. He had not ensured that Napoléon could place his army between the British and the Prussians. Napoléon, however, was not worried. He had seen no aggressive move from the Prussians, and there was no heavy British presence at Quatre-Bras. He told Ney to occupy the crossroads the next day, June 16.

But at 8:00 A.M. on June 16, everything changed. French cavalry scouts reported that strong Prussian columns were approaching. But only three of Blücher's corps—84,000 men—were assembling around the village of Ligny, along Ligny Creek. His 4th Corps of 31,000 men was still far away, and Wellington, at Brussels, could not possibly help him. Blücher had handed Napoléon the chance to attack only three-quarters of his army.

Napoléon quickly developed a battle plan. He had just 68,000 men at Ligny, but he sent only his cavalry to confront Blücher's easternmost corps along the creek. This allowed him to concentrate his two corps in a direct frontal attack against the two Prussian corps around Ligny. With the odds even, Blücher would have to use all his reserves to stop the attacks.

This would leave Blücher unable to defend against the decisive blow that Napoléon planned to deliver against Blücher's right rear. Napoléon expected the job of seizing Quatre-Bras to be easy, and figured that Ney could send one of his corps to deliver the blow on Blücher's right rear at Brye, five miles southeast of Quatre-Bras and two miles northwest of Ligny. While this strike was being delivered, Napoléon planned for his Imperial Guard, an elite force of veterans reserved for culminat-ing attacks, to smash through the center of the Prussian line at Ligny. Napoléon expected these two near simultaneous assaults to destroy the two westernmost of Blücher's corps and compel the easternmost corps to fall back toward the Prussian supply base at Liège to the northeast—and thus entirely out of the campaign.

In his confidence that Ney would carry out his part of the plan, Napoléon did not order forward his reserve force, the 6th Corps of

10,000 men, under Georges Mouton, comte de Lobau. It remained at Charleroi. This was an inexcusable mistake. If Lobau had been moved up to a point a few miles west of Ligny, he could have swung onto the right rear of the Prussians, and Ney need not have been called on. Napoléon finally ordered the 6th Corps to Fleurus, just south of Ligny, late in the afternoon, but it arrived too late to play any role in the battle. Napoléon never explained this, the first in a number of severe tactical errors that he was to make in this campaign. In the aftermath of Waterloo, few observers recognized these blunders, and no one asked Napoléon to justify or excuse them.

In the meantime. Wellington had made a bad judgment when he learned that French forces had been spotted along the frontier. He assumed erroneously that Napoléon was going to advance on Mons, thirty-five miles southwest of Brussels, and then turn northward on Brussels to try to cut off his communications with England. This was a most illogical conclusion, since the main British supply base was the great deepwater port of Antwerp, north of Brussels, and an attack by Napoléon from the south would merely drive Wellington back on his supplies.

Wellington's incorrect decision illustrates why it is important to find out the enemy's plans before committing one's army. By failing to determine Napoléon's true intention, Wellington violated a cardinal Sun Tzu principle: do not assume the enemy will do what one thinks he will do, but find out what he is actually going to do. Wellington should have waited until Napoléon showed his hand before committing himself in any direction.[18]

Fortunately for the British, Napoléon reasoned that Wellington would do the sensible thing and move his army toward Quatre-Bras and junction with the Prussians. So his original dispositions were aimed at meeting the British at Quatre-Bras. Assuming that the enemy will make the rational decision might, in theory, be a violation of Sun Tzu's rule first to ascertain the enemy's actual plans. In the absence of sure knowledge, however, the safest choice is the correct choice. In Napoléon's case, this was to assume that Wellington would move on Quatre-Bras at the first opportunity, and to make preparations accordingly.

After issuing his orders to turn south from Brussels, Wellington went to a ball being put on by the duchess of Richmond on the evening of June 15. During the party he got word that Napoléon had reached Charleroi, thirteen miles north of the frontier, with his entire army. Wellington and the duke of Richmond went into the study to examine a map. Wellington at once realized that Napoléon was threatening to place himself between the British and the Prussian armies. "Napoléon has humbugged me, by God!" he shouted. "He has gained twenty-four hours march on me."[19]

Wellington now directed the British army to Quatre-Bras. But many of his officers were at the duchess's party, and the army endured extreme confusion getting on the march. It was late on the afternoon of June 16 before strong British forces arrived at Quatre-Bras.

Therefore, Marshal Ney had plenty of time to seize Quatre-Bras on the morning of June 16. But Napoléon's choice of the wrong left-wing commander now had portentous consequences. Ney did precisely nothing until 11:00 A.M., when he at last ordered the 2nd Corps, under Marshal Comte Honoré-Charles Reille, to move forward and seize the crossroads. At the same time, he ordered the 1st Corps, under Marshal Jean-Baptiste Drouet, comte d'Erlon, to advance to Gosselies, seven miles south of Quatre-Bras.

Accordingly, when Wellington arrived at Quatre-Bras at 10:00 A.M. on June 16, he found one of his divisions in possession, but no enemy. While the rest of his army was frantically trying to reach the crossroads, Wellington rode over to Brye, five miles southeast of Quatre-Bras and a couple of miles west of Sombreffe, where he met with Blücher at 1:00 P.M. Wellington agreed to come to Blücher's assistance, provided he was not attacked himself. After looking over Blücher's defensive preparations around Ligny, Wellington remarked to his military attaché, "If they fight here, they [the Prussians] will be damnably mauled."[20]

When Wellington arrived back at Quatre-Bras around 3:00 P.M., the situation had become critical. All thought of helping Blücher vanished. The crossroads were being held by only 7,800 infantry and fourteen cannons. Reille's 22,000-man 2nd Corps backed up by sixty cannons had appeared around 2:00 P.M. Reille could easily have seized the position, but he moved so slowly that a large number of British troops arrived in time to stop the advance.

Reille was now slightly outnumbered, and despite heavy fighting, he was unable to break through. Ney was impatiently awaiting the arrival of d'Erlon's corps, but he had been so tardy in ordering it forward that the corps was still some distance away.

Meanwhile, beginning at 2:30 P.M., the French 3rd Corps attacked the Prussians at St. Amand, two miles southwest of Ligny, while the 4th Corps assaulted Ligny. But Prussian resistance was extremely strong. Around 3:30 P.M. Napoléon sent a note to Ney to dispatch d'Erlon's corps onto the Prussian right rear at Brye immediately.

By 5:00 P.M. Blücher's reserves were exhausted. He had committed nearly all of his men, except his cavalry, while Napoléon still had 10,000 men of the Imperial Guard uncommitted. He expected to hear the sound of d'Erlon's guns on the Prussian rear around 6:00 P.M. This is when he intended to launch the Guard against the Prussian center at Ligny.

However, Charles Huchet, comte de la Bédoyère, the messenger sent by Napoléon, had completely misunderstood his instructions. When he found d'Erlon on the road to Quatre-Bras, he ordered him to turn about and to march—not on the Prussian rear—but on the *French* rear!

While Napoléon was making final preparations for the Guard to assault Ligny, General Dominique-René Vandamme, commander of the 3rd Corps, rode up and announced that a heavy enemy force was approaching Fleurus, directly behind the French line. Napoléon at once suspended the Guard attack and set up blocks to stop the expected assault. But—something Vandamme himself had not done—he sent an aide to find out for certain whether this column was an enemy force. The aide came back at 6:30 P.M. with the news that it was d'Erlon's corps.[21]

It was now too late to send the corps onto the Prussian rear. Napoléon decided to go ahead and launch the Guard attack. It went in at 7:30 P.M. just as a heavy thunderstorm erupted, making it impossible to fire muskets. The Guard drove the Prussians out of Ligny with naked bayonets.

When the rain ceased, Blücher assembled all of his cavalry and, with him at their head, launched charges against the Guard, which had formed up in battalion squares with bayonets projecting to repel cavalry assaults. The attacks failed, and in the resulting melee, Blücher's horse was struck by a bullet and rolled over its rider. His aide dragged the seventy-three-year-old commander, bruised and half-conscious, to safety. If he had not rescued Blücher, the battle of Waterloo would have had an utterly different outcome.

The 1st and 2nd Prussian Corps fell back west of Sombreffe, just as Napoléon had expected.[22] If d'Erlon had been on hand, they would have been destroyed. Even so, Ligny was a great French victory, costing the Prussians 25,000 men and the French about 11,000. Some 10,000 of the Prussian losses consisted of deserters, however, who made for Liège. These were largely men from former French provinces, and their sympathies were with Napoléon.

At 9:00 P.M., the fight at Quatre-Bras ended in a draw. Losses were 4,000 on each side. The British still held the field, but they would have to retreat the next day, because, with the Prussians defeated, the French could sweep around their rear and cut them off from Brussels.

Despite the blunders of Ney, Napoléon had driven Blücher from the field. He had every reason to believe the Prussians would retire on their supply base at Liège to the northeast, and Napoléon could turn against Wellington in safety. On the morning of June 17, 1815, Napoléon sent Grouchy with his two corps (3rd and 4th) and his cavalry to find the Prussians and report back. The campaign of Waterloo now took on a life of its own, unrelated to the plans of Napoléon, and dependent on the flawed visions of the two wing commanders, Grouchy and Ney. Both men began to make one disastrous blunder after another.

Grouchy's first cavalry reports were that the Prussians were in full retreat on Liège. But he didn't realize that these were the deserters who had fled the field at Ligny. He also didn't know that the Prussian army actually had retired on Wavre, north of Ligny. The Prussian chief of staff had found that many of the troops had moved in that direction, and it was a convenient rallying point. When Blücher recovered, he took advantage of this unanticipated decision and resolved to go to the aid of the British if attacked.

Meanwhile, Ney, at Quatre-Bras, was doing precisely nothing. Wellington received a Prussian officer at 9:00 A.M. on June 17, who informed him of Blücher's retreat and asked Wellington's intentions. The duke replied that he was falling back to the low ridge of Mont-Saint-Jean, just south of the village of Waterloo, about fifteen miles from Brussels. There he would offer Napoléon battle if Blücher would support him with one corps.

At 10:00 A.M. the retreat began. The British troops were unmolested because Ney had ignored Napoléon's order to attack at first light. Ney's troops were still in bivouac when Napoléon rode up at 1:00 P.M. Livid, he got the pursuit under way at 2:00 P.M. The British had a good head start, their advantage increased by a huge thunderstorm that kept the French from advancing across the country to cut them off and force them to stand.[23]

Before nightfall, the British had pulled up on Mont-Saint-Jean. At 6:30 P.M. on June 17, Napoléon's vanguard arrived at La Belle Alliance on the next low ridge south and, sending cavalry forward, found Wellington's army.

Meanwhile Grouchy had finally discovered that the Prussians were at Wavre, nine miles east of Mont-Saint-Jean. At 2:00 A.M. on June 18, Napoléon received a message from Grouchy: "If I find the mass of the Prussians is retiring on Wavre, I shall follow them, so as to prevent their gaining Brussels and to separate them from Wellington."[24] This was gratifying news. It indicated that Grouchy was fully aware that his job was to place his two corps between the Prussians and the British and so prevent the Prussians from reinforcing Wellington.

But it turned out that Napoléon's faith in Grouchy's good judgment was misplaced.

Napoléon replied to Grouchy, describing the situation at Waterloo, and telling Grouchy to head for Wavre, push the Prussians before him, and keep in touch. The message was not clearly written, but Napoléon assumed that the right-wing commander understood that he must block the Prussians from advancing on Waterloo. Yet, as events were to show, Grouchy incredibly did not see something that was plain common sense. His idea was to press on the *rear* of the Prussian army with a small force.

At 11:30 A.M. on June 18, Grouchy and Marshal Étienne-Maurice Gérard, commander of the 4th Corps, were standing in the town of Walhain, seven miles south of Wavre. They heard gunfire from the direction of Mont-Saint-Jean. This was the opening round of the battle of Waterloo, and Gérard said, "I think we ought to march on the cannons," thus interposing Grouchy's wing between Waterloo and Wavre.[25]

But Grouchy said there was no cause to do anything. The bombardment, he said, was merely a delaying action by the retreating British rear guard. Gérard argued on the contrary, that the cannonade signified impending battle. Grouchy's two corps, he insisted, should be between the two hostile armies. If they stayed where they were, on the rear of the Prussians, a small defending force could stop them, and the Prussian main body could advance directly to aid the British. But Grouchy refused to move.

If Grouchy had heeded Gérard, his two corps could have struck Blücher's left, or southern, flank as he was turning westward toward Waterloo. This would have prevented Blücher from reinforcing Wellington.[26]

Instead, Grouchy continued to march north on Wavre with a single column. This column launched timid attacks on the tail of the Prussian army and accomplished nothing. By his stupidity, Grouchy had eliminated the entire right wing of Napoléon's army on the day when the destiny of Europe was being decided.

Wellington's move to Waterloo exemplified an important injunction of Sun Tzu: to select and occupy a battlefield first, forcing the enemy to attack under conditions favorable to the defender and unfavorable to him.

Early on the morning of June 18, 1815, Wellington received a message that Blücher's 4th Corps, under Friedrich Wilhelm von Bülow, would march to his support, followed by a second corps. Wellington thus knew that if he could hold on, an attack was coming on the right, or eastern, flank of the French army.

Napoléon was not happy that the inaction of Marshal Ney had permitted the British army to get away from Quatre-Bras on June 17 and establish itself in a strong position at Waterloo. But he had every reason to congratulate himself. He had sent the Prussian army flying at Ligny. He believed the remaining Prussians were being blocked from marching to the relief of the British. He had assembled a stronger army at Waterloo than Wellington: 72,000 men against Wellington's 67,000 men.

Napoléon had attained this numerical superiority because of a perfectly senseless decision by Wellington. The duke had posted an entire corps, 17,000 men under Frederick, prince of Orange-Nassau of the Netherlands, at Halle and Tubize, a dozen miles west of Waterloo. He had put the corps there for fear that the French might advance directly on Brussels from the south. This was far-fetched reasoning. Once Napoléon concentrated at La Belle Alliance, the ridgeline just south of the British center, it was certain he would not move on Brussels. Wellington's decision was a flagrant violation of the principle of concentration of force. Prince Frederick's corps was so far away that it could not possibily take part in the battle at Waterloo.

Napoléon intended to combine his superiority of force with a huge battery of eighty cannons that he had mounted at La Belle Alliance. His intention was to pound the British positions with artillery fire and then to make a massive, overwhelming assault directly on the left center of the British line. Napoléon believed he could drive the British back in disorder to Brussels and then turn and destroy the Prussian army.

But several things were wrong with this scenario. Napoléon was not aware that the utter failure of Grouchy guaranteed a massive strike on his right, or eastern, flank. He also was continuing to rely on Marshal Ney to direct the attack on the British line, and he had seen how Ney had already failed time after time. There was every reason to expect Ney to fail again.

But the single greatest thing wrong was that Napoléon was planning to violate one of his own fundamental rules of battle. Ever since his first campaign in Italy in 1796–1797, Napoléon had tried to avoid frontal attacks, and instead had tried to swing around on the enemy's flank or rear.

Such turning movements are part of Sun Tzu's primary two-element method for winning battlefield victories. Sun Tzu postulates a *zheng*, an orthodox, direct element that fixes the enemy in place, and a *qi*, an unorthodox, indirect element that flanks or encircles the enemy and achieves victory. *Zheng* at Waterloo would have been the main assault on the British main line along the Mont-Saint-Jean ridgeline. *Qi* would have been a simultaneous assault on Wellington's flank.[27]

Napoléon had a splendid opportunity to make a flank attack at Waterloo. Wellington's left, or eastern, flank was protected by the presence of the Prussian army nine miles away at Wavre. Even though Napoléon did not know the Prussians were approaching, it would have been perilous to launch a flank move in that direction. Wellington's right, or western, flank, on the other hand, was bare and fully exposed, since Prince Frederick's corps was a dozen miles away and would have been unable to arrive in time. Napoléon could have launched one of his corps around this flank while Wellington was wholly absorbed in containing Napoléon's frontal attack against the left center of his line. It would almost certainly have shattered the British army well before the Prussian corps could arrive on the scene.

On this day of Waterloo, however, Napoléon intended to attack headlong into the teeth of the waiting British army. This plan was not only a repudiation of Napoléon's own doctrine but also a violation of a Sun Tzu principle. "Do not attack well-regulated formations," Sun Tzu advises. He also admonishes armies to go around obstacles. "To avoid the substantial, strike the vacuous."[28]

The failure of Napoléon to follow this rule at Waterloo is most baffling and has never been explained. He committed virtually all of the errors that he himself had avoided in the years past and that Sun Tzu would have warned against. Perhaps Napoléon was confident that he could smash the British line with ease. But that is scarcely a reason. There are many imponderables in warfare. Why he ignored his own canon at Waterloo remains one of the greatest imponderables of all.

The focal point or junction of the British position was located where the north-south Brussels-Charleroi road crossed the east-west Mont-Saint-Jean ridgeline. British positions ran southwest for a little over a mile to the walled château, or farmstead, of Hougoumont. The line extended east of the junction for about the same distance along the road to Wavre. It was anchored on the east by the walled and solidly built farmstead of Papelotte and the nearby hamlet of La Haye.

Wellington had no possibility of doing more than defending against a direct attack. By placing Prince Frederick's corps so far west, he had eliminated any chance of using it at Waterloo.

Prior to the frontal attack on the British line, Napoléon sent in a diversionary attack on Hougoumont with a division commanded by his brother Jérôme. Napoléon's intention was to draw additional British troops into this fight in order to weaken the British center.

This was not sensible reasoning, because it tied up French troops in a static, pointless battle. An attack on a fortified position like Hougoumont is directly contrary to Sun Tzu principles. The lowest realization of warfare, according to Sun Tzu, is to attack fortified cities, which is the same as attacking strongly fortified positions. "If you attack cities, the troops' strength will be exhausted," Sun Tzu says.[29]

The attack was further hamstrung by the failure of Jérôme to bring along artillery to blast holes in the solid walls enclosing the farmstead. As a result, he repeatedly assaulted the walls with infantry and was repeatedly thrown back. Later, French batteries did move up and bombard the farmstead, setting fire to most of the buildings. The fight grew into a bloody confrontation involving 14,000 French soldiers and 12,000 British and German soldiers. But it contributed nothing to the battle.

Meanwhile, Napoléon prepared for Marshal d'Erlon's 1st Corps of 19,000 men to assault Wellington's left wing east of the Brussels-Charleroi road. While doing so, he spotted "a dark cloud" emerging from the woods of Chapelle-Saint-Lambert, four miles to the east. A moment later a rider came up with the news that it was the advanced guard of Bülow's 31,000-man corps. Napoléon was surprised, but he was confident he could ruin Wellington long before the Prussians could arrive. He ordered two cavalry divisions to slow Bülow's advance, and detailed Marshal Lobau to follow with his small 6th Corps of 10,000 men to hold the Prussians in check.

When Marshals Ney and d'Erlon launched their frontal attack, they committed a series of blunders that played a major role in the outcome.

Ever since the French army had been reorganized after the French Revolution, tactical doctrine had been to advance battalions of 500 to 600 men in column (or tight marching) formation into battle. Troops moved much faster in this way than in extended lines of battle. The enemy waited in line of battle, for it was the least vulnerable to artillery fire. If a cannon ball hit a British line of battle, only two men would be lost, since the British line was two men deep. If a shot hit a massed column, on the other hand, all the men in a file would be bowled over. This could affect ten or more men.

As French battalions neared the enemy, they deployed into battle lines three men deep. Just before deployment, doctrine called for the French cavalry to threaten the enemy, forcing the enemy to form open or hollow squares, with bayonets projecting outward on all four sides. Cavalry could seldom break these squares. But a square was generally four men deep, and it had only a fraction of the fire power of the same unit in line of battle.

Doctrine called for the French infantry, now in line of battle, to pour their much heavier fire on the enemy squares, while also pounding them with case or grape shot from light regimental cannons pushed forward with the infantry. Case and grape shot consisted of deadly metal balls sprayed into enemy formations. Once the squares were thrown into confusion, doctrine called for the cavalry to charge and scatter the fugitives.

No one knows why, but Ney and d'Erlon completely disregarded French doctrine. They employed no light artillery and no cavalry in the attack. They also drew up two divisions and two brigades in formations 200 men wide, with one battalion close behind the other. These huge masses were too close together to deploy easily into separate battalion lines of battle when they got close to the enemy. It was an absurd method of attack, and it defied common sense. Sun Tzu emphasizes that selection of wise generals is vital in war.[30] The lack of judgment of Ney and d'Erlon was fateful for the French cause.

Meanwhile one French brigade advanced against the walled farmstead of La Haye Sainte on the Brussels-Charleroi road, just below the summit of Mont-Saint-Jean, and another brigade advanced against the farmstead of Papelotte and the hamlet of La Haye on the east. But neither had any light artillery or cavalry support.

These attacks exemplify Sun Tzu's admonition against attacking fortified places. Although the action against La Haye Sainte isolated the defenders, 400 soldiers of the King's German Legion under Major George Baring, the French could neither capture the place nor advance beyond it. Likewise, a German force of 900 men at Papelotte and La Haye held on doggedly to both places all day.

Wellington had pulled all his men—except a Dutch-Belgian brigade of 2,500 men—off the ridgeline to lie down on the reverse slope, where they were virtually immune to the French artillery fire. When the French lines approached the summit, Wellington's men had only to stand up, advance a few paces, and deliver a withering volley.

This combination of Wellington's defensive tactics and Ney's and d'Erlon's abandonment of the rules of engagement placed the French in a desperate tactical position. Without cavalry and light artillery, the allied formations could not be forced into squares. Thus, the allies' lines of battle gave them maximum fire power, whereas the French had a difficult time moving from their mass formations into lines of battle, with consequent loss of time, fire power, and cohesion.

As the French neared the hedgerow-bordered road to Wavre running along the ridgeline—behind which the British were hiding—they forced the Dutch-Belgian brigade to retreat hastily. As the French attempted to deploy into lines of battle, the British infantry pushed forward to the road and delivered crushing volleys at a forty-pace range. Even so, the French gave as good as they got, and the battle was degenerating into a bloody stalemate all along the roadway.

At this moment, two British cavalry brigades, about 2,000 men, charged at full gallop, bounded over the road, and drove straight at the French. Since the French had insufficient time to form defensive squares, they took to their heels. Most rushed back down the slope to safety, but numbers of them surrendered. Meanwhile the British cavalry continued their wild charge, climbing the slope of La Belle Alliance and making for the huge French battery of eighty guns. Here French cavalry counterattacked.

In a wild melee the British horsemen were driven back in complete defeat, losing a large part of their strength in this brief, mad encounter. The Royal Scots Greys, for example, returned with only 50 of their original 300 men. The wasteful charge on the French guns left the British cavalry weak for the remainder of the battle. At 3:30 P.M., Napoléon ordered Ney to capture the walled farmstead of La Haye Sainte. Napoléon intended to use it as the base from which to launch a grand advance.

But Ney was able to get together only two brigades, and the attack failed. Now Ney made a blunder of monumental proportions. He saw British ammunition wagons streaming to the rear. They were actually carrying off wounded, but Ney jumped to the conclusion that the British were retreating. He ordered 5,000 French cavalry to charge the British.

This attack—like d'Erlon's infantry assault—was carried out completely contrary to doctrine. Cavalry operating alone could only force the enemy into squares, which horsemen could not crack. But Ney had not brought cavalry and light guns along in the infantry attack, and now he didn't bring infantry and light guns along in the cavalry attack.

The French cavalry also blundered. As they swarmed up the slopes of Mont-Saint-Jean, the British infantry formed into squares, but Wellington ordered the gunners to keep firing case and grape shot until the last moment, then to rush into the center of the squares with their horses. The gunners fled as the French horsemen climbed toward them, but the French had made no preparations to spike the cannons they now captured. This could have been done quickly by driving headless nails into the priming tubes through which the gunpowder was ignited. The guns remained as potent as ever.

The cavalry charged the infantry squares with great valor. Captain Rees Howell Gronow, of the English Foot Guards, described the scene: "We saw large masses of cavalry advance like an overwhelming, long, moving line. In a short period they were within twenty yards of us, shouting '*Vive l'Empereur!*' The word of command, 'Prepare to receive cavalry,' had been given, every man in the front ranks knelt, and a wall bristling with steel, held together by steady hands, presented itself to the infuriated cuirassiers."[31]

When Henry William Paget, Lord Uxbridge, Wellington's cavalry commander, saw that the French attacks were failing, he hurled his remaining horsemen at the French, driving them back. The gunners rushed out of the squares, manned their pieces, and poured case and grape shot into the retreating enemy, causing great losses.

Napoléon was preoccupied with the arrival of Bülow's Prussian corps on his right flank. Afraid that the cavalry repulse might panic the army, he ordered Marshal François-Étienne de Kellermann to support Ney in another attack with his cavalry corps. Thus Napoléon also disregarded tactical doctrine in sending forward cavalry almost totally unsupported. His fault illustrates that no commander can think of everything in the stress of battle.

More than 9,000 French cavalry formed up, filling nearly all the space between the farmsteads of Hougoumont on the west and La Haye Sainte on the Brussels-Charleroi road. This attack was backed up by only a single artillery battery.

This second cavalry assault met with the same fate as the first. The gunners fled into the infantry squares, and the squares withstood the cavalry charges. Once the attack was repulsed, the gunners rushed out and pounded the retreating horsemen. But the strain on the British was immense. Wellington had used up his reserves.

Around 6:00 P.M., Napoléon ordered Ney to seize the farmstead of La Haye Sainte, irrespective of cost. This he finally achieved, but only because the defending King's German Legion, which had held the place without support all day long, finally ran out of ammunition. Only a few of the German defenders survived.

Ney now moved a few horse artillery pieces toward Wellington's center and began to pulverize the infantry, still in squares, with case shot. The effect of the fire shows what might have happened if Ney had used more cannons and had brought up infantry in his cavalry assaults.

An eyewitness, Alexander Cavalié Mercer, a British battery commander, reported on the rapidity of fire and precision of a single battery set up on a knoll ahead of La Haye Sainte. "Every shot took effect, and I certainly expected we should be annihilated," he reported. "The whole livelong day had cost us nothing like this."[32] Cannon all but destroyed three British regiments. The center of the British line of battle was so weakened that it could not have withstood a strong assault. The 27th Regiment of Foot, for example, lost two-thirds of its men. The men were lying dead, still in rows in their square.

Wellington was deeply perturbed, but he was determined to hold on to his position until the Prussians arrived.[33]

Ney sent to Napoléon an urgent request for troops. Despite the vast accumulation of mistakes by Ney and others, the moment of decision had arrived. One more push and the French could penetrate the British line and win victory.

Napoléon, however, was unable to make this final push because the advance of the Prussians on his right flank had produced a crisis. French cavalry and Lobau's corps had struck Bülow's columns soon after they emerged from the Paris Wood at Chapelle-Saint-Lambert at 4:00 P.M. But the French were outnumbered three to one, and Lobau withdrew to Plancenoit, a mile east of the Brussels-Charleroi road and directly in the rear of the French line. Prussian infantry drove Lobau's troops out of the village, and Prussian batteries opened fire on the Brussels-Charleroi road. Part of the Imperial Guard retook Plancenoit, but it was thrown out again about the time Ney was pleading for troops. With disaster facing him, Napoléon formed eleven battalions of the Imperial Guard in as many squares and posted them as a shield in a north-south line facing Plancenoit. Meanwhile two battalions of the Guard advanced on the village, with bayonets fixed. Without firing a shot, the Guards drove the Prussians out of Plancenoit once more.

It was now past 7:00 P.M. Napoléon decided to strike a final blow before the sun set. He assembled five battalions of the Guard, 2,500 men, to assault the Mont-Saint-Jean ridgeline. But the decisive moment had passed. While the Guard was recapturing Plancenoit, Wellington had brought up two cavalry brigades and the Dutch 3rd Division under David Henrik, Baron Chassé, from other parts of the line. He placed Chassé's division immediately behind a weak defending line of British, German, and Dutch regiments just west of the Brussels-Charleroi road. Just to the west of the Dutch was the Guards Brigade under Sir Peregrine Maitland, and just west of Maitland's Brigade was the Light Brigade under Sir Frederick Adam. The men, all in line of battle, sheltered themselves from cannon fire by crouching in the ditch along the Wavre road.

Each Imperial Guard battalion formed a separate unit, each deployed in six lines of 80 or so men. The Guards were accompanied by two horse artillery batteries of six guns each, but no cavalry. So this assault, like the other assaults all day, was contrary to doctrine. Without cavalry threats, the British could not be forced into squares.

The five Imperial Guard battalions separated into three forces. On the east, two battalions of grenadiers overran the weak British, German, and Dutch regiments, but they were stopped by Chassé's Dutchmen, shattered by volleys, and sent flying.

Just to the west, two Imperial Guard chasseur battalions approached the 1,500 men of Maitland's Brigade. An eyewitness. Captain H. W. Powell, First Foot Guards, described the collision: "Suddenly the cannon fire ceased, and as the smoke cleared away a superb sight opened on us. A close column of Guards were ascending the rise shouting '*Vive l'Empereur!*' They continued to advance till within fifty or sixty paces of our front, when the brigade was ordered to stand up. Whether it was from the sudden and unexpected appearance of a corps so near them, which must have seemed as starting out of the ground, or the tremendous heavy fire we threw into them, *Le Garde*, who had never before failed in an attack, suddenly stopped."[34] The fire crippled the column, and a bayonet charge broke it apart. The surviving guardsmen turned and fled, leaving dead and dying across the field.

A short time later the last Guard battalion moved up on Adam's

Light Brigade. As this battalion neared the ridgeline, Sir John Colborne ordered two regiments to wheel forward at a right angle and to pour fire into the flank of the Guards as they passed. The Guards suffered heavily, but turned and delivered devastating volleys on the two regiments, knocking down hundreds of British soldiers in a couple minutes.

Wellington came up at this moment and ordered Colborne to charge the Guard. The British soldiers rushed at the French column with wild shouts. As an eyewitness reported, "In the next ten seconds the Imperial Guard, broken into the wildest confusion, and scarcely firing a shot to cover its retreat, was rushing toward the hollow road in the rear of La Haye Sainte."[35]

Wellington, sitting on his horse and watching the enemy's increasing confusion, decided to finish the day. He spurred to the edge of the ridgeline, stood in his stirrups, took off his hat, and waved it in the air. The signal was understood at once, and a general advance of the entire British army began to pour down the slope and up toward the main French line on La Belle Alliance ridgeline.

The French position collapsed in minutes as soldiers abandoned their guns and fled. Protected by remaining soldiers of the Guard, Napoléon escaped, first to Charleroi, then to Paris on June 21. The next day he abdicated.

The casualties on the memorable day of Waterloo were staggering. Napoléon lost 25,000 men who were killed or wounded; another 8,000 were captured. Wellington lost 15,000 killed or wounded; Blücher 7,000.

On July 15, 1815, Napoléon climbed on board the British warship *Bellerophon* in Rochefort harbor and began his journey to exile on St. Helena in the South Atlantic. He died there in 1821.

We can see in the case of Napoléon that a great commander can fail in the end when he is unable or unwilling to apply just one or two of the rules of war. Most of the principles that Napoléon read about or discovered on his own were the same ones Sun Tzu preached. Napoléon followed them during most of his career. Although he ignored some of the rules at crucial times, his one great failure as a field commander was his inability to delegate authority. This is what undid him at Waterloo.

During the Napoleonic era, armies became several times larger than those in the dynastic wars that preceded it. In this environment, subordinate commanders had to be extremely capable, and they had to have the authority to act on their own. But Napoléon, unwilling to raise leaders who might oppose him, would not accept independent field commanders. Therefore, it was only a matter of time before he made some mistake that would cause his rule to collapse.

Sun Tzu and all great philosophers urge states to find wise leaders who do not make fatal blunders. This, of course, is the counsel of perfection, and human beings are incapable of attaining it. We must do what we can to choose the best leaders possible, but we must realize that—as happened to Napoléon—human frailty can demolish the best-laid plans.

FOUR

The Civil War
Campaigns of 1862

Three transformative changes in warfare—railroads, the electric telegraph, and the Minié-ball rifle—came into use between the end of the Napoleonic era in 1815 and the American Civil War of 1861–1865. Railroads made it possible to move men and supplies in unlimited quantities from one location to another with hitherto unimagined rapidity. The telegraph permitted almost instantaneous communication between distant points, increasing greatly the capability of commanders to make quick decisions. The Minié-ball rifle revolutionized the nature of combat because it had an effective range of 400 yards, four times that of the standard infantry weapon, the smoothbore musket.

Commanders rapidly adjusted to the logistics of the railroad and to the speed of the telegraph. They were less able to change infantry tactics. For over two centuries, the standard method of reaching a decision had been to march long lines of soldiers up to a defending enemy force. Both sides then discharged volleys of fire. When one side began to waver, the other side usually won the battle by launching a bayonet charge. In the Civil War, commanders could think of no other way of deciding a battle. But casualties were unprecedented because advancing forces were subjected to accurate fire for several times the distance they had to endure from muskets. In the Civil War as a whole, six out of seven attacks failed.

Only one officer, the Confederate general Thomas J. "Stonewall" Jackson, devised an alternative solution to the offensive battle. But he faced tremendous difficulties in trying to convince his superiors to follow it.

If there ever was an intellectual descendant of Sun Tzu, it was Stonewall Jackson. His methods in the campaigns of 1862 embodied virtually all of Sun Tzu's primary axioms: avoid strength, strike at weakness, go around the enemy, use deception not power to overcome, seize something the enemy must seek to recover, and induce the enemy to attack well-prepared positions and be defeated.

Jackson also sought to strike at the heart of Union power, its factories, cities, and railroads. This embodied Sun Tzu's most profound advice: to destroy the very will of the enemy to resist.[1] A drive into the North could have won the war for the South in weeks. But Jackson was unable to induce the Confederate president, Jefferson Davis, and his military adviser, Robert E. Lee, to carry out this campaign. Davis and Lee abandoned Jackson's war of maneuver and took up a long war of attrition, of slowly wearing down resistance. This was a war that the South, with one-eleventh of the industry and one-third of the manpower of the North, was bound to lose.

Therefore the campaigns of 1862 display in very graphic form the distinctions between what was achieved when commanders adopted policies that were consistent with the doctrines of Sun Tzu and what was lost when they did not adopt such policies. For this reason, the 1862 campaigns constitute the most illuminating textbook we possess on the conduct of war. In that fateful year, when Davis and Lee refused the admonitions of Jackson, the destiny of the United States of America was determined.[2]

The year opened with a remarkable strategic situation. Since the

Confederate victory at Manassas on July 21, 1861, the new Union commander, George B. McClellan, had been building an army around Washington. It now numbered nearly 240,000 men, including garrisons manning a series of forts he established encircling the capital. His field forces were well over twice the size of the Confederate army under Joseph E. Johnston around Fairfax in northern Virginia.

On March 13, 1862, McClellan got the approval of President Abraham Lincoln to carry out a dramatic campaign to capture the Confederate capital of Richmond and to destroy the Confederate army in the east. McClellan took advantage of Union command of the sea to move about 100,000 Union soldiers by way of the Chesapeake Bay to Fort Monroe, a U.S. Army post at the tip of the peninsula between the York and the James rivers. Fort Monroe had never been surrendered and could form a base from which to advance up the peninsula to capture Richmond.

McClellan's initiative presented the Confederacy with a potentially disastrous situation. As his army moved up the peninsula, other Union forces were poised to descend on Richmond from the north and west. South of Harpers Ferry on the Potomac River, a 23,000-man army under General Nathaniel B. Banks was to dispose of a small army of 4,600 men under Stonewall Jackson at Winchester and then was to clear the whole Shenandoah Valley. From the Allegheny Mountains to the west, a 15,000-man army under General John C. Frémont was to advance on Staunton in the valley and from there drive eastward across the Blue Ridge to Charlottesville and on to Richmond. Meanwhile a 38,000-man corps under General Irvin McDowell around Alexandria was to march southward, first to Fredericksburg and then directly on Richmond. Between these forces the much weaker Confederate army was to be ground to dust and the rebellion crushed.[3]

Johnston's Army of Northern Virginia retreated to a more defensible position on the Rapidan River, north of Orange Court House and Gordonsville. As soon as McClellan's intentions were revealed,

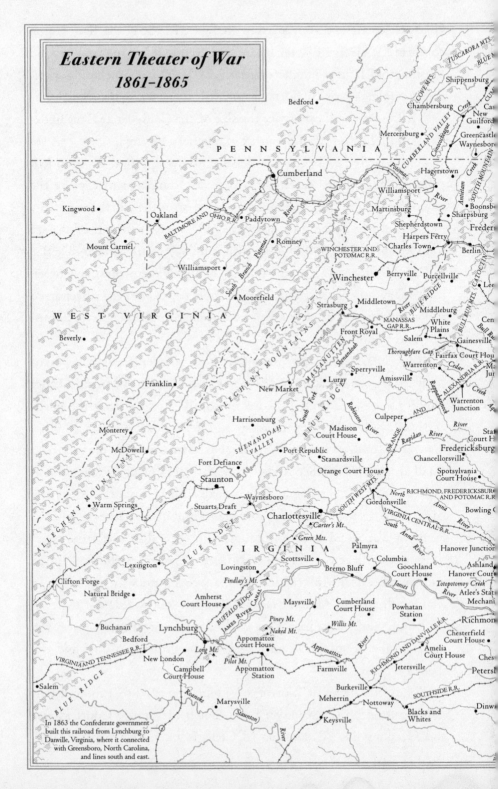

**Eastern Theater of War
1861–1865**

PENNSYLVANIA

Bedford

Shippensburg

Chambersburg

New Guilford

Mercersburg

Greencastle

Waynesboro

CUMBERLAND VALLEY

TUSCARORA MTS.

COVE MTS.

BLUE M

Cumberland

Williamsport

Hagerstown

Martinsburg

Boonsb

Sharpsburg

Shepherdstown

Frede

Kingwood

Oakland

Paddytown

BALTIMORE AND OHIO R.R.

Mount Carmel

Romney

Harpers Ferry

Charles Town

Berlin

Lee

WINCHESTER AND POTOMAC R.R.

Williamsport

Winchester

Berryville

Purcellville

Moorefield

Strasburg

Middletown

Middleburg

WEST VIRGINIA

Beverly

Front Royal

MANASSAS GAP R.R.

Salem

White Plains

Gainesville

Bull R

Cen

Thoroughfare Gap

Fairfax Court Hou

MASSANUTTEN

Franklin

New Market

Luray

Sperryville

Warrenton

Amissville

Cedar

Ma

Ju

ALEXANDRIA R.R.

Warrenton Junction

Harrisonburg

Madison Court House

Culpeper

AND

A

Monterey

ALLEGHENY MOUNTAINS

SHENANDOAH VALLEY

Port Republic

Stanardsville

Orange Court House

ORANGE

Rapidan River

Sta

Court H

Fredericksburg

McDowell

Fort Defiance

Chancellorsville

Spotsylvania Court House

Staunton

Waynesboro

SOUTH WEST MTS.

North

RICHMOND, FREDERICKSBUR AND POTOMAC R.R.

Warm Springs

Stuarts Draft

Gordonsville

VIRGINIA CENTRAL R.R.

Bowling C

Charlottesville

Carter's Mt.

Anna

Green Mts.

South Anna River

Hanover Juncti

Lexington

VIRGINIA

Palmyra

Lovingston

Scottsville

Columbia

Ashland

Hanover Cour

Clifton Forge

Bremo Bluff

Goochland Court House

Totopotomoy Creek

Natural Bridge

BUFFALO RIDGE

Amherst Court House

Maysville

Cumberland Court House

Powhatan Station

Atlee's Stat

Mechani

Buchanan

Findlay's Mt.

JAMES RIVER CANAL

Piney Mt.

Willis Mt.

James

Richmo

Lynchburg

Naked Mt.

Bedford

Long Mt.

Appomattox Court House

Appomattox River

Chesterfield Court House

VIRGINIA AND TENNESSEE R.R.

New London

Pilot Mt.

RICHMOND AND DANVILLE R.R.

Amelia Court House

Ches

Campbell Court House

Appomattox Station

Farmville

Jetersville

Petersl

Salem

BLUE RIDGE

Roanoke

Burkeville

SOUTHSIDE R.R.

Dinw

Marysville

Meherrin

Nottoway

Blacks and Whites

(Staunton)

Keysville

River

In 1863 the Confederate government built this railroad from Lynchburg to Danville, Virginia, where it connected with Greensboro, North Carolina, and lines south and east.

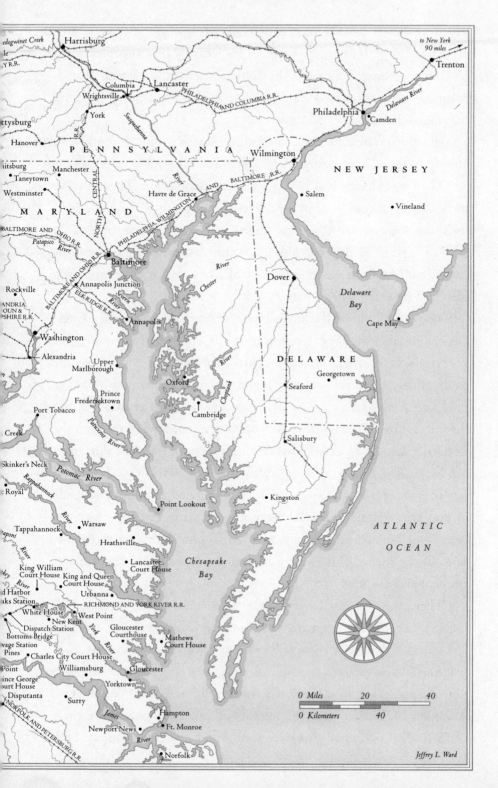

Jeffrey L. Ward

Johnston moved 57,000 men to Richmond, leaving only the 8,000-man division of Richard S. Ewell in the vicinity of Culpeper, north of Orange. Johnston sent 13,000 Confederates under General John B. Magruder to form a weak defensive line at Yorktown, a few miles up the peninsula from Fort Monroe.

Johnston's retreat forced Stonewall Jackson to withdraw southward, quickly followed by the advance of Banks and his army up the valley.[4]

The Confederacy was facing imminent dissolution. There was no force to stop the advance of McDowell directly on Richmond. Jackson's tiny army of 4,600 was considered to be entirely too small to do anything against Banks. And only a 2,800-man detachment under General Edward Johnson stood in the way of Frémont's army approaching Staunton from the Alleghenies.

Magruder, holding the flimsy line at Yorktown, presented the single tactical glimmer of hope. Celebrated in the old army for his amateur theatricals, he now put on a great show that deceived McClellan. He made blustering threats to attack, and marched the same Rebel unit time after time past a spot on a road under Union observation to give the impression of great strength, sending the unit around through the woods so it could repeatedly pass the open spot in the same direction.

McClellan, who could have broken the Yorktown line easily, instead settled down for a long siege. McClellan violated a fundamental rule of Sun Tzu because he did not determine the actual state of the enemy in front of him. It is imperative, Sun Tzu says, to ascertain the dispositions of the enemy. Otherwise, a commander is blind and cannot make reasonable decisions.[5]

There was one intellectual glimmer of hope visible to Stonewall Jackson, but it was not apparent to President Davis or to General Lee. Jackson saw that even though Union superiority of force was massive, the North suffered one weakness in its strategic plan. Abraham Lincoln possessed an exaggerated fear for the safety of Washington. Although McClellan had left a number of troops, as well as the circle of fortresses, around Washington, Lincoln felt insecure. The vast bulk of the Union army was on the peninsula and could not come to the aid of the capital if a Confederate force struck. To McClellan, such a fear was groundless. The fortresses alone could contain any likely attack. Far more important, he was confident that every Confederate soldier would be committed to protecting Richmond, not raiding Washington.

At this moment Stonewall Jackson emerged as a great general. A great general can see a situation as a whole, not merely his own circumstances. Sun Tzu says that "the highest realization of warfare is to attack the enemy's plans."[6] Jackson, looking at the entire eastern theater of war, saw that anything he could do in the Shenandoah Valley or elsewhere to raise Lincoln's anxiety about Washington would reduce the Union forces pressing on Richmond. But his military superiors only partially recognized this opening.

A golden opportunity emerged on March 21, 1862. When General Banks arrived in Winchester and discovered how tiny Jackson's army was, he got permission to leave 9,000 men in the valley under James Shields, and began to move the remainder of his army east toward Manassas. Banks's new orders were to protect Washington and the line of the Potomac. Once McClellan was secure on the peninsula, he was to seize Warrenton, on the Orange & Alexandria Railroad southwest of Manassas, and reopen the Manassas Gap Railroad from Manassas to Strasburg to ensure supplies for Union forces that remained in the valley.

Jackson's cavalry chief Turner Ashby had been monitoring the withdrawal of Union forces, and he reported that all of Banks's army except for four of Shields's regiments had departed.

Jackson set his little army in motion at once. The pace of Jackson's marches was already legendary. His men called themselves the "foot cavalry." But this time, Jackson outdid even himself. He marched so fast that only 3,000 of his men remained in ranks at 2:00 P.M. on Sunday, March 23, when he came up on Ashby, who was skirmishing with Federal artillery at Kernstown, four miles south of Winchester.[7] Ashby assured Jackson that the force visible to the east of the Valley

Pike (present-day U.S. Route II) was a rear guard. The rest of Shields's division, he said, had already left the valley.

While Ashby continued to demonstrate with his artillery, Jackson moved the bulk of his force three miles to his left, or west, up a long, low wooded hill called Sandy Ridge, hoping to get on the flank of the Union troops and evict them from their position.

But Ashby had been wrong. Shields's entire division of 9,000 men

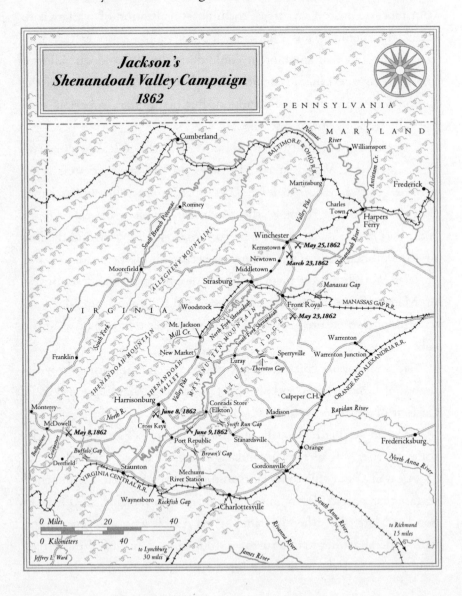

was hidden north of Kernstown. The force was under the temporary command of Colonel Nathan Kimball since Shields had been wounded. Kimball sent two brigades onto Sandy Ridge to stop Jackson. Realizing he was facing a much larger force than his own, Jackson ordered his last three regiments to come forward. But before they could arrive, the commander of his Stonewall Brigade, Richard B. Garnett, fearing his line was about to break, ordered withdrawal.

Jackson tried to stem the frenzied retreat. But when a force has to withdraw under pressure, the retreat usually turns into a rout. This happened to Jackson's men. They fled several miles southward, having lost 718 men, compared to the Federals' loss of 590. Nearly one-fourth of his infantry had fallen or been captured.

Jackson relieved Garnett of his command for withdrawing without orders. But the Federals regarded the encounter at Kernstown as anything but a Confederate defeat. Lincoln concluded that Jackson would not have attacked unless he had been greatly reinforced. Accordingly, Lincoln ordered Banks's entire army back into the valley, and he directed that a 10,000-man division under Louis Blenker, scheduled to move to McClellan on the peninsula, be diverted to Frémont's army in the Alleghenies. Even more significant, he ordered Irvin McDowell's 38,000-man corps to remain in the vicinity of Alexandria. Secretary of War Edwin M. Stanton instructed McDowell, "You will consider the national capital as especially under your protection and make no movement throwing your force out of position for the discharge of this primary duty."[8]

Thus, Banks was returned to challenge Jackson, and 48,000 Union troops who might have been used to defeat the Confederates at Richmond were diverted to other purposes. Rarely in history has so small a force brought about such a massive strategic dislocation.

The denial of McDowell's corps had a paralyzing effect on McClellan. Hesitant to a fault under the best of conditions, he complained bitterly to Lincoln. Exasperated, the president replied that McClellan had 100,000 men and said, "You must act."[9] But McClellan did not act. He continued to wait for McDowell. Thus Jackson's blow at Kerns-town gave the Confederate leaders time to devise a strategy to prevent disaster. But the question was, would they seize the opportunity?

Stonewall Jackson withdrew southward up the Shenandoah Val-ley, hoping to find an opportunity to strike at Banks. But the Federal commander moved slowly to Woodstock, about thirty miles south of Winchester. The huge agricultural resources of the valley were vital to the Confederacy, and to preserve them Jackson had to keep Staunton from being captured. The town was on the Virginia Central Railroad, which ran from Richmond to Clifton Forge. If Frémont and Banks met at Staunton, the valley would be lost, and the two forces would have an open road to Charlottesville and Richmond.

Jackson had increased his little "Army of the Shenandoah" to 6,000 men through recruitment. And President Davis and General Lee had told Jackson he could use Richard Ewell's 8,000-man division, if neces-sary. This force, plus Edward Johnson's small detachment at Staunton, raised Jackson's total numbers to about 17,000, or well less than half the number of men in the combined Union armies converging on the valley.

Under pressure from Washington, Banks finally pushed up the macadamized Valley Pike to New Market on April 17, forcing Jackson back to Harrisonburg, eighteen miles to the south and twenty-five miles north of Staunton. Banks's advance to New Market opened up a stra-tegic opportunity for Jackson that changed everything. Set down in the midst of the Shenandoah Valley is a high massif known as Massanut-ten Mountain, running forty-five miles north and south. It had exactly one road crossing over it, from New Market in the broad main valley to Luray in the narrow Page or Luray Valley, squeezed between Massa-nutten and the sharply rising Blue Ridge to the east. Down this valley runs the South Fork of the Shenandoah River. The South Fork meets the North Fork at Front Royal, the northern terminus of Massanutten, and from there the Shenandoah flows as one stream to the Potomac at Harpers Ferry.

On April 19, Jackson abruptly moved his army from Harrisonburg eastward just below the southern escarpment or face of Massanutten to Conrad's Store (now Elkton). Leaving a detachment to guard the bridge over the South Fork there, Jackson bivouacked his army in Elk Run Valley at the foot of Swift Run Gap, in the Blue Ridge east of Conrad's Store.

Ewell now had guaranteed access to the Shenandoah Valley. Jackson sent young Henry Kyd Douglas, a member of his staff, across the Blue Ridge to find Ewell and alert him.

To all appearances, Jackson's withdrawal from the main valley had opened the way for Banks to march straight up the Valley Pike to Staunton and join with Frémont, whose only opposition was Edward Johnson's tiny force. But Jackson had actually locked Banks in place. When Banks looked at his map, he saw that if he moved on Staunton, Jackson could march north from Conrad's Store to Luray, turn onto the one road over Massanutten Mountain, and emerge at New Market. There, Jackson would cut Banks's line of supply and route of retreat. If Banks struck out for Staunton, he would fall into a trap and could lose his entire army. Jackson's positioning, by taking spectacular advantage of the terrain, exemplifies one of Sun Tzu's maxims.[10]

Jackson had dealt with Banks, but he still had to confront Frémont. His advanced brigade had reached Monterey and was getting ready to march the thirty-five miles to Staunton. General Joe Johnston's orders had obligated Jackson to remain close to the railway, so he could move to help defend Richmond if McClellan broke through the lines at Yorktown. General Johnston saw Jackson's force only as a source of potential reinforcements. But Robert E. Lee had a wider vision. On April 21, Lee wired Jackson: "If you can use General Ewell's division in an attack on Banks, it will prove a great relief to the pressure on Fredericksburg [where Lincoln, no longer anxious about Jackson, had allowed McDowell to move preparatory to a march on Richmond]."[11]

This message liberated Jackson.[12] He embarked on one of the most mystifying moves in military history. On April 30, he called on Ewell to move at once to Elk Run Valley and to remain there unless Banks marched on Staunton. Jackson told Turner Ashby merely to "feel out" the Federals toward Harrisonburg. When Ewell arrived at Elk Run Valley, Jackson and his little army had vanished, no one knew where. The people of Staunton, with Frémont descending on them, were baffled and dismayed.

On Saturday, May 3, worse news came: Jackson's army was crossing the Blue Ridge at Brown's Gap, southeast of Port Republic, and he was abandoning the valley to the enemy. The people of Staunton were now plunged into despair.

When General Banks received the report that Jackson was in retreat, he wired Secretary of War Stanton that he was certain "Jackson is bound for Richmond."[13] Banks suggested that he depart the valley, cross the Blue Ridge, and clear the whole country north of Charlottesville.

But Jackson's disappearance aroused a totally different concern in Stanton's mind. Jackson might be "bound for Richmond," but he also might be heading for Fredericksburg to challenge McDowell. Stanton wired McDowell not to move until Jackson's intentions were better known. Stanton then ordered Banks to send James Shields's division to McDowell as a precaution. Banks's army was thus nearly cut in half.

By disappearing, Jackson placed a new brake on McDowell, and McDowell's halt kept McClellan from moving. Jackson, by a distant, indirect maneuver, once more had blocked the North from taking action.

On May 4, Jackson emerged at Mechums River Station on the Virginia Central Railroad, about nine miles west of Charlottesville. Trains were waiting, and the soldiers were sure they were headed to either Richmond or Fredericksburg. But when the trains started off, they steamed *west* to Staunton. In a matter of hours, Jackson landed in the central position between the two Federal armies! It was precisely the kind of advance that Napoléon had planned to seize Quatre-Bras in the Waterloo campaign of 1815. If Jackson had advanced directly on Staunton from Elk Run Valley, he would have given away his intention, and Frémont and Banks could have crushed his army between them. But Jackson had moved so secretly that both Federal armies remained inactive and far apart, and neither commander could do a thing to counter him.

Jackson joined with Edward Johnson and marched into the Alleghenies to confront Frémont's advance unit. Frémont had weakened his own situation by allowing his 25,000-man army to spread out in four segments down the South Branch of the Potomac River. Accordingly, on May 8, Jackson confronted only 4,000 Federal troops at the little village of McDowell, twenty-seven miles west of Staunton.

The commanders, Robert C. Schenck and Robert H. Milroy, had worsened their situation by setting up their defenses in the village, which lay in a deep hollow surrounded by high mountains. All Jackson had to do to dislodge them was to move on their rear. He made preparations to do so. Meanwhile, some of Jackson's soldiers occupied steep Sitlington's Hill, overlooking the village on the east. Milroy concluded that Jackson was moving cannons atop the hill to bombard the village. This was not true, but Milroy convinced Schenck that the Federals should attack the hill. It was a senseless move. But that was how the unnecessary battle of McDowell was fought. The attacks failed, and at the end of the day, Milroy and Schenck realized they were in a trap and hastily abandoned the village.

Jackson pressed after the fleeing Federals, but he wasn't interested in catching them. He wanted merely to drive Frémont far back in the mountains so that he could not join Banks or capture Staunton. This done, Jackson returned to the Shenandoah Valley to deal with Banks.

Meanwhile McClellan had finally broken through the flimsy Confederate line at Yorktown and had moved to within twenty miles of Richmond. The South had abandoned Norfolk and scuttled its sole ironclad, the *Virginia* (generally known by its original name, the *Merrimac*). It had too deep a draught to move up the James River, which Union gunboats now ascended to reach Drewry's Bluff, six miles below Richmond, where Confederate batteries barred passage.

The Confederate capital was now in a desperate situation. Military stores were removed and archives packed and ready to go. Robert E. Lee wrote Jackson on May 16: "Whatever movement you make against Banks, do it speedily, and if successful drive him back towards the Potomac, and create the impression, as far as possible, that you design threatening that line."[14]

Jackson was already moving to do just that. Banks had withdrawn northward to Strasburg, where he posted 7,400 of his men to build strong entrenchments facing the Valley Pike, down which he expected the Confederates to attack. Banks placed 1,000 of his men at Front Royal, ten miles east of Strasburg, to guard the Manassas Gap Railroad.

General Johnston wired Jackson to release Ewell to reinforce the defense of Richmond. Jackson wired back that he needed Ewell to deal with Banks. Johnston responded that Banks should be left "in his works," and that Ewell should come east.

Attacking Banks "in his works" was not in the least what Jackson had in mind. He telegraphed Lee: "I am of opinion that an attempt should be made to defeat Banks, but under instructions from General Johnston I do not feel at liberty to make an attack. Please answer by telegraph at once."[15] Lee responded authorizing Ewell to remain in the valley.

To give Banks's spies the impression that he was massing his forces to march down the Valley Pike to Strasburg, Jackson directed Ewell to send his Louisiana Brigade from Conrad's Store around the base of Massanutten Mountain to New Market. Meanwhile, Jackson's force moved onto the Valley Pike and marched to New Market.

On the morning of May 21, the men moved north through New Market expecting to march directly on Strasburg. Just at the edge of the village, however, Jackson quietly turned the head of the column to the right—up the long, sloping road (present-day U.S. Route 211) leading over Massanutten Mountain to Luray. The Rebel army had turned completely away from Banks and was marching eastward.

Sun Tzu would have recognized the move at once. It was a classic expression of his principal military movement, his combination of a *zheng*, an ordinary or direct force, and a *qi*, an extraordinary or indirect force. The infantry didn't know it, but Jackson had already applied his *zheng* force by directing his cavalry under Turner Ashby to drive straight north down the Valley Pike, giving the impression that it represented the advance elements of Jackson's whole army marching on Banks's "works." By this means, Jackson held Banks in his position at Strasburg. The *qi* force meanwhile marched over Massanutten Mountain. It emerged hours later at Luray, where the remainder of Ewell's division was waiting. In one swift move, Jackson had consolidated all of his infantry and guns, and they now descended as one body on the isolated and hopelessly outnumbered Union outpost at Front Royal.

Jackson's move was utterly unanticipated by the Federals. In numerous telegrams back and forth, the field commanders and Lincoln and Stanton kept reassuring themselves that things were going splendidly. The Confederates had not followed up on the attack on Frémont. Banks felt fully secure behind his fortifications at Strasburg. McClellan was boasting of imminent success. McDowell had already crossed the Rappahannock River at Fredericksburg with a portion of his troops and was beginning to move to Richmond. Lincoln and Stanton, expecting the forthcoming fall of Richmond, were to leave for Fredericksburg the next day.

On the morning of May 23, Confederate troops stormed Front Royal, where Federals were guarding the wooden railroad viaduct and bridges over the Shenandoah River. The fight was one-sided, and all but a few of the 1,000-man garrison were killed or captured. Jackson was now as close to Banks's rear base at Winchester as was Banks himself. But Banks was strangely unmoved. He concluded it was only a cavalry raid. Even when presented with the facts, he was unwilling to admit that he had been fooled. Only around 10:00 A.M. on May 24 did he finally realize that he was in a trap, and at last ordered an immediate withdrawal from Strasburg to Winchester, abandoning a mountain of supplies.

In the race that followed, most of Banks's infantry got away to Winchester on the hard Valley Pike, but numbers of cavalry had to escape by small roads westward and were of no use in defending Winchester. At Winchester, Banks's situation was desperate. He had no more than 7,500 discouraged men. Jackson had about 16,000 gleeful soldiers invigorated by success.

Although the Federals put up a stout defense on May 25, they were quickly overwhelmed, and the entire army fled northward. The Confederates captured 3,000 men and might have captured more except that Turner Ashby's cavalry had moved eastward without orders and was not available to pursue the fugitives.

Even so, Banks's army had been driven in panic to the Potomac River. The news created consternation throughout the North. Abraham Lincoln feared that Jackson might capture Washington. Seasoned generals like McDowell told Lincoln this was not possible. Jackson's army was much smaller than the combined forces around Washington, and he would not be able to mount an offensive unless he was reinforced.

Slightly mollified, Lincoln decided to become a military strategist himself and trap Jackson in the northern end of the Shenandoah Valley. He wired McDowell to stop his advance on Richmond and to send forces to seal off Jackson's retreat at Strasburg. He ordered Frémont to assist from the west. Here Lincoln made a fearsome error. McDowell at Fredericksburg was in the central position between Jackson and Joe Johnston. If McDowell moved to Richmond, he could join McClellan and probably force Johnston's army to surrender. Jackson's small army would then be isolated in the Shenandoah Valley and could be destroyed at leisure.

McDowell saw this, but Lincoln did not. He remained focused on the danger of Jackson, and not on the opportunity that was available at Richmond. Accordingly, McDowell turned Shields's division, followed by other forces, toward Strasburg. Once more Jackson's indirect move had stopped McClellan in his tracks.

At this point Stonewall Jackson made a concerted effort to change Southern strategy and to prevent a collision of Confederate forces with McClellan's army at Richmond.

From the start of the war, President Davis had been pursuing a policy of passive defense. He held that the South was only defending itself against aggression. In his view, all it had to do was to fend off Northern attacks until the Northern people became weary, or Britain and France intervened to protect their textile industries, which depended on Southern cotton. It is always a mistake to rely on the anticipated actions of other people to achieve one's goals. For the South, this was especially unwise. Abraham Lincoln and the Radical Republicans were bent on invading the South and beating down resistance by main force. British and French politicians were unwilling to incite the ire of their own textile workers, who were very poorly paid, to support the South, whose cotton field slave workers were not paid at all.

The war was going to be won or lost entirely by the South. And it could not win by main strength. Its only hope was to develop a strategy that could neutralize the North's vastly superior resources.

The North, confident of its power, had developed no plans to counter a possible invasion. Lincoln, to be sure, was constantly afraid of a Southern strike against Washington, but strategically this made no sense whatsoever. Any direct blow would run up against the ring of fortresses that McClellan had built. These would slow a decision until the North's material ascendancy could be brought to bear.

Stonewall Jackson saw from the outset that the key to the outcome was not the capture of Washington, but the will of the Northern people to pursue the war,. The resolve of the North could be attacked by destroying its factories, railroads, farms, and commerce. Washington need not even be approached. It could be captured *indirectly* by severing the single rail corridor that reached the city from the north—the Baltimore & Ohio Railroad. Cutting this line would deprive the capital of food and other supplies and would force the Republican administration to evacuate the city.

The giant flaw in the North's strategy was that it had nothing to protect its interior. The vast bulk of its military forces were pressing into the South. They would be unavailable in the event that a Southern army invaded the North. Jackson saw this very clearly. He had already proved in the Shenandoah Valley that he could march rings around Northern armies. He was confident he could do the same in the North, where there were few Union forces of any consequence. Jackson's plan illustrates the most important advice that Sun Tzu gives about warfare: neutralize the enemy's strategy.[16]

Jackson had already proposed an alternative to Davis's passive defense. In mid-October 1861 he had approached Gustavus W. Smith, a division commander in the Army of Northern Virginia, and asked Smith to help him to convince Davis to develop a new policy. Smith was unable to do so, and Davis ignored the idea.

This original proposal embodied all of the ideas that would have nullified Northern strength and given the South victory. Jackson told Smith, "McClellan, with his army of recruits, will not attempt to come out against us this autumn. If we remain inactive, they will have greatly the advantage over us next spring. Their raw recruits will have become an organized army, vastly superior in numbers to our own. We are ready at the present moment for active operations in the field, while they are not. We ought to invade their country now, and not wait for them to make the necessary preparations to invade ours. If the president would reinforce this army by taking troops from other points not threatened, and let us make an active campaign of invasion before winter sets in, McClellan's raw recruits could not stand against us in the field.

"Crossing the upper Potomac, occupying Baltimore, and taking possession of Maryland, we could cut off the communications of Washington, force the Federal government to abandon the capital, beat

McClellan's army if it came out against us in the open country, destroy industrial establishments wherever we found them, break up the lines of interior commercial intercourse, close the coal mines, seize and, if necessary, destroy the manufactories and commerce of Philadelphia and of other large cities within our reach, take and hold the narrow neck of country between Pittsburgh and Lake Erie, subsist mainly on the country we traverse, and making unrelenting war amidst their homes, force the people of the North to understand what it will cost them to hold the South in the Union at the bayonet's point."[17]

Jackson's proposal was an eloquent expression of one of Sun Tzu's most important axioms: "Attaining one hundred victories in one hundred battles is not the pinnacle of excellence," Sun Tzu says. "Subjugating the enemy's army without fighting is the true pinnacle of excellence."[18]

On May 30, 1862, while watching skirmishers firing at Harpers Ferry, Stonewall Jackson presented his plan once more. He asked an old friend, Colonel Alexander R. Boteler, a former congressman, to carry the proposal to President Davis, whom he knew well, and to General Lee. If his command was increased to a total of 40,000 men, Jackson told Boteler, he would cross into Maryland, "raise the siege of Richmond and transfer this campaign from the banks of the Potomac to those of the Susquehanna."[19]

The concept was even more feasible now than it had been in the fall of 1861, because McClellan had isolated on the peninsula between the York and the James rivers the largest Union army—the only force that could defeat Jackson. Even if Lincoln ordered it to move at once, it would take two weeks at least, probably much longer, to assemble a superior army in Maryland.

Although there were more than 60,000 troops arrayed against Jackson at the moment, they were scattered. Jackson expected to slip through the trap Lincoln was trying to set at Strasburg and to withdraw south far up the Shenandoah Valley. From there, if he got the reinforcements he was asking for, he could burst through or go around any

Union forces still in the valley, cross the Potomac, and have almost free rein until McClellan extricated his army from the peninsula and came to confront him. By then, Jackson felt, it would be too late.

If Jackson's plan was adopted, the North would be in an almost impossible dilemma. The combination of McClellan's extreme slowness and Jackson's extreme speed indicated that even if McClellan managed to assemble an army in Maryland or Pennsylvania, Jackson could out-maneuver him, defeat isolated parts of his army, and halt the Northern war effort. At the very least a drive into the North would terminate the siege of Richmond without a single additional Southern soldier being sacrificed. It would throw the North onto the strategic defensive. It might win the war in a matter of weeks.

Jackson and Boteler took the train back to Winchester, where Jackson got together papers explaining his proposal, and Boteler set off to see Davis.

Meanwhile, on May 31 to June 1, Joe Johnston was attacking McClellan immediately east of Richmond. The event, known as the battle of Seven Pines in the South and the battle of Fair Oaks in the North, demonstrated persuasively that Johnston did not know how to conduct a battle. His performance was so poor that the projected major strike by James Longstreet's division on the right, or northern, flank of two Union corps lined up facing Richmond did not land at all. Instead, Longstreet came in behind D. H. Hill's division two miles south and merely blocked other Confederate troops from going into action. D. H. Hill, left unsupported, crashed headlong into the defending Federal troops on Williamsburg Road (present-day U.S. Route 60), suffered fearsome casualties, and achieved nothing. Johnston himself sustained two wounds that were not fatal but put him out of action for six months. At the end of the engagement President Davis realized that Johnston was an inadequate commander. Though reluctant to lose his right-hand man, he appointed Robert E. Lee commander of the Army of Northern Virginia. Lee thus became its final chieftain.[20]

Jackson was not in the least perturbed about Lincoln's plans to block him at Strasburg. Converging two armies on a single point from two different directions is one of the most difficult tasks in warfare. The ordinary general sees a trap waiting to be sprung at every crossroad. Each general is ignorant of the other's movements and intentions. This uncertainty causes commanders to become timid and hesitant. These ordinary fears were doubled and redoubled in the minds of Frémont and Shields, for they were trying to cage a general who already had shown astonishing speed and bewildering movements.

Accordingly, Shields reached Front Royal, but he was afraid to advance ten miles farther to Strasburg. Frémont likewise stopped at Cedar Creek, six miles west of Strasburg, where he did nothing but demonstrate against Ewell's division. Jackson's army streamed unmolested through Strasburg and headed southward on June 1.

Frémont pursued the Confederates south up the Valley Pike, while Shields moved up the Luray Valley, hoping to get behind Jackson's army, either at New Market or at Harrisonburg. But Jackson had already dispatched cavalry to burn the two bridges over the South Fork of the Shenandoah River at Luray and the single bridge at Conrad's Store. This kept Shields east of the South Fork and completely separated from Frémont.

Jackson pulled his army back to Port Republic, where another of his cavalry teams had secured the last remaining bridge over the river. Now Jackson was once more in the central position, this time between Shields on the east and Frémont on the west. Since Jackson held the only bridge, neither could help the other.

On June 8, 1862, Frémont came up against Ewell's division at Cross Keys, five miles west of Port Republic. Frémont's actions were weak and tentative, and he backed off entirely when the brigade of Isaac R. Trimble swung around his left flank. The next day Jackson sent two brigades of Shields's division flying in a tightly contested battle at Port Republic.

That was the end of the Shenandoah Valley campaign. Jackson marched his army to safety into the lower cove of Brown's Gap in the Blue Ridge. On June 10, Shields withdrew to Luray, while Frémont retreated hastily to Harrisonburg and, ultimately, all the way to Middletown, ten miles south of Winchester. Jackson, left alone and unmolested, brought his men down from the Blue Ridge on June 12, pitched camp below Port Republic, and gave them a much-needed five-day rest.

Shortly before he arrived at Port Republic, Jackson received a bare message from President Davis regretting that he could not send additional troops for the proposed offensive into the North. Jackson was disappointed, but he didn't give up. The day after he brought his army down from the Blue Ridge, he called in Colonel Boteler again and asked him to take a letter to General Lee to explain his plan and to solicit troops. Jackson was deeply opposed to a headlong battle with McClellan. If he could strike into the North, he told Boteler, "Richmond can be relieved and the campaign transferred to Pennsylvania."

Boteler got nowhere when he presented Jackson's plan to Lee. "Colonel," Lee said, "don't you think General Jackson had better come down here first and help me to drive these troublesome people away from before Richmond?" When Lee sent Jackson's proposal to President Davis, he wrote, "I think the sooner Jackson can move this way [toward Richmond] the better—The first object now is to defeat McClellan."[21] Davis agreed.

So Lee and Davis possessed an entirely different view than Jackson. Jackson wanted to *pull* the Union away from Richmond by posing a vastly greater danger to the North—invasion of its cities, and breakup of its economy—that would force McClellan to withdraw. Jackson was proposing a plan consistent with one of Sun Tzu's fundamental axioms: the way to avoid what is strong is to strike what is weak.[22] Union strength was McClellan's army massed at Richmond. Union weakness was the undefended Northern population, industry, railroads, and farms. Lee, with Davis's approval, intended to do precisely the opposite of what Jackson proposed. He wanted to *drive* McClellan's army back by main force. While Jackson pressed for an indirect approach, Lee believed that destruction of the enemy's army by direct, headlong attack was the best strategy.

When Jackson got the news, he made no comment. Leaving his cavalry to guard the Shenandoah Valley, he secretly set his army in motion for Richmond.

Military command structure requires subordinates to present all of their proposals for action to their superiors. Since the first of June 1862, Stonewall Jackson, through his emissary Colonel Boteler, had been trying to get President Davis and General Lee to listen to his proposals to transfer the war to Maryland and Pennsylvania and entirely avoid a collision with McClellan. But he had failed. The minds of Davis and Lee were fixated on the Army of the Potomac at the gates of Richmond. They could see nothing else.

Accordingly, the battles of the Seven Days, which followed, were fought precisely as Lee wished. He concentrated the Confederacy's power and confronted the enemy's strength directly. The operation started on June 26, 1862, with an attack on Fitz John Porter's Union corps located north of the Chickahominy River. Five battles of headlong assault followed. A. P. Hill's division, aided by D. H. Hill's division, attacked Union fortifications along Beaver Dam Creek just east of the village of Mechanicsville. The attack failed, but Porter withdrew to new positions along Boatswain's Swamp, about four miles east. This battle, known as Gaines Mill, finally succeeded in driving Porter across the Chickahominy, but with appalling losses. Next, a direct attack at Savage Station got nowhere, but McClellan was retreating to Harrison's

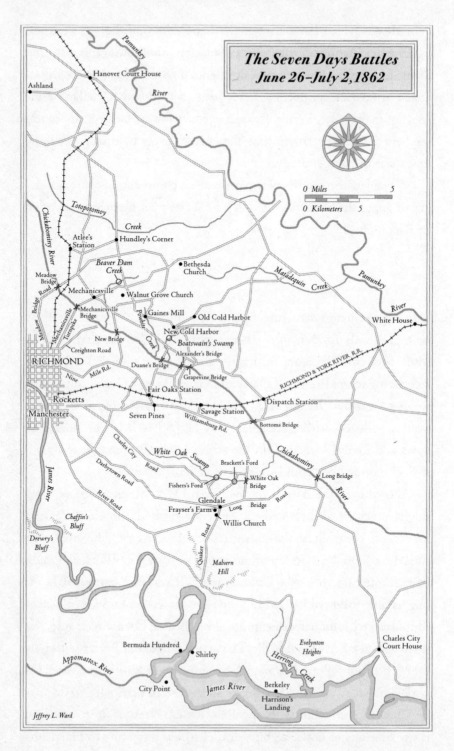

The Seven Days Battles
June 26–July 2, 1862

Jeffrey L. Ward

Landing on the James River, twenty-five miles southeast of Richmond, so his forces withdrew. Then came another direct attack at Frayser's Farm at Glendale. This attack also failed. Finally Lee launched a frontal assault against the massed strength of the Union army at Malvern Hill, on July 1. This attack failed as well. McClellan was able to withdraw with impunity to Harrison's Landing, where he could not be dislodged.

Only one of Lee's direct assaults succeeded. The Seven Days cost the Confederacy 20,000 men, nearly all killed or wounded. This was one-quarter of Lee's entire army. McClellan lost 8,800 men, killed or wounded, plus 6,000 more who were captured. Since prisoners of war were routinely exchanged, the real Federal cost was less than half that sustained by the Confederates. With losses like this, the South, with a third the population of the North, was bound to lose.

In the Seven Days battles, General Lee established the pattern that he was to follow throughout the war. On the offensive, he wanted to attack the enemy in front of him. Indirection was meaningless to him. Lee was possessed with the idea of direct assault.

Lee's methods represented a profound violation of Sun Tzu's principles and a repudiation of Napoléon Bonaparte, who said, "A well-established maxim of war is not to do anything which your enemy wishes—and for the single reason that he does so wish. You should therefore avoid a field of battle which he has reconnoitered and studied. You should be still more careful to avoid one which he has fortified and where he has entrenched himself. A corollary of this principle is, never to attack in front a position which admits of being turned."[23] Instead of charging directly into enemy strength, as Lee did, the English strategist Basil H. Liddell Hart said that the goal of the general should be the same as that of Paris in the Trojan War of Greek legend. Paris avoided any obvious target on the foremost Greek champion Achilles, but instead aimed his arrow at Achilles' only vulnerable point, his heel.[24]

Jackson had been deeply troubled by Lee's methods in the Seven Days. On July 7, 1862, he called on his old friend, Alexander Boteler, to make one more plea to President Davis to invade the North. The South was far too weak in manpower to overwhelm the Union army by sheer power, he said. The only solution was to avoid the enemy's strength and force the Northern people, faced with destruction of their property, to accept peace. Jackson pointed out that McClellan's army would pose no danger until it was reorganized and reinforced. The South should concentrate 60,000 men and march into Maryland.

But once more President Davis rejected the idea. Jackson at last realized that Davis would never accept the strategy, nor would Lee.

Abraham Lincoln called an officer from the western theater, Henry Wager Halleck, and consolidated all Union forces under his direction. He also called another officer from the west, John Pope, to form a new "Army of Virginia" of 60,000 men out of various separate commands spread across the map. While George McClellan threatened Richmond with 90,000 men at Harrison's Landing, Lincoln instructed Pope to march on Richmond by way of the Orange & Alexandria Railroad, thus approaching the Confederate capital from the west.

Pope's cavalry occupied Culpeper Court House, only twenty-seven miles north of Gordonsville, on July 12, 1862. Lee sent Jackson with 12,000 men, soon raised to 24,000, to block him. Gordonsville was on the Virginia Central Railroad. Its loss would sever connections with the Shenandoah Valley and must be prevented at all costs.

Pope was having difficulty consolidating the various elements of his new command, and Jackson saw a chance to shatter parts of it. On August 9, he collided with Banks's isolated corps at Cedar Mountain, about seven miles south of Culpeper. When Banks attacked, Jackson sent the corps flying. But other Union forces arrived to reinforce Banks, and Jackson withdrew to the Rapidan River, just north of Orange.

When McClellan found that Jackson had advanced to Gordons-ville, his proper move would have been to attack Lee's weakened army

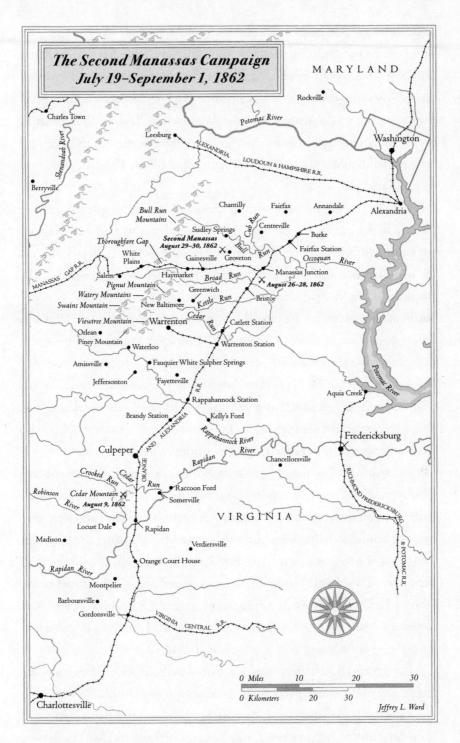

The Second Manassas Campaign
July 19–September 1, 1862

MARYLAND

Rockville

Charles Town

Potomac River

Leesburg

Washington

ALEXANDRIA,

LOUDOUN & HAMPSHIRE R.R.

Shenandoah River

Berryville

Chantilly   Fairfax   Annandale

Alexandria

Bull Run
Mountains   Sudley Springs   Centreville

Cub Run

Burke

Thoroughfare Gap   **Second Manassas**
August 29–30, 1862   Fairfax Station

White
Plains   Gainesville   Groveton   *Occoquan   River*

MANASSAS GAP R.R.   Salem   Haymarket   *Broad   Run*   Manassas Junction

Pignut Mountain   **August 26–28, 1862**

Watery Mountains   Greenwich

Swains Mountain   New Baltimore   *Kettle   Run*   Bristoe

Cedar
Viewtree Mountain   Warrenton   *Run*   Catlett Station

Orlean
Piney Mountain   Waterloo   Warrenton Station

Amissville   Fauquier White Sulpher Springs

Aquia Creek

Jeffersonton   Fayetteville

R.R.

Rappahannock Station

Brandy Station   Kelly's Ford

Fredericksburg

ORANGE AND ALEXANDRIA   *Rappahannock River*
River

Culpeper   *Rapidan*

Chancellorsville

Crooked   Run   *Cedar*
Robinson   *Run*   Raccoon Ford

RICHMOND, FREDERICKSBURG

Cedar Mountain ✗   Somerville
August 9, 1862

River

V I R G I N I A

Locust Dale   Rapidan

Madison   Verdiersville

Rapidan River   Orange Court House   *& POTOMAC R.R.*

Montpelier

Barboursville
Gordonsville   *VIRGINIA   CENTRAL   R.R.*

0 Miles   10   20   30

Charlottesville   0 Kilometers   20   30

Jeffrey L. Ward

at Richmond. But Jackson had been right. McClellan was not going to move on his own volition. Halleck and Lincoln concluded that McClellan's army should be evacuated from Harrison's Landing and brought back to Washington, or sent to reinforce Pope in central Virginia. Strategically this was a senseless move, because the Union abandoned a highly advantageous position within striking distance of Richmond. The decision allowed Lee to move with most of the Confederate army to join Jackson.

On August 15, Lee met with Jackson and James Longstreet. Jackson already had a plan. One of Sun Tzu's principles is to find out the enemy's dispositions and, using them, to make his own plans. Jackson, on his own, reached the same conclusion now. When Pope stopped at the Rapidan River, he had massed his army on the Gordonsville-Culpeper road (present-day U.S. Route 15). Pope was convinced that if Jackson advanced, he would come up the road to Culpeper. Pope had left entirely unguarded fords to the east over the Rapidan. His failure to take this elementary precaution flew in the face of Sun Tzu's maxims and of common sense. Sun Tzu says that a general should never rely on chance but should ascertain the enemy's capabilities and correct his own weaknesses. This will prevent the enemy from mounting a surprise attack.[25]

Jackson told Lee that by crossing Somerville Ford (on present-day U.S. Route 522) and Raccoon Ford, two miles farther east, the Confederates could sweep around Pope's left, cut his supplies and stop any troops coming to help, drive his now-isolated force against the Rapidan or against the mountains to the west, and either destroy it or force it to surrender. This was precisely the sort of sweep that Jackson had made around Banks's army at Strasburg, and it could have been even more devastating because the Confederates could quickly imperil Pope's army by severing the Orange & Alexandria Railroad.

Lee accepted Jackson's proposal, but—without telling Jackson—he didn't accept crucial aspects of it. Jackson wanted the Confederates to cross the fords the next night, August 16. Longstreet, however, insisted on more time to accumulate food. Jackson offered to give Longstreet enough biscuits for the march, but Lee delayed the approach to the fords to August 17 and the sweep around Pope until August 18. To Jackson, it was imperative to move quickly before Pope learned of the movement.

Then Lee postponed the attack again. Longstreet still didn't have enough biscuits, and Lee's cavalry chief, J. E. B. (Jeb) Stuart, had not, as ordered, burned the railroad bridge at Rappahannock Station. In fact, Lee was not thinking of driving Pope's army against the Rapidan or the mountains at all, but merely of forcing Pope to withdraw. He wrote President Davis nearly at the end of the campaign that his entire purpose had been to maneuver Pope out of Virginia, not destroy his army. But he disclosed none of this intent to Jackson.

Lee's delay was fatal to Jackson's hopes. One of the great chances in the war was lost. On August 18, Pope got word of the planned attack from an order he found on a captured Confederate officer and from a spy who reported that the Rebel army was assembling near the eastern fords. Accordingly, Pope moved his army back to the Rappahannock River, twenty-five miles north. On August 20 it was firmly arrayed along the river from Rappahannock Station (present-day Remington on U.S. Routes 15 and 29) to Kelly's Ford, four miles downstream.

Only a short time remained before Pope's army grew too large to handle. Elements of McClellan's army were already landing at Aquia Creek, on the Potomac near Fredericksburg. Soon his entire force would be available. A strike by Stuart's cavalry to break the railroad bridge at Catlett Station, fourteen miles north of Rappahannock Station, failed. On August 24, Lee told Jackson to take his whole corps, 23,000 men, move on Pope's rear, and break the railroad line, forcing Pope to retreat.

For Jackson, this was an opportunity not to be missed. Instead of edging around Pope's line just east of the Bull Run Mountains (as the Catoctin chain is known in this part of Virginia) and cutting the railway at the nearest point, Jackson swung west of the mountains, moved twenty-five miles north to Thoroughfare Gap, and struck straight east to Manassas Junction, the main Federal supply depot on the Orange & Alexandria Railroad. It was a stunning strategic surprise that not only shattered Pope's entire supply system, but also, by landing less than thirty miles from Washington, posed a direct threat to the national capital.

The news forced Pope to flee from the Rappahannock River. Pope, however, thoroughly underestimated Jackson. He concluded that Jackson was now stuck at Manassas and could be "bagged" by converging Federal forces from the south, west, and north. But when Union forces marched into Manassas on the morning of August 28, 1862, they found that their quarry had flown, and that the entire Federal supply depot was a mass of smoking ruins. It had been consumed by Rebel-set fire.

Only at the end of the day did the Federals discover that Jackson was occupying the heights just west of Groveton, eight miles northwest of Manassas and three miles northeast of Gainesville, where Lee's army, now marching through Thoroughfare Gap, was to emerge the next day. Thus Jackson had arranged for the entire Confederate army to consolidate at Groveton. But he had also arranged to test a new theory he had developed on how to defeat the Union army in battle. He was certain that he could induce Pope to attack him, because—in accordance with the admonition of Sun Tzu—he seemed to have fled in panic from Manassas and now appeared to be cowering in fear at Groveton. "Warfare is the way of deception," Sun Tzu writes. "Although you are capable, display incapability to the enemy. When committed to employing your forces, feign inactivity."[26]

Jackson had realized that a new approach to battle was necessary because headlong assaults, like those Lee had ordered in the Seven Days, were too deadly. Direct attacks crashed straight into the heart of enemy strength. They were also failing because of the effectiveness of the Minié-ball rifle and of the light canister-armed cannons rolled up to the firing line, which sprayed a deadly cloud of metal fragments at assaulting troops. These two weapons made the practice of lining up

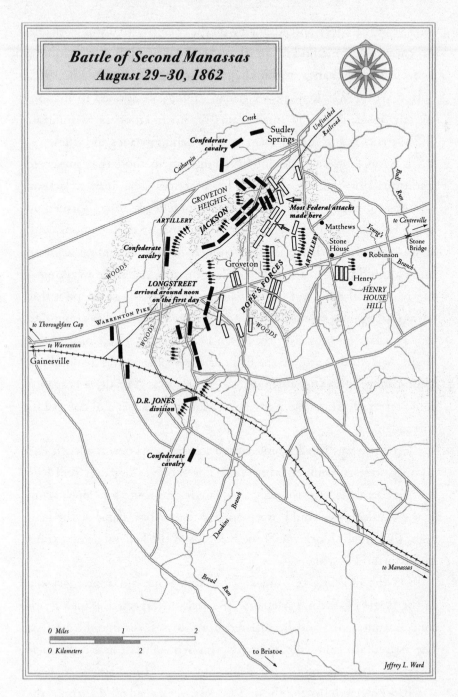

Battle of Second Manassas
August 29–30, 1862

Creek

Sudley
Springs

Unfinished
Railroad

Confederate
cavalry

Catharpin

GROVETON
HEIGHTS

Most Federal attacks
made here

ARTILLERY

JACKSON

Matthews

to Centreville

Bull
Run

Confederate
cavalry

Stone
House

ARTILLERY

Young's

Stone
Bridge

Robinson

Branch

WOODS

Groveton

POPE'S FORCES

Henry

LONGSTREET
arrived around noon
on the first day

HENRY
HOUSE
HILL

to Thoroughfare Gap

WARRENTON PIKE

WOODS

WOODS

to Warrenton

Gainesville

D.R. JONES
division

Confederate
cavalry

Branch

Dawkins

Broad
Run

to Manassas

0 Miles   1   2

0 Kilometers   2

to Bristoe

Jeffrey L. Ward

forces two men deep and advancing on the enemy virtually unworkable. An entirely new method of attack had to be devised. But this required a revolutionary change in thinking. The solution came only in 1915, during World War I, when a German captain abandoned formations entirely, instead sending small teams of storm troopers to infiltrate Allied trenches and rolling them up with hand grenades and rifles.

Jackson, however, had found an interim method that preserved traditional formations and orthodox practices. The answer, Jackson saw, was to induce the enemy to attack Confederate forces formed up in a pre-selected, strong defensive position anchored by cannons, with at least one flank that was open enough for the defending army to move around it when the battle ended. Because defensive weapons—the Minié-ball rifle and canister-firing cannons—were so powerful, any attack against a determined and organized defender was bound to fail, as had been proved in the Seven Days battles. The Confederates could then advance around the flank of the weakened and demoralized Union army and either force it into chaotic retreat or drive it against some terrain feature, like a river or a mountain range, and compel its surrender.[27]

Groveton was an admirable site to test Jackson's new theory. It had an open western flank at Gainesville. The Stone Bridge over Bull Run in the Federal rear was the only adequate retreat route for Pope's army. If the Confederates could sweep around the western flank of the Federals, they might block the Stone Bridge, pin the Federal army against Bull Run, and destroy it.

On the morning of August 29, 1862, Pope did attack Jackson, in the battle of Second Manassas. As Jackson expected, Pope's headlong assaults failed and he suffered heavy losses. Around 11:30 A.M., Lee arrived at Gainesville and swung his army almost at a right angle to Pope's army, facing his left flank. But Lee did not attack, as Jackson had expected. Instead, he and Longstreet argued all day about the feasibility of attacking and finally decided against it. A giant opportunity had been lost. But Pope tried to attack Jackson again the next day.

Once again Jackson's forces stopped the direct assaults. Once again Lee refused to advance on Pope's totally exposed flank. Only toward the end of the day, when Pope's failed attacks started to disintegrate his army, did Lee at last call for an advance on Pope's flank. But it was too late. The Confederates were unable to seize Henry House Hill, just above the Stone Bridge, before nightfall, and Pope's army was able to get away. Lincoln, recognizing Pope's incompetence, sent him out west to fight Indians and reinstated McClellan.

What could have been the total destruction of a Federal army became merely a defeat of that army. Jackson had shown Lee a method that could win the war in one or two engagements. But Lee had not grasped it and had not followed through. Jackson did not give up. He looked for other opportunities where Lee might accept his system. But a great chance had been lost at Second Manassas.

Lee now decided to invade Maryland. His aim, just as it had been in the Seven Days, was to attack George McClellan's army. Jackson had just demonstrated at Second Manassas how to defeat the enemy by standing on the defensive and *then* attacking the repulsed and demoralized Federals. But this lesson had not sunk in on Lee.

On September 3, 1862, Lee turned his columns toward Leesburg and the fords over the Potomac River. He halted at Frederick, Maryland, forty miles northwest of Washington. There he held a conference with Jackson and Longstreet. Jackson emphatically urged that the Confederate army take up a strong defensive position with an open flank somewhere east of Frederick. Lincoln—always fearful of an attack on the capital—was certain to require McClellan to keep the Union army between Lee and Washington. Therefore, the road would be open for the Confederates to move eastward to Baltimore or Philadelphia. Because of this peril, McClellan would be obliged to attack Lee at the first opportunity. When he did, Jackson said, he would lose.

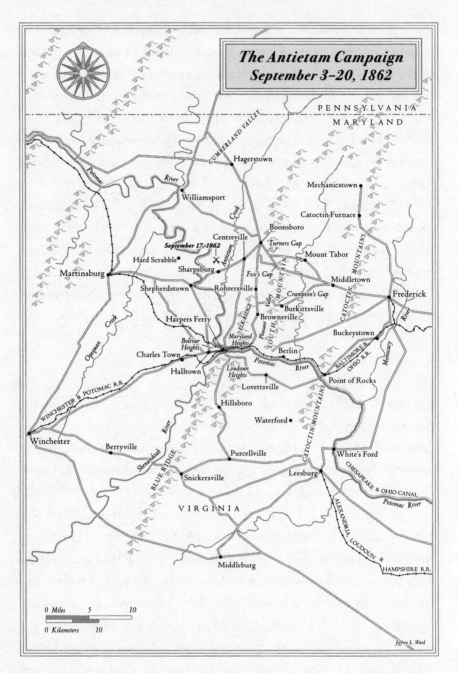

The Antietam Campaign
September 3–20, 1862

PENNSYLVANIA
MARYLAND

CUMBERLAND VALLEY

Potomac River

Hagerstown

Williamsport

Mechanicstown

Catoctin Furnace

Centreville

Boonsboro

September 17, 1862

Turners Gap

Mount Tabor

Hard Scrabble

Martinsburg

Sharpsburg

Fox's Gap

Middletown

Shepherdstown

Rohrersville

Crampton's Gap

Frederick

Harpers Ferry

Burkittsville

Brownsville

Bolivar Heights

Maryland Heights

Berlin

Charles Town

Buckeystown

Opequan Creek

Halltown

Loudoun Heights

Potomac River

Point of Rocks

BALTIMORE & OHIO R.R.

WINCHESTER & POTOMAC R.R.

Lovettsville

Hillsboro

Waterford

Winchester

Berryville

Purcellville

White's Ford

Shenandoah River

Snickersville

Leesburg

CHESAPEAKE & OHIO CANAL

Potomac River

VIRGINIA

BLUE RIDGE

CATOCTIN MOUNTAINS

SOUTH MOUNTAIN

ELK RIDGE

Pleasant Valley

CATOCTIN MOUNTAINS

Monocacy

Middleburg

ALEXANDRIA, LOUDOUN & HAMPSHIRE R.R.

0 Miles   5   10
0 Kilometers   10

Jeffrey L. Ward

Jackson's proposal was totally logical and compelling. Nine-tenths of Northern industry was located along the rail corridor from Baltimore to southern New Hampshire. The Northern population was also concentrated there. A threat in this direction would be decisive.

McClellan saw the danger clearly. In his official report a year later, he wrote, "One battle lost and almost all would have been lost. Lee's army might have marched as it pleased on Washington, Baltimore, Philadelphia, or New York. It could have levied its supplies from a fertile and undevastated country, extorted tribute from wealthy and populous cities, and nowhere east of the Alleghenies was there another organized force to avert its march."[28]

Despite Jackson's overwhelming argument, Lee refused. He resolved to move *west* across South Mountain, the extension into Maryland of the Blue Ridge, and then march north to Harrisburg and break the railroad bridge over the Susquehanna River there! It was an appallingly inconsequential strategic move. No real damage could be done to the Northern war effort. And Lee's resolve to attack McClellan—not for McClellan to attack him—would repeat the disastrous results of the Seven Days.[29]

In the campaign that followed, Lee decided to send most of his army to seize bypassed Harpers Ferry, then to reassemble it west of South Mountain in Maryland. The attack, led by Jackson, succeeded very well, forcing 11,500 Union soldiers to surrender. But Lee's order scattering his army was discovered discarded (probably by General D. H. Hill) at the former Rebel campsite at Frederick. McClellan, knowing Lee's dispositions, defeated the small Confederate defending force on South Mountain, forcing it to retreat. Lee's proper course now was to withdraw back into Virginia. However, with an army only half the size of the Union army, he resolved to fight along Antietam Creek, just east of Sharpsburg, on September 17, 1862.

In doing so, Lee violated a fundamental tenet of Sun Tzu—he did not ascertain the terrain on the battle site. The Confederate army was wedged in a cul-de-sac formed by a bend of the Potomac and was incapable of maneuver. The army could do nothing but fight for its life. It succeeded, primarily because of the military ineptitude of McClellan, but it was the bloodiest single day in the Civil War, and it gave Lincoln the opportunity to issue the Emancipation Proclamation, which turned the war into a moral crusade. The Maryland campaign of 1862 was a calamity, and it was wholly the fault of Robert E. Lee.

The final event in 1862 that proved Lee's strategic blindness was the Fredericksburg campaign. Lincoln ousted McClellan but named in his place an even more incapable officer, Ambrose E. Burnside. The only thing Burnside could think to do was to launch a headlong attack against the Confederate army that had emplaced itself on the heights just south of the Rappahannock River at Fredericksburg.

Lee resolved to defend this position, but Jackson opposed fighting there. Jackson told Lee that the Confederates would win, but they could not swing around the defeated Federals and shatter their army because the Union guns on Stafford Heights, just opposite the town on the north bank of the river, dominated the entire battlefield and would prevent a Confederate counterblow. Moreover, it would be impracticable to maneuver against Burnside's most vulnerable point, his supply line, because his base at Aquia was only twelve miles away. Burnside could easily withdraw to Aquia Creek before the Rebels could isolate his army.

Jackson proposed instead that the Confederates withdraw to the North Anna River, twenty-five miles south. Here the Federals, advancing from Fredericksburg, would expose their right flank and their supply line for the entire distance from Aquia Creek, thirty-seven miles. If they attacked on the North Anna and were defeated, as Jackson was confident would be the case, they would have to retreat all the way back to Aquia Creek. At numerous points along the way, Confederate cavalry could slow the Federal withdrawal, giving the infantry ample time to swing onto the enemy rear, sever the Union supply line, and force the Federals to attack once again and once again be defeated. It was a chance to destroy the entire Union army.

"I am opposed to fighting on the Rappahannock," Jackson said to General D. H. Hill. "We will whip the enemy, but gain no fruits of victory. I have advised the line of the North Anna, but have been overruled."[30]

So once again Lee refused the advice of Jackson. The Confederates indeed did win the battle of Fredericksburg on December 13, 1862. Burnside's headlong attacks failed utterly, costing him 12,600 men. But the North could replace its losses easily. And the South, as Jackson had predicted, gained nothing.

The 1862 campaigns show conclusively that when the military plans were consistent with Sun Tzu's maxims, tremendous gains resulted. When they were not, the effects ranged from lost opportunities to catastrophe. For example, spectacular success followed Stonewall Jackson's use of an indirect approach (Sun Tzu's *qi*) to overwhelm Banks's army at Strasburg. A great loss came when Lee refused to use this same approach to corner Pope's army on the Rapidan. Another great gain came when Jackson knew and exploited the geography of the Shenandoah Valley (in accordance with another Sun Tzu axiom) and stopped Banks from advancing on Staunton because he could sever Banks's supply line at New Market. An irretrievable loss occurred at Antietam when Lee failed to do the same, to find out that the Potomac River's course boxed in the Confederate army and eliminated any possibility of swinging on the Union flank.

F I V E

Gettysburg,
1863

In May 1863, the new Union commander, "Fighting Joe" Hooker, concentrated a huge force of 70,000 troops at Chancellorsville, on the left flank of the Confederate army at Fredericksburg. Robert E. Lee accepted the urging of Stonewall Jackson to swing his entire corps onto the unguarded western flank of Hooker's force, drive it away from United States Ford, the only available passage over the Rappahannock River, and force its surrender.[1]

Jackson's strike was completely successful. But Jackson was mortally wounded as he was organizing the final movement to block United States Ford, and this decisive strike was never carried out. The Union army was severely defeated, but it was able to retreat back across the Rappahannock.[2]

Now Jackson was gone. None of the officers Lee had left possessed anything like Jackson's stature. A hobbled Confederate army took up the task that Lee now assigned it: invasion of the North to seek a decision in the war. Lee reorganized his army into three corps under the command of James Longstreet, Richard S. Ewell, and A. P. Hill.

Longstreet had absorbed some of Jackson's thinking. He tried to get Lee to resolve not to attack the enemy, but to give battle only when Confederate forces were in a strong defensive position. Other Confederate leaders were thinking along the same lines. Porter Alexander, Longstreet's brilliant artillery chief, observed that when all of the Army of Northern Virginia's corps were together, nothing could successfully attack them.[3]

Longstreet thought he got Lee's promise to stand on the defensive in the campaign in the North. In the event, Longstreet's understanding turned out to be completely wrong.

On June 10, 1863, Lee launched his army northward. Avoiding Union army strength and following the line of least resistance, Lee slipped around to the west of the main Federal forces protecting Washington and moved into the Cumberland Valley of Maryland and Pennsylvania. Preceded by far-ranging cavalry that nearly reached the Pennsylvania capital of Harrisburg, the leading Confederate corps under Ewell seized Carlisle, twenty miles west of Harrisburg, on June 27, while Jubal Early's division pressed on through York to Wrightsville on the Susquehanna River, about thirty miles southeast of Harrisburg.

In this first stage of the invasion, Sun Tzu could have only applauded Lee's actions. He had seized the strategic initiative by maneuvering to a nearly unassailable position. In doing so, Lee had demonstrated Sun Tzu's single most profound injunction: "The way to avoid what is strong is to strike what is weak," and its closely related axiom, "As water seeks the easiest path to the sea, so armies should avoid obstacles and seek avenues of least resistance."[4]

Lee thus struck into virtually undefended space. Now well north of the Union army, he could move in any direction while his Federal opponent, newly appointed (June 28) Army of the Potomac commander George G. Meade, could do little more than react to Lee's initiatives.

Lee had two particularly promising strategic options. He could consolidate his army at Carlisle, forcing Meade to attack strongly defended

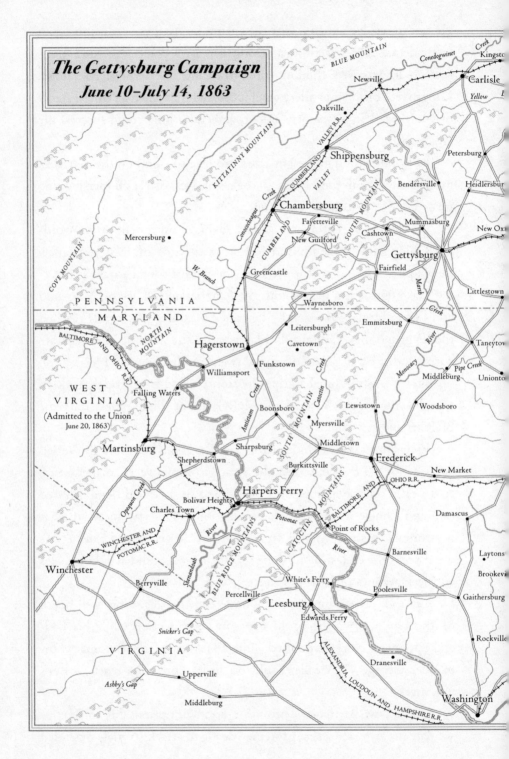

The Gettysburg Campaign
June 10–July 14, 1863

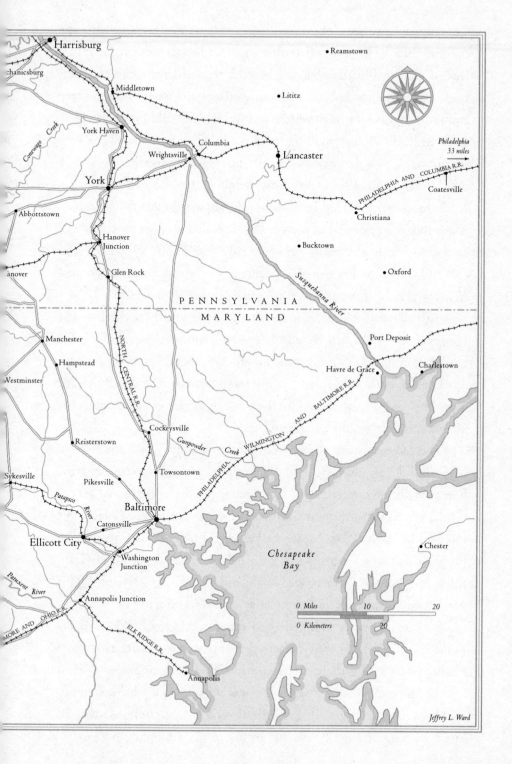

Jeffrey L. Ward

Confederate positions on well-chosen ground; or he could turn the Susquehanna River into a defensive moat and strike out on the undefended road to Philadelphia, the North's second-largest city and vital north-south railway hub. The loss of Philadelphia would be a military and political disaster from which the North likely could not recover. A strike at Philadelphia would have been consistent with Sun Tzu's prescription. He says that a good general "offers something that the enemy must seize."[5] Philadelphia was most definitely that "something."

Meade, whose army had cautiously advanced only to Frederick, Maryland, was powerless to prevent Lee from taking either choice. If Lee elected to remain at Carlisle, he would have days to find a suitable elevation and prepare an impregnable defense before Meade's army could possibly reach him. If Lee decided to strike out for Philadelphia—he was closer to the city than Meade and it was by far his best choice—the Union army would be obliged to race after him. Anywhere along the road, Lee could pull up his army on an easily defended elevation with open flanks, build field fortifications, mount cannons, and wait. Meade would be forced to attack under the most desperate circumstances. He almost certainly would be defeated.

The campaign was all but won. But, incredibly, Lee did not see it. Nor did he make any effort to play on Meade's anxieties and confuse him as to his intentions. Lee did not even realize he had achieved a spectacular strategic position at Carlisle. We know this is true because the moment he learned that Meade had reached Frederick, Lee abandoned his gains and sent his army in forced marches to concentrate at Cashtown, in southern Pennsylvania, eight miles west of Gettysburg. This was a most destructive and completely counterproductive decision.[6]

Lee's troops were compelled to force-march toward the rallying point (his three corps were dispersed twenty to forty miles away from Cashtown). Getting there was an exhausting and disorienting exercise for the troops. No one knew what was waiting at Cashtown. It was a plunge into darkness. In his official report, Lee confessed that he knew nothing about the size of enemy forces advancing on Gettysburg, nor what their intentions were. Once he got to Cashtown, Lee stumbled into a meeting engagement with Meade's army that sacrificed every advantage he possessed. This led to a totally unnecessary battle at Gettysburg.

Sun Tzu says that an army should move in accordance with a thought-out plan, not react to unexpected events. "If the entire army contends for advantage," Sun Tzu writes, "you will not arrive in time." This means that one should never rush into battle but should maneuver into a tactically advantageous position before challenging the enemy. Lee's actions were directly to the contrary. He rushed to a rallying point about which he had no information. The terrain was not even known. He had no definite target or objective. Lee placed his army in an extremely dangerous position before its first encounter with the enemy.[7] It was absolutely uncalled for.

Sun Tzu says that generals should not proceed in haste to some unfamiliar place. Having a purpose and sticking to it establishes order and cohesion. Lee should not have reacted to the news that Meade was pursuing him by rushing to Cashtown. Of course Meade was pursuing him! What else could he do? But it would take days before Meade could challenge him. In fact, the farther Lee was away from Meade, the longer it would take Meade to reach him and the greater preparations Lee could make to receive him. By rushing to Cashtown and thus *toward* Meade, Lee threw away this priceless advantage of time. Lee should have already figured out where the Confederate army was heading, and he should have continued with his intent. This would have forced Meade to conform to Lee's plans, not Lee to conform to Meade's.

It's quite apparent, however, that Lee did not have any objective when he moved into Pennsylvania. The strategic positions the Confederate army achieved were not in accordance with a thought-out design by Lee; they were gained by the bold actions of subordinate commanders. Lee did not even recognize what they had done.

A Sun Tzu maxim is perfectly suited to Lee's situation: "The victorious army first realizes the conditions for victory, and then seeks to engage in battle. The vanquished army fights first, and then seeks victory." This is precisely what Lee did. He fought first and then sought victory. He hastened back to Cashtown without any plan. He stumbled into a battle at Gettysburg. Every action during the three days of the battle was an improvisation. He compounded these blunders by also rushing into combat against an enemy already in possession of the battlefield. Sun Tzu warns that "first on the battlefield waits for the enemy fresh," while "last on the battlefield charges into the fray exhausted."[8]

The battle of Gettysburg began in an odd way. Harry Heth's division in Hill's 3rd Corps struck out from Cashtown on July 1, foraging for much-needed footwear rumored to be at Gettysburg. Instead of shoes, however, the Confederates found the Union cavalry division of John Buford waiting for them. Hill pushed more units toward Gettysburg to sweep the Yankees out of town, but he encountered infantry from the 1st Corps arriving in time to back up Buford's cavalrymen.

Like a magnet, this unplanned meeting engagement drew the two armies together. When Lee arrived on the scene, he quickly abandoned any thought of defense and moved directly to an offensive battle.

Lee had scant knowledge of the battleground and even less information on the force gathering to oppose him. In total violation of Sun Tzu's maxims, he entered into a billowing battle with no idea of how to win it. Suffering heavy losses, Lee drove Union defenders off McPherson Ridge to the west of Gettysburg and occupied Seminary Ridge, southwest of the town. Meanwhile Ewell, coming down from Carlisle, drove other Federal defenders from the town and onto Cemetery and Culp's hills just to the south.

Gettysburg started as an accidental battle. It need not have expanded into a full-scale engagement. As soon as he realized that Gettysburg was occupied by an unknown number of Union troops, Lee should have pulled back to South Mountain, just west of Cashtown, concentrated

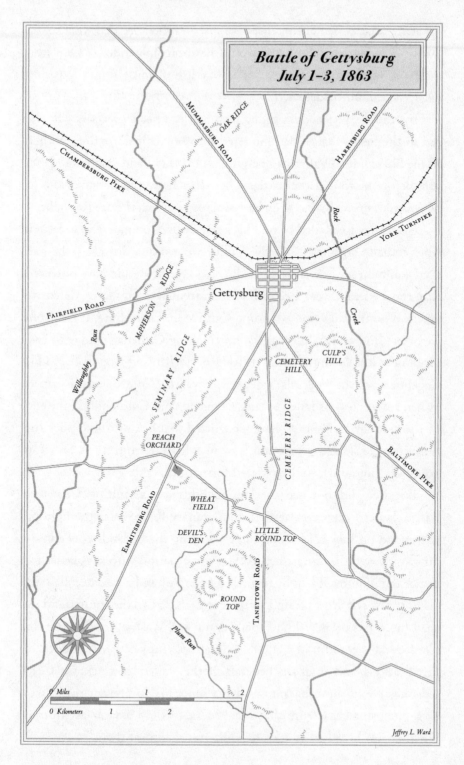

Battle of Gettysburg
July 1–3, 1863

Jeffrey L. Ward

his army, ascertained enemy dispositions, and then decided what to do. This is exactly what Sun Tzu would have recommended. "One who excels at warfare," he writes, "first establishes himself in a position where he cannot be defeated."[9]

Instead, Lee rushed headlong into battle. This is precisely what he did in the Seven Days. He blundered into one collision after another. In the Shenandoah Valley campaign, on the other hand, Stonewall Jackson, before he fought the battles, knew that he would be victorious at McDowell, Front Royal, Winchester, Cross Keys, and Port Republic.

Even after Lee failed to pull back to South Mountain and ascertain what actually lay ahead, he still could have avoided disaster if he had used common sense at the end of the first day. He should have observed that the Federals were occupying an extremely formidable defensive position on the ridgeline extending south from Gettysburg. It ran from Cemetery and Culp's hills on the north along Cemetery Ridge to two prominent knolls on the south, Little Round Top and Round Top. This ridgeline gave the Federals a decided advantage in a defensive battle. When Ewell's troops failed to rush Cemetery and Culp's hills at the end of the first day, Lee should have recognized that he must not attack the ridgeline. He should go around it or march away from it. As Sun Tzu says, "Do not attack well-regulated formations."[10]

But Lee did not see the impossibility of assaulting Cemetery Ridge. James Longstreet arrived on Seminary Ridge after the fighting had ended on July 1. He found Lee watching the Federals concentrate on Cemetery Hill. Longstreet studied the situation with his glasses for five or ten minutes. Then he turned to Lee. "All we have to do," he said, "is to throw our army around by their left [that is, to the south], and we shall interpose between the Federal army and Washington." There the Confederates could find a suitable elevation, emplace guns, build field fortifications, and await the Federals. If they failed to attack, the Confederates could move back toward Washington. To prevent this, however, Longstreet was sure that the Federals would assault as soon as possible. "When they attack," he said, "we shall beat them."[11]

Lee strongly resisted Longstreet's argument. Longstreet argued back just as forcefully. He and Lee knew that Lincoln always insisted on the Union army remaining between the capital and the Confederate army. But Lee now had the chance to place his army closer to Washington than Meade's army. Meade would be certain to attack immediately; otherwise, he'd be ousted from his job.

General Lee finally concluded the argument: "They are there in position [pointing to Cemetery Hill and Ridge], and I am going to whip them or they are going to whip me."[12]

What an astonishing refusal to face the facts! The thinking of Sun Tzu and Napoléon Bonaparte, and common sense, all lead to the identical conclusion: do not attack head-on a superior enemy in position on a highly defensible elevation. This was all the more true because both armies were employing the Minié-ball rifle and light cannons rolled up to the defending line and firing canister at attacking troops. Defenders were also shielding themselves behind field fortifications, if they had time and materials to build them, or behind natural barriers like stone fences. The advantage had swung overwhelmingly to the defense.

An army should go around roadblocks, fortifications, and defended strong points, Sun Tzu says. "The army's disposition of force avoids the substantial and strikes the vacuous," he says.[13] Napoléon said never to make a frontal attack if one could do otherwise, and always to move on the enemy's rear, even if it fails, because a rear maneuver will shake enemy morale and force him into a mistake. Instead, Lee fell back into the pattern of headlong assault he had exhibited since he first took command in June 1862.

Meade realized, the moment he arrived on Cemetery Hill just before midnight on July 1, that Lee could dislodge him merely by moving between him and the capital. Abner Doubleday, commander of the Union 1st Corps, also saw the danger. "Lee could easily have maneuvered Meade out of his strong position on the heights, and should have done so," he wrote.[14]

On the second day of the battle, July 2, Lee insisted that James Longstreet's 1st Corps attack Cemetery Ridge from the southwest. Lee had decided that the Union army was occupying only Cemetery Hill and Culp's Hill, and Confederate forces could mount the supposedly unoccupied slopes of Cemetery Ridge just to the south and roll up the Union forces on the two northern hills. Longstreet protested, but to no avail.

Lee ordered the attack without first gaining definitive battlefield intelligence. Sun Tzu writes, "Determine [the enemy's] disposition of force to know the tenable and fatal terrain. Probe them to know where they have an excess, where an insufficiency."[15]

During the morning of July 2, Lee sent two engineer officers to determine whether enemy troops were occupying lower Cemetery Ridge and the Round Tops. They reported back that isolated individuals but no Union forces were present. Neither Lee nor Longstreet made any further reconnaissance, a profound failure on the part of both officers. As the day wore on, the situation changed entirely. Meade ordered Daniel Sickles to occupy Cemetery Ridge with his 3rd Corps. But Sickles thought a better place was the elevated Peach Orchard on the Emmitsburg Road between Seminary and Cemetery ridges. He moved his corps west, creating a deep salient with the Peach Orchard as its apex.

Longstreet only discovered Sickles's corps at 3:30 P.M. He had planned to install his artillery at the Peach Orchard to cover his advance on Cemetery Ridge. The Confederates now could not possibly seize Cemetery Ridge quickly and roll up the Federal line. The Confederates would have to seize the Peach Orchard first. This would take time and give the Federals an opportunity to strengthen defensive positions on Cemetery Ridge. Sickles's advance invalidated Lee's entire plan. But Longstreet, angry that he had been overruled, sent no message informing Lee. Instead, he obdurately held to the original orders.

Longstreet's circumstance is a recurring factor in warfare. Military command structure requires a subordinate to obey the orders of his superior, even if he disapproves of them. It is the subordinate's duty to carry out his commander's wishes to the best of his ability. However, Longstreet now had positive information that Lee's original premise was incorrect. The Federals most certainly occupied Cemetery Ridge, and they had advanced into the valley to the west of it. It was Longstreet's responsibility to inform Lee of these developments. Whether it would have changed Lee's mind is unknown, but Longstreet's silence was a dereliction of duty.

Just at this time, McIvor Law, a brigade commander in John Bell Hood's division, offered Longstreet a far better plan—an alternative that could have won the battle in a day. Law discovered that Round Top was unoccupied. It rose, Law wrote, "like a huge sentinel guarding the Federal left flank, while the spurs and ridges trending off to the north of it afforded unrivaled positions for the use of artillery."[16]

Cannons placed on Round Top would be able to deliver enfilade fire—or fire on the *side* of the Union positions—along the entire Union line from Little Round Top to Cemetery Hill. Enfilade fire is almost impossible to defend against. The only solution is to withdraw. Porter Alexander described well the advantages: "A battery established where it can enfilade others need not trouble itself about aim. It has only to fire in the right direction and the shot finds something to hurt wherever it falls. No troops, infantry or artillery, can long submit to enfilade fire."[17] So mounting cannons on Round Top would have been decisive because the Union army would have been compelled to abandon the ridgeline.

Law told Hood that Round Top was the true base for the Confederate army, and that his brigade could seize the hill, block the Taneytown road, a quarter of a mile to the east, and cut the Baltimore Pike, a couple of miles beyond. This would unhinge the entire Union position. Law said occupation of Round Top would compel the enemy to change front, leave his strong position on the ridgeline, and attack the Confederates on Round Top. Law was right. His brigade could strike where the enemy was not, and seize the one position that dominated the entire Union line.

Hood endorsed Law's proposal, but when Hood advanced the idea, Longstreet replied that Lee was already fretting with him over the delay in attacking, and he was unwilling to add to it by offering further suggestions. So Longstreet compounded his dereliction of duty by refusing to propose Law's plan to Lee.

If Lee had known, what would he have done? It's evident that Lee had missed or disregarded the importance of Round Top, although he had been observing the terrain for more than a day. Seizing Round Top would have led to a defensive battle, and Lee wanted to attack. We do not know for certain, of course, but Lee most probably would have ignored Law's plan just as he had ignored Longstreet's plan to move south.

The battle of Gettysburg provides enlightening instruction on how generals estimate terrain and evaluate the dispositions of the enemy. What they *see* varies enormously among individuals. An observant person looking at the landscape of Gettysburg is struck almost at once by the dominance of Round Top at the southern end of the ridgeline. The hill soars above the other terrain features. For a person with imagination—most especially for a seasoned military officer who should have special knowledge about enfilade fire—it stands forth as the true place for cannons. But quite clearly either Lee did not see it or he ignored it. The same is true for Meade, who made no effort to seize Round Top.[18]

But McIvor Law did see it only a short time after he arrived on the field. Law was a subordinate commander, however. The person who *must* see is the senior commander. As Sun Tzu advises, a successful general is one who can take in an entire scene.[19] Napoléon Bonaparte understood this necessity quite well. He said a superior general has *coup d'oeil*, or the ability to see things at a glance.

The presence or absence of commanders with true vision largely determines the outcome of battles, and usually of wars. If a general who can see is opposed to one who cannot see, the general with vision will almost certainly prevail. This was the case with Stonewall Jackson in the battles he fought as senior commander. When a commander who can't see clashes with an opposing commander who also can't see, the outcome will depend on other factors. This was the case at Gettysburg.

Lee not only couldn't see but also was unable to make reasoned choices. Throughout the war, Lee focused on the enemy in front of him. He seldom saw anything else. This is why the Seven Days battles played out as they did. This is why Lee couldn't fathom Stonewall Jackson's strategy to sweep around John Pope's army and drive it against the Rapidan River or the mountains. This is why he sat for nearly two days on the undefended flank of the Union army at Second Manassas and did not attack.

One of the most remarkable aspects of the battle of Gettysburg is that the Confederates actually captured Round Top, but nothing was done to exploit the feat. Colonel William C. Oates, commanding two Alabama regiments, seized Round Top in minutes after Longstreet launched Hood's division at 5:00 P.M. Oates had not been party to the dispute with Longstreet. But as soon as he reached the summit, Oates realized that the Confederates could evict the Federals from their entire position. All they had to do was to cut down some trees and drag cannons to the top. No attack on Little Round Top, Cemetery Ridge, Cemetery Hill, or Culp's Hill was necessary.[20]

But a staff officer reached Oates and ordered him to follow Lee's original attack plan and advance on Little Round Top, preparatory to climbing Cemetery Ridge. Oates protested, but he obeyed the orders. His men collided with the 20th Maine Regiment that had just arrived on Little Round Top. The 20th Maine repulsed repeated attacks by Oates's regiments. Ironically, Law was in command of this operation. Hood was badly wounded shortly after the attack started, so Law took charge of the division. He spent the rest of the day trying to follow Lee's orders. Therefore, no senior officer was able to focus on Round Top, and it was never exploited.

Longstreet waited an hour and a half before sending Lafayette McLaws's division against the Peach Orchard at 6:30 P.M. After fierce and sustained assaults, the Confederates cracked the center of Sickles's line at the orchard, forcing the entire Union corps, plus reinforcements, to withdraw in disorder. The Rebels were stopped by darkness and a gun line established by Federal cannoneers along Plum Run, just west of Cemetery Ridge.[21]

The attacks cost the Confederates 4,000 casualties, but the effect was merely to drive Sickles back to Cemetery Ridge, the *real* Union defensive line. Longstreet thus rectified a line that Sickles had overextended in the first place.

Because of Lee's faulty actions, the advantages the South had gained by invading the North had been washed away by the evening of July 2, 1863. Since Lee once more refused Longstreet's plea on the morning of July 3 to move the Confederate army to the south, the only reasonable course left was to withdraw back into Virginia while the South still possessed some offensive power. But Lee refused to do this. Instead he insisted on launching a headlong assault against the very center of the Union position—an action that has gone down in history as Pickett's Charge. Of all the counterproductive actions Lee took in the war, this was by far the most damaging.

Sun Tzu might have been speaking of a situation similar to what happened on Gettysburg's climactic day, July 3, when he said, "One who knows when he *can* fight, and when he *cannot* fight," will be victorious. Sun Tzu emphasizes that "there is terrain for which one does not contend."[22] There is no better example of such terrain than the strong Union positions running from Cemetery Hill and Culp's Hill, along Cemetery Ridge, and anchored at Little Round Top on July 3. Lee should have realized that a frontal attack targeting the center of the Union line on Cemetery Ridge—"terrain for which one does not contend"—was an action that his army "cannot fight."

Longstreet tried with all of his argumentative skills to talk Lee out of making the attack. But Lee adamantly refused. Stonewall Jackson might have persuaded Lee to follow a wiser course of action, but Longstreet could not do so.

In a lost fragment of *The Art of War* discovered in an ancient tomb years after the original text was written, Sun Tzu answers a question from the king of Wu that supports Longstreet's logic: "Suppose the enemy arrives first, occupies the strategic positions and holds the advantageous ones with selected troops. What should we do? If the enemy has gained a position, then be careful not to attack it. Draw him away by pretending to go off. The enemy will certainly come forth to rescue the endangered target. What others want we will give them; what they abandon we will take."[23]

Depending on his men to win the day, Lee launched 13,500 of them in a frontal assault against the center of the Union position. What a tragic refusal to face his responsibilities! How desperately the South needed the wisdom of Sun Tzu that day! He says: "One who excels at warfare seeks victory through the strategic configuration of power, not from reliance on men."[24]

A general's plans and their execution should accomplish his goals. A general should never depend on his soldiers to accomplish with their blood what his own strategy and tactics have failed to achieve. Lee's dispositions at Gettysburg were atrocious, and victory could be achieved only if the men exhibited superhuman valor. This was impossible, and failure resulted. Men should never be put into a position where they must save a situation. They should be used to exploit a situation.

A great general *preserves* the lives of his men by placing them in positions where their presence and their actions achieve victory. A great general does not descend into desperate straits where he can succeed *only* by sacrificing the lives of his men. In the Gettysburg campaign, Lee had a number of chances to move his army to places where it would have been impossible for him to be defeated—and where he then could have swept around the enemy and defeated him. He could have stood on the defensive at Carlisle or on the road to Philadelphia. He could have concentrated on South Mountain just west of Cashtown. Once committed to Gettysburg, he could have moved to the south of Cemetery Ridge, forcing the Federals to evacuate. He even could have stood on the defensive on Seminary Ridge, the main Confederate position at Gettysburg, and forced the Federals to attack him—and be defeated, just as he was defeated when he attacked them.

Porter Alexander saw this opportunity clearly. "It does not seem improbable that we could have faced Meade safely on the 2nd [of July] at Gettysburg without assaulting him in his wonderfully strong position," he wrote. "We had the prestige of victory with us, having chased him off the field and through the town. We had a fine defensive position on Seminary Ridge ready at our hand to occupy. It was not such a really wonderful position as the enemy happened to fall into, but it was no bad one, and it could never have been successfully assaulted." Alexander added that "the onus of attack was upon Meade anyhow. We could even have fallen back to Cashtown and held the mountain passes with all the prestige of victory, and popular sentiment would have forced Meade to take the aggressive."[25]

But Lee relied totally on his men to achieve what was manifestly unachievable: to cross a bullet- and shell-strewn field more than half a mile wide and overcome an emplaced superior enemy in an elevated position. To order such an attack was a monstrous failure of leadership.

Porter Alexander was in charge of a tremendous preparatory artillery bombardment from 138 Confederate guns disposed around the Peach Orchard and along Seminary Ridge. Alexander was directing this fire from a point out in the valley in front of Seminary Ridge.

Longstreet came out alone to where Alexander was standing. "I don't want to make this attack," he told his artillery chief. "I believe it will fail. I do not see how it can succeed. I would not make it even now, but that General Lee has ordered and expects it."

Alexander believed Longstreet was on the verge of stopping the attack, "and even with slight encouragement he would do it." But Alexander, a colonel, wrote, "I was too conscious of my own youth and inexperience to express any opinion not directly asked. So I remained silent while Longstreet fought his battle out alone and obeyed his orders."[26]

The Confederate infantrymen from divisions commanded by George Pickett, Johnston Pettigrew, and Isaac Trimble stepped off around 2:00 P.M. on July 3. Pickett's Charge was bloodily repulsed, with half of the men being killed or wounded. Realizing that the battle was irretrievably lost, Lee met the survivors of the charge with the lament, "It is all my fault." He spoke the truth.

Pickett's Charge should be seen as a vastly magnified version of the Charge of the Light Brigade at Balaclava in the Crimean War—as an act of lunacy or perversity by a commander who ignored better counsel and brought on a disaster that could and should have been avoided.

Of the more than 150,000 Confederate and Union soldiers taking part in the three-day battle, nearly 50,000 became casualties. Both sides suffered about the same number of losses, but they represented 30 percent of Lee's army and 25 percent of Meade's force. While the Union army could readily replace its Gettysburg losses—and add tens of thousands more fresh combat troops to its field forces—the Confederate army could not.

Lee brought his defeated army back to Virginia, evading Meade's half-hearted pursuit and crossing the rain-swollen Potomac River the night of July 13–14. The remainder of the war played out to its inevitable end. Nearly two years after leading the Confederate army to its "high tide" at Gettysburg, Lee surrendered at Appomattox Court House on April 9, 1865.

What would Sun Tzu have done if he had been in command of the Southern army at Gettysburg those fateful days in July of 1863? It is safe to say that he would not have fought the battle at all.

Battle of the Marne,
1914

The decisive battle of the Marne in early September 1914 is one of the great examples in history of how and how not to apply the fundamental strategic concept of Sun Tzu: his idea of combining orthodox (*zheng*) and unorthodox (*qi*) forces. In this battle the German chief of staff, Helmuth von Moltke, ignored the original battle plan, which exemplified Sun Tzu's concept, and instead turned the *qi* force intended to circle spectacularly around Paris into a direct *zheng* force that charged directly into French strength. The consequence of this disastrous decision was the loss of World War I by Germany.

Virtually all military operations—from the smallest local engagement to the biggest strategic campaign—can be reduced to how or whether a commander applies *zheng* and *qi*. Uncounted commanders over the ages have been ignorant of the concept of orthodox and unorthodox forces, or they have disregarded it. All but a few of the generals on both sides in the American Civil War were such officers, and they made headlong attacks that relied on brute force to achieve their goals. That is why six out of seven of their assaults failed.

On the other hand, practically all successful commanders through-out history have applied the rule of *zheng* and *qi*. Combining these two approaches causes the enemy to divide his own strength, allowing the decisive blow to be delivered against a fraction of the enemy's power, not —as in the case of a direct attack—against the vast bulk of his power.

"In warfare," Sun Tzu writes, "the strategic configurations of power do not exceed the unorthodox and the orthodox, but the changes of the unorthodox and the orthodox can never be completely exhausted. The unorthodox and orthodox mutually produce each other, just like an endless cycle. Who can exhaust them?"[1]

In general, the orthodox is the main force that engages the enemy and holds him in place, while the unorthodox is the smaller force that attacks the enemy at a different, unexpected, place, usually flank or rear, forcing him to disintegrate.

But this normal arrangement can be reversed. In the 1805 cam-paign leading up to the battle of Austerlitz, for example, a small French cavalry force under Joachim Murat pressed through the Black Forest of southern Germany and locked in place the Austrian army under Karl Mack von Leiberich at Ulm on the Danube River. Meanwhile, the main French army under Napoléon Bonaparte moved through Ger-many farther north and descended on the rear of Mack, forcing his surrender. In this case, Murat was the orthodox, or *zheng*, force, while the French Grand Army was the unorthodox, or *qi*, force. A simi-lar application of the principle occurred in Napoléon's Italian cam-paign of 1796–1797. He drew the Austrian army to Valenza on the Po River in Piedmont, Italy, with a huge demonstration, while his main army marched sixty miles down the Po and crossed at Piacenza, where it threatened Austria's main base of Milan, forcing the Austrians to withdraw eastward in disorder. The Valenza demonstration was the *zheng* force, while the Piacenza crossing was the *qi* force.

The cause of World War I was economic rivalry. After Germany unified in 1871, its industrial production multiplied several times over. By the turn of the twentieth century, it surpassed Britain in industrial development and overall economic power. Germany began seeking a large colonial empire and expanding international trade. Most of these advances came at the expense of Britain.

German leaders on the right began to challenge Britain's leading role in world trade. To gain more of this trade, they induced Germany to embark on a fateful program to challenge the Royal Navy. Britain, whose empire was founded on sea trade, was unwilling to tolerate any threat to its navy. The result was a fierce naval arms race. By 1909 Britain had won. Its navy was twice the size of Germany's, and the disparity was growing, not shrinking. But Britain, fearful of Germany's intentions and anxious about its economic growth, had signed a series of agreements with France in 1904 that grew into a secret military alliance, and it had signed a similar agreement with Russia in 1907.

In 1907 Arthur Balfour, who had been British prime minister from 1902 to 1905, told an American diplomat, "We are probably fools not to find a reason for declaring war on Germany before she builds too many ships and takes away our trade."

American President Woodrow Wilson remarked in 1919, "This war was a commercial and industrial war. It was not a political war." About the same time, the English economist John Maynard Keynes wrote that Britain had destroyed a trade rival in the war. "Do you want to know the cause of the war?" the automaker Henry Ford asked. "It is capitalism, greed, the dirty hunger for dollars."[2]

Although the economic collision with Britain was the underlying cause of the war, Germany also faced severe challenges on the Continent. As a result of the defeat of France in the Franco-Prussian War of 1870–1871, Germany had annexed the French provinces of Alsace and Lorraine. This covetous avarice of Germany turned France into a mortal enemy bent on revenge. Along with the danger in the west, Germany faced a potential enemy in the east. Russia was seeking to expand into the Balkans at the expense of Germany's only reliable ally, Austria-Hungary.

All that was needed to set off conflict was a spark. It came when a cell of Serbian terrorists bent on creating a "greater Serbia" shot the Austrian archduke Franz Ferdinand and his wife on a street in Sarajevo, Bosnia, on June 28, 1914. Austria wanted to exploit the assassinations to destroy Serbia. Germany covertly supported Austria. But Serbia was backed by Russia. After a month of intense negotiations, Austria-Hungary declared war on Serbia, and Russia mobilized. Germany tried to get Russia to restrict its troops to the Austro-Hungarian frontier, but Russia refused. Accordingly, Germany declared war on Russia on August 1. Within a few days Britain, France, and Russia were at war with Germany and Austria-Hungary.

The fear of a two-front war had long agonized the German General Staff. It sought a way to eliminate one threat before having to face the other. Since Russia was notoriously slow in mobilizing its forces, and since the heart of German industry was the Ruhr, just east of Holland, the impetus grew to throw up a temporary shield against Russia and to concentrate most of Germany's power to defeat France quickly and thoroughly. Then the danger of Russia could be dealt with at leisure.

But defeating France, especially since it would likely have the help of Britain, was no easy matter. With this in mind, Count Alfred von Schlieffen, chief of the General Staff from 1891 to 1906, developed plans for a *Vernichtungskrieg*, or war of annihilation. His aim was to avoid a frontal attack by a deep concentric encircling movement around the French flank in order to drive French forces into a pocket or caldron where they had to either surrender or be annihilated.

Although Schlieffen knew nothing of Sun Tzu, his idea exactly mirrored Sun Tzu's concept of combining *zheng* and *qi*. That is, Schlieffen called for one German force (*zheng*) to hold the main enemy force in place, while another German force (*qi*) swung around to the flank or rear of the enemy and forced his destruction.

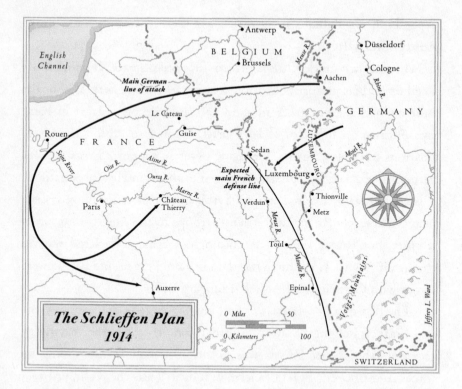

Such an operation was impossible along the restricted frontier with France, which ran only 150 miles. French forces would be so numerous and formidable that any attack would have to be frontal, leaving little scope for a flank attack. The only alternative was to hold the main French army along the frontier with a small force (*zheng*) and to swing the main German attack (*qi*) through Belgium and Luxembourg onto the rear of the French army.

Astonishingly, Schlieffen modeled this extremely ambitious plan on a single battle—Leuthen in Silesia—fought in 1757 by Frederick the Great of Prussia. Frederick exploited the fact that Prussian troops marched faster than other armies. Consequently, he developed his "oblique order" in which a small force held the enemy army in position by threatening one wing with attack, while the main force marched on the other wing and destroyed it. At Leuthen, Prussian cavalry demonstrated against the northern flank of the Austrian army, while the Prussian infantry marched on the southern flank and rolled it up.

Schlieffen planned to use this same method on a vast scale. While a small force challenged the French in Alsace-Lorraine, inducing the French army to attack, the main German offensive was to roll over the plains of Belgium and northern France, cross the Seine River near Rouen, circle around south of Paris, then turn back to the northeast, and press onto the rear of the French armies, which had meanwhile advanced through Alsace-Lorraine to or almost to the Rhine River. Schlieffen conceived that the French armies would be caught between German masses on both sides and be forced to surrender.[3]

While an enemy commander was likely to anticipate an ordinary battlefield flanking movement, the French command was less likely to fathom an "oblique order" of attack over such a huge expanse of geography. Space could create obscurity and veil intent.

The Schlieffen Plan called for concentrating the vast bulk of German strength on this great right-hand pincer movement. Of the seventy-two German divisions expected to be available, fifty-three were to be allocated to this wing, ten to form a pivot around Verdun, and only nine to be held in Alsace-Lorraine along the French frontier. Schlieffen's object was to keep the German left wing so weak that the French would be encouraged to attack. The farther the French drove forward, the more difficult it would be to extricate their forces when the German flanking movement swept onto their rear.

By happenstance, the French were about to play into German hands. In the years shortly before the war, a new school of theorists, led by Ferdinand Foch, had become fixated on the idea that wars could be won by quick offensive action. The school preached that the French would be bound to win if they attacked forcefully. French obsession with this *offensive à outrance*, or all-out attack, paid no attention to the lessons learned in the American Civil War, which proved that defensive weapons fired from behind strong field fortifications could stop practically any attack. It also ignored the developments of extremely formidable defensive weapons after the Civil War. These included the magazine bolt-action rifle, with an effective range of a thousand yards;

the machine gun, perfected by Hiram Maxim in 1884; much more powerful explosives, commencing with Alfred Nobel's dynamite, invented in
1866; and quick-firing artillery equipped with newly developed hydrau-
lic recoil mechanisms, which could launch shells miles from the front
lines (and thus were invulnerable to enemy rifle and machine-gun fire).

Although the Schlieffen Plan was an essential part of German strategy to survive a two-front war, Helmuth von Moltke, who became chief
of staff in 1906, did not understand it. No one in the German leadership had any inkling of this astounding fact. Moltke was the nephew
of the like-named Helmuth von Moltke, the brilliant Prussian chief
of staff who had led Germany to unification in 1871. The younger
Moltke's military training had been of the best, and his credentials
were impeccable. Everyone assumed that Moltke understood warfare in
general and Germany's secret military plans in particular. But this was
not true. Because selection of leaders depends on many factors, which
can vary as circumstances vary, individuals incapable of understanding
warfare can become senior leaders. Moltke was such an officer.

Only a tiny fraction of Germany's leaders were privy to the Schlieffen Plan, and no one raised suspicions when Moltke began altering the
plan in the years prior to the war. Of nine new divisions that became
available, he allocated eight to the left wing and only one to the right.
When the war started, he altered the plan even more.

Moltke sent forward only thirty-four divisions—not the fifty-
three Schlieffen had planned—in three armies (1st, 2nd, and
3rd) through Belgium to commence the wide-arcing advance. Against
them the French had only thirteen divisions in the 5th Army, plus
the small four-division British Expeditionary Force (BEF). The German advance should have progressed with little trouble, because the
Allies thought the Germans were aiming straight at Paris, and left
the extreme west virtually undefended. Thus, the path was almost
wholly open for the Germans to swing well to the west and to avoid
the French and British forces.

But Moltke began making profound blunders from the start. He diverted seven divisions from the western wing to stand guard over the Belgian army and to seize the old French fortresses of Givet and Maubeuge. The Belgians had withdrawn to Antwerp and were interested only in their preservation, not attacking the German army. The old fortresses were useless for holding up the German advance and could easily have been left to follow-on reserve troops. Moltke also sent another four divisions to East Prussia, to aid in stopping the Russians, though they were not needed and had not been called for.

At the same time, it became clear that Moltke had neglected to explain the Schlieffen Plan to the commanders of the three German armies on the west. They didn't understand what the plan called for, and instead of trying to avoid the French and British forces, they continually attacked them head-on.

Alexander von Kluck's German 1st Army collided with the BEF at Le Cateau in northern France in a full-scale attack on August 25–27. The BEF fought off a double envelopment by Kluck's entire army. It was the biggest British battle since Waterloo. The 40,000 British troops succeeded in disengaging, but the BEF suffered 7,800 casualties.

To relieve pressure on the BEF, the French 5th Army fought a series of successful engagements around Guise, fifteen miles south of Le Cateau, on August 29. These collisions caused the German armies to shift their direction directly against the defending French forces.

Meanwhile, as the Germans advanced into Belgium, the French launched an offensive into Lorraine on August 14, 1914, with nineteen divisions, just as Schlieffen had anticipated. Departing radically from Schlieffen's plan, however, Moltke diverted six newly formed divisions to this wing. They should have gone to strengthening the western wing. He also allowed the commander of the eastern wing, Rupprecht Maria Luitpold Ferdinand, crown prince of Bavaria, to go over to the attack himself. This violated the entire premise on which the Schlieffen Plan was based, namely, that the eastern wing at first should *withdraw* to lure the French into advancing.

The French forces were overwhelmed by August 20 not only by

powerful German forces but also by the utterly false idea that offensive spirit could overcome machine-gun bullets and fast-firing artillery shells. The nineteen French divisions were shattered, and the few survivors fell back on the Vosges Mountains and the French fortress chain based in Epinal, Toul, and Verdun. Here French reserves easily repulsed Prince Rupprecht's further attacks. The French were able to send troops to form a new 6th Army to reinforce the French western flank.

Now Moltke made the fatal mistake that destroyed any hope of carrying out the Schlieffen Plan. The German western wing, continuing to ignore Schlieffen's directive to keep moving to the west and south, was marching southeast, colliding with French forces every step of the way.

Instead of ordering the wing to return to its original path and to swing around these enemy forces, Moltke abruptly changed the entire strategy. On August 28, 1914, he told the armies that the objective of the campaign "must be to advance as rapidly as possible on Paris, not to give the French army time to recover, to prevent it from forming fresh units, and to take from France as many of its means of defense as possible."[4] In other words, Moltke outlined a policy of direct attack that was completely at odds with the Schlieffen Plan. Instead of going *around* any resistance that materialized, Moltke ordered the 2nd and 3rd Armies to attack the enemy frontally.

Only the 1st Army on the extreme west was to continue the original plan. Moltke ordered it to move in a southwesterly direction on a path that would lead about twenty-five miles west of Paris. But he told the 2nd Army to advance directly on Paris, and the 3rd Army to turn southeast to Château-Thierry on the Marne River fifty-five miles *east* of Paris. Moltke foreshadowed his real intent by adding that it might be necessary to abandon the flanking movement altogether and wheel the 1st Army directly south if the enemy put up strong resistance on the Marne.

These actions proved that Moltke did not understand the Schlieffen Plan at all. He had entirely missed the significance of a wide sweep to the west to avoid enemy forces and to allow the west wing to get south of Paris without resistance, so it then could move up on the rear of the French armies defending the German frontier. Instead, he charged directly *into* the heart of Allied resistance.

In the event, the German 2nd and 3rd Armies moved well to the east of Château-Thierry, creating a gap of several miles between the 1st and 2nd Armies. The final destruction of the Schlieffen Plan was accomplished by Kluck, commander of the 1st Army. When Karl von Bülow, commander of the 2nd Army, asked for assistance to help push back the French, Kluck, with the ready approval of Moltke, complied at once, turning eastward on August 31. In doing so, Kluck exposed his right flank. He also abandoned the concept of swinging around west and south of Paris. This ended the envelopment and sent the entire western wing of the German army into a direct assault against emplaced French forces along the Marne. It was a total renunciation of the Schlieffen Plan and played directly into the hands of the French and British defenders.

On September 5, the French 6th Army, which had been assembling in Paris, advanced on Kluck's right flank along the Ourcq River, a tributary to the Marne, about thirty-five miles northeast of Paris and about twenty miles west of Château-Thierry. Quick action by Kluck's right-flank corps commander, Hans von Gronau, saved the 1st Army from envelopment. Kluck did not realize the danger immediately, but by September 7 he had grasped it and turned his whole army westward in a savage counterattack that forced the 6th Army on the defensive. Only the arrival of 6,000 reinforcements from Paris, carried by 600 Parisian taxicabs, permitted the 6th Army commander, Michel Maunoury, to stem the German advance.

Kluck's shift westward widened the already existing gap between the 1st and 2nd Armies to thirty miles. Kluck was not worried, because the 70,000-man BEF under Sir John French, which was supposed to have covered this gap, had been retreating at full speed since the battle of Le Cateau, and was well south of the Marne. But on September 7, the BEF at last turned about and commenced a slow advance north-ward, threatening to move between the German 1st and 2nd Armies. Fighting now became general along the Marne, with the three German armies colliding with the French 6th and 5th Armies and another new French army, the 9th, on the east. Schlieffen had intended a blood-less sweep around the Allied armies. What the campaign had become, through the stupidity of Moltke, was a headlong confrontation with the Allied armies.

Moltke was getting few reports from the front. Worried by rumors and pessimistic fragmentary messages, he sent an officer from his staff, Lieutenant Colonel Richard Hentsch, to inspect the front on Septem-ber 8. Hentsch's orders were verbal, and they remain somewhat a mys-tery. But Moltke gave this junior officer full authority to issue orders in the chief of staff's name. Hentsch arrived at 2nd Army headquarters just as news came in that the right flank of the army was being turned by a vigorous night attack by Franchet d'Espèrey's French 5th Army. Bülow was about to retreat. Kluck was making headway against Mau-noury's 6th Army on the northwest, but the BEF's threatened advance into the gap between both armies imperiled Kluck's left and rear.

Hentsch approved Bülow's retreat, and later the same day, in Moltke's name, he ordered the 1st Army to withdraw as well. Moltke now realized that his offensive had failed, and he ordered a general retirement to the Aisne River, some thirty miles north. This was an unnecessary retreat. The German armies could easily have contained the Allied advances. But the withdrawal was actually the most sensible action. Since Moltke had already destroyed any possibility of carrying out the Schlieffen Plan, backing up to the Aisne allowed the Germans to construct a solid defensive line and reorganize their forces.

Moltke is said to have reported to Kaiser Wilhelm II after the bat-tle, "Your Majesty, we have lost the war." This was the truth, though it took both sides four years and millions of casualties to realize it. Once the Germans were stopped, the Allies were able to throw up defensive entrenchments, and the war of movement quickly ended. On September 14, Kaiser Wilhelm relieved Moltke and replaced him with General Erich von Falkenhayn.

Thereafter ensued the "race to the sea" as each side tried to go around the other's western flank, finally ending on the Strait of Dover at Nieuwpoort, Belgium, a few miles east of the French port of Dunkirk. At the same time, the defensive front extended eastward as well, becoming a continuous line of entrenchments from Switzerland to Belgium and ending mobility in the West. This line of trenches soon solidified into a rigid, almost impenetrable complex of field fortifications backed by machine guns and massed artillery. Neither side thereafter could open enough space to reinstitute a war of movement.

The defeat on the Marne was one of the most decisive battles in world history. If it had ended differently, the course of the twentieth century would have been altered fundamentally. The outcome was due to Moltke's total misunderstanding of Schlieffen's strategy. Through his inept generalship he ruined a brilliant plan that, if carried out correctly, almost certainly would have succeeded.

But this was not the prevailing opinion that came out of the war. Because the German offensive was widely advertised as being the Schlieffen Plan, and because the offensive had ended in disaster, most observers concluded that the plan itself was at fault. Few knew that it was not the plan, but Moltke's implementation of it, that had failed.

The concept of a wide-ranging strategic offensive fell out of favor in the years after 1918. This attitude was most prevalent among the winning generals on the Allied side. They discouraged imaginative thinking and choked off new ideas. Military theory in Britain, France, and the United States focused on the meticulous method of attack that the Allies had worked out in the war. Attacks were preceded by heavy bombardment of enemy positions, followed by a "rolling barrage" of shellfire that stayed ahead of the infantry who came out of their trenches and advanced behind the shell blasts.[5] The method was a form of direct attack and of attrition warfare, designed to wear down the enemy. Though it often was successful, it caused immense casualties and was incapable of achieving complete breakthroughs. Advances were slow because shellfire shattered towns and villages and cratered the landscape, virtually prohibiting wheeled transport. This gave the enemy time to throw up new barriers to block further advances.

Nevertheless, most Allied commanders concluded that continuous trench lines and field fortifications would extend along an entire front in future wars, and that such lines could be broken or pushed back only by the "rolling barrage" attack system. Accordingly, they went into World War II in 1939 with the idea of repeating the methods of painstaking advance they had followed in the previous war.

Leaders of the defeated German army did not want to duplicate the failed results of World War I, but they were as conservative as Allied commanders and continued to think in terms of long main lines of resistance and painstaking attacks with infantry and artillery to gain small objectives.

However, a few inventive thinkers in the German army had not been deceived into believing the Schlieffen Plan had failed because its concept was wrong. They sought ways to circumvent the continuous trench lines of World War I and to return to mobile warfare. They saw the answer in the further development of the "storm troop" or "infiltration" tactics that the Germans had developed during the war. In this method, one small group of soldiers held down an enemy trench position or strong point with heavy directed fire.[6] This was Sun Tzu's orthodox *zheng*, or holding, force. Once the enemy was driven under cover, one or more well-trained teams of eight to twelve "storm troopers" (Sun Tzu's unorthodox *qi*, or flanking, force) infiltrated the trench line or sneaked up on the strong point, and "rolled it up" with grenades and small-arms fire. This system could be extended to several storm troop teams operating together to attack a fairly large sector.

Storm troopers finally solved the problem of assault that had stymied commanders in the Civil War, because they eliminated military formations altogether and gave soldiers specific assignments. The system became the standard "fire-and-maneuver" tactical method that armies use to this day. It overcame enemy guns and fortifications and returned movement to the battlefield.

But the storm troopers had not won the war for Germany. Although they could occasionally break the enemy line, they moved on foot and could not advance fast enough to create a strategic penetration before enemy forces coming up on railways could close the gap.

One additional element was needed. In the years after the war, the small group of original thinkers recognized that the *zheng* and *qi* tactics of the storm troops could be exploited by creating divisions of fast-moving tanks and motorized forces that could penetrate a breach faster than enemy reinforcements could seal it. It was a brand new idea, but it was to bring mobility back to warfare.

S E V E N

German Victory
in the West, 1940

One of the most successful applications of the Sun Tzu axiom to avoid strength and strike at weakness occurred when Nazi Germany overran the Low Countries, defeated France, and ousted Britain from the Continent in six weeks in 1940. The Germans feinted with a massive decoy attack into northern Belgium and Holland, which drew in most of the mobile Allied forces. Meanwhile, the actual strategic advance went almost unnoticed through the heavily forested Ardennes Mountains of eastern Belgium and Luxembourg and emerged at Sedan, France, *behind* the Allied armies.

The Allies were totally surprised. They had not anticipated a main blow through the Ardennes. In 1933, Marshal Henri Philippe Pétain, then minister of war and a hero of World War I, had told the French Senate that the Ardennes could not be crossed by substantial German forces.

The Germans' success created an almost uncontested path to the English Channel 160 miles away. When they arrived, they cut off all of the Allied armies in Belgium. Most surrendered, but—because of the inexplicable refusal of the German dictator, Adolf Hitler, to allow his armor to seize Dunkirk—the British were able to evacuate their Expeditionary Force, along with 120,000 French soldiers.

The campaign nevertheless was the greatest victory in the twentieth century. But it did not win the war for Germany because Hitler completely misunderstood its significance and squandered its fruits.[1]

The German plan was the brainchild of a low-ranking fifty-three-year-old major general, Erich von Manstein. His ideas were rejected by the German high command, which wanted to fight a war very much like the one it had lost in World War I. It was only through the intervention of three even lower-ranking German officers that Manstein's ideas were brought to the attention of Hitler. He ordered their implementation, but he did not grasp their scope.

Although Manstein knew nothing about Sun Tzu, he was a brilliant strategist, and he arrived on his own at one of Sun Tzu's most fundamental concepts: "make an uproar in the east but attack in the west." Manstein saw that deception is the most dependable way of achieving victory. By staging an "uproar" at one place, a general can induce his enemy to commit his strongest forces there, and thereby ensure that the general's actual target somewhere else will be poorly defended or not defended at all.[2]

Manstein's idea was not original. It goes back to the beginning of warfare and is the intellectual foundation of Sun Tzu's concept of the orthodox, or direct, *zheng* force working in conjunction with the unorthodox, or indirect, *qi* force.

Germany's original plan was extremely modest. It aimed only to defeat large portions of the Allied armies and gain territory in Holland, Belgium, and northern France "for successful air and sea operations against Britain and as a broad protective zone for the Ruhr" industrial region east of Holland.[3]

This was not a sensible plan. The Allies already anticipated that the

Germans would come through Belgium because a direct attack across the French frontier was impracticable. In the 1930s France had constructed the Maginot Line from Switzerland to Luxembourg, a barrier of interconnected reinforced concrete fortifications and casemated cannons that could be overcome only by direct attack, if at all, and with catastrophic troop losses.

Once the Germans moved into Belgium, the Allies intended to throw forward nearly all of their mobile formations to meet the Germans along the north-flowing Dyle River, a few miles east of Brussels. At best the Germans could expect to drive the Allies back to the westward-flowing Somme River in northern France, but not achieve a decision in the war.

When Manstein, chief of staff for Army Group A, saw the German plan in October 1939, he declared that it would be a crime to use the German army for a partial victory, leading to a long war of attrition. Since the Allies had command of the sea, they had access to resources from Asia, Africa, and America. Blockaded Germany did not and therefore would likely lose a long war of attrition.

Manstein proposed that a major attack be launched in northern Belgium and Holland to bait the Allied armies, but that the main effort be shifted to the Ardennes—and that the attack be conducted almost entirely by the new German panzer, or armored, divisions, supported by a new aerial weapon, the Stuka dive bomber. Neither the commander of the German army, Walther von Brauchitsch, nor the chief of staff, Franz Halder, recognized the revolutionary impact of these two weapons, however. They also did not believe that tanks could break through the Ardennes or cross the deep Meuse River at Sedan without massive infantry and artillery support.

Orthodox German thinking followed closely the Allied doctrine developed in World War I. It held that tanks should assist infantry in carrying out assaults *on foot* against enemy objectives. Accordingly, the British and French put their emphasis on short-range, heavily armored monsters—like the British Matilda and the French Char B—that could deflect most enemy fire but moved at about the pace of a walking infan- tryman. Allied commanders believed any enemy breakthrough would take place on a narrow front, and they could move up individual tanks, along with infantry and artillery, to seal it. They had many more tanks than the Germans, which they largely spread in "penny packets" among their infantry divisions. Thus the French and to a large degree the Brit- ish were aiming to fight the same sort of war they had fought in World War I.

French army doctrine required a continuous front, strongly manned by infantry and backed up by artillery. The French expected the enemy to attack this front fruitlessly and wear down his strength. Only when the enemy was stopped did doctrine permit the French to go over to the offensive.

When the infantry attack started, it had to come behind a mas- sive artillery barrage. The foot soldiers could advance only 1,600 yards before stopping to allow the artillery to shift its fires. After several such bounds, they had to stop until the guns could be moved forward. All this required a great deal of time.

Heinz Guderian, the German officer who founded the German armored force, thought this method of warfare was hopelessly out- moded. He had built the panzer arm on the teachings of two English experts, J. F. C. Fuller and Basil H. Liddell Hart. During the 1920s, they developed very advanced concepts of concentrating armor into large units. Their ideas made little impact on British military thinking, however, and Guderian's similar ideas did not much interest the Ger- man high command.

But Adolf Hitler expressed enthusiasm for tanks shortly after he came to power in 1933. This gave Guderian the opening to induce the army to put all armor into panzer divisions. He also convinced the German high command to adopt only long-range tanks that were "fast runners." These tanks had less armor than French and British tanks, but they could travel at twenty-five to thirty miles an hour. They could make quick penetrations into the enemy rear and keep on going.

Guderian added greatly to the power of the panzers by inducing the high command to include motorized infantry, artillery, and engineers in every panzer division. Thus all arms could work together in battle groups, and they could advance at the same speed as the tanks.

Guderian preached a new doctrine that panzer divisions alone, or with the help of dive bombers, could penetrate any enemy main line of resistance. Erwin Rommel, who was to become famous as a panzer leader, produced the best one-sentence description of the theory: "The art of concentrating strength at one point, forcing a breakthrough, rolling up and securing the flanks on either side, and then penetrating like lightning deep into the enemy's rear, before he has had time to react."[4]

The whole concept was a speeded-up version of the storm troops developed by lower-ranking German officers in World War I. They figured how to break through enemy trench lines by laying down heavy fire on a particular point, while one or more teams of *Stosstruppen*, or storm troopers, infiltrated the trench line and "rolled it up" with grenades and small-arms fire. The *Stosstruppen* had not won the war because they advanced on foot, and the Allies were always able to close the gaps with troops brought up by railways. Guderian saw that this fatal flaw could be overcome by using panzers. Unlike the storm troopers, they could keep on going, disrupting the enemy's entire main line of resistance.

The Junker Ju 87B Stuka dive bomber was a slow (240 mph) aircraft, but it could make pinpoint attacks on enemy battlefield positions and could serve the same purpose as artillery. The Allies had seen no need for a dive bomber. Their bombers were designed to drop bombs over a wide area, not strike individual targets.

⚞

Manstein and Guderian were certain that the Meuse River could be breached quickly at Sedan with only panzer divisions and Luftwaffe (German air force) bombers. They believed the French would not have time to bring up enough troops or guns to stop them. Speed would ensure that few enemy units would be in place to block the panzers as they drove right across France to the English Channel.

But the army high command, the *Oberkommando des Heeres*, or OKH, refused to accept Manstein's proposal. As Manstein continued to bombard OKH with his argument, Halder reassigned Manstein to command a new infantry corps that had only a minor role in the upcoming campaign. That would take care of Manstein and his ideas, Halder thought.

Back at Army Group A's headquarters in Koblenz, however, two of Manstein's assistants rose in revolt. When Hitler's chief military aide, Colonel Rudolf Schmundt, visited in late January 1940, Colonel Günther Blumentritt and Major Henning von Tresckow laid Manstein's whole idea out to him.

Schmundt explained the ideas to Hitler. He liked them, but to ensure their acceptance, Schmundt engineered a "working breakfast" with Hitler and five new corps commanders, including Manstein, along with Rommel, who had just been named commander of the 7th Panzer Division. After the breakfast, Manstein explained the whole idea to Hitler. The dictator accepted the concept and ordered its implementation.

In the OKH's final plan, Army Group B was to make an "uproar" north of the Liège-Charleroi line to draw as many Allied elements toward it as possible. Meanwhile, Army Group A was to make the real attack through eastern Belgium and Luxembourg south of this line.

Of Germany's ten panzer divisions, OKH allocated seven (with 1,800 of Germany's 2,400 tanks) to Army Group A. Lieutenant General Heinz Guderian's 19th Corps with three panzer divisions (1st, 2nd, and 10th) had the primary task of thrusting through the Ardennes to emerge at Sedan. Major General Hans Reinhardt's 41st Panzer Corps with two panzer divisions was to strike Monthermé on the Meuse a few miles north of Sedan. Lieutenant General Hermann Hoth's 15th Panzer Corps with two panzer divisions, one of them Erwin Rommel's 7th, was to cross the Meuse at Dinant about forty

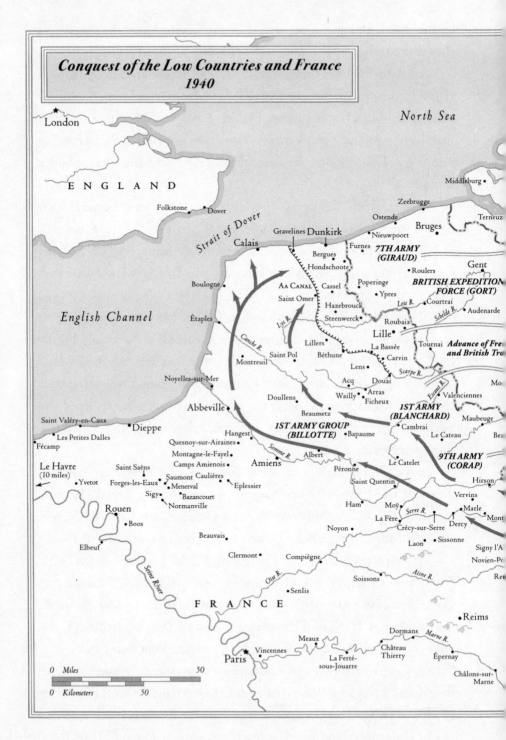

Conquest of the Low Countries and France
1940

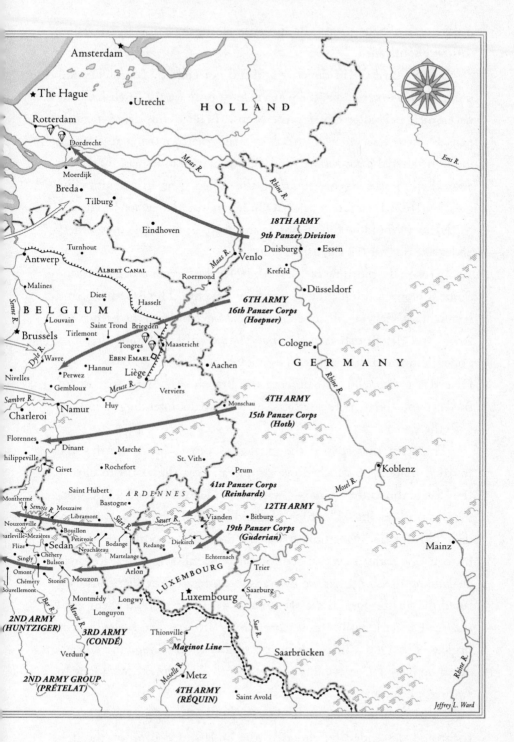

Jeffrey L. Ward

miles north of Sedan, with the aim of shielding any effort by the Allies to strike southward.

But the final OKH directive still did not embody Manstein's and Guderian's injunction that the panzers must push for the English Channel immediately after crossing the Meuse. Halder considered it indispensable first to secure bridgeheads over the river by moving up infantry divisions after the panzers crossed. But delaying ran the risk of giving away the opportunity of encircling the Allied wing in Belgium. The great question, therefore, was what Guderian would do when he crossed the Meuse. Would he follow orders and stop, or would he defy orders and strike out for the English Channel?

Early on the morning of May 10, 1940, the Germans delivered sensational blows in Holland and northern Belgium. The Allied supreme commander, General Maurice Gamelin, at once ordered the French 1st Army and the British Expeditionary Force (BEF) of nine divisions under John Standish Verecker, Viscount Gort (Lord Gort), to rush to the Dyle River. Gamelin also ordered the French 7th Army to rush to Breda, about thirty miles southeast of Rotterdam, intending to link up with the Dutch.

The event that created the greatest "uproar" in the north—the frenzied reports of which drove people all over the world to cluster transfixed around their radios—was the sudden descent of 4,000 German paratroops into "Fortress Holland" around The Hague, Rotterdam, Utrecht, and Moerdijk. It was the first great airborne invasion in history. The paratroops grabbed four airports, allowing a 12,000-man air-landing division to arrive by transport aircraft. The Germans captured the key bridges in the region and were able to hold them until the 9th Panzer Division broke through the frontier and rushed to the bridges. The Dutch now had no possibility of resisting, and surrendered on May 15, 1940, forcing the French 7th Army to withdraw to Antwerp, Belgium.

Other paratroops seized bridges over the Albert Canal near Maastricht and descended by glider on the undefended roof of the Belgian fortress Eben Emael, five miles south of Maastricht. The troopers sealed the gun ports and imprisoned the garrison, which surrendered the next day.

Led by Erich Hoepner's 16th Panzer Corps of two divisions (the 3rd and 4th), the German 6th Army encircled the Belgian fortress of Liège and pressed the Allies to Antwerp and to their defensive line along the Dyle River. The German 18th Army, which had moved into Holland, turned on Antwerp as soon as the Dutch surrendered, and evicted the 7th Army. The French cavalry that had advanced east of the Meuse to slow the Germans made little impression and withdrew behind the main Allied positions.

Thirteen French infantry divisions, with 800 tanks scattered in small groups among the units, moved up to hold the "Gembloux gap," the twenty-mile space between Wavre on the Dyle and Namur on the Meuse. A two-division French "Cavalry Corps" with 400 tanks lined up to challenge Hoepner's panzers around the village of Hannut, a few miles northeast of Gembloux.[5] Although the French commander had spread out his tanks in a long line, which made it impossible for them to work in concert, they nevertheless stopped the first German panzers. When more German tanks came up, however, the commanders saw the weakness of the French dispositions, concentrated their tanks at one point, broke through, and shattered the entire line along the Gembloux gap.

The Belgians and the Allies fell back to the Schelde River, forty to fifty miles west. The German high command didn't want to hurry the Allies into too rapid a retreat before the net had been stretched across their rear. Accordingly, it took Hoepner's panzer corps away to back up the drive through the Ardennes, and also withdrew Luftwaffe support.

While the world's attention was riveted on the breathtaking battles in Belgium and Holland, the actual *Schwerpunkt*, or center of gravity of the German offensive, plunged almost unnoticed through the Ardennes toward Sedan and the weakest point of the French line, sixty miles

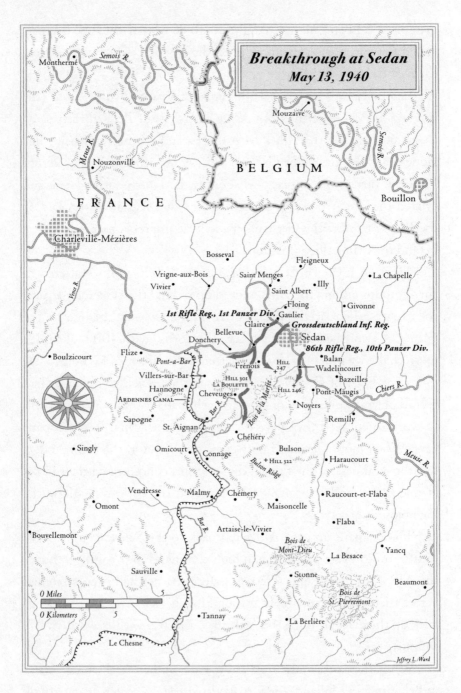

Breakthrough at Sedan
May 13, 1940

away. The leading element was the 1st Panzer Division of Guderian's corps. Allied air power ignored the movement.

The 1st Panzer Division encountered only sporadic resistance and seized the north bank of the Meuse at Sedan on the evening of May 12. The French defenders were stunned and were unprepared the next day when Guderian's infantry crossed the river in rubber boats, helped by a massive bombardment by Luftwaffe bombers. The infantry penetrated more than five miles south by the end of the day. But it took until the morning of May 14 before the Germans finished a pontoon bridge and got the first tanks across.

Reinhardt's 41st Panzer Corps gained a narrow foothold across the Meuse at Monthermé. But the terrain was extremely steep there, and Reinhardt had a hard time holding on under strong French pressure. Rommel's 7th Panzer Division, on the other hand, forced a large breach farther north at Dinant.

Guderian pressed to get as many tanks and guns as possible across his one pontoon bridge. He assumed the French were rushing reinforcements forward for a powerful counterattack. But the French command had been so distracted by the unexpected appearance of a major force at Sedan that its response was extremely slow. Only forty French tanks and a single infantry regiment moved forward at 7:00 A.M. on May 14 to attack the 1st Panzer's infantry around Bulson, about five miles south of Sedan. The Germans slowed the French long enough for the first German tanks and guns to come up. By 10:45 A.M., few of the French tanks remained, and the surviving tanks and infantry retreated rapidly south.

Meanwhile British and French aircraft tried bravely to destroy the pontoon bridge at Sedan, but lacking dive bombers, they were unable to hit that pinpoint target and lost many aircraft to German antiaircraft fire.

German infantry were approaching high ground at Stonne, about ten miles south of Sedan. This ridge dominated the country to the south and guarded the Meuse crossings. Guderian turned over capture of Stonne to Gustav von Wietersheim, whose two motorized divisions of his 14th Corps were still caught in traffic in the Ardennes. Guderian left the 10th Panzer Division and the attached Grossdeutschland Infantry Regiment to secure Stonne.

Guderian met with the commanders of the 1st and 2nd Panzer Divisions. With their eager concurrence, he ignored Halder's orders to halt and wait for the infantry divisions to catch up, and ordered the panzers to turn west, break through the French defenses, and drive full out for the coast. Guderian saw that the French were paralyzed by the speed of the German advance. He resolved to follow the idea of Manstein, to strike without pause for the English Channel and total victory.

The same evening, General André Corap, commanding the French 9th Army, the only force now blocking the panzers, made a fatal mistake and ordered the entire army to abandon the Meuse and withdraw to a new line some fifteen to twenty miles to the west. He made this decision not only because of the breakthrough at Sedan, but also in response to reports that "thousands" of tanks were pouring through Rommel's breach at Dinant, although Hoth's entire corps counted only 542 tanks.

When the French arrived on the new line, Rommel's and Guderian's panzers were already in some of the positions the 9th Army was supposed to occupy, while the withdrawal opened the way for Reinhardt, whose tanks drove westward along an unobstructed path, shattering the 9th Army's dispositions and throwing the army into chaos.

On May 16, the new British prime minister, Winston Churchill, arrived in Paris to find panic setting in. Staff in government offices were burning their papers, expecting the capital to fall at any moment. The turmoil slowly abated as word spread that the panzers were heading west, not toward Paris. In a meeting with the French premier, Paul Reynaud, and Churchill, General Gamelin reported that he had no more reserves, and no ideas on how to stop the Germans.

Reynaud took over the defense establishment, relieved Gamelin, and appointed General Maxime Weygand, who had just arrived from Syria, to command the armies. He also named the ambassador to Spain, Marshal Henri Philippe Pétain, as vice premier. Weygand went to the front on May 21, but he was unable to conceive any plan to reverse the disaster unfolding. The fundamental reason was that the French command structure was too rigid and too slow to respond to the rapidly moving panzers. The plans it developed were out of date well before they could be transmitted to the troops and carried out in the field.

Guderian's and Reinhardt's panzers were rolling toward the English Channel against virtually no opposition. On the roads, panicked civilians and fleeing soldiers were all mixed together, creating chaos. Infantry divisions had relieved the mobile forces fighting for the Stonne heights, but Wietersheim was having a difficult time getting his motorized divisions forward to seal the flanks. Rundstedt was doing everything possible to bring forward the infantry divisions, but they were marching on foot and the pace was slow. To the orthodox soldiers who made up the German high command, dangers threatened the flanks with every mile that the panzers pressed westward.

The German generals were as bewildered by the pace of the advance as the Allies. They were unable to comprehend what was actually happening. No one had ever seen anything like this. They could not understand that an unprecedented victory was unfolding, and that the speed of the panzer advance alone made it impossible for the French to respond.

Rather, they feared that a disaster was about to descend on the German army in the form of some tremendous counteroffensive launched from somewhere on the flanks. Hitler, above all, was on the verge of

distraction. Despite the fact that he had approved the strategy, Manstein's (and Sun Tzu's) concepts of uproar east and attack west and of
striking into weakness were entirely alien to him. Now that they were
succeeding beyond his wildest imagination, he became terrified and
uncertain.

Hitler hurried to see Rundstedt at Charleroi, Belgium, and urged
him to be cautious. Rundstedt, a very conventional soldier, was also
worried. He ordered Ewald von Kleist to stop the panzers in order for
the infantry to catch up. Kleist commanded the panzer group made up
of the corps of Guderian, Reinhardt, and Wietersheim.

Kleist did not convey the anxieties in the high command to his
corps commanders. He simply told them to halt. But Guderian and
Reinhardt saw that victory could be ensured only if they continued to
drive west at full throttle and not give the confused French a chance
to draw a breath, assemble their scattered forces, and actually launch a
strike on the flank.

After a heated argument with Kleist, Guderian was able to get him
to allow the advance to continue for another twenty-four hours. Guderian then ordered his troops to spring forward without hesitation and
without stopping. By nightfall on May 16, Guderian's spearheads were
at Marle and Dercy, on the Serre River fifty-five miles west of Sedan,
while his and Reinhardt's reconnaissance elements were all the way to
the Oise River, another fifteen miles west.

Guderian assumed that this spectacular success had quieted the
fears back at headquarters, and he sent a message that he intended
to continue the pursuit the next day, May 17. Early in the morning,
Guderian received a radio flash that Kleist would be flying into Guderian's airstrip at Montcornet, a few miles east of Marle, at 7:00 A.M.
Kleist arrived promptly, didn't even bid Guderian good morning, and
launched into a tirade for his disobeying orders. Guderian at once asked
to be relieved of his command. Kleist, taken aback, agreed and told him
to turn over his command to the next-senior officer.

Guderian radioed Rundstedt's army group to relay what had happened, and said he was flying back to report. Within minutes, a message came back telling him to stay where he was. General Wilhelm List, 12th Army commander, was coming to clear up the matter. List reinstated Guderian with Rundstedt's approval and told Guderian that the halt order had come from Rundstedt. List was in agreement with Guderian's desire to keep going and authorized him to make "reconnaissance in force,"[6] a subterfuge that did not defy Rundstedt's order but slipped around it.

Deeply appreciative, Guderian unleashed his panzers, and they surged forward. Rundstedt finally called off his stop order, and the 1st Panzer Division forced a bridgehead over the Somme River near Péronne, forty miles west of Marle, on May 19.

Although the speed of the panzer drive had utterly confused the French high command, the newly formed French 4th Armored Division under Charles de Gaulle came forward on May 17 with a few tanks and attacked Montcornet. But his was only a glancing blow, and the division was severely repulsed. Throughout the campaign, neither the French nor the British were able to get organized enough to mass any substantial armored force. The unbelievable speed of the panzers so destabilized Allied decision-making that all the commanders could think to do was to hold stolidly in place, or retreat when German tanks rushed toward them. Yet, the Allies still had formidable armored strength. If they had concentrated it at a single place, they might have plunged it into the side of the German advance and brought it to a halt.

The Allies never pulled their armor together, however. The French had formed four armored divisions but wasted them in isolated engagements like de Gaulle's attempt at Montcornet. Most of the 3rd Armored Division had been dispersed among the infantry south of the Meuse at Sedan, where it never was able to play a decisive role. The 1st had run out of fuel and had been shattered by the 5th Panzer Division just west of Dinant. Noncombatant parts of the 2nd had fled south of the Aisne River to Rethel, while the remainder was delivered by rail to various stations in the vicinity of Hirson, and these isolated fragments were bypassed or overrun by Guderian's and Reinhardt's corps.

In Belgium, the British had ten battalions of tanks that were parceled out to the infantry divisions, as were those of the three French mechanized divisions and a number of independent French tank battalions. The French tanks assembled at Gembloux had been strung out in a long, unsupported line. Each tank, in effect, had to fight alone, or with the help of tanks nearby. Despite this atrocious tactical formation, they had performed excellently, showing what might have been achieved if they had been massed and used in a concerted attack.

Once German headquarters had released him, Guderian stopped for nothing. On May 20, the 1st Panzer seized Amiens and pressed southward to form a bridgehead four miles deep across the Somme. During the afternoon, the 2nd Panzer reached Abbeville, and that evening a battalion of the division passed through Noyelles-sur-Mer and became the first German unit to reach the Atlantic coast. Only ten days after the start of the offensive, the Allied armies had been cut in two.

After the Allies had retreated in haste from the Dyle River line, they had formed a line along the north-flowing Schelde River. Their southern flank rested at Arras, on the Scarpe River, a tributary to the Schelde. Arras was only twenty-five miles north of Péronne on the Somme. Thus the Germans had only this narrow corridor through which to feed their panzers and their offensive.

The Allies still had a chance. If they could close the gap, they could isolate the panzers, reunite the armies in Belgium with forces to the south, and bring the German offensive to a halt.

Meantime, Lord Gort, commander of the BEF, was getting worried about the safety of British forces holding Arras. He instructed Major General Harold E. Franklyn to form the 5th and 50th Infantry Divisions and the 1st Army Tank Battalion and to cut off German access to the city on May 21.

Lord Gort was losing confidence that his French allies were capable of organizing any response to the German offensive. He had already alerted the War Office in London that he was thinking of retreating to the coast and evacuating the army back to England. This dire prospect caused the British cabinet to send General Sir Edmund Ironside, chief of the Imperial General Staff, to Belgium on May 20 to order the BEF to move south on Amiens, on the other side of the gap, and to attack all enemy forces it encountered. Given the circumstances, this was a most ridiculous order.

Lord Gort told Ironside that most British forces were trying to hold off the German 6th Army on the east, and any attack southward would have to be done in conjunction with the French. Ironside and Gort's chief of staff, Lieutenant General Sir Henry Pownall, went to see General Gaston Billotte, commander of the French 1st Army Group. Billotte ordered two French divisions to attack the next day, May 21. But the French were slow and said they couldn't mount the attack until May 22.

Since the French were not ready, General Franklyn's operation to protect Arras went on as planned on May 21. Franklyn sent most of his forces to the Scarpe River east of Arras. He thought only minor German forces were south of Arras, so he ordered just two infantry battalions and fifty-eight Mark I Matilda tanks armed with only a single machine gun and sixteen Mark II Matildas armed with a high-velocity two-pounder (40-millimeter) gun to clear them out. Matildas were slow infantry tanks, but with 75 millimeters of armor they were much more resistant to enemy fire than the lighter-skinned panzers.

In fact, Rommel's 7th Panzer Division had arrived south of Arras, and he swung his tanks around northwest of Arras on the morning of May 21, with the intention of then striking for Lille, some twenty miles north. Since the division's artillery and infantry were lagging behind, Rommel rode back to urge them forward.

The British formed up west of Arras in the afternoon and attacked southeast. They ran into Rommel's isolated artillery and infantry and began to inflict heavy casualties. The Germans found their 37-millimeter antitank guns to be useless against the Matildas. The British tanks overran the antitank guns but were stopped by Rommel's frantic effort to form a "gun line" of field artillery and especially high-velocity 88-millimeter antiaircraft guns, which materialized as a devastating new weapon against Allied tanks. The artillery and the "88s" destroyed thirty-six tanks and broke the back of the British attack. The British fell back into Arras and attempted no further attack.

The British effort had been too weak, but it showed what could have been done if commanders had mobilized a major counterattack. Nevertheless, the attack at Arras deeply alarmed the German high command, especially Adolf Hitler. Rommel's division lost 387 men, four times the number of casualties suffered until that point. The attack stunned Rundstedt. His anxiety fed Hitler's similar fears and led to momentous consequences in a few days.

On May 22, Guderian struck north from Abbeville, aiming at the English Channel ports and the rear of the British, French, and Belgian armies, which were still facing eastward against Fedor von Bock's Army Group B. Reinhardt's panzers kept pace on the east. Guderian's tanks isolated Boulogne and Calais, both of which surrendered after German attacks. This brought Guderian to Gravelines, barely ten miles from Dunkirk, the last port from which the Allies in Belgium could evacuate.

Reinhardt also arrived twenty miles from Dunkirk on the Aa (or Bassée) Canal, which ran from Douai on the Scarpe River past La Bassée and Saint-Omer to Gravelines. The panzers were now closer to Dunkirk than most of the Allies.

Meanwhile, the right flank of the BEF withdrew from Arras to La Bassée on May 23 under pressure of a thrust northward by Rommel toward Lille. On May 24, Army Group B broke the Belgian army's line at Courtrai (Kortrijk), only thirty miles from Ostend and Dunkirk, leaving a gaping hole in the Allied front. King Leopold of Belgium surrendered four days later. Despite the Belgian defection, the BEF withdrew by stages to Dunkirk.

The news of German advances had been good, but Rundstedt gave Hitler a gloomy report on the morning of May 24, laying emphasis on the tanks the Germans had lost and on the possibility that the Allies might attempt an attack bigger than the one at Arras. These fears reinforced Hitler's anxieties. Yet Guderian's, Reinhardt's, and Rommel's fast exploitations were preventing both resistance and a flank attack. The Germans had been out of danger from the first day, but to Hitler (and to most of the senior German generals) it seemed too good to be true.

There were few Allied forces in front of Guderian and Reinhardt. They had an easy task to seize Dunkirk and close off the last possible port from which the Allies could evacuate. This would force the capitulation of the entire BEF and the French 1st Group of Armies, more than 400,000 men.

On this day, May 24, the war took a bizarre and utterly bewildering turn. Rundstedt, fearful that the Allies would launch an attack on his flanks, wanted the infantry divisions to catch up with the panzers for protection. Hitler, sharing Rundstedt's paranoia, agreed and ordered the panzers to halt along the Aa Canal. Guderian and Reinhardt protested vehemently, but they received curt messages to remain where they were. While the BEF and many parts of the French armies rushed to Dunkirk, forming a solid defensive shield, and while the Royal Navy organized frantic and highly successful efforts to carry the soldiers back to England, the German panzers sat idle. It was unbelievable.

The British used every vessel they could find, 861 in all, many manned by civilian volunteers, to carry the troops away. The soldiers had to leave all of their weapons and vehicles on shore, but between May 26 and June 4 the vessels evacuated 338,000 troops, including 120,000 French (who were promptly shipped back to unoccupied

France). Only a few thousand members of the French rear guard were captured.

To this day, no one has been able to fathom Hitler's decision. With victory already within his grasp, he threw it away. The BEF was the *only* army that Britain possessed. Virtually all the British army leaders were in Belgium. If the BEF had been lost, Britain would have found it virtually impossible to create another army for a very long time. At least as important, passage of this army into captivity would most probably have induced the British leadership to conclude a peace with Hitler in order to free its soldiers. Churchill was defiant, but other leaders would have been willing to make peace in order to get the men home—especially since Hitler had already signaled that he would permit Britain to retain its navy and its empire, demanding solely that Britain grant Germany a free hand on the Continent.

Brauchitsch and Halder tried without success to get the halt order lifted. But Hitler voiced a very offhand view of the situation to Brauchitsch, saying that the Luftwaffe would foil any attempt to embark troops from Dunkirk and would sink any boat that reached the open sea. This was manifestly not possible. The Luftwaffe had suffered heavy losses during the campaign, a fact known to all the senior chiefs. The Luftwaffe caused much damage, but it could not stop the evacuation.

The most credible explanation of Hitler's decision is that he thought the British would view evacuation as a decisive defeat that would bring them to terms. He did not see it the way the British saw it, as deliverance from certain disaster. The "miracle of Dunkirk" revived British morale and hopes for victory. But Hitler was totally self-absorbed. He stated his belief immediately after the evacuation that the British had been defeated, and that they would "come to their senses" and conclude a peace with him. Hitler could see no other point of view but his own.

Indirection and subtlety were alien to Hitler's thinking. His practice was to attack the enemy head-on. Only once did he choose an indirect method—his approval of Manstein's advance through the Ardennes. He did not see that the Germans were successful because they were *avoiding* enemy strength. He was incapable of understanding a doctrine like Sun Tzu's combining *zheng* direct forces with *qi* indirect forces. He followed the same headlong path for the remainder of the war, making one disastrous decision after another.

Hitler was a polar opposite of Sun Tzu. His inability to envision alternative ways of achieving his goals was the cardinal reason for his destruction.

The end in France came swiftly. In three weeks, the Germans had captured a million prisoners, while suffering 60,000 casualties. The Belgian and Dutch armies had been eliminated, and the French had lost thirty divisions, nearly a third of their total strength and the best and most mobile part. They had also lost the assistance of nine British divisions, now back in Britain, with all of their equipment gone. Only one British division and part of another remained in France south of the Somme.

General Weygand was left with sixty-six divisions, most of them understrength, to hold a front along the Somme and Aisne rivers and the Maginot Line, which was longer than the original. Most of the mechanized divisions had been lost or badly shattered. On the other hand, the Germans quickly brought their ten panzer divisions back to strength and deployed 130 infantry divisions, only a few of which had been engaged.

OKH promoted Guderian to command a new group of two panzer corps, and ordered him to drive from Rethel on the Aisne to the Swiss frontier. Kleist kept two panzer corps to strike south from bridgeheads over the Somme at Amiens and Péronne, but these later shifted eastward to reinforce Guderian's drive. The remaining armored corps, under Hermann Hoth, was to advance between Amiens and the sea.

The offensive opened on June 5, and France collapsed quickly. Not all the breakthroughs were easy, but the panzers soon ranged across the countryside, generally avoiding or bypassing villages, towns, and forests where Weygand had set up all-around hedgehog defenses. The almost unobstructed advances created chaos and caused French soldiers to surrender by the hundreds of thousands.

One advance involved the movement of Erwin Rommel's 7th Panzer Division. On June 5 it crossed the Somme near Hangest between Abbeville and Amiens. The division already had moved so fast and materialized at points so unexpectedly that the French had named it the "ghost division." On June 6, at Quesnoy-sur-Airaines, a few miles southwest of Hangest, the entire division lined up on a 2,000-yard front, with the panzer regiment in the lead, and advanced across the country. Two days later it reached the Seine River near Rouen, a drive of seventy miles. Then Rommel turned northwest and raced to the sea at Saint-Valéry-en-Caux, where he captured most of the British 51st Highland Division, and three French divisions. Later the division raced from near Rouen to Cherbourg in the longest one-day advance in history, seizing the port shortly after the last British troops had departed.

Guderian's panzers cut off northeastern France with a rapid drive on the Swiss frontier. The troops defending the Maginot Line retreated and surrendered almost without firing a shot.

The Germans entered Paris on June 14 and reached the Rhône River valley on June 16. That same night, the French asked for an armistice. Reynaud resigned as premier and was replaced by Marshal Pétain.

Meanwhile General Alan Brooke, who had taken command of all British forces in France after Dunkirk, hurriedly evacuated 150,000 British troops, along with 18,000 French, 24,000 Poles, and 5,000 Czechs, from numerous ports along the Atlantic coast. Many of the French joined the Free French movement under Charles de Gaulle, who had arrived in Britain, vowing to fight on against the Germans.

On June 22, the French accepted the German terms at Compiègne, a few miles north of Paris, in the same railway car where the defeated Germans had signed the armistice ending World War I in 1918. On June 25, both sides ceased fire. The greatest military victory in modern times had been achieved in six weeks.

Germany occupied northern France. In unoccupied southern France, centered around the watering spot of Vichy, a government under Marshal Pétain was set up. "Vichy France" became a collaborator with Nazi Germany.

Hitler had been unable to see how capture of the BEF could have ended the war with a spectacular victory for Germany. He was also unable to understand that he still could have parlayed his partial victory into a complete triumph. The way was plain to see—through North Africa and the Middle East. Britain was largely without weapons. It was defending the Suez Canal with only a single understrength armored division.

If Hitler had sent just four panzer divisions to Libya, a colony of his "Axis" partner, Italy, he could have occupied French North Africa (Morocco, Algeria, Tunisia) and seized the Suez. This would have forced the Royal Navy out of the Mediterranean, turning it into an Axis lake.

Panzers could have swept across the entire Middle East from Palestine to Iran, gaining an unlimited supply of oil, Germany's single most-needed commodity. Turkey would have been forced to come to terms.

Occupation of Iran would have closed off Britain's and America's only feasible supply route to the Soviet Union. German forces in northern Iran would have been within easy striking distance of the Soviet oil fields in the Caucasus and along the shores of the Caspian Sea. Oil was mandatory to conduct modern war, and Joseph Stalin would have gone to any length to prevent a German attack on his oil.

He would have supplied Germany with grain and delivered rubber, nickel, and other needed commodities from southeast Asia by means of the Trans-Siberian Railway.

In other words, Germany—by merely sending four panzer divisions into North Africa—could have neutralized the threat of the Soviet Union and created a virtually unassailable empire encompassing all of Europe west of Russia, North Africa down to Dakar in Senegal, and the Middle East.

Although a number of Hitler's advisers saw this opportunity and tried to convince him to seize it—especially his navy chief, Erich Raeder—Hitler refused. Instead he launched a headlong assault against the Soviet Union in June 1941. This was his fatal error. From that point on, Germany was on the road to disaster. Adolf Hitler understood none of the indirection reflected in Sun Tzu's *Art of War*. This blindness saved the world from being dominated by one of the most malignant monsters ever to appear on earth.

E I G H T

Stalingrad,
1942

The primary reason why the Allies won World War II is that Adolf Hitler was incapable of seeing paths to victory pointed out to him by his senior commanders. These paths were consistent with the fundamental axioms laid out long ago by Sun Tzu. But in a dictatorship, the only vision that counts is that of the dictator. If he cannot see and follow the most intelligent strategies, then he will fail. Therefore, as night follows day, Germany was doomed to be torn to pieces for its crime of obeying such a mad and irresponsible leader.

The battle of Stalingrad in 1942 is one of the supreme examples in world history where a leader defiantly ignores wiser counsel and engineers his own destruction. At the end of this disastrous battle—which cost Germany 250,000 men—Allied leaders knew Hitler was incapable of making correct military judgments. They then knew they would prevail.

Hitler's military education consisted entirely of service as a private soldier, finally a corporal, in the trenches of World War I. From his point of view, war was a headlong collision of giant forces. The stronger force finally pushed back the weaker force and gained a devastated battlefield. Field Marshal Erich von Manstein perceived this defect of Hitler very clearly. "He was a man who saw fighting only in the terms of utmost brutality," Manstein wrote. "For the *art* of war he substituted brute force."[1] Hitler never rose above this elementary and quite incomplete concept of war. For him the greatest of campaigns was nothing more than a vastly larger version of the continuous, lethal frontal attacks on the Western front.

The admonition to approach one's objective indirectly was entirely foreign to Hitler. His method was a straight test of strength. His frontal assault on Stalingrad was an absolute example of this thinking. Sun Tzu, on the other hand, abhors frontal attacks and he most especially abhors attacking "fortified cities."[2]

Hitler regarded Germany's military achievements early in the war as his own. He never gave Manstein any credit for his plan to defeat France in 1940. In Manstein's judgment, Hitler's misplaced self-congratulation caused him to lose all sense of proportion in assessing his own capabilities. "Thus he was not prepared to see a really responsible military adviser alongside himself," Manstein wrote. "He wanted to be another Napoléon, who had only tolerated men under him who would obediently carry out his will. Unfortunately he had neither Napoléon's military training nor his military genius."[3]

In addition to strategic blindness, Hitler was possessed, at least from the early 1920s, by two consuming demons. They wiped out what little logical, rational thinking he retained. One demon was his insane, relentless hatred of Jews. The other was an equally insane, relentless desire to destroy the Soviet Union. These paranoias led Hitler to attack the Soviet Union head-on in June 1941 and then to kill or starve millions of Slavs to provide *Lebensraum*, or space for German settlers. They also led to the *Einsatzgruppen* he sent in the wake of his armies to murder all the Jews they could find, and to the gas chambers at Auschwitz and other death camps where he killed millions more.

We can draw from these facts an inescapable truth: a successful commander must be able to take into consideration all the factors in a given situation, and then act on them.

Hitler's intellectual incapacities negated all the ideas of his senior commanders; he simply could not fathom what they were trying to achieve. Hitler was thus the exact opposite of the intelligent commander espoused by Sun Tzu who makes reasoned judgments based on all contingencies, dangers, and opportunities. Instead, for Hitler the war came down to the very sort of contest he had experienced in the trenches.[4]

Hitler's crippling incompetence can be seen in the requirements he set for the attack on the Soviet Union in June 1941. Although Germany's forces were less than half the size of the Soviet forces, Hitler expected not only to destroy the Soviet army but also to seize a million square miles of western Russia in the summer and fall of 1941. This was an area as large as the United States east of the Mississippi River.

Hitler demanded that the German army undertake three simultaneous offensives in three totally different directions: one to Leningrad (St. Petersburg) in the north, one to Moscow in the center, and one to the Ukraine in the south. Achieving just one of these targets would have been an extremely demanding accomplishment. Achieving all three at once was impossible.

The offensives petered out in the snows of the Russian winter in front of Moscow in December 1941. Seven months of war left more than one million men killed, wounded, or captured, accounting for one-third of the entire German army in the Soviet Union.

The gains the Germans did achieve were due as much to the disastrous placement of the Red Army by Joseph Stalin as to the success of German arms. Stalin lined up his army along the frontier, with few reserves behind. When the German panzers punched holes in this front, they were able to swing around the largely immobile Russian infantry and create caldrons, trapping hundreds of thousands of Russian soldiers, who were forced to surrender.

With the entry of the United States into the war after the Japanese attacked Pearl Harbor on December 7, 1941, a new strategic challenge faced Germany. Should Hitler continue to attack the Soviet Union, or should he switch to the defensive there and focus on preventing American and British forces from reaching the continent of Europe?[5]

The German navy chief, Erich Raeder, presented a strategy that answered both questions. He proposed two primary goals for 1942: Erwin Rommel, commander of the Africa Corps in Libya, should be given enough forces to capture Egypt, the Suez Canal, and the Middle East, and the German army in the east (*Ostheer*) should seize the Soviet oil fields in the Caucasus and along the western shore of the Caspian Sea centering on the city of Baku. Germany had the power to achieve both of these goals, Raeder said. It did not have the power to do much more.

If Germany gained the oil fields, the Soviet Union's capacity to carry on modern warfare would be drastically reduced.[6] It had few other sources of oil. With limited fuel, Soviet tanks and trucks would be unable to sustain long offensives. If Germany controlled the Suez Canal, the Royal Navy would be forced to vacate the Mediterranean, and Germany could occupy all of North Africa. Germany could then turn its strength to building submarines and aircraft to interdict the flow of supplies and troops from America. Any effort by the Western Allies thereafter would be extremely difficult and highly problematical. Winston Churchill understood this quite well. In a message to President Franklin D. Roosevelt, Churchill said that if Egypt and the Middle East were lost, continuation of the war "would be a hard, long, and bleak proposition."[7]

Rommel strongly endorsed Raeder's plan and told Hitler he could seize Egypt and the Middle East with just three more divisions—or about 45,000 men and 360 tanks. After receiving reinforcements early in 1942, the *Ostheer* numbered 2.4 million troops and thousands of tanks and new self-propelled guns.

Raeder's proposals were by far the best option Germany possessed. But Hitler rejected sending more forces to Rommel. He accepted Raeder's proposal to seize the oil fields, but made it clear that he was not content merely to neutralize the Soviet Union, which capture of the oil fields would largely do. He wanted to *destroy* the Red Army. This was his primary goal. Capturing the oil fields was by comparison a low priority. He was unable to see how an indirect strike into the Caucasus with overwhelming forces would gain him nearly everything he truly needed in the east, preserving most of his remaining strength to counter the rising power of the United States.

Hitler could have achieved his purpose by an offensive with only a few mobile forces from Kursk eastward to Voronezh on the upper Don River. This would have drawn off most Soviet troops. Major German formations then could have moved southward and swept over the Caucasus. The Germans would have been moving on shorter interior lines. The Soviets, moving on much longer exterior lines, would have found it extremely difficult to reinforce the south before German forces could seize it. A strike at Voronezh would have been a Sun Tzu *zheng*, a direct holding move. A strike at the Caucasus would have been a Sun Tzu *qi*, an indirect move that brings victory. But Hitler never considered this or any similar deceptive strategy.

Manstein, who dealt intensely with Hitler during this period, wrote that Hitler never grasped an essential element about warfare: that one can never be too strong at the crucial spot and that one may have to dispense with less vital fronts to achieve a decisive aim. Instead, Manstein wrote, Hitler "seized on almost any aim that caught his fancy, causing him to fritter away Germany's strength by taking on several objectives simultaneously."[8]

Instead of sending every possible soldier and tank against the oil fields, he sent most of his forces against the city of Stalingrad (now Volgograd) on the Volga River. This place had virtually no strategic importance, but Hitler insisted on seizing it. Stalingrad was irrelevant to gaining the oil fields. It faced the vast open steppes of Eurasia. Even if captured, it would gain him nothing but empty space.

The only reason Hitler gave for demanding its capture was to interdict oil tanker traffic up the Volga. But if the oil fields were captured,

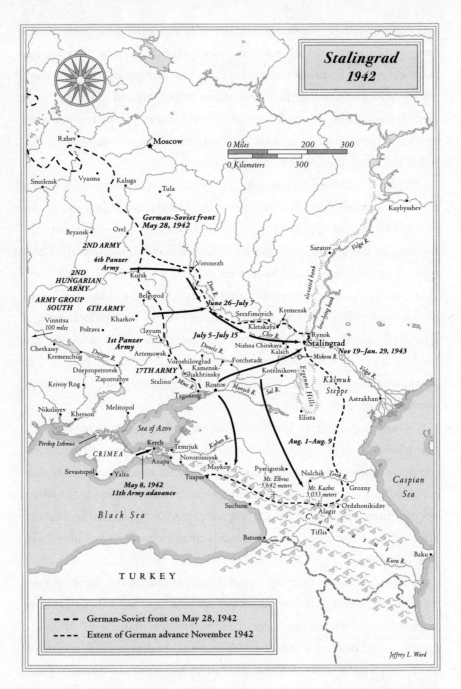

Stalingrad
1942

German-Soviet front
May 28, 1942

- - - German-Soviet front on May 28, 1942
- - - - Extent of German advance November 1942

Jeffrey L. Ward

the traffic would cease in any case. Most observers believe that Hitler's primary motivation was that Stalin had renamed the old city of Tsaritsyn in honor of himself in 1925. Attacking a city because of its name sounds like the reasoning of a lunatic. But Hitler insisted on capturing Leningrad in 1941—it too was not strategically important—because the Communist revolution started there in 1917 and it was named after Vladimir (Nikolai) Lenin, leader of the revolution.

Hitler's original dispositions called for four armies to seize the Caucasus and for just one army to capture Stalingrad. But he quickly changed focus and turned three armies (the 2nd, 6th, and 4th Panzer) against Stalingrad and sent only two armies into the Caucasus. These armies (the 17th and the 1st Panzer) were too weak to overcome the frantic resistance of the Soviet armies, and they quickly stalled in the high passes of the Caucasus Mountains.[9]

All the seasoned commanders in the German army saw that this was madness. Franz Halder, the chief of staff, protested vehemently, but Hitler paid him no attention. Hitler insisted on believing that the Red Army was on the verge of collapse, and he ignored evidence of powerful Soviet formations to the east of the Volga and in the Caucasus. He screamed at Halder when the chief of staff informed him that the level of Soviet tank production was three times that of German production. "He would not believe what he did not want to believe,"[10] Halder wrote in his diary. Hitler transferred his headquarters to Vinnitsa in Ukraine and took over direct command of the southern part of the front.

Hitler's 1942 campaigns violated virtually all of Sun Tzu's rules of war. Instead of one objective, Hitler designated two. Instead of concentrating his forces, he fatally divided them. Instead of deception, he revealed his plans quite openly to the Soviets. Sun Tzu says that a skilled general must confuse the enemy while concealing his own dispositions and intent. But Hitler was plainly aiming at two completely different targets hundreds of miles apart.

Accordingly, the Soviets could ignore German formations elsewhere and mass all their reserves to contest these two offensives. This was clearly inconsistent with a Sun Tzu maxim. "Before he gives battle," Sun Tzu writes, "the superior general causes the enemy to disperse. When the enemy disperses and attempts to defend everywhere he is weak everywhere, and at the selected points many will be able to strike his few."[11] Hitler made no deceptive move to force the enemy to disperse. Likewise, he presented no *zheng* direct force to hold the Russians in place and no *qi* indirect force to descend on the Russian flank or rear and to win by surprise. Everything was frontal, head-on, and obvious.

On June 28, 1942, Hermann Hoth's 4th Panzer Army broke through Soviet defenses east of Kursk and captured Voronezh in a few days. While the 2nd Army moved into Voronezh, the 4th Panzer Army rolled down the dry steppe west of the Don River toward Kalach at the great bend of the Don, forty-five miles west of Stalingrad. It was followed by the huge 6th Army with twenty divisions under Friedrich Paulus. As the 4th Panzer turned south briefly, the 6th Army pressed toward Stalingrad. Paulus's mobile spearheads reached Kalach on July 28, 1942, but could not break through fierce Soviet resistance and cross the Don until August 23.

Meanwhile, Hoth's 4th Panzer Army had turned back north and was pressing through Elista in the Kalmuk Steppe toward Stalingrad. About fifty miles south of the city, Hoth's attack broke down against fierce resistance by two Soviet armies.

On July 28, Stalin issued a *"Ni shagu nazad!"* ("Not a step back!") order and sent the Stalingrad commander, Andrei I. Eremenko, eleven infantry divisions and nine Guards brigades of elite troops to reinforce his five depleted armies. Stalin set up supply bases in the steppe east of the Volga. Eremenko mobilized thousands of civilians in the city to assist the military, including boys aged thirteen to sixteen years. But he evacuated 200,000 people who were too old or too young to fight.

Stalingrad was not a fortress. It was a mixture of old buildings, industrial plants, railroad yards, and barrack-like apartments. It spread fifteen miles along the west bank of the Volga and two to four miles back from it. Good defensive positions were provided by the high western bank of the Volga, by numerous *balkas* (dry ravines or gullies with steep banks), and by railway embankments.

On August 24, Stuka attacks on Stalingrad caused massive damage, killing civilians, turning whole blocks into rubble, and setting fire to wooden structures. While the Stuka attacks were going on, the 16th Panzer Division swept aside modest Russian resistance west of the city and reached the Volga near Rynok, ten miles north of Stalingrad, at 6:30 P.M. on August 24. Hitler's stated purpose had thus been accomplished: German artillery on the high bank of the Volga could stop tanker traffic on the river.

But Hitler insisted on the capture of the entire city. This required hand-to-hand, building-by-building combat of the closest and most intense kind. It was military insanity. All the senior officers in the campaign agreed that—when Stalingrad was not seized in the first rush—it should have been masked with defensive troops and ignored.

In extremely hot weather (it had not rained for two months), German forces were forced to mount individual assaults against the barricades that the Russians threw across nearly every street. The going was incredibly difficult. The Russians hid machine guns and mortars in shattered buildings and sealed off entire streets and neighborhoods with their fire. Every factory and solid building became a savagely defended fortress. German losses were heavy, and the advance slowed to a crawl. Supplies and ammunition were slow to arrive and insufficient.

As panzer leader Friedrich-Wilhelm von Mellenthin wrote, Hitler played directly into the hands of the Russians.[12] In this environment, the ill-trained but dogged Russian soldiers were a match for the most elite German forces. Fighting was close, sometimes face to face, and relied on brute force. All the German advantages of mobility, high troop skills, and precisely executed maneuvers were sacrificed. The battle degenerated into a stalemate.

One of Germany's best formations, the massive, well-armed 6th Army, was immobilized in the chaotic rubble of the Stalingrad salient, where even tanks found it hard to move. But on either side of this salient the lines were being held for 150 miles along the Don to the west by decidedly second-rate, ill-equipped allied troops, the Romanian 3rd Army, the Italian 8th Army, and the Hungarian 2nd Army, and for an equal distance to the southeast by the small, ill-equipped four-division Romanian 4th Army guarding the Kalmuk Steppe.

It was obvious to all of the seasoned German generals that this situation could not be sustained. Erich von Manstein wrote, "A far-sighted leader would have realized from the start that to mass the whole of the German assault forces in and around Stalingrad without adequate flank protection placed them in mortal danger of being enveloped as soon as the enemy broke through the adjacent fronts."[13]

The Russians were certain to be building forces on both sides of the salient in order to launch offensives to seal off Stalingrad and imprison the 6th Army.

Franz Halder, the chief of staff, assembled unimpeachable intelligence proving that this was taking place. When he insisted on telling Hitler, the führer dismissed him on September 24. The new chief of staff was Lieutenant General Kurt Zeitzler, a tank expert who saw that Hitler was not interested in the truth, and did nothing to challenge his insistence on keeping the 6th Army in its exposed position.

Hitler also sacked Wilhelm List, commander of the 17th and 1st Panzer Armies (Army Group A), because he had not captured all of the Caucasus. Instead of appointing a new commander, Hitler directed the group himself, in his spare time. Here was convincing evidence of Hitler's divorce from reality. From his headquarters at Vinnitsa, he issued orders for his troops to carry out operations deep in the mountains of the Caucasus that were impossible to execute. He never himself set foot in the the region, and knew nothing of the hopeless conditions his troops were facing there.

On November 19, 1942, in thick fog, N. F. Vatutin, commander of the Soviet Southwest Front, launched a massive tank-led offensive against the Romanian 3rd Army at Kletskaya and Kremensk on the Don eighty miles west of Stalingrad. The Romanians had no tanks of their own and no antitank guns that could penetrate the thick armor of the Soviet T-34 tanks. They lasted only briefly before the entire army disintegrated into headlong retreat. The next day, General Eremenko launched a similar T-34-led attack against the Romanian 4th Army in the Kalmuk Steppe. It too disappeared in chaos. The entire rear behind Stalingrad had been opened to the Soviet armor.

On November 22, two Soviet tank corps joined near Kalach and closed the pincers on the 6th Army. With this, 250,000 men were sealed within a pocket measuring thirty miles east and west and twenty-five miles north and south.

If the 6th Army had been allowed to break out, it almost certainly could have gotten away intact. But Hitler refused to allow the army to move. He ordered it to curl up like a hedgehog and defend itself in place. Hermann Göring, a crony of Hitler and chief of the Luftwaffe, promised grandiloquently that the air force would supply the army until a new battle group could be formed to break the caldron. Senior Luftwaffe officers said it couldn't be done, but Hitler ignored their warnings.

As Soviet troops formed a double ring around Stalingrad, one to hold the 6th Army, the other to forestall rescue efforts, Soviet gunners posted 395 antiaircraft guns along the air corridor the Luftwaffe had to fly, while 490 fighter aircraft assembled to shoot down Luftwaffe transports.

The daily needs of the 6th Army totaled 700 tons, but Colonel Fritz Morzik, Luftwaffe air transport chief, said that at best his transports could fly in 350 tons a day. This proved that air supply was impossible, but Hitler refused to look at the facts. The Luftwaffe could not even deliver one-half of the 6th Army's needs. Though air officers made extreme efforts, they set down just 269 tons from November 25 to 29, and only 1,267 tons from November 30 to December 11. Ammunition supplies dropped, fuel became scarce, and the men began to starve.

Meanwhile another, even more dangerous, enveloping movement was threatening. The blunders of Adolf Hitler had opened a vast opportunity for the Soviets to win the war in a few months, if not weeks. After the Soviets overran the Romanian 3rd Army at Kletskaya and Kremensk, Manstein withdrew the main German defensive line to the Chir River, some 50 miles south of the Don and to the west of Stalingrad. Defending the upper Chir was the six-division Italian 8th Army. The Italian army was just 200 miles northeast of Rostov on the lower Don next to the Sea of Azov. If a Soviet army could crash through the Italians and drive to Rostov, it could cut off and destroy not only the beleaguered 6th Army at Stalingrad but also both German armies in the Caucasus and the German forces along the Chir. In other words, if the Russians could reach Rostov, they could destroy *all* the German forces and their allies on the southern front. If these forces were lost, Germany could no longer defend itself. The war would be lost. The senior commanders in the German army saw this peril clearly, but Hitler did not.

German intelligence services were providing irrefutable evidence that the Soviets were, in fact, massing for just such a war-winning move. Army group Voronezh Front under F. I. Golikov was gathering on the upper Chir opposite the pitifully inadequate Italian 8th Army.

Despite the danger, Manstein saw that the immediate problem was to extricate the 6th Army from its trap at Stalingrad. Hitler had already handed him the task of relieving the army. If this immense force could be extricated, it could blunt a strike toward Rostov.

Manstein found a narrow avenue along which a relieving force could advance—from Kotelnikovo southwest of Stalingrad. He had immense difficulties assembling a strike force but finally acquired just one panzer corps, the 57th, to break a hole and advance to Stalingrad. He launched the attack on December 12. It caught the Russians by surprise and made good progress, although the Soviets brought up troops and counterattacked time after time.

Meanwhile, the Soviets unleashed their offensive toward Rostov on December 16. The Soviet 1st Guards Army overran the Italians with ease. The Italian army disintegrated, and a sixty-mile-wide rupture opened in the front, through which Soviet tanks poured, aiming straight for Rostov. Manstein ordered General Karl-Adolf Hollidt, commanding along the Chir, to pull back to guard the crossings over the Donetz River at Forchstadt and Kamensk-Shakhtinsky, the only barrier now in front of Rostov.

Despite the danger, Manstein held steadfastly to his advance on Stalingrad. He called on the army high command (OKH) to order the 6th Army to break out toward the advancing 57th Panzer Corps. If both forces exerted their utmost strength, they could crack through the defensive shield and meet.

But Hitler refused to sanction a breakout. It was beyond belief, but he ruled that the 57th Panzer Corps was to continue to attack, while the 6th Army was to remain in place. Manstein slowly realized that Hitler intended to hold onto Stalingrad and supply it by a land corridor. This was a manifest impossibility, but Hitler was totally unable to understand that the 6th Army could survive *only* if it withdrew from Stalingrad. Manstein could not believe that Hitler was so stupid, and hoped he could get him to change his mind.

The critical moment came on December 19. The 57th Corps reached the narrow Miskova River, just thirty miles from the siege front. Manstein sent an urgent message to 6th Army commander Paulus and to Hitler: the 6th Army must disengage and drive southwest to join the 57th Panzer Corps.

Hitler took hours to reply. He finally said the 6th Army *could* break out, but it still had to hold existing fronts north, east, and west of the city. This was patently impossible. Hitler's refusal to allow the 6th Army to extricate itself was a death sentence. For seven days the 57th Panzer Corps had run every conceivable risk to open a door and keep it open. For seven more days Manstein held the corps at the Miskova River, trying desperately to get Hitler to change his mind. But he refused. Manstein could leave the corps exposed no longer. On December 27, he pulled his severely weakened force back toward Kotelnikovo. The attempt to relieve Stalingrad had failed—not because the troops had failed, but because Hitler could not see reality.

The German 6th Army now proceeded to die. Food supplies dwindled to virtually nothing. Russian attacks drove the Germans out of most of their shelters. The survivors huddled in the ruins close to the Volga. On February 2, 1943, the last resistance ceased. The Luftwaffe had evacuated about 25,000 wounded and specialists, but about 160,000 men died and 91,000 were captured. Most of the prisoners soon succumbed to exposure and typhus. Only 6,000 saw their homeland again, after twelve years of captivity.

Erich von Manstein turned his attention to saving the rest of the German army in the south. The Soviet offensive aimed at Rostov was proceeding at full force. Dogged defense in front of the Donetz River temporarily held up the Russian advance.

At this lowest point of German fortune, Manstein saw an opportunity to turn devastating defeat into spectacular victory. His concept was pure Sun Tzu: deception and striking a massive blow from a wholly unexpected direction.

Manstein recognized that all of the gains in the south in 1942 were going to be lost. Army Group A could not remain in the Caucasus. Once the Russians seized Rostov, they would be cut off. The few German forces remaining west of Stalingrad would have to retreat.

Accordingly, he proposed to Hitler that—while Hollidt temporarily held the Russians at bay in front of the Donetz—all the German forces on the southern front be withdrawn in stages to the lower Dnieper River, 220 miles west of Rostov. Manstein was certain that the Russians would perceive a massive withdrawal as a collapse of German will. They would believe that they could destroy the German army by a swift offensive aimed at cutting the Germans off from the essential Dnieper crossings of Dnepropetrovsk and Zaporozhye, where any evacuations must take place and where all supplies came through. Manstein was certain that the Russians would make every effort to sweep around the Germans and get to the crossings first. This would create a vastly extended, extremely fluid Russian front stretching across the lower Ukraine.

Manstein proposed that, in the meantime, a powerful German force be concentrated near Kharkov, 250 miles northwest of Rostov and 125 miles northeast of Dnepropetrovsk. When the Soviets extended themselves westward, the German forces around Kharkov would drive into their northern flank. This movement, Manstein told Hitler, would "convert a large-scale withdrawal into an envelopment operation" that would push the Russians against the Sea of Azov to the south and destroy them.[14]

It was a brilliant concept, as brilliant and as deceptive as Manstein's strategy to strike through the Ardennes against the Western Allies. It would throw the Russians on the defensive and transform the strategic picture in the south.

But Hitler refused. He didn't want to give up his summer conquests, transient as they were. Manstein concluded that the dictator "actually recoiled from risks in the military field."

"Obstinate defense of every foot of ground gradually became the be all and end all of Hitler's leadership," Manstein wrote. "Hitler thought the arcanum of success lay in clinging at all costs to what he already possessed."[15]

It was only because of Manstein that all the German armies, except the 6th, got away. Manstein ignored Hitler's orders for the troops to remain in place, finding one subterfuge after another to justify his actions. He pulled back the German armies in a series of masterful retreats. The Germans abandoned Kursk in the center and withdrew beyond Kharkov, 430 miles west of Stalingrad. Manstein held Rostov long enough for the Germans to withdraw from the Caucasus. Even so, Hitler insisted on keeping the 17th Army in the Kuban region of the northwest corner of the Caucasus, where it served no purpose but later was able to evacuate across the Strait of Kerch to the Crimea. Manstein formed a new line along the Mius River, forty miles west of Rostov, and stopped the Russian advance.

Manstein achieved the last success of German arms on the eastern front. On March 14, 1943, he enveloped overextended Soviet forces at Kharkov and recaptured the city.

Admiral Raeder and Generals Halder and Manstein had conceived their own strategies and policies that mirrored axioms of Sun Tzu. They had urged these measures on Hitler. But he had ignored them all, and thereby had brought about the most devastating defeat suffered by German arms in the war. With the loss of a quarter of a million of his best troops at Stalingrad and his refusal afterward to carry out a strategic withdrawal and counteroffensive, Hitler lost the initiative. He now was condemned to a deadly defensive war on all fronts. This was a war that Germany was increasingly incapable of pursuing because its arms production was nowhere close to that of the Western Allies and the Soviet Union. Stalingrad is a textbook case of the contrast between what a campaign following the axioms of Sun Tzu could have achieved, and what actually happened when these axioms are disregarded. In the direction pointed out by Admiral Raeder lay at least a stalemate and possibly a negotiated peace. In the direction followed by Hitler lay inevitable defeat.

NINE

The Liberation of France, 1944

Both the Allies and the Germans violated Sun Tzu principles in the campaign to liberate Europe that began with the invasion of Normandy on June 6, 1944. These failures led to disastrous losses and consequences on both sides.[1]

The first and most decisive German blunder was to not learn about and accommodate to the capabilities of the enemy, in this case the strength of Allied air power—a breach of one of Sun Tzu's maxims.[2] Accordingly, the Germans held in the interior the ten panzer or panzer-grenadier "fast divisions" (*Schnelldivisionen*)[3] that Adolf Hitler had allocated to defend the West, intending to launch them at the beaches once the Allies had landed. But Allied air power kept these divisions from reaching the beachheads while the Allies were still weak and vulnerable and could have been overrun. This failure permitted the Allies to consolidate their hold on Normandy and ultimately achieve victory.

The Allied blunders also began prior to the invasion with their failure to ascertain in advance the nature of enemy terrain and to adapt to it—a breach of another of Sun Tzu's rules.[4] The Allies did not anticipate the barriers created by the hedgerow-bordered fields of the

Norman *bocage* country. These enclosed fields became individual battle-fields that stymied the Allied advance for seven weeks and cost 200,000 casualties.

When the Americans finally broke through the hedgerow country on July 25, 1944, Hitler made the ruinous decision to hold his armies in Normandy when he should have evacuated them at once.[5]

The Allied senior commanders then rejected the proposal of General George S. Patton Jr. to encircle the Germans and force their surrender. Instead, they tried to seal off the German escape route. This was poorly executed. Though the Germans suffered much from Allied air power, the vast bulk of them got away, allowing Hitler to pursue the war for eight more deadly months. In these decisions, the senior Allied generals violated a fundamental tenet of Sun Tzu. They did not investigate objectively Patton's proposal, and they did not follow through in preventing the German escape. An intelligent commander, Sun Tzu says, *creates* opportunities for victory, taking advantage of events as they occur. He does not depend on fortuitous victory. He never relies on chance.[6]

The decision as to where the panzer and panzer-grenadier divisions were to be stationed pitted against each other the two greatest armored commanders in history, Heinz Guderian, father of the panzers, and Erwin Rommel, the "Desert Fox" who achieved renown as commander of the Africa Corps in Libya and Egypt in 1941–1942.

Guderian, along with General Leo Geyr von Schweppenburg, chief of panzer training in the West, proposed that the ten fast divisions be stationed north and south of Paris. This would be far enough inland from the Atlantic coast that they could be switched to the main invasion front once it had been identified. Both officers recognized the superiority of Allied air power, but they believed the problem could be overcome by moving at night. They received approval from Gerd von Rundstedt, commander in chief West.

Guderian thought the Allies should be allowed to land where they chose and to make a penetration. Then the Allies could be thrown back into the sea by a counteroffensive on a giant scale. This was how the Germans had successfully countered Soviet offensives in Russia. Neither he nor Geyr had any idea how Anglo-American command of the air could restrict panzer movement.

Rommel did. He knew from his experiences with superior air power in North Africa that Allied aircraft could shatter vehicles, break bridges, and tear up roads leading to the front, thereby slowing motorized movements day or night. Rommel, who, as commander of Army Group B, was in charge of defending the Atlantic coast, insisted on stationing panzer divisions very close to the beaches. He told Guderian that the day of mobile warfare for Germany had passed because of superior Allied air power and because Germany had not kept pace with the Western Allies in the production of tanks and armored vehicles.

In Rommel's eyes, the Germans had to determine in advance where the Allies were going to invade. If German armor could not move, it had to be close to the invasion site. Rommel decided that the Allies would land at the Pas-de-Calais opposite Dover. He ruled out other landing sites because the Pas-de-Calais gave access to a port or ports capable of handling large ships, and because the Allies could provide greater air cover there than anywhere else. "If the enemy once gets his foot in, he'll put every antitank gun and tank he can into the bridgehead and let us beat our heads against it," he told Fritz Bayerlein, commander of the Panzer Lehr Division.[7]

To prevent this from happening, Rommel insisted, the Germans had to fight and win the battle right on the beaches. Reserves could not be posted any great distance inland. They had to be right behind the shore so they could come up quickly irrespective of Allied air power. Accordingly, Rommel began constructing a fortified mined zone from the Pas-de-Calais coast to points five or six miles inland. Rommel built some defensive positions along the Normandy coast, but not many.

Rommel was wrong about the landing site, of course. He was not aware of a brilliant British invention—two artificial harbors (Mulberries) that could serve as temporary ports. The Allies did not have to capture a port to invade the Continent. They could land on the beaches of Normandy, the least likely place that was still under the Allied air umbrella.

Guderian also was wrong about Allied air power. In the winter of 1944, the Luftwaffe was virtually driven from the skies by the American P-51 Mustang fighter. With range-extending detachable wing fuel tanks, it was escorting B-17 bombers in daylight raids deep into Germany. The Luftwaffe was compelled to challenge the P-51s, but their best fighter, the Focke-Wulf 190, was inferior. The Germans lost large numbers of fighters combating the raids. By the spring of 1944, virtually no fighters remained.[8]

The situation called for an intense application of a Sun Tzu axiom. "What is of supreme importance in war," he writes, "is to attack the enemy's strategy."[9] Perhaps because of the heated dispute over where the panzers were to be stationed, the German leaders failed to analyze Allied strategy. If they had done so, they could have figured easily the few places where an invasion would have to come.

Allied strategy was based on superior air power. The Allies had demonstrated in the Mediterranean in 1943 that they would land only on beaches that their fighter aircraft could cover. Since the best British fighter, the Spitfire, had an operating range of a little over 400 miles, all landing sites in Sicily and Italy were within 200 miles of Allied airfields. Although later models of the Spitfire, along with other British and American fighters and fighter-bombers, had somewhat longer ranges, only three locations were within Allied fighter coverage: the Pas-de-Calais, the Normandy beaches, and the Cotentin Peninsula of Normandy.[10] Because the Germans were well aware of the Allied fixation on air cover, they could have used logic to figure out the potential landing sites. And if they had stationed three or four panzer divisions directly behind each of these three sites, they could have moved quickly to drive the Allies off whichever beach they landed on.

Such a compromise would have solved the problem of where to post the panzers. It would have answered Rommel's insistence on having tanks right at the invasion beaches, and it would have given Guderian mobile reserves for unexpected contingencies. It was this need that motivated him to want the tanks posted safely inland.

But this did not happen. Rommel persisted in believing, until shortly before the landing, that the Pas-de-Calais was the only possible site. Since Guderian, Geyr, and Rundstedt believed otherwise, the final decision fell to Adolf Hitler. The führer had already shown in countless cases that he was unable to make up his mind. As Erich von Manstein had observed closely, he seized on anything that struck his fancy or aroused his fears, and made wholly illogical decisions.[11] Seeing dangers at every turn, he spread the ten panzer and panzer-grenadier divisions from northern Belgium to the south of France. In the final allocation, Hitler stationed six fast divisions north of the Loire River and four south of the river, three of them near the Spanish frontier or close to Marseille along the Mediterranean coast. Spreading of the panzers was a flagrant violation of Sun Tzu doctrine to concentrate one's forces. As a consequence, German armored divisions found it impossible to get to Normandy in time to make any difference. Just a single panzer division was near the Normandy beaches, and the commander was so indecisive that he frittered away his chances to snuff out the landings.[12]

The blunder in failing to figure out the three places where the Allies could land resulted in calamity for the Germans. Because of intensive Allied air interdiction, practically every unit ordered to the battle-

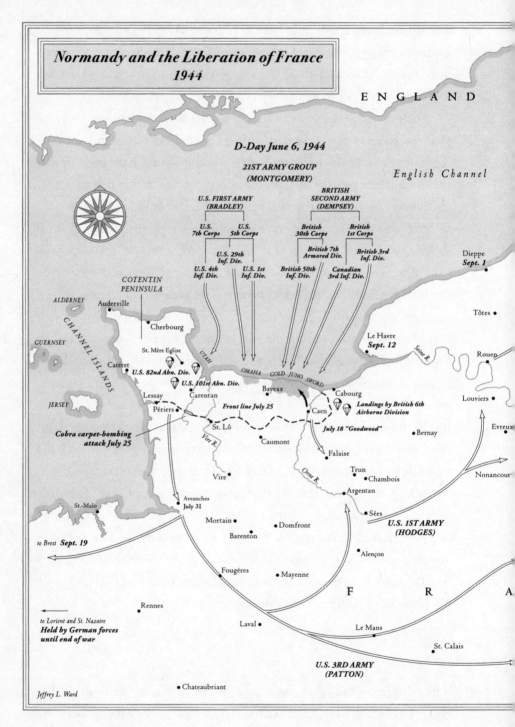

Normandy and the Liberation of France
1944

D-Day June 6, 1944

ENGLAND

English Channel

21ST ARMY GROUP
(MONTGOMERY)

U.S. FIRST ARMY
(BRADLEY)

BRITISH
SECOND ARMY
(DEMPSEY)

U.S.
7th Corps

U.S.
5th Corps

British
30th Corps

British
1st Corps

U.S. 29th
Inf. Div.

British 7th
Armored Div.

British 3rd
Inf. Div.

U.S. 4th
Inf. Div.

U.S. 1st
Inf. Div.

British 50th
Inf. Div.

Canadian
3rd Inf. Div.

Dieppe
Sept. 1

COTENTIN
PENINSULA

ALDERNEY

Auderville

Tôtes

CHANNEL ISLANDS

GUERNSEY

Cherbourg

St. Mère Eglise

UTAH

Le Havre
Sept. 12

Seine R.

Rouen

Cateret

U.S. 82nd Abn. Div.

OMAHA   GOLD JUNO SWORD

Louviers

JERSEY

U.S. 101st Abn. Div.

Bayeaux

Cabourg

Landings by British 6th
Airborne Division

Lessay

Carentan

Caen

Evreux

Périers

Front line July 25

July 18 "Goodwood"

Bernay

Cobra carpet-bombing
attack July 25

St. Lô

Vire R.

Caumont

Falaise

Orne R.

Trun
Chambois

Nonancour

Vire

Argentan

St.-Malo

Avranches
July 31

Sées

U.S. 1ST ARMY
(HODGES)

to Brest Sept. 19

Mortain

Domfront

Barenton

Alençon

Fougères

Mayenne

F   R   A

to Lorient and St. Nazaire
Held by German forces
until end of war

Rennes

Laval

Le Mans

St. Calais

Jeffrey L. Ward

Chateaubriant

U.S. 3RD ARMY
(PATTON)

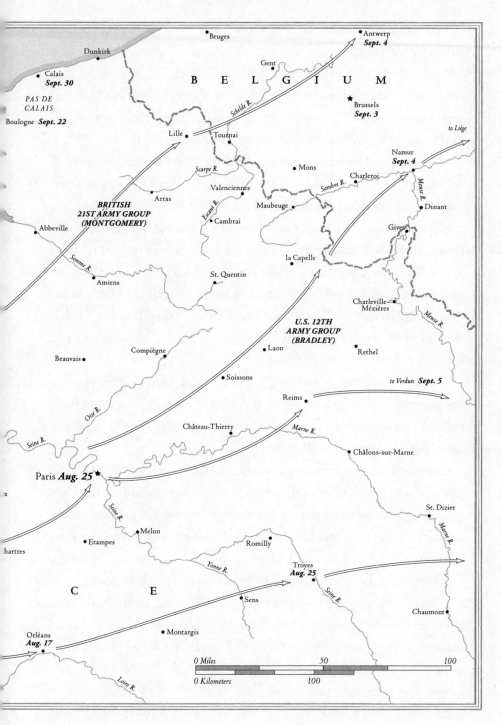

Bruges

Antwerp
Sept. 4

Dunkirk

Gent

Calais
Sept. 30

PAS DE
CALAIS

B E L G I U M

★ Brussels
Sept. 3

Boulogne **Sept. 22**

Schelde R.

to Liège

Lille

Tournai

Namur
Sept. 4

Scarpe R.

Mons

Charleroi

Meuse R.

Valenciennes

Sambre R.

Dinant

Arras

Escaut R.

Maubeuge

Givet

Abbeville

Cambrai

Charleville-
Mézières

Somme R.

la Capelle

Meuse R.

Amiens

St. Quentin

**BRITISH
21ST ARMY GROUP
(MONTGOMERY)**

Beauvais

Compiègne

Laon

Rethel

**U.S. 12TH
ARMY GROUP
(BRADLEY)**

Soissons

to Verdun **Sept. 5**

Oise R.

Reims

Château-Thierry

Marne R.

Châlons-sur-Marne

Seine R.

Paris **Aug. 25** ★

St. Dizier

Melun

Seine R.

Romilly

x

Etampes

Marne R.

hartres

Troyes
Aug. 25

C   E

Yonne R.

Sens

Seine R.

Chaumont

Orléans
Aug. 17

Montargis

0 Miles   50   100

0 Kilometers   100

Loire R.

front suffered heavy damage. Casualties ran to 2,500 to 3,000 men a day. Replacements were few, and the immense losses in tanks and self-propelled guns were never made up. The railway system serving Normandy vanished under Allied bombs. Fighter-bombers smashed anything moving on the roads during the day. The supply system was so damaged that only the barest essentials reached the front.

Rommel and Rundstedt went to Hitler's retreat at Berchtesgaden in Bavaria on June 29 to talk with the führer. They told Hitler the situation was impossible. How, Rommel asked, did Hitler imagine the war could still be won? The question brought on a chaotic argument from Hitler. Rundstedt and Rommel expected to be ousted from their jobs. When Rundstedt got back to Paris on July 1, he received an order from Hitler that "present positions are to be held." He called Hitler's headquarters and told a staff officer he couldn't fulfill this demand. "What shall we do?" the officer asked. Rundstedt replied, "Make peace, you fools."[13]

On the next day a messenger from Hitler handed Rundstedt a handwritten note relieving him of command because of "age and poor health." His successor was Günther von Kluge, who quickly took the same gloomy approach as Rundstedt.

Rommel, to his surprise, remained at his post. About this time Rommel and his chief of staff, Hans Speidel, concluded that the Germans should commence peace talks with the Western Allies. But before any action could be taken, Rommel was severely wounded by a low-flying American aircraft near Livarot on July 17.

Three days later, on July 20, 1944, a bomb exploded under a table at Hitler's headquarters in Rastenburg, East Prussia, where Hitler was meeting. Colonel Claus von Stauffenberg, a leader of the secret opposition to Hitler, had placed it there. But the führer survived and commenced a wave of terror against anyone suspected of a role in the plot. This led to numerous executions. On October 14, 1944, a deputation from Berlin visited Rommel, who was recovering from his wounds at his home near Ulm. The group gave him a choice. He could be tried by a People's Court, which would have meant execution, or he could take poison and receive a state funeral—and his wife and son would not be persecuted. Rommel chose poison.[14]

Meanwhile the Allies were having great difficulties with the *bocage*— the hedgerow country of Normandy. The hedgerows were a total surprise. None of the planners had thought to find out what the land was like behind the beaches, despite the fact that Normandy had been an extremely popular British travel destination before the war. Virtually the entire American sector, from the coast of the Cotentin Peninsula to the north-south line from Caumont to Bayeux, was *bocage* country. In the British sector to the east, the land was part *bocage* and part rolling countryside.

To protect their crops and their animals against sea winds and to mark boundaries, for centuries Norman farmers had closed their land into fields of only a few acres by raising embankments three or four feet high around each field. Dense shrubbery, brambles, hawthorn, and small trees grew on these banks, forming solid barriers that held in animals. Each field had a gate to admit animals and equipment. Dirt tracks or sunken lanes ("holloways"), largely overgrown and obscured from observation, ran between these hedgerows, permitting troops and weapons to move free from observation from the air or on the ground. The effect was to divide the terrain into thousands of walled enclosures.

The *bocage* was ideal country for defensive warfare. The Germans could hide in the hedgerows. As Allied soldiers or tanks advanced across the small fields, the Germans could launch *Panzerfäuste*, or bazooka rockets, at the vehicles and shatter the infantry with automatic weapons fire. The Germans organized each field as a defensive stronghold. Once they had stopped an attack, they brought down preregistered mortar rounds on the field. Mortars caused three-quarters of the American casualties in Normandy. Camouflaged Tiger tanks, assault guns, and 88-

millimeter antiaircraft guns could knock out any Allied tank up to 2,000 yards distant that ventured onto the main roads or lanes or into the holloways.

The Allied advance ground to a halt. The war was in danger of degenerating into a stalemate. Now the utter failure of Allied planners to anticipate this debilitating terrain feature was being paid for with the blood of Allied soldiers.

We have seen throughout history abundant examples of the incapacity of some commanders to anticipate the environments in which they require their soldiers to fight, and the deadly consequences this can bring. General John Burgoyne's disregard of the entrapping territory of upper New York in 1777, for example, was the fundamental reason for his defeat and surrender—and Britain's loss of the American colonies. Another example is Robert E. Lee's failure to determine that the course of the Potomac River at Antietam boxed the Confederate army into a corner in which its only hope was somehow to survive. It was this disaster that made possible the Emancipation Proclamation and the South's ultimate defeat.

The decisive importance of terrain is why Sun Tzu emphasizes that it is imperative for commanders to know "mountains and forests, gorges and defiles, the shape of marshes and wetlands."[15]

The *bocage* was no secret. Normandy and England had been intimately connected well before the Norman conquest of 1066, and this connection continued in the following centuries. Many thousands of contemporary Britons knew the landscape well. It was therefore inexcusable for the officers in charge of Operation Overlord, the plan to invade Europe, to anticipate the *bocage*.

Vast tracts of southern England were covered with hedgerow-enclosed fields very similar to the *bocage*. If the Overlord planners had recognized what they were dealing with, they could easily have experimented with ways to crack the hedgerows without heavy losses. They could have come up in advance with the solution that individual soldiers discovered on their own in Normandy. The soldiers found that by welding bulldozer-like blades to the front of the standard Allied tank, the Sherman M4A3, it could break through the hedgerows without exposing its thin and vulnerable underside to enemy fire. It was this Achilles' heel that German soldiers exploited to destroy most of the Shermans as they crashed into Norman fields.

Once the soldiers hit on an ad hoc answer, they undertook a prodigious program and equipped 60 percent of the Shermans with the blades by July 25.

But this resolution was still in the works in the weeks after the landings on June 6, and American commanders were frantically searching for some way out of the impasse. Omar Bradley, commander of the U.S. 1st Army, decided to take advantage of Allied command of the air to blow apart a three-mile section of the German line a few miles west of the town of Saint-Lô. If he could break a wide hole in the German line, he hoped the 7th Corps under J. Lawton Collins could rush into the German rear and shatter the German defensive position. The operation, called Cobra, took place on July 25 and involved 1,500 heavy bombers, 380 medium bombers, and 550 fighter-bombers.

Panzer Lehr Division received the brunt of the Cobra attack. The commander, Fritz Bayerlein, reported that all German positions were shattered and that the landscape resembled the moon. One-third of the German combat effectives were killed or wounded, and only a dozen tanks remained in operation. German opposition melted away.

By the end of July 26, American armor had penetrated ten miles, and the next day it went farther. The entire western portion of the German front collapsed. On Collins's right, or west, Troy Middleton's 8th Corps broke through and turned the corner between Normandy and Brittany at Avranches. The *bocage* had been bypassed.

Once the Allies broke out of Normandy, Operation Overlord called for the Allies to capture Brittany and open the Breton ports to supply the Allied armies. Omar Bradley was charged with this task, and on August 1, George Patton's 3rd Army was formally activated to carry it out.

At this moment, Adolf Hitler handed the Allies gratis a means of ending the war well before the end of 1944. He committed another of the catastrophic mistakes that had marked his conduct of the war. He demanded that his panzers drive westward to recapture Avranches. Hitler's aim was to isolate and destroy all American forces that had advanced into Brittany and south of Avranches.

Hitler's decision was a strategic blunder of massive proportions. The American breakthrough had placed all of the German armies in Normandy in grave jeopardy, because Americans were now south of the German armies and could press eastward and encircle them on all sides. The correct military response was for the Germans to retreat at once, first to the Seine River, then to other river and terrain barriers eastward toward the German frontier, thereby preserving the German armies and their weapons to fight another day.

But Hitler was unwilling to give up any territory. He also was deeply distracted because of the attempt on his life on July 20, which showed a willingness of many Germans to end the war as soon as possible.

Patton—by far the most imaginative and capable commander on the Allied side—recognized Hitler's error at once. He saw that a gigantic, swift victory could be achieved. He and other American generals on the spot were sure that they could stop the German panzer attack toward Avranches. Patton saw that the attack would actually imperil the Germans further. It would send many of their forces far westward, making it that much more difficult to extract their armies from the trap that was forming around them in Normandy.

Patton pointed out to Bradley that, since the Americans were now well south of the German armies, the way was open for a massive strike eastward against almost no opposition through the "gap" between Orléans and Paris. American forces could seize Paris swiftly and then drive down the right, or northern, bank of the Seine River to the English Channel and cut off all German forces in Normandy. These armies would be forced to surrender. There would then be few German forces remaining to contest a quick strike for the Rhine River. Once across the river, flying columns could overrun Germany in days. The war could be ended quickly and with few additional casualties.

Patton's plan would permit the Allies to scrap the slow, careful advance that the Overlord planners had expected to conduct against a doggedly defending, formidable German army. Such a move would be a Sun Tzu *qi*, or indirect, strike that would achieve victory, while the remaining Allied troops in Normandy kept the Germans in place with a Sun Tzu *zheng*, or holding, action.

Here was the decisive moment in the campaign to liberate France and end the war. Patton had seen a chance to exploit Hitler's fatal insistence on holding every inch of ground. Patton wanted to use this flaw to isolate and force the surrender of all the German armies in Normandy. But the decision rested not with Patton, but with his superiors: American General Dwight D. Eisenhower, supreme commander; British General Bernard Law Montgomery, Allied ground forces commander; and Bradley, who was extremely cautious, was not given to making bold decisions, and had decided on Cobra only as a desperate measure to break out of the trap of the *bocage*.

All three senior commanders were lacking in strategic sense and imagination. Eisenhower had no battle experience and no grand view of how to win the war. But he was willing to accept responsibility, he was fair and patient, and he had a big grin and an easy, familiar way of talking. People liked Ike. Montgomery had led the British 8th Army to victory in Egypt and Libya. The son of a perfectionist mother and an ineffectual father, Montgomery grew up introverted, tactless, and arrogant. He was highly critical of others, and he refused to compromise, in direct contrast to Eisenhower. Bradley was a self-effacing, homespun Missourian who was often filled with doubt. He had been catapulted over Patton when Patton was nearly sent home in disgrace after slapping two enlisted men he thought were malingering in hospitals in Sicily in 1943. Eisenhower had finally decided to keep Patton, but resolved to give him no higher command than that of an army.

Patton was a polar opposite of Bradley. He was eccentric, erratic, vain, deeply emotional, and a genuine military romantic. Born in California, he was the scion of a prominent Virginia family. His grandfather was a Confederate colonel, and John Singleton Mosby, the famous Confederate partisan leader in Virginia who had become a lawyer in California, frequently visited in the Patton home. Patton grew up hearing stories of Mosby's adventures, and he sought to become a hero in his own right.

But Patton's situation was analogous to Stonewall Jackson's. Jackson understood almost from the outset how to win the war for the South, but, as a subordinate commander, he was unable to carry his strategy into practice. Patton likewise saw a way to victory in the summer of 1944, but, as a subordinate, he depended on superior commanders to accept his proposals.

Bradley, who had now moved up to command the 12th Army Group, took very seriously the Overlord plan to seize the ports of Brittany. But Patton and some subordinate armored generals were clamoring to abandon this methodical plan as unnecessary, and to use the limited number of available troops to launch a full-blown offensive eastward.

Everything had been transformed by the German collapse on the western flank. The Allies were already supplying thirty divisions through the captured Norman port of Cherbourg and the single Mulberry port off Normandy that had survived a channel storm. These ports could supply flying columns under Patton that could race to Paris, and then turn down the north bank of the Seine to the sea.

The war then could be finished by forming a relatively small mobile force that could rush to the German frontier on a very narrow front, cross the Rhine River, and penetrate into the heart of Germany in a series of rapier thrusts. There would be few German forces to stop such a concentrated push. In weeks it could drive a stake in the heart of German resistance and end the war.

As Bradley was contemplating Patton's proposal, the German panzers reached just to the west of Mortain, about twenty miles east of

Avranches, but were halted by strong American forces. Since Hitler still refused to allow withdrawal, the German troops were lodged in a deep salient running from Mortain on the west to the vicinity of Falaise, forty-five miles to the northeast. Falaise was twenty miles south of Caen, the British anchor on the eastern end of the Normandy bridgehead.

However glittering the possibilities of Patton's plan, Bradley could not bring himself to undertake it. Bradley was too conventional a soldier. The plan had blossomed forth in Patton's mind when Hitler attempted to nullify the Cobra breakout with the hopeless strike for Avranches. Neither Hitler's atrocious strategy nor the unexpected bonanza of the German collapse had been anticipated by the meticulous Overlord planners. To authorize it, Bradley would have to exhibit boldness, innovation, and speed. This was not Bradley's way.

Bradley got no help from Montgomery, who had even less imagination than Bradley, and who advised him to continue the original Overlord plan to seize Brittany. Eisenhower stayed aloof from the whole affair.

Bradley thus chose the orthodox option: to devote most of his strength to capturing Brittany. Patton, still on probation from the Sicilian slappings, felt too insecure to raise a formal objection. Montgomery and Bradley failed to recognize the brilliance and imagination exhibited in Patton's idea. They lost a great opportunity to end the war in weeks.

The Breton effort at once became a side show, and it was costly, time-consuming, and utterly futile. It took 20,000 American troops two weeks to seize Saint-Malo on the north coast of Brittany, which was destroyed and made unusable in the process. It took more than three divisions suffering almost 10,000 casualties in a month-long operation to capture Brest, which also was ruined in the fighting. Lorient and Saint-Nazaire remained under German control, ringed about by American troops, to the end of the war. Bradley sent far too many soldiers into Brittany, a useless expenditure of resources, and they fought a bitter campaign for ports that were never used, a tragic waste of effort and of men.

Patton did not say so publicly, but he echoed John Shirley Wood, commander of the U.S. 4th Armored Division. Wood complained that the senior commanders were "winning the war in the wrong way,"[16] because they were moving far too slowly, were undertaking operations of little benefit, and were suffering far too many unnecessary casualties.

With the relatively few American troops that he had not committed to Brittany, Bradley opted for a much less ambitious plan than Patton had proposed. After the failure of Hitler's strike toward Avranches, the Germans were in a perilous situation. To the north were Montgomery's two armies (British 2nd and Canadian 1st) and the U.S. 1st Army, now under Courtney Hodges. To the south was Wade Haislip's 15th Corps, the single element of Patton's 3rd Army not committed to Brittany.

Bradley's plan was for Haislip's corps to reach Alençon, seventy-five miles east of Avranches, and then turn *north* and drive through Argentan to join the Canadians and Poles who were now pressing south from Caen to seize Falaise. If successful, this maneuver would trap whatever German forces were between Mortain and Falaise-Argentan.

Bradley's plan was likely to achieve big dividends only if it was conducted with great force, speed, and persistence. Patton was not impressed because the plan required a junction with Montgomery, who was notoriously slow. As Patton expected, Montgomery did not push the Canadians and the Poles to move on Falaise with any speed, and he also would not allow Patton's Americans to advance on their own to Falaise, because it was in the British sector.

Montgomery, obsessed with keeping a "tidy battlefield," thought an American advance into the British zone was an improper transgression. Bradley could have confronted Montgomery, but he did nothing.[17]

Even getting to Argentan proved difficult for Patton. On August 12, the town was being guarded by only a single German bakery company. The U.S. 5th Armored Division, just a few miles away, was on the way to occupy it. But, in defiance of orders, the Free French 2nd Armored Division, attached to Haislip's corps, usurped the road, keeping the Americans from moving down it. By the time the Americans could get past the French, a powerful German panzer force had secured Argentan.

Thus a huge gap remained open between Falaise and Argentan, which the Germans used to evacuate the pocket. The Germans did suffer from Allied bomber and fighter strikes, but when a company of the U.S. 90th Division met a Polish company in the burning village of Chambois northeast of Argentan on August 19, most of the Germans had gotten away. Even then the juncture did not create a solid barrier. Germans continued to filter through what was only a porous sieve for several more days. More than 240,000 Germans escaped in the last twelve days of August alone. They moved swiftly back toward the German frontier.

The French armored division troops, under Jacques Leclerc, had been uninterested in being at Argentan all along. They wanted to liberate Paris. On August 21, Leclerc, totally without authorization, sent a fast motorized contingent to the capital, a hundred miles away. His action raised a howl from the American command and led to a confrontation between Eisenhower and Charles de Gaulle, chief of the Free French. On August 22, Eisenhower backed down and permitted the whole French armored division to move at once to Paris, abandoning Argentan. This caused a huge rift between the Allied command and de Gaulle. The French division and civilian Parisians swiftly took over Paris. The German commander, Dietrich von Choltitz, surrendered on August 25. De Gaulle arrived in the undamaged city on the same day and took command of the French government.

During the last stages of the battle for the Falaise pocket, the senior Allied commanders were already preoccupied with getting to the Rhine River and with overrunning Germany.[18]

In the drive across France, Eisenhower opted for a "broad-front" strategy to ensure that both Britain and the United States could claim the triumph together. This refusal to decide on a single, war-winning drive guaranteed that neither side would get enough fuel and supplies to win a victory in 1944. This was a profound failure of leadership on Eisenhower's part, and it placed political considerations above military operations and human lives.

If Eisenhower had not taken this course, it would almost certainly have been possible to take advantage of German chaos to penetrate into the heart of Germany—provided that most of the available fuel, ammunition, and other vital supplies were committed to one concentrated blow to cross the Rhine at a single point. This inevitably would have meant that the commander would be Patton, because the 3rd Army was on the east and closest to Germany. Patton most definitely wanted to carry out this operation, but Bradley did not press the matter, and Eisenhower ignored his requests because he did not want to enrage the British.

Montgomery, on the contrary, argued that the major strike should be conducted by his army group. He contended, illogically, that he could drive up the coast and get across the lower Rhine in Holland before the Germans could organize a defense. This route not only was far longer than Patton's but also faced one major river barrier after another. However, the Overlord plan called for eliminating the launching sites of the V-I, the jet-powered flying bomb revenge weapon that Hitler was aiming at England. These sites were located in the Pas-de-Calais. Overlord also called for the capture of Antwerp on the Schelde River in Belgium to serve as a major supply port. Montgomery's move up the coast would uncover the V-I sites, and was one argument for giving him preference. Patton, on the other hand, argued that a strike into the heart of Germany would end the war quickly and stop the V-I attacks as well.[19]

Eisenhower gave the most fuel and supplies to Montgomery and allocated to him the U.S. 1st Army and twelve American divisions, totaling twenty-five divisions. But Montgomery's advance had little chance of ending the war quickly. And Patton, left with fifteen divisions and starved for fuel, had little chance of doing so either. Patton, for example, received 2,000 tons of supplies a day, Courtney Hodges's 1st Army, 5,000 tons. By dividing the gasoline supply between Montgomery's and Bradley's army groups, Eisenhower ensured that all would stop well short of the Rhine.

Bradley turned Patton loose before the end of the Falaise pocket battle. He gained a great deal of territory, but his tanks ran out of gas on the Moselle River near Metz on September 5.

Though Montgomery swept past the Pas-de-Calais and captured Antwerp on September 4, 1944, he failed to secure the seaward approaches to the port, and Antwerp remained unusable. In addition, he made a mess of his abortive effort to cross the lower Rhine at "a bridge too far" at Arnhem, Holland, in the Market Garden operation. This operation failed, with huge numbers of casualties.

American anger erupted over Eisenhower's decision to give Montgomery preference in receiving supplies, thereby hobbling Patton. The anger was especially great since Montgomery failed so miserably. The British charged, on the other hand, that Eisenhower should have authorized only a single, Montgomery-led advance on Berlin. They wanted Patton, who was actually within striking distance of the Rhine, to be stopped entirely, while they wanted Montgomery, who had countless streams and canals to cross, to get all the fuel and supplies.

The British argument had little validity. But—since Patton got some of the gas they thought should have gone to Montgomery—the British possessed an argument that raged on till the end of the war and well beyond it. Eisenhower, in their view, was responsible for the stalemate that came about when the Allies ran out of fuel along the German frontier in September 1944. Critics thus blamed Eisenhower for allowing the U.S. 3rd Army to get bogged down attacking Metz, for the U.S. 1st Army fighting a costly tree-to-tree battle in the Hürtgen Forest just inside the German frontier near Aachen, and for allowing the Germans time to build up strength to attack in the Ardennes during Christmas

1944 in the Battle of the Bulge. These and other clashes along the frontier cost massive Allied casualties.

The British charges against Eisenhower were unfair. But Eisenhower had shown that he did not possess an essential requirement for a successful commander: he was unable to evaluate two opposing arguments and come to a correct decision. Attempting to accommodate the interests and the pride of both the Americans and the British, he guaranteed failure. What is worse, he also guaranteed that the war would go on and that hundreds of thousands of men on both sides would die or be maimed.

Eisenhower violated one of Sun Tzu's most important imperatives. "Warfare," he says, "is the greatest affair of state, the basis of life and death, the way to survival or extinction. It must be thoroughly pondered and analyzed."[20] Eisenhower's duty as supreme commander was to end the war as rapidly and as inexpensively as possible. By dividing his resources instead of concentrating them, he ensured that this would not be done.

The continuation of the war all the way to May 1945, therefore, was largely due to the failure of leadership of Dwight Eisenhower. But another failure had already occurred. This failure was primarily the property of Bradley, though Montgomery shared some of the blame, and indirectly so did Eisenhower, who took no part in the decision. All were unable to grasp the opportunities that Patton presented to them after the Cobra breakthrough.

They could not see that Patton's plan had the potential to end the war in weeks by eliminating the German armies in Normandy, and that it was not necessary to wait to accomplish the task much later along the Rhine River. Both Montgomery and Bradley likewise failed in their conduct of the much less ambitious plan to close the Falaise-Argentan gap. If this effort had been pursued with vigor and determination, they might have captured many of the seasoned German combat troops.[21]

Sun Tzu holds that successful commanders must be able to see ways they can win. Successful commanders can seize unanticipated opportunities when they occur. This requisite vision was not present in the three senior Allied commanders in France in 1944. Only George Patton saw the proper ways forward: first the sweep down the Seine to trap the German armies in Normandy, and then a strike straight for the heart of Germany along the shortest route and on a narrow front.

Thus George Patton's slapping of two psychologically unfit soldiers in Sicilian field hospitals turned out to be a couple of the most costly episodes in the Second World War. They revealed his unstable mental condition. Though Eisenhower finally decided to keep him, Patton was doomed to occupy a subordinate position. If the incidents had not occurred, Patton would have become Eisenhower's closest military adviser, and he would have commanded the American armies in France. Patton as commander would have acted on the opportunities that he saw so clearly, and he would have conducted the kind of full-throttle, fast war of movement that the American army was skilled at and equipped for. Omar Bradley, who moved into the command position Patton would have occupied, had little imagination and never took chances. The result was that the Allies "won the war in the wrong way." They took much longer and they suffered many hundreds of thousands more casualties than were necessary.

TEN

Inchon and the Invasion
of North Korea, 1950

The United States faced a most remarkable problem in the summer of 1950. It found itself in a completely unanticipated war with a small Communist state, North Korea, and it was losing. The North Koreans had attacked the American client state of South Korea on June 25, and shattered its underequipped army. Only the swift intervention of American occupation forces in Japan kept North Korea from overrunning the entire Korean peninsula. But the Americans also were unprepared for war, and were swiftly thrown back to the narrow "Pusan Perimeter" around the southern port city of Pusan.

While American leaders were frantically trying to reinforce the perimeter, and while North Korean soldiers were continuously trying to force their way over the Naktong River, the last major barrier in front of Pusan, General Douglas MacArthur, the chief of the American Far East Command, devised a wholly unlikely riposte that would solve the entire problem, would completely avoid the North Korean army on the Naktong, and was precisely in keeping with the doctrine of Sun Tzu.[1]

MacArthur saw an opportunity that no one else saw. He saw that the North Koreans had entirely disregarded the fact that Korea is a peninsula. While the North Korean leaders were focusing on the *land* of the peninsula, MacArthur looked at the *water* that surrounded it on three sides. He knew that the U.S. Navy could carry out an amphibious landing anywhere it wanted to on the Korean shoreline, and the North Koreans, with no navy of their own, could do nothing about it.

MacArthur then looked at the double-tracked railroad that ran from North Korea through the South Korean capital of Seoul and on to the south. This railroad was supplying practically all of the food, ammunition, and fuel for the North Korean army along the Naktong. If this railroad were cut anywhere above the North Korean army, it would collapse in a matter of days because it would be deprived of nourishment. And not a shot would have to be fired at it.

MacArthur saw that Seoul was only twenty miles east of its port city of Inchon. If the Americans staged an amphibious landing at Inchon, they had only this short distance to go to sever the railroad, liberate the South Korean capital, and destroy the North Korean army. The most remarkable fact about the Inchon landing is that the entire Joint Chiefs of Staff (JCS), the top leadership of the United States, fought MacArthur's plan almost to the last minute. When they were proved to be so mistaken, MacArthur came to be viewed as a military genius, while the status of the Joint Chiefs sank like a stone. The Joint Chiefs were accordingly inhibited from calling down MacArthur only three weeks afterward when he launched an operation to conquer North Korea that was the extreme of irresponsibility and that brought disaster to American arms.

The case of MacArthur is quite unusual. His abilities and his disabilities—his capacity to see broad opportunities and his propensity to disregard plain facts—made for a crippling combination. His ability to see strategic possibilities brought on hugely ambitious operations. His incapacity to see danger led the effort to destroy North Korea into catastrophe. MacArthur was far from being the balanced commander espoused by Sun Tzu, one who can see potentials and dangers in all situations and can accommodate both in his campaigns.[2]

The defect was not apparent at Inchon because the Americans faced only minuscule North Korean forces, and the power of the U.S. Navy was overwhelming. In the subsequent invasion of North Korea, however, the outcome depended on Red China. Would the Red Chinese intervene or would they not? The answer to this question required a dispassionate, reasoned, accurate calculation.

Because MacArthur had become larger than life as a result of Inchon, his judgment carried immense weight. He ridiculed the idea that the Chinese would dare come into the war. This conclusion not only turned out to be wholly wrong, but also disregarded repeated Chinese warnings that they would intervene if American forces entered North Korea. The mistake of President Truman and his political advisers was that they listened to MacArthur and not to the warnings coming from Beijing.

The American decisions to land at Inchon and then to conquer North Korea provide some of the most convincing evidence we possess on how the capacity of human beings to make accurate judgments varies greatly between individuals and does not depend on one's background or training. Three civilian leaders—President Truman; W. Averell Harriman, Truman's closest political adviser; and Louis Johnson, secretary of defense—applauded the decision to land at Inchon. But all of the Joint Chiefs of Staff opposed it. Omar Bradley, JCS chairman, called Inchon a "blue-sky scheme" and said "Inchon was probably the worst place ever selected for an amphibious landing."[3] At the same time, there is a dangerous propensity of some civilian leaders to attribute wisdom in politics to military commanders simply because they are successful in war. This was the case with Truman and his team of political advisers. None stood up to question MacArthur's opinion that the Chinese would not enter the Korean War.

At the end of World War II, in August 1945, U.S. and Soviet officials set up the 38th parallel as a boundary on the Korean peninsula. U.S. troops were to accept the surrender of Japanese troops south of this line; Soviet troops were to accept the surrender of troops north of this line. But this military boundary quickly became a political frontier in the Cold War, with the United States setting up a client state under

Syngman Rhee in the south, and the Soviets establishing a Communist state under Kim Il Sung in the north.

On January 12, 1950, Secretary of State Dean Acheson announced an American defensive perimeter in East Asia that included Japan and the Philippines but excluded Taiwan and Korea. This pronouncement apparently convinced Kim Il Sung that the United States would not intervene if he tried to reunite the peninsula by force. He talked Joseph Stalin, the Soviet dictator, into supplying offensive arms, including 150 Soviet T-34 tanks, heavily armored monsters carrying high-velocity 85-millimeter guns. The T-34 was the best tank to come out of World War II; German panzer leader Heinz Guderian credited it with stopping the 1941 German attack on Moscow.

The Americans, fearful that Syngman Rhee would launch an attack northward, had not given the South Koreans any weapons to stop a tank, neither tanks of their own, nor antitank artillery rounds, nor antitank mines, nor the recently developed 3.5-inch "super bazooka" rocket launcher. As a consequence, the T-34s swiftly overwhelmed the South Koreans and drove them in chaos deep into the south on June 25 and the days thereafter.

President Truman believed that the attack on South Korea was the first effort of a Communist conspiracy led by the Kremlin to conquer democratic lands. He reversed U.S. policy at once, ordered General MacArthur to send American forces occupying Japan to aid the South Koreans, and got official backing from the United Nations, but little help except from the British, for a war to push back the North Koreans. Although the Americans suffered many reverses, they slowed the North Korean advance and by August were holding a tight perimeter around Pusan.

With naval forces, Truman also "quarantined" the Chinese island province of Taiwan (Formosa), which had been occupied in October 1949 by Chinese leader Chiang Kai-shek after his Nationalists were ousted from the mainland by Mao Zedong's Communist forces. Truman believed that the Chinese Reds were a part of what the Western democracies were calling "monolithic Communism," and were part of the Communist conspiracy. This ignored the fact that the Chinese Communist revolution was entirely separate from Soviet Communism, and that the Chinese had no part in the North Korean attack.

American leaders had concluded incorrectly that Communist China was a satellite of the Soviet Union. In fact, the Chinese Communists wanted to complete the unification of their country and to embark on a course of economic development unrelated to the aims of the Kremlin. Protection of Taiwan caused Beijing to conclude that the Americans had formed a secret alliance with Chiang Kai-shek and intended to invade the mainland and drive the Reds out of power. American leaders thus acquired Red China as an unnecessary enemy.

MacArthur's military concept to defeat North Korea reflected pure Sun Tzu doctrine. It required a totally committed North Korean army driving against a UN line, a *zheng* force, that held, but just barely, thereby enticing the North Koreans to fling every ounce of strength against it.

If the North Koreans could be kept focused on trying to eliminate the Pusan Perimeter, the crucial stroke could be delivered by a *qi*, or indirect, force at Inchon, far *behind* the North Korean army.[4]

The Joint Chiefs of Staff fought the Inchon site because of the extremely high tides there and the narrow approach channel. General J. Lawton Collins, the army chief of staff (and noted commander of the U.S. 7th Corps that broke through the Germans lines in Normandy in 1944), and Admiral Forrest P. Sherman, chief of naval operations, urged instead a landing at Kunsan, a small port about a hundred miles south of Inchon and only about seventy miles west of the Pusan Perimeter battle line along the Naktong River.

A landing at Kunsan would have had none of the advantages that a landing at Inchon had. It would have struck the flank of the North Koreans, requiring them only to extend their line across the peninsula.

UN forces then would be required to attack frontally up the length of the peninsula, pressing the North Koreans *on* their supplies and reinforcements, not severing them *from* their supplies and reinforcements.

Both Collins and Sherman misunderstood the purpose of strategy. It is to win while reducing the fighting and killing to the least degree possible. As Sun Tzu says, "Attaining one-hundred victories in one-hundred battles is not the pinnacle of excellence. Subjugating the enemy's army without fighting is the true pinnacle of excellence."[5] MacArthur's plan would virtually eliminate the North Korean army along the Naktong without coming anywhere close to it.

The Joint Chiefs of Staff had been established under terms of the National Security Act of 1947, which unified the command of the armed forces within a new Department of Defense and set up the National Security Council (NSC) and the Central Intelligence Agency (CIA). The Joint Chiefs of Staff were to address all American security needs. They were a committee, however, and committees seldom think creatively. The biggest creative thinker in regard to Korea was MacArthur.

MacArthur began demanding more troops than currently existed. These demands forced the United States to go on war footing. On July 19, 1950, President Truman announced an immense expansion of U.S. forces. This involved a huge call-up of National Guard units and reservists.

On July 13, the Joint Chiefs of Staff sent General Collins and General Hoyt S. Vandenberg, the air force chief of staff, to Tokyo to get more information from MacArthur about his plans. The Joint Chiefs were far more worried about a Soviet military threat to Europe than the North Korean threat to South Korea. But MacArthur pooh-poohed the danger in Europe. The Cold War, he said, would be settled in the Far East. And he argued that he should be given absolute priority over other areas.

When Collins asked MacArthur how many troops he would need to reestablish the 38th parallel border, MacArthur said his intention was to *destroy* the North Korean forces, not merely to repulse them. This was contrary to the UN mandate, which was to restore the status quo ante bellum. The North Korean army could not possibly be destroyed unless the North Korean state was destroyed. This would require invasion of North Korea and reuniting the country.

MacArthur was proposing a radical course of action that required a political decision at the highest level. Red China was certain to oppose a forcible reunion of the country. North Korea constituted a vital buffer between the United States and China. Placing American troops on the China-Korea border at the Yalu River would reinforce existing Chinese fears that the United States intended to invade China and reinstate Chiang Kai-shek.

But the Joint Chiefs did not address this matter, and neither did President Truman. Here was an abdication of responsibility, a violation of the first and most important Sun Tzu doctrine. "Warfare," he says, "is the greatest affair of state, the basis of life and death." War must be pondered deeply before it is risked.[6]

If in July 1950 the American leaders had faced up to the implications of MacArthur's purpose, they might have developed a policy that would have assuaged Red China's fears yet eliminated the military threat of Kim Il Sung. Red China might not have resisted a temporary invasion to topple Kim Il Sung's government, but would have resisted an invasion that absorbed North Korea into South Korea. This would have meant the autocratic rule of Syngman Rhee, who was completely dependent on the United States.

But the Truman administration did not address these issues. It did not make a final decision about what to do until September 27, twelve days after the invasion. Then the decision was based on a domestically popular plan to smash North Korea, not on a careful judgment of long-term American national interests—and not on an analysis of how China's anxieties could be mitigated.

The navy and the marines did not want to land at Inchon. Offshore islands slow tidal surges and produce deep mud flats at Inchon. On only four days, September 15 to 18, were tides high enough to cover the mud flats sufficiently to allow Landing Ships, Tank, or LSTs, to float in to shore. The invasion had to come in mid-September or be postponed indefinitely. Surely, navy chiefs said, there must be a better place to land.

On August 23, General Collins, Admiral Sherman, and other top officers from the Joint Chiefs of Staff met with MacArthur in Tokyo to settle the matter. Collins and Sherman pushed once more for Kunsan as the landing site. Collins made a most amazing argument. Kunsan, he said, was connected to roads that would ensure prompt union with American forces in the Pusan Perimeter! He was thinking of linking up the invasion force (10th Corps) with U.S. troops in the south (8th Army), not about severing the North Korean supply line. The entire purpose of Inchon had escaped him.[7]

MacArthur repeated the premise for the Inchon invasion: the North Koreans had committed practically all their forces against the 8th Army. They had no trained reserves to oppose the landing. A landing at Kunsan would allow the North Koreans to create a new front facing both the 8th Army and the 10th Corps, thus requiring a direct assault against the enemy and a bitter winter campaign.

But Collins and Sherman were not convinced. Back in Washington the Joint Chiefs of Staff inclined toward postponing Inchon until they were sure the 8th Army could hold the perimeter. But President Truman called Inchon a daring strategic conception and was sure it would succeed.

Distracted by the endorsement of the president on the one hand, and their own misgivings on the other, the Joint Chiefs gave MacArthur general approval on August 28, but withheld fixing a definite location and reserved the right to reconsider the landing site.[8]

Meanwhile, the North Korean command, knowing its chances of breaking through to Pusan were declining with every day, unleashed a desperate general offensive all around the Pusan Perimeter. The North Koreans had assembled 98,000 men. Against them the UN Command had about 120,000 combat troops, plus 60,000 support personnel.

UN firepower was overwhelmingly greater than North Korean firepower. Ammunition and fuel were still arriving in reduced quantities to the North Koreans, but they received only enough rations for one or two meals a day. By September 1, most North Koreans showed loss of stamina and impaired combat effectiveness.

Nevertheless these hungry and numerically inferior North Korean soldiers attacked. They broke through at several points. But desperate UN defenses and superior weapons finally blunted the incursions and threw the North Koreans back at all points. The fighting was severe, however, and the outcome still undecided. On September 5, 1950, General Walton H. Walker, commander of the 8th Army, considered retreating to a last-ditch line around Pusan harbor. During the night, however, Walker decided there would be no withdrawal.

The news of a possible flight to a "Dunkirk" evacuation zone around Pusan panicked the Joint Chiefs of Staff. They sent a frightened message to MacArthur on September 7 warning of disastrous consequences if the Inchon landing failed.

The message implied that the whole movement should be abandoned. MacArthur fired back that the chances for success were excellent. To back down now, he said, would "commit us to a war of indefinite duration, of gradual attrition and of doubtful results." The position within the perimeter was not critical, and "the envelopment from the north will instantly relieve the pressure on the south."[9]

MacArthur's message should have laid the JCS fears to rest. But it didn't. After a meeting with President Truman on September 8, they approved the plan, but their agreement remained grudging to the last. Omar Bradley said, "It was really too late in the game for the JCS to formally disapprove Inchon."[10]

After all the drama about the feasibility of landing at Inchon, the actual maneuver went off like clockwork, with few losses and no setbacks. Marines quickly seized the city and swiftly moved on toward Seoul, flanked by army troops. The only real obstacle occurred in the streets of Seoul, where a few desperate North Koreans set up roadblocks that had to be beaten down one by one. The process was never in doubt, but the city suffered great damage. The last North Korean defenders filtered out of Seoul on September 28.

Meanwhile the North Korean army facing the 8th Army in the south disintegrated within days. The survivors, hungry, usually without vehicles and mostly without weapons, streamed northward by every unguarded road and path. The North Korean army had virtually ceased to exist.

So it is quite astonishing that the JCS chief, General Bradley, called Inchon "the luckiest military operation in history."[11] Hardly any operation could have involved less luck and more meticulous elimination of chance.

The Inchon invasion exemplified precisely Sun Tzu's primary strategic doctrine of combining a *zheng* holding force with a *qi* indirect flanking force that achieves victory. Only a single American commander, General MacArthur, had pressed for this strategy. The senior command organization, the Joint Chiefs of Staff, had misunderstood it from the first and opposed it to the last. But a fundamental Sun Tzu maxim had been proved valid.

Now a decision had to be made about the fate of North Korea. What was needed was the application of an axiom that Sun Tzu considers to be the most important of all: a nation should resort to war only if all other methods fail.[12] Compromise, accommodation, acceptance of less-than-perfect solutions, all of these are preferable to combat. The outcome of no war is certain. Losses in war can never be recovered.

At this crucial moment, American leadership failed miserably. All the top leaders followed policies that would have horrified Sun Tzu and that ignored the interests of their country. A war that nobody wanted burst forth. It brought vast costs and tragedy to all participants. It could, and should, have been avoided.

The Truman administration—thinking on extremely narrow lines of what would be most advantageous to the United States—had come up with a plan to reunify Korea through elections in the north and south.[13] This implied an invasion of North Korea.

No one took Red China into account. Here blank ignorance and miscalculation created perilous conditions. The first great blunder was locating where the danger lay. The policy-makers believed that only Russia might intervene, but that this was unlikely. They thought that China would not respond on its own.

Omar Bradley summed up the official attitude. He said that Red China was under the tight control of Moscow, and that "the Russians were not ready to risk global war over Korea." If Red China ever intended to move, it would be to seize Taiwan, not "help solve Russia's problem in North Korea."[14]

But Red China's interest was not to serve the geopolitical aims of the Kremlin. It was to protect what Beijing felt were vital Chinese concerns. As far back as the Han dynasty in the time of Christ, the Chinese emperors had sought to keep Korea as a shield protecting the North China plain. Already, by its neutralization of Taiwan, the United States had shown itself to be an enemy in Red China's eyes. It could not be expected to accept a U.S. military presence on the other side of the Yalu.

It would have been much more profitable for the United States to face this problem squarely and decide where American national interests lay. They in no way would be served if Red China resisted. The United States had no incentive, given its huge concerns about Soviet ambitions in Europe, to get involved in a war with China.[15]

None of these objections were addressed. On September 27, President Truman authorized destruction of the North Korean army and approved military action north of the 38th parallel.

On October 7, the United States got the UN General Assembly to approve a resolution to unify Korea. It called for "all sections" of the population to join to hold elections for a unified government.

The Red Chinese began building up their forces along the Yalu in mid-August 1950. This came immediately after American officials commenced calls for eliminating North Korea. The most strident was a statement on August 17 by Warren R. Austin, U.S. ambassador to the UN Security Council, saying that the United Nations should see to the elimination of a Korea "half slave and half free."[16]

The most significant event, however, was release of a statement by General MacArthur on August 28 that he had sent to a Veterans of Foreign Wars (VFW) meeting in Chicago implying that the United States should develop Taiwan as a military base and level a direct threat at Communist China. This statement flew in the face of President Truman's wary handling of Taiwan.[17] MacArthur issued his statement without any notification to the Joint Chiefs of Staff or the president. It incensed Truman, and he ordered MacArthur to withdraw it, though it had already been published worldwide.

Chinese anxiety became manifest after Inchon. On October 1, while the UN General Assembly was debating the resolution to hold an all-Korea election, the Chinese premier, Zhou Enlai, announced that crossing the 38th parallel was a possible cause for war.

Red China's strongest warning came in the early hours of October 3, 1950. Zhou Enlai summoned the Indian ambassador, K. M. Panikkar, and informed him that the People's Republic (Red China) would intervene if American troops crossed the 38th parallel, but not if South Korean troops did so alone. Zhou's warning reached Washington through British channels on the morning of October 3.

Astonishingly, official Washington disregarded the warning. In a series of blind and thoughtless responses, American leaders called the warning a propaganda trick. The invasion of North Korea went ahead on October 9.

Exactly what sort of accommodation the United States could have made with Beijing is unknown. Zhou Enlai had left a large loophole by telling Panikkar that movement of South Korean troops across the 38th did not matter. South Korean troops were capable of completing the destruction of the North Korean army remnants, especially if they got more artillery, tanks, and air support.

Even after American troops moved northward, there is a possibility that the Chinese might have been satisfied with a judicious halt at the narrow waist of Korea above Pyongyang, thus leaving them with a modest buffer in front of the Yalu. This is not what the Chinese were saying, but they waited until American and South Korean forces were on Manchuria's doorstep before responding. This argues that the United States could have achieved more by negotiations than it was to achieve by two and a half years of bloody war.

The UN offensive had just got under way when President Truman, worried about the Chinese threat, decided he and MacArthur needed a face-to-face meeting. Truman selected Wake Island, a tiny U.S.-owned atoll 2,300 miles west of Honolulu and 2,000 miles southeast of Tokyo.

It was a strange encounter, not least because it seemed to elevate the general to the president's political equal. Dean Acheson, who declined to go, summed up his objections as follows: "While General MacArthur had many of the attributes of a foreign sovereign . . . it did not seem wise to recognize him as one."[18] The Joint Chiefs of Staff also didn't want to go, so General Bradley went along to represent them.

The meeting took place on October 15, 1950. MacArthur said he believed formal North Korean resistance would end by Thanksgiving. He said there was "very little" chance either the Russians or the Chinese would intervene. The Chinese, he said, "have no air force. Now that we have bases for our air force in Korea, if the Chinese tried to get down to Pyongyang, there would be the greatest slaughter."[19]

Although it was President Truman's job, not MacArthur's, to determine Red China's intentions, MacArthur's status had risen so high that neither the president nor anyone else at Wake Island questioned his views.

MacArthur's invasion plan at Inchon was virtually flawless. But the plan he came up with to occupy North Korea was astonishingly bad and poorly thought out. His orders were a direct violation of Sun Tzu maxims, which call for careful calculation and meticulous, accurate planning before launching a campaign.[20] The proper military decision was to send forces in hot pursuit straight for Pyongyang, the North Korean capital, and to dispatch fast forces overland northeast of Seoul to seal off the remnants of the North Korean army that had assembled in the "Iron Triangle" of Chorwon, Pyonggang, and Kumwha just north of the 38th parallel. Both operations required speed.

Instead, MacArthur withdrew his only rested force, the 10th Corps, already concentrated at Seoul, and sent it on a long circuitous and time-consuming voyage to an amphibious landing at Wonsan on the Sea of Japan. He assigned the 8th Army, exhausted and out of supplies after having driven up from the Naktong line, to attack northward toward Pyongyang.

There was little emphasis on speed and no attempt to capture the remnants in the Iron Triangle.

By ordering the 10th Corps—the 1st Marine Division and the army's 7th Infantry Division—to withdraw to Inchon and Pusan and to embark for the amphibious invasion, MacArthur clogged the only ports that could deliver supplies required for the offensive into North Korea. For weeks both divisions were eliminated from the order of battle.

Preparing for the amphibious landing at Wonsan took so long that South Korean soldiers got to Wonsan by foot well before the marines even got into their ships.

MacArthur's plans were woefully and manifestly wrong, and they raised sincere questions as to his judgment. But the Joint Chiefs, intimidated by the general's success at Inchon, approved them without comment.

Once Wonsan was captured, MacArthur diverted the 10th Corps to occupy northeastern Korea. The 1st Marine Division and parts of the 7th Infantry Division landed at Hungnam and moved up a narrow mountain road to the Chosin (or Changjin) Reservoir en route to the Yalu River. The remainder of the 7th Division landed at Iwon, while South Korean forces continued on up the coast of Korea toward the Siberian frontier.

Elements of the 8th Army encountered some North Korean opposition on the west, but reached the Chongchon River, about sixty miles south of the Yalu, on October 22. North Korean resistance had become weak and spotty. MacArthur ordered a quick advance by all forward elements straight to the Yalu. Accordingly, numerous small bodies of UN troops, British, American, and South Korean, each one isolated and with no support on either side, struck out for the river.

The lack of resistance, however, was deceptive. On October 6, 1950, the Chinese Communist party's Politburo decided to send "volunteers" to Korea, although no one actually volunteered, and all forces were regulars from the People's Liberation Army (PLA) dressed in Red Chinese uniforms. But the Politburo's decision to call these troops volunteers preserved the fiction that the war was limited to the Korean peninsula. This forced the United States to treat Red China as a neutral power. At the same time it served American interests, for the United States did not want to expand the war into China with all the danger this represented, especially the possibility that the Soviet Union might intervene.

The movement commenced on the night of October 18. A vast force began to slip into North Korea, completely unseen and undetected by American air reconnaissance. Marching by night and hiding by day, the Chinese forces moved in the west to blocking positions on the southern face of the high mountain mass fifty miles south of the Yalu and a few miles north of the Chongchon, and on the east to positions below the Chosin (Changjin) Reservoir.

As the U.S. 8th Army moved across the Chongchon, three Chinese armies (each with 30,000 men) secretly faced them, while two additional armies lay hidden in reserve in the mountains. On the 10th Corps front, one Chinese army was deployed south of the Chosin Reservoir, but only one of its three divisions was in a position to challenge the marines and soldiers advancing up the narrow road from the coast.[21]

The Chinese struck without warning on October 25. In a series of devastating blows, Chinese forces shredded a three-division South Korean corps, caused a South Korean regiment to vanish from the order of battle, and shattered one American regiment (the 8th Cavalry), causing one of its battalions to be abandoned for lost. The sudden onslaught so alarmed General Walker that he withdrew all forces, except for two small bridgeheads, to the south side of the Chongchon.

On the 10th Corps front, Chinese forces occupied a hill twenty miles south of the reservoir. This hill dominated the only road north. The Chinese stopped repeated attacks of the 7th Marine Regiment to seize it.

The reaction of the 8th Army, MacArthur, and the Far East Command to the appearance of the Chinese was astonishing. Their first response was denial that it could be happening. Even as the attacks resulted in shocking losses, the command was reluctant to believe UN forces were facing organized Chinese units.

Then, on November 6, one of the strangest events in the history of warfare took place. The Chinese army, in the full flush of victory, suddenly broke off contact and withdrew entirely from the fight. Australian soldiers with the British 27th Brigade on the west could plainly see the Chinese forces marching away. By the end of the day, all were gone—back into the mountains.

The only plausible explanation for this astounding event is that the Chinese leadership deliberately attacked the UN forces as a warning, and then withdrew in hopes that the United Nations would reconsider its northward movements and stop.

Whatever Beijing's intention, the reaction in Tokyo and Washington was to disregard the evidence. The Far East Command drew no lessons from the events, and no one in Washington raised a red flag.

MacArthur insisted that the march to the Yalu be continued, as if the Chinese action had not taken place at all.[22] Blame has been heaped on MacArthur because he refused to credit the evidence before his eyes. But the same evidence was before the eyes of the Joint Chiefs of Staff and the administration leaders. What was needed, of course, was a full stop, and a total reappraisal of the situation. But official Washington did nothing.[23]

As American forces were gathering supplies for the lunge to the Yalu, the Chinese concentrated 180,000 men west of the high, trackless extension of the Taebaek Mountains running northward to the Yalu and southward to the coast near Wonsan, and 120,000 men east of the mountains.[24]

Against this force, the UN Command had assembled 247,000 men, most of them Americans.

The UN offensive jumped off on the morning of November 24, 1950. The Chinese met it at once. On the west they executed a perfect Sun Tzu counterblow. Chinese forces attacked all of the UN elements advancing northward across the Chongchon River, holding them fast in a battle embrace. These blows were all classic *zheng* orthodox strikes. Meanwhile another Chinese force executed the decisive blow—a *qi* indirect strike that shattered a South Korean division at Tokchon, on the extreme east near the high mountain ridges. Tokchon was well south of the river and east of the main UN concentration along the Chongchon. This was a massive strategic flanking move designed to dislodge the entire UN position along the river. It achieved total success. The Chinese quickly penetrated into the rear of the 8th Army and unhinged the entire line.

Meanwhile, on the 10th Corps front east of the mountains, Chinese forces likewise used classic Sun Tzu methods against individual marine and army elements, holding them in place with *zheng* attacks, and surrounding them and cutting their lines of retreat with *qi* indirect attacks.

On the 8th Army front west of the mountains, all the UN forces except the 2nd Infantry Division and the Turkish Brigade were able to disengage and escape southward. These two forces were along a section of the upper Chongchong that had no roads leading away from the river. Their only way out was to move downstream for twenty-five miles, where there was a road leading south. The 2nd Division suffered 5,000 casualties and the Turks a large part of their 5,000-man force before they were finally able to break away.

The 8th Army withdrew swiftly. By the middle of December it was nervously in place below the 38th parallel and along the frozen Imjin River only a few miles north of Seoul. The initiative had passed over entirely to the Chinese. It had been the longest retreat in American history, 120 miles.

Meanwhile, around Chosin Reservoir, elements of the 1st Marine Division and 7th Infantry Division finally broke through the Chinese forces surrounding them, then staged a "breakout to the coast." The marines and the soldiers cracked every Chinese roadblock on the way to Hungnam and the sea. It was difficult and exhausting, but the vast majority of the men got through, the last elements arriving at the port on December 11.[25]

While the advance of the marines and soldiers to the coast was going on, all other UN forces in northeast Korea withdrew by ship. A huge fleet evacuated the marines and soldiers from Hungnam. On the day before Christmas 1950, the last troops fired off their last rounds, climbed into waiting landing craft, and pulled away to protecting warships. At 2:36 P.M. December 24, the U.S. fleet turned away and steamed south.

The great effort to conquer North Korea had ended in failure.

Perhaps the most important lesson we can learn from the strange case of Douglas MacArthur is that we should examine every military proposal on its merits, and not assume that a plan is good because a commander has an excellent reputation. If American leaders had been aware of and followed the maxims of Sun Tzu, or if they had merely applied critical judgment to the problem, they would have seen quite plainly that MacArthur's ideas about conquering North Korea were badly flawed.

The first and most blatant error was his disregard of how Red China would respond. Sun Tzu says never to embark on war unless all significant questions about its consequences, most especially its negative consequences, have been answered. Sun Tzu emphasizes that leaders should never allow their anger, hatred, and prejudices to influence them, and equally, should never allow wishful thinking and hope for the best to play a part.[26]

The story of how we blundered into North Korea arouses suspicion that the highest leaders in the United States listened to the assurances of MacArthur, and—because he was brilliant, and they didn't know as much about warfare as he did—they squelched their own misgivings. Sun Tzu's point is that intelligent human beings, whether experts or not, can ask all the important questions about warfare, and by careful analysis, they can get all the answers.

Because of MacArthur's mistakes and because American leaders lis-tened to him, the United States suffered a disastrous defeat, and a war nobody wanted went on for two and a half years. This war finally ended where it had started, around the 38th parallel. The same outcome could have been reached in September 1950.[27]

E L E V E N

The Abiding Wisdom
of Sun Tzu

This book shows how Sun Tzu maxims have or have not been applied in some of the most important military campaigns in the past two and a third centuries, and reveals a most enlightening fact: all the Sun Tzu principles are common sense, sincerely and earnestly applied. Commanders who did not use common sense were likely to fail. Those who did use common sense were likely to succeed.

Sun Tzu tells us to look objectively at all sides of a problem—its pitfalls as well as its possibilities. He urges us to determine what we are trying to accomplish, and to focus our main strength and effort on that goal. All this may seem obvious, but we human beings frequently allow our passions, prejudices, and selfish desires to dictate what we do.

Other maxims are: do not attack "well-regulated formations," but induce the enemy to do so and be defeated; win battles by concentration of force, mobility, and surprise; know the enemy's terrain, disposition of forces, and capabilities; do not advance into territory where one can be cut off; and rely on well-thought-out plans to win, not on the sacrifices of soldiers.

None of the Sun Tzu principles is difficult. Every one, when carried out, appears in retrospect to have been the most obvious thing to do. Success came by using intelligent, careful thought to solve a specific problem.

The following examples demonstrate some of the most important principles of Sun Tzu, and show how they have remained the same, despite the vastly different circumstances and problems faced by each of the affected leaders.

Go to extreme limits to avoid war.

Sun Tzu's first axiom is in many ways his most important. "Warfare is the greatest affair of state, the basis of life and death, the way to survival or extinction," he says.[1] The outcome of war can never be certain. Thus it should be the very last choice. Every other possibility should be pursued to the end. Compromises are far preferable to bloodshed and destruction of property and lives.

In the lead-up to the American Revolution, the British leadership paid little attention to this axiom. (See chapter 1.) The thirteen colonies already had a third as many people as Great Britain, and Adam Smith, author of *The Wealth of Nations*, predicted that America would exceed Britain in importance in a century. The only feasible solution for Britain was to grant the colonies complete equality, including equal representation in Parliament. But British leaders offered the colonists few concessions and embarked on an outright war to smash all resistance.

A similar refusal to look for any reasonable alternative to war occurred just prior to World War I in 1914. (See chapter 6.) Both sides were driven by greed and desire for revenge. The British feared the growing economic power of Germany, and France wanted to regain its lost provinces of Alsace and Lorraine. Germany was pushing aggressively its expansion overseas and was largely oblivious to the anxiety this aroused in Britain, while Austria-Hungary wanted to smash Serbia and exclude Russia from the Balkans. None of the major powers was interested in compromise. The terrible war that followed drastically weakened all five powers and set the stage for cataclysmic disasters in the generation that followed.

The United States had little to gain and much to lose if it destroyed North Korea and reunited it with South Korea in 1950. A unified Korea would not increase the power of the United States to any appreciable degree, whereas elimination of the strategic buffer of North Korea in front of the North China plain would threaten the security of Red China drastically. Beijing warned the United States emphatically that it would go to war to protect this buffer, but the Truman administration and Douglas MacArthur scorned the idea. (See chapter 10.) The administration thought only of what would be most advantageous to the United States, not what would ease tensions in East Asia. The result was a dreadful war nobody wanted that lasted two and a half years, cost the lives of hundreds of thousands of people, and led to a generation of enmity between China and the United States.

Attack the strategy of the enemy.

"The highest realization of warfare is to attack the enemy's plans," Sun Tzu says.[2] This is a primary goal. Few countries win their wars unless they find ways to counter the enemy's strategy. Yet the history of warfare shows that commanders frequently do not do so. They only concern themselves with their own strategy.

One of the most flagrant examples of this failure was that of the British in the American Revolution. The American strategy was to avoid being defeated and to wear down the British army. (See chapters 1 and 2.) This strategy was likely to succeed if the British launched repeated campaigns over the vast extent of the thirteen colonies. To attack this strategy, the British needed to find another way to win. A means lay right before their eyes: they could have occupied or blockaded all the major American ports, and protected them with the Royal

Navy. The Americans had no navy, and they depended on overseas trade to survive. Closing the ports would almost surely have forced the Americans to compromise. But the British leaders did not examine the American strategy. They were convinced their armies could humble the Americans, so they launched one campaign after another into the colonial interior. All of these campaigns failed, and the Americans won the war.

In the American Civil War, the Union strategy was to occupy the Southern states and beat down the rebellion by main force. The North had virtually nothing to protect its own territory, except a ring of fortresses built around Washington, D.C. The Confederate general Stonewall Jackson saw this glaring weakness in the North's strategy and proposed to President Jefferson Davis that a Confederate army should cross the Potomac River, occupy Baltimore, cut off the only railroad corridor to Washington from the north, force the Abraham Lincoln administration to abandon the capital, and by "making unrelenting war amidst their homes, force the people of the North to understand what it will cost them to hold the South in the Union at the bayonet's point." (See chapter 4.) Davis refused to accept Jackson's proposal. Robert E. Lee went on to fight a direct war of headlong assaults against Union armies, a method that was bound to lose.

In June 1863 when Lee invaded Pennsylvania, his army reached Carlisle, just west of Harrisburg, and Wrightsville, on the Susquehanna River. Lee knew President Lincoln would demand that the Union army remain between the Confederate army and Washington. Hence, Lee could attack Lincoln's strategy by striking out at once for Philadelphia, the second-largest city in the Union and one on the vital north-south rail corridor along the east coast. If this corridor were cut, the North would be unable to pursue the war. The Union army would be obliged to attack the Confederate army at the first opportunity. If Lee took up a fortified position on any open ridgeline, the Union army would lose. Thus Lee had already achieved a position of almost certain victory. But he was unable to see what he had gained. Instead he rushed back south and got into a fatal encounter battle with the Union army at Gettysburg. (See chapter 5.) This decision lost the war for the South.

In early 1943, after the German dictator, Adolf Hitler, had lost a 250,000-man army at Stalingrad, Field Marshal Erich von Manstein proposed that German forces withdraw to the Dnieper River, 450 miles west of Stalingrad. This would induce the Red Army to advance quickly to cut off the crossings of the river. Germany could attack this Soviet strategy by forming a large army at Kharkov, 150 miles northeast of the crossings. As the Soviets advanced westward, the German forces could drive into their northern flank. As Manstein told Hitler, this would "convert a large-scale withdrawal into an envelopment operation"[3] that would push the Russians against the Sea of Azov to the south and destroy them. It was a plan to convert defeat into victory, but Hitler could never see strategic advantages and refused. (See chapter 8.) The result was the continued retreat of the German army and defeat.

Combine zheng *direct moves and* qi *indirect moves.*

Zheng, or orthodox, maneuvers and *qi,* or unorthodox, maneuvers are Sun Tzu's fundamental principles leading to success in war, both on the battlefield and in broad strategic maneuvers.[4] In general, one holds the enemy in place with the orthodox, or direct, force and gains victory by striking at a different, usually unexpected, place with the unorthodox, or indirect, force.

The concept embodies a crucial Sun Tzu principle: armies should avoid headlong collisions wherever possible. Instead, they should move like water—going around obstacles, not challenging them frontally. Sun Tzu expresses the same idea in his axiom "The army avoids the substantial and strikes the vacuous."

The battle of Waterloo offers a cardinal example of how commanders on both sides should have used *zheng* and *qi* but did not.

The omission by the British commander, the duke of Wellington, imperiled his army. The omission by Napoléon led to his defeat. (See chapter 3.)

Wellington had lined up the British army along the Mont-Saint-Jean ridgeline, south of Waterloo. Napoléon had formed up one of his corps to assault the left center of this line. Wellington had posted a 17,000-man corps under the Dutch Prince Frederick a dozen miles to the west as a guard force. If, instead, Wellington had moved this corps only a couple miles to the west of the Mont-Saint-Jean line, it would have been in position to crash—as an indirect *qi* force—into the left flank of the French army when it attacked. This would have thrown the French army into chaos. But the move never occurred to Wellington.

Since Wellington had not placed Prince Frederick's corps just beyond his right, or western, flank, Napoléon had an open path to swing one of his own corps in a *qi* strike on the British right flank while Wellington was fully committed to defending against the direct *zheng* French frontal attack. This in turn would have thrown the British army into chaos. But Napoléon also did not think to make this move. Instead his forces crashed headlong against the British and were crushed.

In May 1862, Stonewall Jackson executed a perfect *zheng* and *qi* maneuver against the Union commander Nathaniel B. Banks. (See chapter 4.) Jackson sent his cavalry straight northward down the Valley Pike. This was the *zheng* strike that locked Banks in his entrenchments at Strasburg. Meanwhile Jackson's main force swung around to Front Royal on the northeast, in a *qi* indirect move that placed Banks in danger of being blocked from retreat and forced to surrender. Banks raced northward at the last moment, but his demoralized and weakened army was shattered at Winchester.

In 1940, Erich von Manstein conceived a spectacular *zheng* and *qi* combination when he induced Adolf Hitler to make a loud and convincing *zheng* direct attack into Holland and northern Belgium that absorbed the attention of the Allies, while the decisive *qi* indirect force of panzers struck almost unnoticed through the Ardennes. (See chapter 7.) This move forced the defeat of France and the evacuation of the British army from Dunkirk.

The *zheng* and *qi* concepts are expressed in another of Sun Tzu's axioms: "Make an uproar in the east, but strike in the west." The entire idea is summed up in a single profound sentence: "The way to avoid what is strong is to strike what is weak." *Zheng* and *qi* form a complete system of winning battles and campaigns. Their intellectual foundation is that, with deception, one can induce the enemy to misdirect his strongest forces to defend a place that appears to be the primary target but is not, thereby leaving the actual point of attack poorly defended or not defended at all.

Secure intelligent commanders.

Sun Tzu says that one of the elements mandatory for success in war is the selection and support of generals who are wise, credible, benevolent, and courageous. Armies, he says, can be victorious only if "the general is capable and not interfered with by the ruler."[5]

Selecting political and military leaders depends on many factors. Ability and determination may be present, but charisma and chance may be more important. Elected leaders gain their positions from voters, whose approval is often influenced by emotional or other considerations, not the true talent of candidates. Elected leaders might be good at delegating authority, and they might not. Some elected leaders do not want really able military commanders or other leaders under them who might challenge their authority or might compete with them for elected office. This fear of quality is almost universally true of dictators.

The case with Napoléon Bonaparte is telling. He was always insecure because he gained power by a coup d'etat. Therefore, he appointed field commanders, not because they were competent, but because they would obey him. It was only a matter of time before Napoléon made some mistake that would cause his downfall. It happened at Waterloo. The commanders he chose for the wings of his formation turned out to be incompetent. Although Napoléon failed to use a *qi* flanking force, which could have been decisive, the French still could have won if the wing commanders had seized the opportunities before their eyes. Their failure to do so lost the battle and sent Napoléon into exile on the island of St. Helena in the South Atlantic, where he died—years later. (See chapter 3.)

On July 1, 1863, at the close of the first day of Gettysburg, General Robert E. Lee refused the pleadings of General James Longstreet to move the Confederate army to the south of Cemetery Ridge. This would place the Confederates between the Union army and Washington, a move that would threaten the national capital, and a condition that Abraham Lincoln expressly forbade. It would force the Union army off Cemetery Ridge and obligate it to attack the Confederates— and almost certainly be beaten.

General Lee replied: "They [the enemy] are there in position [pointing to Cemetery Hill and Ridge], and I am going to whip them or they are going to whip me."[6]

Here is one of the signal moments in history when the incompetence of a commander is revealed for all to see. (See chapter 5.)

In August 1944, after the Allies had broken out of the Normandy beachhead, the top three Allied commanders—Dwight D. Eisenhower, Bernard Law Montgomery, and Omar Bradley—took no action when General George S. Patton Jr. proposed a swift move of American armies down the Seine River to the English Channel, cutting off all German armies still in Normandy. Here was an opportunity to end the war in weeks, but they were unwilling to alter the methodical, step-by-step advance to the Rhine River that was called for by the invasion planners. The result was almost nine more months of bitter war and the death of hundreds of thousands of men. (See chapter 9.)

In the summer of 1950, the American Joint Chiefs of Staff fought the plan of General Douglas MacArthur to stage a surprise invasion at

Inchon, near the Korean capital of Seoul, and cut off rail connection to North Koreans pressing UN forces in the south. MacArthur's plan was sure to destroy the North Korean army. (See chapter 10.) But the Joint Chiefs of Staff, unimaginative and unwilling to take chances, were overtaken with fear and fought the plan almost to the end. MacArthur, however, received the backing of President Truman and other civilian leaders, and the invasion was a complete success.

We can draw from these facts an inescapable conclusion: a leader who cannot see is doomed to failure. A Sun Tzu requirement for a successful commander is one who can take into consideration all the factors in a given situation, and then act on them. Finding such leaders should be the goal of all governments and armies. Of course we will sometimes succeed and sometimes fail. But we should always have before our eyes the example of Adolf Hitler. His inability to see drove his nation to ruin, and he is the kind of leader that we must avoid at all costs.

ACKNOWLEDGMENTS

The splendid editing and perceptive advice of Star Lawrence and Melody Conroy brought order, coherence, and a clear direction to this book. I am extremely grateful.

The challenge to the designers was great to represent the unique theme of this book in an appropriate graphic context. Ellen Cipriano conceived a truly beautiful interior typography and layout, and Ingsu Liu at Norton and Joe Montgomery with Wednesday design created a remarkably imaginative jacket design. They have produced a work of art of which I am most proud.

The campaigns and battles described in this book would be incomprehensible without accurate, clear, and illuminating maps. I am most fortunate in having Jeffrey L. Ward as my cartographer. His maps are precise, easy to understand, and lovely to look at. I am deeply appreciative.

I have relied on the astute advice and unerring counsel of my agent, Agnes Birnbaum, for a long time. I am tremendously thankful for her support and her faith in me.

Finally, I wish to recognize my sons Bevin Jr., Troy, and David, and my daughters-in-law Mary and Kim for their sturdy support and unwavering encouragement.

NOTES

In these notes, some references give only the last name of the author or editor or the last name and a short title. These works are cited in full in the Selected Bibliography. References not listed in the bibliography are cited in full the first time they appear in the notes of each chapter and then are cited by author and short title afterward. Numbers in the notes refer to the pages.

INTRODUCTION: To Avoid Strength, Strike Weakness

1. Whether Sun Tzu actually existed is not known. *The Art of War*, the short thirteen-chapter work attributed to Sun Tzu (which means Master Sun), may have evolved over time from the recorded teachings of some unknown strategist or strategists during the Warring States period in China, from the sixth to the late third centuries B.C. Some scholars argued that the work was heavily rewritten or even concocted many centuries after the supposed existence of Sun Tzu (about 400 B.C.). But in the 1970s copies of the text on bamboo and wooden strips were unearthed in two widely separated archaeological sites, in Shandong and Qinghai provinces. The texts dated back to the former Han dynasty, one as early as the second century B.C., and they were very close to the traditional text. The scholar John Minford writes, quoting the French scholar Jean Lévi, that the final text is probably the collective "product of a long process of sedimentation of strategic reflection, which eventually crystallized into the form of the manual." See Minford, xxii–xxiii.

2. Griffith, v. Basil H. Liddell Hart's celebrated concept of the indirect approach to warfare is essentially an application of Sun Tzu's combination of an orthodox holding force (*zheng*) combined with an unorthodox force (*qi*) that strikes indirectly at an unexpected place. "I began to realize that the indirect approach . . . was a law of life in all spheres," Liddell Hart writes. "Its ful-

fillment was seen to be the key to practical achievement in dealing with any problem where the human factor predominates. . . . The indirect approach is as fundamental to the realm of politics as to the realm of sex. . . . As in war, the aim is to weaken resistance before attempting to overcome it; and the effect is best attained by drawing the other party out of his defenses." See Liddell Hart, *Strategy*, 18.

3. *Mao Tse-tung: On Guerrilla Warfare* (New York: Praeger Publishers, 1961), and *Sun Tzu: The Art of War* (New York: Oxford University Press, 1971), both translated and introduced by Samuel B. Griffith. A Jesuit missionary to Beijing, Father J. J. M. Amiot, published a French translation of Sun Tzu's work in Paris in 1771. It was issued again in a French anthology in 1782. There also were four translations into Russian and one into German. Before Griffith's work, there were five translations into English, none of which was satisfactory, including that of Lionel Giles in 1910, which left much to be desired. In recent years a number of good translations have appeared. In this volume, I refer as my main source to Sawyer, *The Seven Military Classics of Ancient China*.

ONE: Saratoga, 1777

1. Frederick Jackson Turner, *The Frontier in American History* (New York: Henry Holt, 1921), 4.

2. Adam Smith gives a full discourse of this concept in the third part of chapter 7 in book 4 of *The Wealth of Nations*.

3. The first two sentences of chapter 1 of Sun Tzu's *Art of War* are, "Warfare is the greatest affair of state, the basis of life and death, the way to survival or extinction. It must be thoroughly pondered and analyzed."

4. "To effect an unhampered advance, strike their vacuities," Sun Tzu says. See Sawyer, 167.

5. Strategically, Americans were quite vulnerable to a blockade. They depended on trading their agricultural, forest, and iron products with the mother country in exchange for the manufactured products that Britain had forbidden or actively discouraged the colonies from producing on their own. Americans exported tobacco, grain, fish, pig iron, lumber, indigo, pitch, tar, sailing ships, rum, and other products, and they imported sugar and molasses, coffee, tea, spices, and many needed manufactured goods. Over time, economic deprivation would have diminished the influence of the patriots and increased the voice of the loyalists in urging the colonies to reach an accommodation with

Britain. In 1759, New England sent to England goods valued at £38,000 and imported goods from England valued at £600,000.

6. A flotilla posted at Portsmouth could have blocked all access to the ports on Chesapeake Bay. Philadelphia and Wilmington, Delaware, need not to have been occupied. These ports could have been blockaded by warships stationed in the upper Delaware Bay.

7. Mahan, 156. Mahan is referring to using the Royal Navy to seal off the Hudson River and Lake Champlain and thus isolate New England. He makes no specific reference to a full-blown blockade of American ports, but the concept is implicit in his comment (p. 157) that if France had not entered the war, Britain "would have been able to reduce the Atlantic seaboard."

8. Ibid., 156.

9. For an analysis of Sun Tzu's thinking on this subject, see Sawyer, 155–56. Sun Tzu admonishes commanders to recognize existing elements that can be exploited or to create opportunities—to not depend on opportunities materializing on their own and to never rely on chance or fortuitous circumstances.

10. Eighteenth-century European armies were largely composed of intensely drilled mercenaries drawn from the dregs of society. Wars were largely between kings to settle dynastic disputes. There was little emphasis on loyalty to one's country. Men were not motivated by patriotism. Few decent men were willing to undergo the ferocious discipline and merciless punishments of military service. Soldiers were taught to fear their officers more than the enemy. They were not allowed to mingle with the civilian population, for fear that they would terrorize the people or desert. In peacetime, soldiers were kept in barracks. They were well fed and clothed but were allowed little freedom. In the field, troops were forbidden to forage, and they were fed from storage depots called magazines. A European army was supposed to carry eighteen days of rations with it. The soldier himself carried bread for three days; the bread wagon that followed each company carried bread for six days; and the wagons of the quartermaster carried flour for nine days. See Delbrück, 409. However, armies generally didn't advance for more than a week because new magazines had to be set up if an army marched into enemy territory. Soldiers were expensive, and generals usually sought to avoid battle. Most campaigns were attempts to force the enemy to withdraw by maneuvering on his line of supply. But once battles were joined, they were fought with fury and tenacity and were usually headlong direct assaults. Casualties could be devastating. In the Seven Years' War, for example, in *each* of four battles involving Prussians, more men were killed than in all of the fighting in the campaigns of the French Revolution up

to and including Napoléon's Italian campaign of 1796–1797. These battles
were Prague, 1757; Zorndorf, 1758; Kunersdorf, 1759; and Torgau, 1760. See
Delbrück, 402. The English duke of Marlborough was key to developing new
offensive battle tactics that characterized eighteenth-century battles. The tactics
were made possible by the flintlock musket (whose flint sparks more reliably
ignited gunpowder than the match of the older matchlock musket), and by the
universal adoption of the socket bayonet in the last years of the seventeenth
century. Firing was usually delivered at close range—thirty to fifty paces—and
under cover of the smoke from the discharges, the assault was driven home
with the bayonet. Marlborough's tactics were to pin the enemy down by persistent infantry attacks, then to break him by shock action of the cavalry, using
the sword or saber only. Marlborough allowed his cavalry only three pistol or
musket shots during an entire campaign, and these were to be used to protect horses while grazing, not in combat. The new tactics were deadly to both
attacker and defender. The most staggering losses occurred to one side when
it buckled from attack and collapsed in disorder. In these circumstances, entire
regiments and sometimes whole wings of a retreating army were destroyed or
forced to surrender. The battle of Blenheim in Bavaria on August 13, 1704,
is an example of the extreme costs of combat when generals decided to fight.
Marlborough, commanding an allied army of English, Dutch, Germans, and
Austrians, met a superior French and Bavarian army on the banks of the Danube River. Marlborough sent infantry to hold in place the enemy garrisons in
two villages. The allied soldiers endured enormous casualties in frontal attacks
on these villages. The resolution of the battle occurred when Marlborough
launched a direct infantry assault on, followed by a cavalry breakthrough of, the
French line between these two villages. The assault crushed French opposition.
Nine French infantry battalions holding this line (about 7,000 men) were cut
down to the last man. The French and Bavarians lost 38,000 men, more than
half of their entire army. The allies lost 4,500 men who died and 7,500 who
were wounded, or about a quarter of the allied force. See Fuller, *A Military History*, vol. 2, 127–55.

11. Sawyer, 162.
12. Strategically this was an excellent plan. New England was politically the most
    important region of colonial America and was the cockpit of the revolution.
    Along with New York, it was the easiest to invade because Canada could be
    used as a base of operations. Besides, the British already possessed New York
    City as their primary power center. If the rebellion could be extinguished in
    New England and New York—and the British army was strong enough to

carry this out—the British generals believed the central and southern colonies could be subdued piecemeal over time.

13. Sawyer, 177.

14. Fuller, *A Military History*, vol. 2, 161–86.

15. Ketchum, *Saratoga*, 86–87.

16. Ibid., 104–5, 260–61. When Howe received Germain's letter, he was on the voyage to capture Philadelphia. Howe replied to Germain on August 30, 1777, that it was already too late to cooperate with Burgoyne's campaign.

17. Sawyer, 169.

18. Ketchum, *Saratoga*, 283.

19. Ibid., 161.

20. Ibid., 158.

21. Burgoyne's goal was Albany, on the right, or west, bank of the Hudson. He crossed to the west bank near Fort Edward because there was no opposition there and because the river broadened as it flowed southward, making it more difficult to cross at lower points. Any farther advance down the east bank would likely mobilize strong American opposition, which would make it difficult to force a lower passage. Since Burgoyne had made no move toward New England, the Americans were certain that Albany was his objective. Thus they were not obliged to divide their troops to protect New England and could concentrate at Bemis Heights.

22. British Major General Charles Grey led 1,200 British troops, mainly light infantry from thirteen regiments, in a night attack against Wayne, who had about twice as many men. Grey ordered his troops to remove flints in order to prevent them from firing their muskets. He was subsequently nicknamed "No Flint" Grey. The attackers used only their bayonets and achieved complete surprise. Wayne's force was routed and fled, losing 53 men who were killed, 113 who were wounded, and 71 who were captured. Here was a successful employment of the British doctrine of winning "with zeal and with bayonets only." However, it was achieved against an American force that was taken unawares. The conditions of the Paoli battle were extremely unusual and not conducive to being repeated widely.

23. Howe had divided his army, sending some troops to seize a river fort (Billingsport) near Chester, detailing others to escort supplies up from Head of Elk, and keeping a large detachment in Philadelphia. The remaining force, about 9,000 men, was encamped at Germantown. General Washington devised a plan to send American forces southward in an attack down four roads to Germantown. Maryland and New Jersey militia were to move down the easternmost

road. Pennsylvania militia were to occupy the western one, or Manatawny Road, near the Schuylkill River. Three divisions under Nathanael Greene would proceed down Limekiln Road and strike the British right, or eastern, flank. John Sullivan's column of three brigades was to head directly into Germantown on the Skippack Road, followed by the division of William Alexander. The main strike was from Sullivan's three brigades. They rolled back the British for two miles. But, getting no help from the east, because Greene was slow to arrive, Sullivan was forced to spread out Anthony Wayne's brigade in that direction. American General Adam Stephen, leading his men westward toward the sound of the guns, blundered into Wayne's men and began firing at them. Believing the British were about to enfilade, Wayne's men fled, panicking the rest of Sullivan's force and causing the entire attack to fall apart. Washington's plan was too sophisticated for officers who lacked much field experience, while many of the American troops were raw and subject to panic. Howe, realizing his mistake in dividing his troops, abandoned Germantown and pulled his army back to Philadelphia.

24. Spain declared war on Britain a year later, on June 21, 1779, but refused to recognize American independence. On December 20, 1780, Britain declared war on the Netherlands because of clandestine Dutch trade with the American states.

TWO: The Carolinas, Yorktown, and Independence, 1781

1. Charles Dickens gives the essence of British class distinctions in *The Chimes*: "Oh let us love our occupations, Bless the squire and his relations, Live upon our daily rations, And always know our proper stations." See Alan C. Jenkins, *A Village Year* (Exeter, England: Webb and Bower, 1981), 50.
2. Sawyer, 161.
3. Catastrophe almost always results when an army attempts to hold a city against a stronger enemy that can sever contact with the outside, cut off the food supply, and commence devastating bombardment. This has been true throughout history. Alexander the Great took months but eventually overwhelmed the Phoenician city of Tyre in present-day Lebanon. The Confederates made the same mistake in trying to hold Vicksburg, and Adolf Hitler lost an entire army of 250,000 men trying to hold Stalingrad in World War II. A weaker army should never allow itself to get bottled up in a city or fortress, but should move into the open where it has the opportunity to maneuver and to fight.

4. Theodore A. Dodge, *Alexander* (New York: Houghton Mifflin, 1890; London: Greenhill, 1991), 657. Citation is to the Greenhill edition.

5. There's an old joke that the people of South Carolina were so convinced of the importance of their main town that mothers taught their children that the Ashley and Cooper rivers come together at Charleston to form the Atlantic Ocean.

6. Mao Zedong, 9–10.

7. Ketchum, *Victory at Yorktown*, 99.

8. It is much more difficult to hit a moving target when one is firing down at it than when one is firing from below at a stationary target silhouetted against the skyline. Aim while firing down is usually much less accurate because the target's elevation (that is, the distance from the firer as well as the angle of fire) is changing constantly.

9. Nathanael Greene and a small American force returned to South Carolina in the spring of 1781 and ousted the British from Camden and three other outposts in the interior.

10. Germain wrote to Clinton on May 5, 1781: "I am commanded by His Majesty to acquaint you that the recovery of the southern provinces, and the prosecution of the war by pushing our conquests from the south to north, is to be considered as the chief and principal object for the employment of all the forces under your command, which can be spared from the defense of the places in His Majesty's possession." See Fuller, *A Military History*, vol. 2, 316.

11. As J. W. Fortescue, the celebrated historian of the British army, writes, "The truth was that Clinton, Cornwallis and Germain were all of them in favor of a campaign in the middle colonies. Clinton wished to await the arrival of reinforcements and of a covering fleet, and meanwhile secure a naval base. Cornwallis was for evacuating New York, transferring the principal base of the British to the Chesapeake, and opening the campaign there at once. Germain desired to combine both designs after some incomprehensible fashion of his own." See ibid., 323, citing J. W. Fortescue, *A History of the British Army*, vol. 3, 396–97.

12. A strategy of holding or blockading the American ports would cause the Royal Navy to disperse its ships to protect each location. Thus, the French could concentrate their fleet to strike at one of these locations and be certain of superiority. However, such a strike almost never could be so sudden as to trap a protecting British squadron in harbor. It could almost certainly put out to sea. Other British ships could be swiftly assembled from other ports to challenge a French fleet, so its superiority at any location would be temporary. A French fleet could break a sea blockade for a short time—in Chesapeake or Delaware bays or covering Newport, as examples—but it would be unlikely to defeat a

British land garrison protecting a port. This was shown most graphically at Savannah, where British defenses turned back a mostly French land attack, causing the French fleet to return to France. In any event, the length of time available for a French fleet to besiege and attack a British-held port would be extremely limited, because all Royal Navy ships within reach would be sailing at top speed to challenge it.

13. Sun Tzu writes, "If I determine the enemy's disposition of forces while I have no perceptible form, I can concentrate my forces while the enemy is fragmented. If we are concentrated into a single force while he is fragmented into ten, then we attack him with ten times his strength." See Sawyer, 167.

14. Luvaas, 80.

15. In 1778, France had 80 ships of the line in good condition, while Spain had 60 ships of the line. The Royal Navy had about 150 ships of the line out of a total of 228 ships of all classes. A ship of the line generally had 74 guns, though a few had more and some had fewer. The French and Spanish ships were superior in size and artillery. A British advantage was unity of aim, whereas naval coalitions are usually unable to work long in concert. But Britain was compelled to fight a war around the globe. It had to divide its sea power to protect the home islands and to cover North America, the West Indies, the Mediterranean, and India and the East Indies. A flotilla in any one of these theaters was limited in size. Thus France, though weaker overall, could concentrate superior force in one theater for a limited period.

16. Washington was not gifted with much strategic insight. He had been focused on the British base at New York since being ousted from the city in September 1776. But a French assault on New York would not likely have been decisive. One problem was that the deep-drafted French ships would have had trouble forging the shallow bar at Sandy Hook. Thus a naval bombardment of the New York defenses would have been difficult. The Royal Navy ships stationed at New York would very likely have been able to escape to the open sea. British fortifications were formidable and probably would have withstood the first French onslaught. De Grasse could not keep his fleet at New York long because all British ships within range would converge on him. Not for a moment did French policy contemplate risking France's largest fleet in an all-out showdown with the British in order to bring about the independence of the United States. France's main goal was humbling Britain, not helping America. When Royal Navy ships arrived in force, the siege would be broken. So the window of opportunity would be small and success problematic. Even in the unlikely event that a French assault was successful and the British garrison forced to surrender,

British naval power could still have been concentrated in the Chesapeake, and Cornwallis could have embarked on the new campaign to subdue the middle colonies. On the other hand, if de Grasse struck for the Chesapeake, not New York, a successful sealing off of the Virginia Capes would be sufficient to force Cornwallis's surrender, with no other action required by de Grasse's fleet.

17. Ketchum, *Victory at Yorktown*, 139.

18. For an analysis of the brilliant work of Benjamin Franklin, John Jay, and John Adams to gain a peace treaty as well as expansion of the American frontiers to the Mississippi River, see Bevin Alexander, *How America Got It Right* (New York: Crown, 2005), 11–14.

19. Sawyer, 157.

THREE: Napoléon at Waterloo, 1815

1. Leonard Krieger, *Kings and Philosophers, 1689–1789* (New York: W. W. Norton, 1970), 18–19.

2 Fuller, *The Conduct of War*, 46.

3. Bevin Alexander, *How the South Could Have Won*, 157.

4. Delbrück, 434.

5. Sun Tzu says to avoid all actions not based on detailed analysis of the situation and study of the combat options, which must take into consideration one's capabilities. Hence prejudices and anger should never be permitted to influence decisions. One should create opportunities for victory. One should never depend on them appearing on their own. See Sawyer, 154–55.

6. Napoléon owed much to French military thinkers who came before him. The most important of them were Pierre-Joseph de Bourcet (1700–1780); Jacques-Antoine-Hypolyte, comte de Guibert (1743–1790); Jean-Baptiste Vaquette de Gribeauval (1715–1789); and Chevalier Jean du Teil (1733–1820). Bourcet conceived a "plan with branches," or dividing an army into several dispersed columns and marching them on separate targets. Since it is impossible for an enemy to be in strength everywhere, a commander can mislead the enemy by dividing his forces, making the enemy believe the main force is coming to a place different from the one he expects. The enemy would be forced to abandon his own plans and disperse his troops to meet the new threats. The enemy also might concentrate on one main point and weaken secondary points. A commander following Boutcet's plan could gain at least one of his objectives. But Bourcet insisted that columns remained close enough so two or more could combine to overwhelm an objective weak-

ened by the enemy's division of his own forces. Guibert conceived of a more mobile form of warfare. He invented the breaking up of solid army columns into separate divisions that could march on a separate route. If an army was divided into a number of divisions moving on different roads, the enemy would be confused, allowing the commander to choose where he could strike with the best chance of success. Guibert also wanted to end the existing practice of private contractors bringing food to troops on the march from magazines or supply bases in the rear. He wanted army officers to learn supply. He also wanted an army to live at the enemy's expense in their own country. The kind of soldier that could operate in the environment Guibert advocated did not exist in the mercenary armies of the eighteenth century. A freer, more self-reliant soldier dedicated to his task and his country was required. This sort of soldier materialized in the largely volunteer French armies that came with the revolution. They could be trusted to forage for food, and not desert at every opportunity. Guibert also advocated reducing the weight of cannons so as to increase their mobility. His aim was to achieve quick concentrations of cannons at a single point on the enemy's line, where they could create gaps for a decisive breakthrough. Finally, Guibert advocated that a commander never attack an enemy headlong, but he should immediately turn or flank the enemy's position. This would force the enemy to move, thereby ending the static warfare that was common in the period. Gribeauval's contribution was in vastly reducing the weight of field artillery, as advocated by Guibert. Du Teil created light horse-drawn smoothbore cannons that could keep up with the troops. His aim was to get a large number of guns quickly to a weak point in the enemy line, and to force a breach there with cannon fire. In 1788–1789 Napoléon, only nineteen years old, commanded a demonstration squad at the Artillery Training School at Auxonne, where du Teil's new artillery theories were being tried out. Here, Napoléon formed the basic of his military thinking by actual practice and by reading military treastises. See Bevin Alexander, *How Great Generals Win*, 97–100.

7. Dodge, 197; Fuller, *The Conduct of War*, 48–49. Napoléon never articulated a coherent analysis of his ideas about war. However, campaigns reveal 1) his invariable reliance on the offensive; 2) his trust in speed to economize time and 3) to effect strategic surprise; 4) his insistence on concentrating superior force on the battlefield, particularly at the decisive point of the attack; and 5) his carefully thought-out protective (or defensive) system.

8. Fuller, *The Conduct of War*, 48–51.

9. Parker, 204–5. Napoléon's great blind spot was his inability to see that a

more perfect peace is the true aim of war. Achieving a just and enduring peace should be the ruling idea of policy, and victory the means toward achieving it. The nineteenth-century Prussian theorist on war, Carl von Clausewitz, was equally blind to the true aim of war. His theory that violence should be pushed to its utmost bounds ends in failure. The English military historian J. F. C. Fuller writes that a far better theory of war is offered by the French philosopher Charles de Secondat, the baron de Montesquieu (1689–1755): "Nations should do each other the most good during peacetime and the least harm during wartime without harming their true interests." See Fuller, *The Conduct of War*, 76.

10. Napoléon wanted Europe to share in the new wealth being created in Britain by the machines of the Industrial Revolution. "Why should they [the English] alone reap the benefits which millions of others could reap as well?" he asked. Napoléon believed that Britain profited solely from trade. He saw Europe as losing. He did not understand that free trade would create more wealth for everyone. For this reason Napoléon set up the Continental System to prevent British trade with Europe. But this system deprived the Europeans of goods that Britain alone could provide. This led to deep opposition to Napoléon's policy and to its ultimate failure. Britain was threatened by loss of trade, but it also felt that a united Europe would jeopardize its survival as the dominant maritime power. This was not necessarily so, and a more open trade policy by Napoléon would have reduced this fear.

11. The English military strategist J. F. C. Fuller understood Napoléon's obsession quite clearly. "In his first campaign in Italy (1796–1797)," he writes, "his aim was to seek out his enemy and destroy him in battle. This, and that he violated neutral territory, lived on the country, made war self-supporting by exactions and plunder, and pressed home his victories with relentless pursuits, shocked his contemporaries, who looked on these unmannerly operations, not as legitimate acts of war, but as the incursions of a barbarian." See Fuller, *The Conduct of War*, 44.

12. Ibid., 54.

13. The narrative on the Waterloo campaign is drawn from Fuller, *A Military History*, vol. 2, 494–539; Creasy, 298–302; Chandler, *On the Napoleonic Wars*, 134–39, and *Waterloo*; Blond, 469–99; Georges Lefebvre, *Napoleon: From Tilset to Waterloo, 1807–1815* (New York: Columbia University Press, 1969), 358–69. See also Colin, and Chandler, *The Campaigns of Napoleon*.

14. Sawyer, 156. Sun Tzu does not specify the central position, but it is implicit in his admonition as one of several ways to maneuver one's army into a tactically

advantageous position, concentrate on focused targets, exploit terrain, and aim at a decisive objective.

15. Ibid., 161, 163. Sun Tzu says to engage the enemy only if one's forces are superior to the enemy's or at least match them. One should retreat otherwise. "A small army that acts inflexibly will become the captives of a large army," he writes. Sun Tzu also says one cannot make the enemy conquerable, one can only make oneself unconquerable. "Being unconquerable lies with yourself, being conquerable lies with the enemy." One can be unconquerable whether one has inferior or superior forces. If inferior, one should withdraw and seek a different approach; if superior, one can contemplate victory, but actual victory will depend on what the enemy does. This implies that victory comes as a result of deceptive actions and inventive strategy, not because one merely has a larger army. Small armies can defeat large armies by strategic or tactical moves that make them superior in critical situations, even if they are weaker overall.

16. Fuller, *A Military History*, vol. 2, 495.

17. Sawyer, 169.

18. This concept is embodied in the following Sun Tzu admonition: "The highest realization of warfare is to attack the enemy's plans; next is to attack their alliances; next to attack their army; and the lowest is to attack their fortified cities [which by inference also means any heavily fortified position]." Finding out the enemy's plans is the same as determining the enemy's strategy. As part of this concept Sun Tzu says to engage the enemy only if one's forces are superior to the enemy's or at least match the enemy's. Otherwise, one should retreat. See ibid., 161.

19. Fuller, *A Military History*, vol. 2, 503.

20. Ibid., 510.

21. Fear that they were about to be assaulted on their rear unhinged the soldiers of Vandamme's 3rd Corps. Many took flight, and one of Vandamme's division commanders turned his cannons on fugitives who were running away. The Prussians took advantage of the disorder in the 3rd Corps and assaulted St. Amand vigorously. Had the Young Guard of the Imperial Guard not arrived to counterattack, the entire 3rd Corps would probably have disintegrated.

22. By driving into the Prussian line at Ligny, Napoléon pushed the two westernmost Prussian corps westward, the only direction they could go initially to avoid the Imperial Guard and pursuing French cavalry. They then could move

north. Napoléon assumed that, once clear of the battlefield, they would turn northeast toward their supply base at Liège.

23. Michel Ney was the preeminent example of Napoléon's refusal to raise up responsible military leaders. By appointing only commanders who would obey him, he never developed leaders with great military skill who were capable of taking charge and winning battles on their own. At Waterloo, therefore, Napoléon had few choices, none of high capability. Ney had a record of outstanding bravery but no record of outstanding leadership. Only Marshal Louis-Nicolas Davout exhibited high command capability, and Napoléon never advanced him to positions where he might threaten his authority. Ney was known as a touchy and temperamental commander. He was so impulsive while serving in Spain that he was sent home in near-disgrace in 1811. After Waterloo, Napoléon acknowledged that it had been a great mistake to employ him. See Ney, Michel, *Encyclopaedia Britannica*, 15th edition, Macropedia (Chicago: 1978), vol. 13, 55–57; Fuller, *A Military History*, vol. 2, 494–95.

24. Fuller, *A Military History*, vol. 2, 519–20.

25. Ibid., 521.

26. Grouchy had actually learned at 10:00 P.M. on June 17 that the Prussians were concentrating at Wavre. That's when he sent off his message to Napoléon. He should have recognized that the two armies were only nine miles apart and could readily unite. He should have turned his two corps northwest between Wavre and Mont-Saint-Jean at once. If he had moved immediately, he would have had time to block the Prussians entirely from aiding the British. By 11:30 A.M. on June 18, the Prussians already had moved so far toward Mont-Saint-Jean that he could only strike the flank of the advancing corps.

27. Sawyer, 164–65.

28. Ibid., 168, 170.

29. Ibid., 159.

30. Ibid., 157.

31. Account of Captain Rees Howell Gronow, at http://en.wikipedia.org/wiki/Battle_of_Waterloo.

32. Fuller, *A Military History*, vol. 2, 532.

33. Ibid., 530.

34. Waterloo, 18 June 1815: Charge of the Imperial Guard, 7 P.M., Captain H.W. Powell, First Foot Guards, at http://home.iprimus.com.au/cpcook/letters/pages/waterimp.htm.

35. Fuller, *A Military History*, vol. 2, 537–38.

FOUR: *The Civil War Campaigns of 1862*

1. This concept is spelled out by Sun Tzu: "If I dare ask, if the enemy is numerous, disciplined, and about to advance, how should we respond to them? I would say, first seize something that they love for then they will listen to you." Two other related admonitions: "If the enemy opens the door, you must race in." "Attack what they love first." See Sawyer, 179, 183.

2. The narrative on the 1862 campaigns is largely drawn from Bevin Alexander, *Lost Victories, Robert E. Lee's Civil War,* and *How the South Could Have Won.*

3. It never occurred to General McClellan that the Confederate army around Fairfax should have been challenged with a strong move directly against it. This would have held the Rebel army in place and prevented it from interfering with the decisive Union movement by sea to Fort Monroe and a drive up the peninsula to Richmond. A Union frontal confrontation would have been a Sun Tzu *zheng,* or orthodox direct movement. McClellan's march up the peninsula would have been a Sun Tzu *qi,* or unorthodox indirect movement. With the main Confederate army unable to extricate itself, McClellan would have faced little opposition. By ignoring the opportunity, McClellan permitted Joseph E. Johnston's Rebel army to march to Richmond and to challenge him with nearly its full strength. McClellan's peninsula campaign, therefore, was a complete violation of Sun Tzu's fundamental method of achieving victory in battle. The North had ample forces to carry out such a move. Nathaniel B. Banks's army of 23,000 men and Irvin McDowell's corps of 38,000 men, if combined, would have been only slightly inferior to Johnston's army, and troops from the forts encircling Washington could have been called upon. McClellan's army of 100,000 men would have been unaffected.

4. Since Shenandoah Valley streams drain northward into the Potomac River, movement southward in the valley is up, not down.

5. Sun Tzu says, "One who does not know the plans of the feudal lords [that is, the enemy] cannot prepare alliances beforehand. Someone unfamiliar with the mountains and forests, gorges and defiles, the shape of marshes and wetlands cannot advance the army. One who does not employ local guides cannot gain advantages of terrain." See Sawyer, 169. Magruder's strength as well as his defensive fortifications could readily have been determined by spies. In any event, Magruder's manpower could not have been but a fraction of McClellan's because McClellan had positive information that the bulk of the Confederate army was at Richmond.

6. Ibid., 161.

7. In the Civil War and in most wars up to World War II, soldiers marched on foot to their destinations. They marched in formations, usually columns or files (front to back), and in a number of ranks (across, usually three or four files marching beside each other)—hence the term "rank and file" for private soldiers as a body. The military term for this moving in formation was "marching in ranks." Since troops had to "remain in ranks" in order to march with the formation, anyone who dropped by the wayside "fell out of ranks," while those who did not "remained in ranks."

8. Allan, *History of the Campaign*, 85.

9. Goodwin, 432.

10. Sun Tzu says, "Configurations of terrain are an aid to the army. Analyzing the enemy, taking control of victory, estimating ravines and defiles, the distant and near, is the way of the superior general." This means that a skillful general estimates fully the difficult and the easy aspects of terrain, the advantageous and the harmful, the distant and the near. "One who knows these and employs them in combat will certainly be victorious. One who does not know these nor employ them in combat will certainly be defeated." See Sawyer, 177.

11. *The War of the Rebellion*, vol. 12, part 3, 859. See also Bevin Alexander, *Lost Victories*, 59, note 16.

12. Jackson's first proposal to Lee was to ask for 5,000 reinforcements to send to Edward Johnson to stop Frémont's advance temporarily. Jackson then intended to march his army northward to Luray, cross at Thornton Gap (present-day U.S. Route 211) to Sperryville on the eastern slope of the Blue Ridge, and from there turn north, leaving the enemy in doubt as to whether he was aiming at Front Royal to the northwest or Warrenton to the northeast. Warrenton was only twenty-five miles from Centreville and the main Federal positions guarding Washington. This march along a single line would immobilize the Washington garrison, keep Irvin McDowell's 38,000-man corps from marching to the aid of McClellan, and force Banks to retreat, since his lines of supply would be threatened—all with practically no casualties. Lee could not promise any more troops, however, and Jackson was forced to abandon this plan. But it demonstrates Jackson's strategic brilliance in a most graphic manner.

13. Henderson, vol. 1, 288. Citation is to the Konecky and Konecky edition.

14. *The War of the Rebellion*, vol. 12, part 3, 892–93; Allan, *History of the Campaign*, 88.

15. *The War of the Rebellion*, vol. 12, part 3, 896–98. There is no record of Lee's response, but he probably got President Davis's approval. See Bevin Alexander, *Lost Victories*, 76, note 7.

16. Sawyer, 161.

17. Henderson, vol. I, 174–76. Citation is to the Konecky and Konecky edition. Henderson's source for Jackson's proposal was a personal letter he received from General Smith.

18. Sawyer, 160.

19. All of Jackson's proposals to Colonel Boteler are recorded in a narrative by A. R. Boteler in *Southern Historical Society Papers*, Richmond, Va., vol. 40, 165, 172–74.

20. The first commander of the Army of Northern Virginia was Pierre G. T. Beauregard of Louisiana, who commanded at the battle of First Manassas, or First Bull Run, on July 21, 1861. His preparations for the battle were poor, and he was duped by the Union commander, Irvin McDowell, who unleashed a surprise strike on the Confederate left flank. Beauregard avoided disaster only because McDowell made one mistake after another in the conduct of the battle. The South's top leadership recognized that Beauregard was incapable of independent command and sent him off to the western theater, replacing him with Joseph E. Johnston. In the west Beauregard failed to produce results and was relieved. Later in the war, however, he served with distinction in subordinate roles where he was not called on to make major independent judgments.

21. *Southern Historical Society Papers*, vol. 40, 172–74. Jackson's proposal, with Lee's and Davis's comments written on it, was reproduced as a manuscript in *The Centennial Exhibit of the Duke University Library* (Durham, N.C.: Duke University, 1939).

22. Sawyer, 168. Sun Tzu admonishes the general to avoid the substantial and to attack the vacuous. Therefore, a general almost never should attack an enemy headlong. "All warfare," Sun Tzu says, "is based on deception. Supreme excellence consists in breaking the enemy's resistance without fighting." To achieve this, Sun Tzu recommends that the successful general "march swiftly to places where he is not expected."

23. Major Thomas R. Phillips, ed., *Roots of Strategy* (Harrisburg, Penn.: Military Service Publishing, 1941), 407–41.

24. Liddell Hart, *Strategy*, 363. Liddell Hart describes this concept more fully in a 1925 book, *Paris, or the Future of War*.

25. Sawyer, 154.

26. Ibid., 158.

27. We know that Jackson devised this new tactical system immediately after the Seven Days battles, because Jackson's actions during the campaign against Union General John Pope were directed at getting the enemy to attack, not for

the Confederates to attack. Jackson was so reticent at explaining his theories, however, that we can get only a hint of his thinking in his comment just prior to the battle of Fredericksburg in December 1862 to Heros von Borcke, a Prussian officer on the staff of cavalry chief Jeb Stuart. When Borcke wondered aloud whether the Rebels could stop an assault by the vast Federal army arrayed in front of them, Jackson replied, "Major, my men have sometimes failed to take a position, but to defend one, never!" After the battle of Chancellorsville, in the spring of 1863, Jackson said much the same thing to his medical officer, Hunter McGuire: "We sometimes fail to drive them from position, they always fail to drive us." The conclusion we can draw is that since Rebel soldiers could always defend attacks, the Confederates should avoid direct assaults themselves and induce the enemy to attack. See Bevin Alexander, *How the South Could Have Won*, 106.

28. *The War of the Rebellion*, vol. 19, part I, 65.

29. Lee's determination to attack McClellan is proved by a statement Lee made to historian William Allan on February 15, 1868, in Lexington, Virginia: "Had McClellan continued his cautious policy [of advancing] for two or three days longer [after the Confederates seized Harpers Ferry], I would have had all my troops reconcentrated on the Maryland side, stragglers up, men rested, and intended then to attack McClellan, hoping the best results from the state of my troops and those of the enemy." See Allan, *The Army of Northern Virginia in 1862*, 440–41 (citation is to Da Capo Press edition); Freeman, *Lee's Lieutenants*, vol. 2, 715–23.

30. Robert Lewis Dabney, *Life and Campaigns of Lieut.-Gen. Thomas J. (Stonewall) Jackson* (New York: Blalock & Company, 1866; Harrisonburg, Va.: Sprinkle Publications, 1983), 595. See also Bevin Alexander, *How the South Could Have Won*, 300, note 9.

FIVE: Gettysburg, 1863

1. Lee wanted to swing around the Union army at Antietam, but he did not have the space to do so. The battle at Chancellorsville is the only other time that Lee accepted Jackson's proposals to carry out such flank attacks. His decision was forced on him because Hooker had placed a huge force on Lee's left, or western, flank, while threatening his right, or eastern, flank at Fredericksburg with another huge force. There was no other way (except retreat southward) to prevent these two forces from converging on the Confederate army. A strike on Hooker's western flank emerged as a possibility when Lee's cavalry chief, Jeb

Stuart, reported that the western end of Hooker's line was "floating in the air," meaning it had no defensive emplacements facing west. But Jackson, not Lee, proposed the exact location of the strike, its size (Jackson's whole corps), the resolve to roll up the Union western flank, and the aim of cutting off Union access to United States Ford.

2. The narrative on the Gettysburg campaign is largely drawn from Bevin Alexander, *Lost Victories, Robert E. Lee's Civil War*, and *How the South Could Have Won*.

3. Edward Porter Alexander, *Fighting for the Confederacy*, 230. Standing on the defensive followed a Sun Tzu maxim. "One who cannot be victorious assumes a defensive posture," Sun Tzu writes. "In these circumstances, by assuming a defensive posture, strength will be more than adequate, whereas in offensive actions it would be inadequate." See Sawyer, 163.

4. Sawyer, 168.

5. Ibid., 165.

6. Lee gave the reason for doing this as protecting his Cumberland Valley supply line. But by that time. he had already abandoned it, since his army found much more food by foraging in Pennsylvania than could be brought up from war-ravaged Virginia. At the same time it was unreasonable to think that Meade might abandon his position between Lee's army and Washington and move into the Cumberland Valley. Such a move would be directly in violation of orders from President Lincoln.

7. Sawyer, 156, 169.

8. Ibid., 164, 166.

9. Ibid., 164.

10. Sun Tzu says, "In order await the disordered; in tranquility await the clamorous. This is the way to control the mind. When near await the distant; with the rested await the fatigued; with the sated await the hungry. This is the way to control strength. Do not intercept well-ordered flags; do not attack well-regulated formations. This is the way to control changes." See ibid., 170.

11. Johnson and Buel, vol. 3, 339. Longstreet is quoted from Edward Porter Alexander, *Military Memoirs*, 386-87. Freeman, *R.E. Lee*, vol 3, 75, citing *Annals of the War, Written by Leading Participants North and South* (Philadelphia: Times Publishing Co.,1879), 421, gives this quotation from Longstreet: "If he is there, it is because he is anxious that we should attack him—a reason, in my judgment, for not doing so."

12. Johnson and Buel, vol. 3, 340.

13. Ibid., 168.

14. Abner Doubleday wrote that it was an open secret that Meade disapproved of

the battleground Winfield Scott Hancock, Union left-wing commander, had selected. Meade had approved Hancock's request to concentrate forces at Gettysburg. But he was a new commander, and he had already decided to go on the defensive along Pipe Creek, a westward-flowing stream in Maryland, some eighteen miles south of Gettysburg. A line at Pipe Creek was comparatively safe. Moving up to Gettysburg was a dangerous, uncertain move, made only at Hancock's recommendation. Meade had not seen the site, but he did know that the Federals had been knocked off their positions to the west and had been driven out of the town. When he got there, he disapproved of the battleground because he spotted the same fatal weakness that Longstreet did: all the Confederates had to do to evict him was to move to the south. See Bevin Alexander, *How the South Could Have Won*, 308, note 28.

15. Sawyer, 168.

16. Johnson and Buel, vol. 3, 320–21.

17. Edward Porter Alexander, *Fighting for the Confederacy*, 251.

18. On the morning of July 2, General Meade ordered General Sickles to locate his 3rd Corps down Cemetery Ridge to Little Round Top, "provided it is practicable to occupy it." Meade displayed no interest in Round Top. Sickles found soggy ground between the end of Cemetery Ridge and Little Round Top and decided to move west to the Peach Orchard. In the afternoon, just before Longstreet ordered his assault, Meade sent his chief engineer, General Gouverneur K. Warren, to "the little hill off yonder"—Little Round Top—to make sure it had troops protecting it. Warren found the elevation unoccupied except for a signal station. But he saw long enemy lines on the south outflanking the Union position. All at once comprehending that the Federals had to hold Little Round Top, Warren rushed off word to Meade and began searching for troops to occupy it. See Bevin Alexander, *Robert E. Lee's Civil War*, 204, 209. Warren made no effort to seize Round Top. Neither Warren nor Meade recognized its significance.

19. Sun Tzu admonishes generals to know the enemy's plans and the terrain in advance, not to rely on learning them as one moves along. "One who does not know the plans of the feudal lords [the enemy] cannot prepare alliances beforehand. Someone unfamiliar with the mountains and forests, gorges and defiles, the shape of marshes and wetlands cannot advance the army. One who does not employ local guides cannot gain advantages of terrain." See Sawyer, 169.

20. Harry W. Pfanz, *Gettysburg: The Second Day* (Chapel Hill: University of North Carolina Press, 1987), 217–19.

21. Lee ordered Richard S. Ewell to strike Cemetery and Culp's hills on the north

as soon as he heard Longstreet's cannons, while A. P. Hill was to engage the enemy directly on Cemetery Ridge. Ewell waited until almost dark to attack in the north. He occupied part of Culp's Hill but accomplished little. Hill did even less, but Ambrose R. Wright's Georgia brigade in Hill's corps seized the center of Cemetery Ridge during the afternoon when most Union forces had been pulled off to defend against Longstreet's attack on the south. The breakthrough could have broken the Union line, but neither Hill nor Lee exerted any effort to support Wright, and the Georgians were forced to retreat.

22. Sawyer, 162, 171.

23. Ralph D. Sawyer, *Sun Tzu: The Art of War* (Boulder, Colo.: Westview Press, 1994), 239–40.

24. Sawyer, 166.

25. Edward Porter Alexander, *Fighting for the Confederacy*, 233–34.

26. Ibid., 261.

SIX: Battle of the Marne, 1914

1. Sawyer, 165.

2. Fuller, *A Military History*, vol. 3, 173–74; Bevin Alexander, *How America Got It Right*, 80.

3. The narrative on the battle of the Marne is drawn from Fuller, *A Military History*, vol. 3, 171–227, and *The Conduct of War*, 131–60; Liddell Hart, *The Real War*, 3–70, and *Strategy*, 167–79; and Walter Goerlitz, *History of the German General Staff, 1657–1945* (New York: Praeger, 1953), 143–65. A number of observers have compared the Schlieffen Plan to the battle of Cannae on August 2, 216 B.C., when the Carthaginian commander Hannibal surrounded a Roman army and massacred it. Schlieffen conceived only a single flanking movement, however, not the double envelopment and closing in on the rear of the Romans that Hannibal accomplished. Schlieffen's actual plan was to repeat on a vast scale what Frederick the Great called his "oblique" method of attack—that is, he marched on one wing of the enemy while holding the other wing in place. His was actually an ancient technique. The Theban commander Epaminondas used similar tactics at the battle of Leuctra in 371 B.C. The same concept is embodied in Sun Tzu's *zheng*, or direct, holding force and his *qi*, or indirect, flanking force. Frederick's oblique force was a *qi* element.

4. Fuller, *A Military History*, vol. 3, 213–14.

5. For a detailed analysis of how linear battles were fought, see Paul Herbert, "The Battle of Cantigny," *On Point: The Journal of Army History*, vol. 13, no. 4 (Spring

2008), published by the Army Historical Association. The article describes the first offensive of the U.S. Army in World War I at the village of Cantigny, seventy miles north of Paris, on May 28, 1918. The 1st Infantry Division's 28th Infantry Regiment carried out the attack. It followed precisely the doctrine of linear warfare that had been worked out by the French. To seize the Cantigny plateau, the division attacked with a single regiment, its three battalions advancing abreast, each in its own zone. The American line was just beyond the village of Villers-Tournelle, and the Americans had to cross a "no man's land" of 1,500 yards to reach Cantigny. The center battalion was reinforced by twelve slow-moving French Schneider tanks that had the primary job of clearing German troops from the village of Cantigny. The attack was preceded by a heavy bombardment by 75-millimeter guns and 155-millimeter howitzers. Then the Schneider tanks crossed the American trenches at pre-selected passages. The barrage of 75-millimeter guns shifted from the village to the line of departure for the American infantry, blasted there for three minutes, then moved forward in a "rolling barrage" that stayed ahead of the infantry, who came out of their trenches and advanced more or less abreast a fixed distance behind the shell blasts. The aim of the rolling barrage was to force the enemy to keep under cover and not be able to arrest the advance of the infantry. To everyone's surprise, the attack met spotty German resistance, and the Americans were able to capture the village. The French tanks could not enter the village because of rubble from explosions, and were soon withdrawn. The success of the attack depended on the weight of the artillery barrage on German positions, and surprise.

6. The storm troop system is explained fully by Bruce Gudmundsson in his *Stormtroop Tactics* (Westport, Conn.: Praeger, 1989).

SEVEN: German Victory in the West, 1940

1. The narrative for this chapter is drawn largely from Bevin Alexander, *Inside the Nazi War Machine*, and *How Hitler Could Have Won*, 1–35.

2. Sun Tzu says, "Attack where [the enemy] is unprepared; sally out when he does not expect you." See Griffith, 69. He also says, "Now an army may be likened to water, for just as flowing water avoids the heights and hastens to the lowlands, so an army avoids strength and strikes weakness." See ibid., 101. The most telling metaphor for this concept—"make an uproar in the east, but attack in the west"—was produced by Mao Zedong, the Chinese Communist leader who based his highly successful guerrilla warfare methods on Sun

Tzu's teachings. Around 1936, Mao wrote, "Ingenious devices such as making a noise in the east while attacking in the west, appearing now in the south and now in the north, hit-and-run and night action should be constantly employed to mislead, entice, and confuse the enemy." See ibid., 51. For exposition of Sun Tzu's concepts of *zheng* and *qi*, see Sawyer, 164–65.

3. Frieser, 61.

4. Rommel, 124.

5. The two-division French "Cavalry Corps" at Hannut was comparable to a panzer corps. It contained 239 Hotchkiss tanks mounting 37-millimeter guns, and 176 Somua tanks carrying 47-millimeter guns, the best tank cannon in the world at the time. In duels, especially with the French Somuas, the Germans lost in a shocking fashion. The Somuas had 55 millimeters of armor and the Hotchkiss tanks had 45 millimeters, compared to 30 millimeters on the Panzer IIIs and IVs, the German battle tanks. Many experts considered the Somua the best battle tank at the time.

6. Guderian, 110.

EIGHT: *Stalingrad, 1942*

1. Manstein, 280.

2. Sawyer, 161. Sun Tzu says: "The highest realization of warfare is to attack the enemy's plans; next is to attack their alliances; next to attack their army; and the lowest is to attack their fortified cities." Samuel B. Griffith in his essay on Sun Tzu's *Art of War*, summarizes Sun Tzu's strategic thinking as follows: "By selection of a devious and distant route he may march a thousand *li* without opposition and take his enemy unaware. Such a commander prizes above all freedom of action. He abhors a stable situation, and therefore attacks cities only when there is no alternative. Sieges, wasteful both of lives and time, entail abdication of the initiative." See Griffith, 41.

3. Manstein, 283.

4. There is no evidence that Hitler, despite serving almost all of World War I on the western front, was ever aware of the storm troop or infiltration tactics developed by a German captain, Willy Martin Rohr, in 1915. Storm troop tactics were an indirect means of winning battlefield victories. The entire concept was lost on Hitler, however. This is shown in the fact that Hitler never understood the intellectual basis of Erich von Manstein's strategy for a decoy attack on the north to draw off Allied forces in 1940, while the main attack went through the Ardennes to Sedan. Manstein's plan was a strate-

gic application of Captain Rohr's battlefield method. For a full exposition of Rohr's conception, see Bruce Gudmundsson, *Stormtroop Tactics* (Westport, Conn.: Praeger, 1989).

5. The narrative for this chapter is drawn largely from Bevin Alexander, *How Hitler Could Have Won*, 126–30, 145–64.

6. The Soviet Union had few other sources of oil in 1942. The oil fields of Siberia were not discovered until after the end of World War II. The only other major oil field in operation during World War II was the so-called Second Baku field between the Volga and the Ural mountains, which was discovered in 1929 but was disappointing in its production. See Heinrich Hassmann, *Oil in the Soviet Union* (Princeton, N.J.: Princeton University Press, 1953). Although there were some oil wells in western Kazakhstan east of the Caspian Sea, extraction methods were technologically inferior to Western techniques and produced little oil. The vast Tengiz oil field of western Kazakhstan was not discovered until 1979.

7. Shirer, 829; Warren E. Kimball, *Forged in War: Roosevelt, Churchill, and the Second World War* (New York: William Morrow, 1997), 84.

8. Manstein, 275–76.

9. Hitler assembled a million men in fifty-four divisions. In addition there were about 200,000 men in twenty allied divisions (six Hungarian, eight Romanian, and six Italian). The allied divisions were deficient in modern weapons and training. The main striking forces were 1,500 tanks in nine panzer and seven motorized (now designated as panzer-grenadier) divisions. Also, cannons mounted on tank chassis (self-propelled guns) were coming on line. Unlike previous campaigns, *Schnellen Truppen*, or fast troops, were not concentrated but were divided among the five armies (2nd, 6th, 17th, and 1st and 4th Panzer). The panzer armies had three armored and two motorized divisions apiece, but also thirteen infantry divisions between them. All the infantry divisions relied on horse-drawn wagons and the legs of the soldiers. The Soviets assembled about 1.7 million men and 3,400 tanks, 2,300 of them superior KVs and T-34s.

10. Liddell Hart, *The Other Side of the Hill*, 296–98.

11. Griffith, 42. Sun Tzu says, "The excellent general weighs the situation before he moves. He does not blunder aimlessly into baited traps. He is prudent, but not hesitant. He realizes that there are some roads not to be followed, some armies not to be attacked, some cities not to be besieged, some positions not to be contested, and some commands of the sovereign not to be obeyed. He takes calculated risks, but never needless ones. When he sees an opportunity he acts swiftly and decisively." See ibid., 43.

12. F. W. von Mellenthin, *Panzer Battles* (Norman: University of Oklahoma Press, 1956), 160.

13. Manstein, 302.

14. Ibid., 372. Manstein explains this concept fully. "A grave crisis," he writes, "could have been turned into victory!"

15. Ibid., 277, 279.

NINE: The Liberation of France, 1944

1. The narrative for this chapter is drawn from Bevin Alexander, *How Hitler Could Have Won*, 233–75, and Martin Blumenson's *Breakout and Pursuit* (Washington, D.C.: Office of the Chief of Military History, 1961), *The Duel for France* (New York: Houghton Mifflin, 1963), and *The Battle of the Generals: The Untold Story of the Falaise Pocket—The Campaign That Should Have Won World War II* (New York: William Morrow, 1993).

2. Sawyer, 162. Sun Tzu says, "One who knows the enemy and knows himself will not be endangered in a hundred engagements." This signifies that one should ascertain the enemy's capabilities and intentions to the maximum degree possible before making one's own plans. One then should accommodate one's own plans to the possible actions of the enemy.

3. By 1944, panzer and panzer-grenadier divisions were fairly close to being comparable. Panzer divisions had a few more tanks and tracked assault guns than the panzer-grenadier divisions, the latter having a few more mobile infantry, but both were formidable, fast-moving, heavily armored forces of all arms, and they were employed interchangeably in attacks.

4. Sawyer, 169. Sun Tzu says one should know the enemy's plans and the terrain in advance; one should not rely on learning them as one moves along. This makes for ill-considered decisions. "One who does not know the plans of the feudal lords [the enemy] cannot prepare alliances beforehand. Someone unfamiliar with the mountains and forests, gorges and defiles, the shape of marshes and wetlands cannot advance the army. One who does not employ local guides cannot gain advantages of terrain."

5. Ibid., 171. Sun Tzu's admonitions in this context are common sense. He writes, "There are roads that are not followed. There are armies that are not attacked. There is terrain for which one does not contend." All of these rules applied to the German armies placed in jeopardy by the Allied breakthrough on July 25, 1944. Hitler's only viable option was to withdraw the armies at once. Other-

wise they risked being surrounded by Allied troops on their south moving eastward through the huge hole opened in the western front.

6. Ibid., 155.

7. Rommel, 468.

8. The Germans had built a thousand new Me-262 twin-engine, jet-propelled fighters. This aircraft had a speed (540 mph) and armament (four 30-millimeter cannons) far exceeding those of any Allied fighter. However, the pool of experienced Luftwaffe pilots had been virtually wiped out in the effort to stop the P-51s. The Luftwaffe could produce only 500 crews, most poorly trained. In addition, production of aircraft fuel fell to only 10,000 tons a month by September 1944, while the Luftwaffe's minimum requirements were 160,000 tons a month. Also Allied airmen discovered that the jets needed excessively long runways to take off, and they began bombing these long strips. Accordingly, very few of the Me-262s ever flew against the Allies.

9. Griffith, 77.

10. A strike into Holland would encounter hard-to-cross rivers and canals, and land below sea level that could be flooded. The Brittany peninsula might be sealed off, and the French coast south of the Loire River was much too far away.

11. Manstein wrote that Hitler had an intense fear of denuding secondary fronts or subsidiary theaters "in favor of the spot where the main decision had to fall, even when a failure to do so was palpably dangerous. . . . Whenever he was confronted with a decision which he did not like taking but could not ultimately evade, Hitler would procrastinate as long as he possibly could. This happened every time it was urgently necessary for us to commit forces to battle in time to forestall an operational success of the enemy or to prevent its exploitation." See Manstein, 278.

12. One panzer division, the 21st, south of Caen, was within immediate striking distance of the beaches. The division had 150 tanks, 60 assault guns, and 300 armored troop carriers. Its commander, Edgar Feuchtinger, formed part of the division to attack British paratroops east of the Orne River near Caen on the morning of June 6, but he received countermanding orders to attack west of the river. This caused delay, and only 50 tanks and a battalion of panzer-grenadiers struck toward the British beaches about midday. The tanks finally reached the unguarded coast between Juno and Sword beaches at 8:00 P.M. Meanwhile, Feuchtinger was sending another 50 tanks to reinforce this advance when overhead he saw the largest glider-borne force in the war, 250 transports, coming to reinforce the British 6th Airborne Division a

few miles east. Feuchtinger assumed incorrectly that the gliders were landing in his rear, and he recalled all his tanks. This ended the last chance the Germans had to smash the beachheads. It goes without saying that if Rommel had been in command of the 21st Panzer that day, he would not have called off the attack and would have overridden the two British beaches. At the critical moment, an indecisive German officer was in command; the result was failure. The *Oberkommando der Wehrmacht*, or OKW, the German armed forces command, ordered the SS Panzer Hitler Jugend Division, west of Paris, to advance on Caen during late afternoon on June 6, 1944. It did not complete its 75-mile journey until 9:30 A.M. on June 7. Friedrich Dollmann, 7th Army commander, ordered Panzer Lehr Division, near Chartres, 110 miles from the front, to drive in daylight on June 7 toward Villers-Bocage, 15 miles southwest of Caen, to block British movement in that direction. Fritz Bayerlein, Panzer Lehr commander, protested in vain. Both divisions suffered heavy damage from Allied air attacks. Panzer Lehr, the only division in Normandy at full strength, lost 5 tanks, 84 self-propelled guns and half-tracks, and 150 trucks and fuel tankers. Both Panzer Lehr and SS Hitler Jugend were unable to deliver attacks when they arrived.

13. Blumenson, *The Battle of the Generals*, 100.

14. Rommel opposed assassinating Hitler, and insisted that the führer be brought to trial for his crimes. After the failed bomb attack of July 20, a dragnet sought out anyone suspected of participating. One of the plotters, Carl-Heinrich von Stuelpnagel, blurted out Rommel's name after a botched suicide attempt. Another conspirator, Caesar von Hofacker, admitted under Gestapo torture that Rommel was involved. A leader of the resistance, Carl Goerdeler, wrote in several letters that Rommel was a potential supporter.

15. Sawyer, 169.

16. Blumenson, *The Battle of the Generals*, 163.

17. Patton tried every maneuver to get the stop order rescinded, but Bradley was adamant. At last, Patton convinced Bradley's headquarters to telephone Montgomery's headquarters on August 13 and ask directly that Patton's troops be allowed to proceed into the British zone. Montgomery's chief of staff, Francis de Guingand, responded, "I am sorry," and refused even to refer the matter to Montgomery for reconsideration. Bradley did not press the issue.

18. Neither Bradley nor Montgomery was much concerned with trapping the Germans in Normandy. They were losing interest in the pocket, believing the Germans were in chaos and could still be stopped before they could cross the Seine.

Those few who got over the Seine, they thought, would flee back to Germany and would not be able to organize a solid defense barrier anywhere, even along the Siegfried Line or West Wall. This was dangerous overconfidence, and it turned out to be incorrect, but both officers acted on it. See Blumenson, *The Battle of the Generals*, 238.

19. The first V-1 flying bombs were launched against England on June 12–13, 1944. They had a range of 140 miles, a speed of 350 mph, and an 1,800-pound warhead. They were accurate only within an eight-mile radius. Of 9,200 launched against England, antiaircraft fire and fighters destroyed 4,600. The V-1s killed 7,800 people and injured 44,400. The V-1 attacks against England largely ceased when the Allies captured the Pas-de-Calais in early September 1944. The V-2 was a rocket-propelled ballistic missile with a range of 200 miles and a 2,200-pound warhead. It flew at 2,200 mph, beyond the speed of sound, and gave no warning. It was less accurate than the V-1. The first V-2s were fired on September 8, 1944, not from the Pas-de-Calais, which was being overrun by the Allies. The Germans fired 1,300 V-2s against Britain. They killed 4,100 people and injured 8,400. See Zabecki, ed., *World War II in Europe*, vol. 2, 1054–57.

20. Sawyer, 157. Sun Tzu says that the intelligent commander must not be interfered with by the ruler. See ibid., 162. The commander must resist political pressures of all kinds in order to accomplish the very critical purposes of war. It is fundamentally wrong for a commander to allow the "ruler" (that is, government leaders or particular national interests or desires) to influence military decisions. Eisenhower's proper course in this situation was, not to accommodate both sides, but to decide how best to end the war and to allocate all possible resources to achieve this best choice.

21. In late November 1944, Eisenhower also halted a proposal by Lieutenant General Jacob Devers to launch an attack across the Rhine River into southern Germany by his 6th Army Group, which had invaded France on the Mediterranean coast in August and had moved up to Alsace and to the Rhine at Strasbourg. If the 6th Army Group (U.S. 7th Army and French 1st Army) had breached the Rhine, it might have come up behind the German 1st Army opposing Patton's 3rd Army. The full story of this proposal is told by David B. Colley, *Decision at Strasbourg: Ike's Strategic Mistake to Halt the Sixth Army Group at the Rhine in 1944* (Annapolis, Md.: Naval Institute Press, 2008). Eisenhower did not want to cross the Rhine until the bulk of the German troops west of the river had been defeated or pushed back to the east bank. Any crossings

would be against the Ruhr industrial area opposite Holland. This intention was in keeping with Eisenhower's broad-front strategy. See Colley, *Decision at Strasbourg*, 139.

TEN: *Inchon and the Invasion of North Korea, 1950*

1. The narrative of this chapter is drawn largely from Bevin Alexander, *Korea*, 148–373.

2. Sawyer, 154, 157. Sun Tzu says to avoid all actions not based on detailed analysis of the situation and the combat options available. Hence leaders should not allow labels, anger, hatred, prejudice, or wishful thinking to influence their decision-making. Decisions should be based on ascertainable facts and realities.

3. Omar Bradley and Clay Blair, *A General's Life: An Autobiography* (New York: Simon & Schuster, 1983), 544.

4. Sawyer, 164. This is Sun Tzu's fundamental strategic method. The orthodox is generally the main force that engages the enemy. The unorthodox is usually the smaller force that attacks the enemy at a different, usually unexpected, place, forcing the enemy to disintegrate. The various possibilities of where the unorthodox force can strike make it virtually impossible for the enemy to know in advance. In general, the orthodox force holds the enemy in place, while the unorthodox attacks his rear or flank. This is how it occurred in Korea.

5. Ibid., 161.

6. Ibid., 157.

7. The opposition of Lawton Collins, Forrest Sherman, and the other members of the Joint Chiefs of Staff demonstrates that high-ranking officers can be blind to strategic purposes and can miss elementary facts. This implies that nations cannot always rely on their designated experts to make intelligent decisions about warfare. In some cases, intelligent civilians have better judgment than professionals and can see strategic opportunities that are invisible to so-called experts. Collins, in his book *War in Peacetime*, recounts that at the August 23 conference, he questioned the ability of the forces defending the Pusan Perimeter (U.S. 8th Army) to make a quick junction with the forces landing at Inchon (10th Corps). "There was a serious question," Collins writes, "whether the 8th Army could break through the North Korean cordon along the Naktong River and drive on Inchon quickly enough before the enemy could concentrate an overwhelming force against the amphibious attackers." This sentence reveals a complete misunderstanding of what the Inchon invasion was all about. Almost all of the North Korean combat forces were in the south

pressing against the Pusan Perimeter. There were *no* significant enemy forces to the north. Thus, where was this "overwhelming force" to come from? It didn't exist. MacArthur's strategy guaranteed that there would be no substantial forces capable of opposing the Inchon landing. Collins had failed utterly to understand this. See J. Lawton Collins, *War in Peacetime: The History and Lessons of Korea* (Boston: Houghton Mifflin, 1969), 120, 124–25. Even if the North Koreans denuded the Pusan Perimeter and sent some troops to Inchon, they would have taken days to arrive. U.S. command of the air precluded movement of enemy forces by day, thus lengthening greatly the time it would take to reach Inchon or Seoul. Actually, it made little difference whether North Korean forces moved toward Inchon or stayed and fought the 8th Army. The key was to deprive the North Koreans of their ammunition, fuel, and food, and thus render them unable to fight. Cutting the supply lines ensured that this would happen. See Bevin Alexander, *Korea*, 174–75.

8. The Joint Chiefs of Staff message: "After reviewing the information brought back by General Collins and Admiral Sherman we concur in making preparations and executing a turning movement by amphibious forces on the west coast of Korea either at Inchon in the event the enemy defenses in vicinity of Inchon prove ineffective or at a favorable beach south of Inchon if one can be located. We further concur in preparation, if desired by CINCFE [Commander in Chief, Far East: MacArthur], for an envelopment by amphibious forces in the vicinity of Kunsan. We understand that alternative plans are being prepared in order best to exploit the situation as it develops. We desire such information as becomes available with respect to conditions in the possible objective areas and timely information as to your intentions and plans for offensive operations." See ibid., 181.

9. Ibid., 189.

10. Bradley and Blair, *A General's Life*, 556.

11. Ibid., 557.

12. Sawyer, 154.

13. On July 17, Truman instructed the National Security Council (NSC) to propose what to do "after the North Korean forces have been driven back to the 38th parallel." NSC 81 was completed on September 1 and proposed that the United States seek unification of Korea through free elections by the United Nations and that the South Korean government of Syngman Rhee be recognized as the only lawful government in the country. Secretary of State Dean Acheson got an amendment that MacArthur had to clear operations north of the 38th with Truman, and American forces should not be used close to

the Korean border with China, although this was not a requirement. Truman approved the paper on September 11.

14. Bevin Alexander, *Korea*, 231.

15. In Senate hearings on American policy in the Far East beginning in May 1951, Omar Bradley opposed an even bigger war, which MacArthur had threatened on March 24, 1951, and which would have extended to the Chinese mainland. Truman relieved MacArthur of his command on April 11, 1951, and brought him home. Bradley testified that a broader conflict with China would involve the United States "in the wrong war, at the wrong place, at the wrong time, and with the wrong enemy." However, he and the other Joint Chiefs of Staff had done nothing to prevent the *first* war with China that began in late October 1950. This was also the "wrong war." See ibid., 414–17.

16. Ibid., 238–39.

17. MacArthur's statement to the Veterans of Foreign Wars read in part, "Nothing could be more fallacious than the threadbare argument by those who advocate appeasement and defeatism in the Pacific that if we defend Formosa [Taiwan] we alienate continental Asia. Those who speak thus do not understand the Orient. They do not grant that it is in the pattern of Oriental psychology to respect and follow aggressive, resolute and dynamic leadership—to quickly turn on a leadership characterized by timidity or vacillation—and they underestimate the Oriental mentality. Nothing in the last few years has so inspired the Far East as the American determination to preserve the bulwarks of our Pacific Ocean strategic position from future encroachment, for few of its people fail accurately to appraise the safeguard such determination brings to their free institutions." MacArthur's VFW message chopped at the foundations of a carefully put together administration edifice, only barely holding up, that was designed to assure world opinion that the United States had no aggressive intentions against Red China, even as it was denying the Chinese Communists access to a province that everyone, including the Nationalist Chinese, agreed was an integral part of China. See ibid., 176–78.

18. Dean Acheson, *Present at the Creation* (New York: W. W. Norton, 1969), 456.

19. Bevin Alexander, *Korea*, 247.

20. Sawyer, 154–55. Sun Tzu says to avoid all actions not based on detailed analysis and the combat options available within one's own capabilities. This is a part of Sun Tzu's admonition to create the opportunity for victory, which is unlikely unless adequate plans and preparations are made in advance.

21. The Chinese had little artillery and relied on small arms and mortars. They had little motorized transport and generally walked into battle, carrying on their

backs what few supplies they had. Yet the Chinese army had already shown itself to be an extremely formidable force. The primary reason was that the soldiers practiced infiltration of enemy positions at night, envelopment on the sides of enemy units, and roadblocks in the enemy rear. All of these represented Sun Tzu maxims, were stunning in their effect, and in the earlier clashes had disarrayed or routed UN troops time after time.

22. In a message to the Joint Chiefs on November 7, MacArthur wrote, "It would be fatal to weaken the fundamental and basic policy of the United Nations to destroy all resisting armed forces in Korea and bring that country into a united and free nation." He rejected out of hand a British proposal to set up a buffer zone in extreme North Korea between the Chinese and UN forces. This, he said, was equivalent to giving the Sudetenland in Czechoslovakia to Nazi Germany in 1938. Rather, MacArthur urged, the United Nations should condemn Red China for defiance of its resolutions and should threaten military sanctions—presumably attacks on Chinese territory—if Chinese forces were not withdrawn. See Bevin Alexander, *Korea*, 293–94.

23. MacArthur had assumed a damn-the-torpedoes mentality that brooked no compromise. He informed the Joint Chiefs that occupying all of Korea provided "the best—indeed only—hope that Soviet and Chinese aggressive designs may be checked before these countries are committed to a course from which for political reasons they cannot withdraw." So there it was. MacArthur held that the *only* way to keep the Chinese from entering the war was to advance to the Yalu. No better evidence of MacArthur's divorce from reality could be offered. See ibid., 297.

24. For supply, Americans depended on their numerous trucks. When these failed because of bad or blocked roads, they called for air supply, either drops by parachute or ferrying of supplies to forward airfields. The general abundance of supply permitted Americans to be wasteful in their use of ammunition, a habit that could be disastrous when Chinese roadblocks cut off trucks and air supply was not feasible. The Chinese had to rely on human or animal transport to move supplies to forward areas. The ubiquitous A-frame wooden racks that Koreans and Chinese used to haul loads on their backs were a common mode of carriage. The Chinese, therefore, got much less resupply than the Americans, but they were not dependent on the roads. As a consequence, the Chinese could move through the mountains or on steep tracks and through roadless valleys to emerge behind UN forces to set up roadblocks and cut off or envelop forward troops. Americans, largely tied to their main supply routes (MSRs), were vulnerable to the semi-guerrilla tactics of the Chinese.

25. But the costs were very high. About 1,000 men were killed, wounded, or missing in the breakout, most of them marines. In the battles around Chosin Reservoir before the breakout, the marines suffered 2,665 casualties—383 killed or dead of wounds, 159 missing, and 2,123 wounded. The three 7th Division battalions cut off and shattered east of the reservoir lost over 2,000 men, killed, wounded, or missing, while 100 more army troops were killed or wounded in other engagements. Thus, including losses to a British marine commando unit attached and the few South Koreans, about 6,000 of the 25,000 troops in the campaign were casualties.

26. Sawyer, 154–55.

27. One of the most significant failures in American history to avoid war whenever possible and to end it as quickly as possible once it has been undertaken—one of Sun Tzu's maxims—occurred in early July 1951. When talks to end the war in Korea were first being negotiated, the Chinese Communists proposed a complete cease-fire along the battle line. This would have ended the war at once. The talks to reach a final conclusion and a peace treaty then could have proceeded, but no more lives would have been lost. General Matthew B. Ridgway, the recently appointed Far East commander, however, refused to accept the Communist offer, and insisted that the fighting go on while the peace talks proceeded. Ridgway was afraid the Communists would build up their forces during a cease-fire and might launch an offensive. But of course the Americans could have done the same thing. The Communists were willing to take the chance. But Ridgway was not. Ridgway got the backing of the Joint Chiefs of Staff and President Truman. This American intransigence deeply soured the peace talks, which started at Kaesong and later were transferred to Panmunjom. Worse, the war went on for two more years, and hundreds of thousands of young men on both sides were killed and maimed. It was totally unnecessary. The war could have ended in early July 1951. See Bevin Alexander, *Korea*, 426–32.

ELEVEN: The Abiding Wisdom of Sun Tzu

1. Sawyer, 157.
2. Ibid., 161.
3. Manstein, 372.
4. Sawyer, 164–65.
5. Ibid., 157, 162.
6. Johnson and Buel, vol. 3, 340.

SELECTED BIBLIOGRAPHY

Alexander, Bevin. *How Great Generals Win.* New York: W. W. Norton, 1993.

———. *How Hitler Could Have Won World War II: The Fatal Errors That Led to Nazi Defeat.* New York: Crown, 2000.

———. *How the South Could Have Won the Civil War: The Fatal Errors That Led to Confederate Defeat.* New York: Crown, 2007.

———. *How Wars Are Won: The 13 Rules of War—From Ancient Greece to the War on Terror.* New York: Crown, 2002.

———. *Inside the Nazi War Machine.* New York: New American Library, 2010.

———. *Korea: The First War We Lost.* New York: Hippocrene, 1986, 2000.

———. *Lost Victories: The Military Genius of Stonewall Jackson.* New York: Henry Holt, 1992.

———. *Robert E. Lee's Civil War.* Holbrook, Mass.: Adams Media, 1998.

Alexander, Edward Porter. *Fighting for the Confederacy: The Personal Recollections of General Edward Porter Alexander.* Edited by Gary W. Gallagher. Chapel Hill: University of North Carolina Press, 1989.

———. *Military Memoirs of a Confederate: A Critical Narrative.* New York: Charles Scribner's Sons, 1907.

Allan, Colonel William. *The Army of Northern Virginia in 1862.* Boston: Houghton Mifflin & Co., 1892; New York: Da Capo Press, 1995.

———. *History of the Campaign of Gen. T.J. (Stonewall) Jackson in the Shenandoah Valley of Virginia.* Philadelphia: J. B. Lippincott & Co., 1880; New York: Da Capo Press, 1995.

Becke, Capt. Archibald F. *Napoleon and Waterloo.* 2 vols. Freeport, N.Y.: Books for Libraries Press, 1971.

Blond, George. *La Grande Armée.* Translated by Marshall May. London: Arms and Armour Press, 1995.

Brett-James, Antony, ed. *The Hundred Days.* New York: St. Martin's Press, 1964.

Chandler, David G. *Atlas of Military Strategy: The Art, Theory and Practice of War, 1618–1878.* London: Arms and Armour Press, 1980, 2000.

———. *The Campaigns of Napoleon.* New York: Macmillan, 1966.

———. *On the Napoleonic Wars.* London: Greenhill Books; Mechanicsburg, Penn.: Stackpole Books, 1994.

———. *Waterloo: The Hundred Days.* London: Osprey; New York: Macmillan, 1980.

Chidsey, Donald Barr. *Victory at Yorktown.* New York: Crown, 1962.

Colin, Jean. *The Transformations of War.* Translated by L. H. R. Pope-Hennessy. London: Hugh Rees, 1912.

Creasy, Sir Edward. *Fifteen Decisive Battles of the World.* New York: Harper, 1951; Harrisburg, Penn.: Stackpole Company, 1960.

Delbrück, Hans. *The Dawn of Modern Warfare. History of the Art of War*, vol. 4. Translated by Walter F. Renfroe Jr. Lincoln: University of Nebraska Press, 1985.

Dodge, Theodore Ayrault. *Great Captains.* Boston: Houghton Mifflin, 1889. Reprint: Whitefish, Mont.: Kessinger Publishing, n.d.

Freeman, Douglas Southall. *Lee's Lieutenants: A Study in Command.* 3 vols. New York: Charles Scribner's Sons, 1942–1946.

———. *R.E. Lee, A Biography.* 4 vols. New York and London: Charles Scribner's Sons, 1934–1935.

Frieser, Karl-Heinz, with John T. Greenwood. *The Blitzkrieg Legend. The 1940 Campaign in the West.* Annapolis, Md.: Naval Institute Press, 2005. Copyright *Militärgeschichtlichen Forschungsamt* (of the German Army), 2005. Originally published as Karl-Heinz Frieser, *Blitzkrieg Legende. Der Westfeldzug 1940.* Munich: Oldenbourg (2nd edition), 1996.

Fuller, J. F. C. *The Conduct of War, 1789–1961.* New Brunswick, N.J.: Rutgers University Press, 1961; New York: Da Capo Press, 1992.

———. *A Military History of the Western World.* 3 vols. New York: Funk and Wagnalls, 1954–1957; New York: Da Capo Press, n.d.

Gilbert, Martin. *The First World War.* New York: Henry Holt, 1994.

Goodwin, Doris Kearns. *Team of Rivals: The Political Genius of Abraham Lincoln.* New York: Simon & Schuster, 2005.

Greene, Jerome A. *The Guns of Independence: The Siege of Yorktown, 1781.* New York: Savas Books, 2005, 2009.

Griffith, Samuel B., trans. *Sun Tzu: The Art of War.* New York: Oxford University Press, 1971.

Guderian, Heinz. *Panzer Leader.* New York: E. P. Dutton, 1952.

Henderson, Colonel G. F. R. *Stonewall Jackson and the American Civil War.* 2 vols. New York: Longmans, Green & Co., 1898; 1 vol., New York: Longmans, Green &

Co., 1936, 1937, 1943, 1949; 2 vols., New York: Konecky & Konecky, 1993.

Hibbert, Christopher. *Redcoats and Rebels.* New York: W. W. Norton, 1990.

Johnson, Robert U., and C. C. Buel, eds. *Battles and Leaders of the Civil War.* 4 vols. New York: Century Magazine, 1887–1888; reprint, Secaucus, N.J.: Castle, n.d.

Keegan, John. *The First World War.* New York: Alfred A. Knopf, 1999.

———. *The Second World War.* London: Hutchinson, 1989; New York: Viking Penguin, 1989.

Ketchum, Richard M. *Saratoga: Turning Point of America's Revolutionary War.* New York: Henry Holt, 1997, 1999.

———. *Victory at Yorktown: The Campaign That Won the Revolution.* New York: Henry Holt, 2004.

Lewis, Paul. *The Man Who Lost America.* New York: Dial Press, 1973.

Liddell Hart, Sir Basil H. *History of the Second World War.* New York: Putnam's, 1971.

———. *The Other Side of the Hill.* London: Cassell, 1951. Published in the United States as *The German Generals Talk.* New York: William Morrow, 1948.

———*The Real War, 1914–1918.* Boston: Little, Brown, 1930, 1964.

———. *Strategy.* New York: Praeger, 1954.

Luvaas, Jay. *Napoleon on the Art of War.* New York: Touchstone, 1999.

Luzader, John F. *Saratoga: A Military History of the Decisive Campaign of the American Revolution.* New York: Savas Beattie, 2008.

Mahan, Alfred Thayer. *The Influence of Sea Power upon History, 1660–1805.* Englewood Cliffs, N.J.: Prentice Hall, 1980.

Manstein, Erich von. *Lost Victories.* Chicago: Henry Regnery, 1958.

Mao Zedong. *Mao Tse-tung on Guerrilla Warfare.* Translation and introduction by Brig. Gen. Samuel B. Griffith. New York: Praeger, 1961.

May, Ernest R. *Strange Victory: Hitler's Conquest of France.* New York: Hill and Wang, 2000.

Minford, John, ed. and trans. *The Art of War: Sun-tzu.* New York: Viking, 2002.

Morrissey, Brendan. *Yorktown 1781: The World Turned Upside Down.* New York: Osprey, 1997.

Paret, Peter, ed. *Makers of Modern Strategy.* Princeton, N.J.: Princeton University Press, 1986.

Parker, Geoffrey. *The Cambridge History of Modern Warfare.* New York: Cambridge University Press, 2005.

Pimlott, John, ed. *Guerrilla Warfare.* New York: Military Press, 1985.

Rommel, Field Marshal Erwin. *The Rommel Papers.* Edited by B. H. Liddell Hart. New York: Harcourt, Brace, 1953; London: Collins, 1953.

Sawyer, Ralph D. *The Seven Military Classics of Ancient China.* Boulder, Colo.: Westview Press, 1993; New York: Basic Books, 2007.

Shirer, William L. *The Rise and Fall of the Third Reich.* New York: Simon & Schuster, 1960.

Southern Historical Society Papers. 50 vols. Richmond: 1876–1953.

Spring, Matthew H. *With Zeal and with Bayonets Only: The British Army on Campaign in North America, 1775–1783.* Norman: University of Oklahoma Press, 2008.

The War of the Rebellion: A Compilation of the Official Records of the Union and Confederate Armies. 128 parts in 70 vols., and atlas. Washington, D.C.: Government Printing Office, 1880–1901. Available online at Cornell University Library Digital Library Server, Making of America Collection, http://cdl.library.cornell.edu.

Zabecki, David T., ed. *World War II in Europe: An Encyclopedia.* 2 vols. New York: Garland Publishing, 1999.

INDEX

5/11

GO
WILD

GO
WILD

FREE YOUR BODY AND MIND FROM THE AFFLICTIONS OF CIVILIZATION

JOHN J. RATEY, MD
and RICHARD MANNING

Foreword by David Perlmutter, MD

LITTLE, BROWN AND COMPANY
New York   Boston   London

Copyright © 2014 by John J. Ratey, MD, and Richard Manning
Foreword copyright © 2014 by David Perlmutter, MD

Little, Brown and Company
Hachette Book Group
237 Park Avenue, New York, NY 10017
littlebrown.com

First Edition: June 2014

Little, Brown and Company is a division of Hachette Book Group, Inc. The Little, Brown name and logo are trademarks of Hachette Book Group, Inc.

The publisher is not responsible for websites (or their content) that are not owned by the publisher.

The Hachette Speakers Bureau provides a wide range of authors for speaking events. To find out more, go to hachettespeakersbureau.com or call (866) 376-6591.

The photograph on page 11 is reprinted with permission of Getty Images / Nat Farbman.

ISBN 978-0-316-24609-5
Library of Congress Control Number 2014936317

10 9 8 7 6 5 4 3 2 1

RRD-C

Printed in the United States of America

Contents

Foreword

On March 7, 2009, NASA launched the *Kepler* space observatory with the goal of discovering earthlike planets orbiting stars in our galaxy. Almost immediately, the data produced by this venture revealed the presence of planets orbiting stars in the "Goldilocks zone," a term used to describe an ideal distance between a planet and its parent star that is "neither too hot nor too cold"—what scientists have more formally termed the "habitable zone." By November 2013, the mission scientists concluded that in our galaxy alone there may exist as many as *forty billion* planets that could support life.

Applying some clever mathematics to their observations of these planets, the *Kepler* team learned something surprising: They discovered that planets actually deform the orbits of the very stars around which they revolve. And the denser the planet, the more it affects the orbit of the parent star.

In 1543, Nicolaus Copernicus challenged the prevailing notion that the earth was the center of the universe. In his publication *De Revolutionibus*, he presented his observations concluding that the earth actually rotated around the sun. His rejection of geocentrism was ultimately denounced by religious leaders who held to the biblical proclamation of the primacy of the earth. What followed thereafter must surely have been a debate of great intensity, with both sides fervently digging in their heels.

We now know that these seemingly irreconcilable theories are actually both right and wrong. And this paradox is elegantly resolved by the *Kepler* observations of distant planets. Like the newly discovered planets, our earth distorts the orbit of a star, our sun. Thus the delineation of master and subordinate becomes blurred. In the mutually distorting dance of sun and earth, each participant influences the other.

In the pages that follow, you will be exploring the many dances that define our species. Through metaphor and anecdote, science and educated speculation, you will gain a deep understanding of the profound influence that our interactions with our environment have upon charting our destiny as well as our momentary well-being. And you will discover how, like our small planet's tug on the sun, each of us in turn influences all that surrounds us.

We humans are a polarized lot. Whether we're debating the center of celestial movement or the importance of genes versus environmental influence in human development, there is often little common ground. But now we are learning that, like planets and stars, genes and environment influence each other. It has become clear that our lifestyle choices—including food, sleep, exercise, relationships, and even acts of compassion—feed back a constant flow of information to our DNA and actually modify the expression of what had been considered an immutable code. As the science of epigenetics reconciles seemingly disparate theories about our health destiny, we are learning to embrace the notion of the dance and to accept that we must design our lives accordingly.

Go Wild shows us how we can do just that, by tapping into nature's design for us. Our genetic array evolved and refined itself over millions of years to manifest health almost perfectly in response to a fairly predictable set of cues from the environment. But we've turned the tables on our life code by providing confusing social, nutritional, and chemically toxic signals. Go Wild reveals the depth of our current evolutionary discordance, awakening us to how our lifestyle choices foster maladaptive gene expression and thus pave the way for disease.

The mission accomplished by this wonderfully empowering book is nothing short of revolutionary. Ratey and Manning provide us with the tools we need to reestablish evolutionary concordance and eliminate the conflict that we have unknowingly created between the boundless potential imparted to each of us and the maladaptive influences that now hinder its manifestation.

—David Perlmutter, MD

GO
WILD

Introduction

Go *Wild*. This title at first might suggest scenes such as college kids run amok on spring break, so it's fair to ask up front: What do we mean by this? If not college kids, then maybe survivalists foraging on an island? Loinclothed hunters pitching spears at antelope or fleeing lions? We mean nothing nearly so lurid, but you're getting warmer. "Wild" is one of those overworked words with layers of loaded meanings, but we intend to strip it to its core in order to make it useful—useful even to your own personal well-being.

Our meaning is easy enough to grasp. Think of wild versus tame, wolf versus dog, bison versus cow. We have the same sort of distinction in mind now when we ask you to expand this with the somewhat revolutionary notion of applying the idea to humans. Wild humans. It's not as odd as it sounds. In fact, through deep history, through tens of thousands of years, everyone was a wild human. The very same forces that tamed wolves and made them dogs tamed humans. Call these forces civilization, and yes, obvious and abundant benefits came with the deal. We're not here to dispute those blessings. Our bedrock point has more to do with genes, evolution, and time. Human evolution occurred under wild conditions, and this made us who we are. The modern human still operates on those same genes, almost wholly unchanged. We are designed to be wild, and by living tamely we make ourselves sick and unhappy.

We are going to tell you a number of fascinating details about that design: that you are born to move with grace, born to embrace novelty and variety, born to crave wide-open spaces, and, above all, born to love. But one of the more profound facts that will emerge is that you are born to heal. Your body fixes itself. A big part of this is an idea called homeostasis, which is a wonderfully intricate array of functions that repair the wear and tear and stress of living. This ability lies at the very heart of what we mean by "going wild."

We're going to make our case by first showing you the real, sweeping, catastrophic consequences of taming. The world's leading causes of death and suffering—killers like heart disease, obesity, depression, and even cancer—are the price we pay for ignoring our genetic code, our design. But fixing this, especially fixing this on the individual level, in your life, is not as overwhelming as it sounds. That's where homeostasis comes in. The task at hand is to get out of the way and let your body's wonderfully evolved abilities for self-repair do their job. The steps are simple and doable, even in our modern world. This is not speculation. Lots of people have taken these steps, including the authors. We'll tell you about them in detail, but we also have something more planned for you. If you trace these ideas along with us through this book, we think you will come away with a new appreciation for the human condition.

One of the realizations we hope to deliver is how everything—

how you eat, move, sleep, think, and live—is connected. All of it is relevant to your well-being. This seems a simple enough idea, but it flies straight in the face of the fundamentals of Western thought, of science, and especially of modern Western medicine. The tame idea is to break down a problem into components, find out which component is malfunctioning, and fix that problem—an idea that works well enough with machines, but we are not machines. We are wild animals. The wild idea is to embrace complexity.

The fact is, your depression is not solely a condition of mind and is not isolated in the brain. It may be directly and firmly a fault of your exercise routine or choice of vegetables and protein. Your obesity may be caused by your diet or it may be linked to bacteria or lack of sleep—or, even more curiously, your maternal grandmother's low birth weight. Your failure at your job may be cured by long walks in the mountains with your dog.

Even the child's song knows that the leg bone is connected to the thigh bone; we mean to press this idea a lot further to provide some appreciation of the enormous complexity and interconnectedness of the various elements of human life.

The chapters that follow will begin to assemble the case by breaking down our various topics into subcategories, and some are the usual suspects. We will begin with the basics, by examining diet and then exercise, but that's not to say we will deliver up the usual advice. Rather, we are going to use some emerging realizations in both of these areas to establish a habit of mind, a method of thinking about the human condition. We'll build on that case by looking at a broader set of behaviors: sleep, mindfulness, tribalism, relationships, and contact with nature. As the case builds, you will notice a couple of themes. First, it will quickly become apparent that the boundaries of our categories are porous indeed. We will begin talking about nutrition, and suddenly there is a firm, physical link through an identifiable pathway to, say, brain function or the immune system. This is as it should be, because this is the reality.

But more important, you will also notice that each of these categories is a pathway, and each path leads eventually to the brain and the mind. Of course it does: the mind is the seat of well-being. Which leads us to a set of fundamentally contradictory ideas that will channel what follows. Each of these contradictory ideas is correct in its own way, and each has much to teach us.

The first of these emerges in a whole slew of statements through the years, but it's perhaps best stated in a sentence attributed to Native Americans: "Every animal knows way more than you do." The contradictory statement to this one has a long and robust tradition in Western thought, explicitly articulated even at the very root of the Judeo-Christian tradition: you, as a human, are the crown of creation, better, "more evolved," and therefore somehow separate from and superior to all other animals.

Maybe it's best to hear the first case from a field biologist, because these are often the people who, like traditional Native Americans, truly understand the idea. The act of close observation of a given species of wild animal does nothing so much as instill a deep appreciation for the inherent abilities that attune animals to the environment. The biologist was expressing this very idea to an observer one time when the observer challenged him. "Okay, if owls are so smart, why don't they build houses, cars, and computers?" The biologist's instant response was "They're so smart that they don't have to."

The same idea emerges in a more common event. You don't have to be a biologist to make a close study of an animal, and many of us do. We study our dogs. And many of us have had the experience of watching the familiar family pet deliver a litter of pups. Being proper dog surrogate parents, we research the coming event as thoroughly as possible. We make trips to the vet, we prepare for the various procedures we will need to follow to ensure each pup's first breath — there's a series of defined and specific steps to effect a clean entry into the world: clear obstructions and mucus and then stimulate, stroking gently to encourage those first few magical breaths. We think we have to, because our dog, smart as she may be, has never mothered pups before and has no access to how-to books or the instructions we printed from the Internet. And then the pups come and the supposedly ignorant first-time mother flawlessly executes each complicated step precisely as the instructions specified, and then she looks at us as if to say, "What are you here for?" The dog doesn't need to read the manual, because every animal knows way more than you do.

This is an especially important example, because it involves hormones, in this case oxytocin. Dogs have them. So do all animals, including humans, and oxytocin will figure in much of this book — even, in fact, in some surprising areas like business transactions, exercise, and violence.

But we are not restricted in thinking about instinctive knowledge of well-being in other animals, a statement that lies at the very heart of our argument. Somehow, we have gotten to the point of believing that we must ensure our personal well-being by a series of complicated gyrations and contortions, whole shelves of self-help books, multiple gym memberships, moon-launch-capable gear and telemetry, daily attention to the health section of the newspaper, support groups, and a constant count of calories. Yet imagine for a second a group of Masai men—the storied herders of Kenya—making their way across the Serengeti, an effortless trot of lithe, formed bodies, perfect conditioning, and a beauty and economy of motion that would be the envy of every dedicated gym rat. When do the Masai count calories or read the manuals? Where are their personal trainers? Or, for that matter, how do we explain the apparent well-being of the hunter-gatherer groups so assiduously studied for centuries by anthropologists and universally reported to be fit, thin, and happy? Hunter-gatherers are wild humans. Like every wild animal, they know way more than we do, which flies straight in the face of the crown of creation argument, and we do indeed mean to, at least at first, challenge that notion. Much of the damage that we inflict on ourselves, on others, and certainly on the natural world stems from extreme adherence to the notion of human exceptionalism.

Nonetheless.

The jury is still out on the question of whether the human brain is the pinnacle, the best thing evolution has ever done. The experiment has been in progress for only a couple of million years, and we have yet to see all the downsides, although a few are coming clearly into view. However, it is a simple matter of fact (and wonder) that the human brain is the most complicated and profound organ ever. In the early days of thinking about human evolution, or even today, much of what we consider exceptional about our brain is our cognitive abilities: using tools, planning, being clever — that sort of thing. These abilities are marvelous and unique. We don't mean to understate them here, but it may help to begin thinking about some other abilities as well. For instance, the purpose of all brains — not just ours, but in all sentient beings — is to allow movement, locomotion, coordination, and manipulation. We're exceptionally good at these skills as well.

Yet our cleverness, recall, learning, and grasp of fact are not all that complex as brain functions go. It turns out — and we know this because of sophisticated tools that measure and assess brain activity — that some activities we take for granted (empathy, language, and everyday social skills) are exceedingly complex; they light up the whole brain, a buzzing glow of unimaginably dense neural networks. This is what we do and what no other species can do. We'll unpack this idea slowly as we go, but know up front that what makes us human is our unprecedented ability to get along with one another. This is our crowning achievement.

And this is what interests us, but also offers a model or framework for the case we will build in the following chapters. We are going to talk about components of human activity, like diet, sleep, and exercise. But, as we have said, there are important connections among these components. More to the point, each of these activities supports the brain. Each of them in meaningful, measurable, tangible, nameable ways supports the brain and the brain's ability to light up that hypercharged network of neural pathways. These are the neural pathways that sponsor and record your well-being and ultimately your ability to connect to other humans. Light up the whole system, and you will feel better.

This book builds its case in succeeding chapters along just this path of logic. We'll begin by laying out a baseline, a summary of what we know about initial conditions and the details of human evolution. What exactly is the human condition and what is human nature? And we'll make the overarching case, by updating a more-than-century-old inquiry into "diseases of civilization," that violation of those initial conditions has made us ill. Most of what ails us today are precisely these afflictions: diseases of civilization. Then in successive chapters we'll look at the subsets of human activity: diet and exercise, sleep, tribalism, contact with nature, relationships, and mindfulness. We'll then summarize with a chapter of practical advice on the personal level.

"Wild." This is the word we need now. Before civilization, everything was wild, including humans. The polite term of anthropology is "hunter-gatherer," but calling our ancestors "wild" explains so much more. Before there was farming and cities, we were wild humans. Ever since, more and more of us have been tamed, and this is what is making us ill. All that unfolds in the following chapters will be the case for honoring the design of our bodies that evolution gave us, but the easier way to say it is this: Go wild.

Worldwide, there is a growing and necessary trend toward restoring wild systems via ecological restoration. The Europeans call this process "re-wilding." We are arguing that the human body is every bit as complex and biodiverse, it turns out, as any wild ecosystem, and like an ecosystem, it works best when restored to wild conditions. So think of this book as instructions for re-wilding your life, and maybe even an introduction to ideas that may change the way you think about life.

In the beginning, though, it may help you to imagine three scenes. You'll want to recall them every now and again throughout this book to see how different they appear. Like old-style chemical photo developing, the narrative that follows should reveal more detail in these images as our story unfolds. At first, the images will seem fuzzy and disconnected; if we do our work correctly in the pages to come, they will begin to reveal much about the human condition.

Here's one:

This is a photograph that we encountered years ago but that kept popping into mind as we thought about this project. There's probably a good reason it persisted, and it must begin with the fact that this is a classic photo of a band of hunter-gatherers recorded in 1947, before encroachment by civilization had compromised their way of life—and civilization did indeed make these people as sick as the rest of us in a very short time. But this is a "before" photo, and it shows a group of San people of Africa's Kalahari gathered in conversation or, probably more accurately, in storytelling, an activity that has bound us and defined our humanity for longer than we can imagine. The nakedness, of course, strikes us first, but that's a normal enough state for most of humanity for most of history. But beyond that, notice what the nakedness reveals: the lithe, fit bodies, upright and strong. Count ribs. But then check out the guy telling the story: the animation, the affect, the engagement. See what his face is doing, that he radiates a sort of magnetism that holds the circle together, engaged and involved. Who among us today communicates so well? And the circle itself? Notice that it is mostly children, that it hangs together, almost literally. There is an undeniable and readily apparent bond. There is trust.

The second image derives from a video readily available on YouTube, but anyone who has trained in developmental psychology has already seen it and heard it discussed at length, because its content explains a crucial issue of human development. But no need to go to the actual video: the scene it shows is normal enough and repeated often in every child's upbringing, at least every child lucky enough to have a reasonably normal upbringing. The scene is easy to imagine. A mother and a toddler are alone in a room full of attractions and distractions for the toddler—brightly colored toys and other objects of fascination. But it's a strange room. Toddler clings to mom but eyes attractions surreptitiously. Then courage builds, bolstered by mom's affection, and toddler leaves mom to engage an attractive object, maybe a big block. The block falls and makes a noise, and toddler immediately bolts for mom, goes through an interval of comforting, and then works up the nerve to once more go exploring, to venture off in search of the unknown.

All of this is exactly as it should be, now and from the beginning of human time. This pattern of balancing between comfort and exploration of the unknown is how we build our brains, and it is enabled by the presence of a mother's affection and support. It is the normal state of affairs, and we will need this image later, because it is not just about toddlers; it is about each of us.

The third image would at first blush seem to be about very few of us—a special case. We mean to address human well-being here as a universal, but autism is not universal. Most of us see it from afar and categorize it as one of those unlucky twists of fate that trouble a few people, maybe a genetic problem, but what has this to do with me? Yet we will build the case here that the relevance of this neurological problem goes well beyond the social costs. Autism may well be a disease of civilization, placing it right at the heart of the issues we trace here.

We were particularly struck on a visit to the Center for Discovery, in upstate New York; it's a residential facility that serves 360 people with autism, many of them too violent or disruptive to function in a normal family setting. Not all autistic people are violent or this disruptive, but the few who are wind up in places like the Center for Discovery. On the day we visited, staffers escorted us in and out of a series of classrooms, and we engaged some students without a second thought. Staffers told us that a month or so earlier this openness and access would not have been possible, that some of these people might have erupted. The staff credited the remarkable improvement in large part to an exercise regimen, and we watched people run, jump, and dance. This was their treatment: running, jumping, and dancing with one another. But just as important, this new routine built on a long-standing practice at the center of ensuring sound nutrition and connection with nature.

The scene we keep coming back to, however, was in a single tiny classroom, where four adolescent boys were seated in a row facing a simple bell and wood block that they each played in turn. A slight, dark woman with a cherubic face and a pageboy haircut sat at a small electric piano and tickled out a simple refrain, over and over again, as repetitive and simple as it had to be to engage the boys to ring the bell or strike the block, each in strict simple time to the beat laid down by the piano player. The words of the refrain echoed the activity: "Ring the bell, ring the bell, ring the bell," on and on and on. Rhythm and music, melody, meter, keeping time. This is the rhythm that calls forth a brain retreated from social engagement—the hallmark of autism.

But then we noticed the piano player, that she must perform this repetitious exercise for hours on end each day, because that is what is required of her. We noticed, too, that she was not treating this like repetition, that she was putting something of herself into each phrase, throwing in little embellishments and improvisations, that she sang from her center and, like all good singers, from the core of her emotional self. She was summoning a ray of hope to make music—not just sound, not even just melody and rhythm, but music—and doing it again and again and

14

again in a situation that most of us would find hopeless. She was every bit as engaged and invested with the circle around her as the !Kung San storyteller. She was living the moment. She was mindful.

Appropriate, then, that this image came to us in this place, the Center for Discovery, because this was the site of one of two major turning points in each of our own stories. We have long said that there is no reason to write a book unless the process of doing so changes the author's life. Forever. Fair enough, because we hope that this book will change your life. Eventually, we will report how this happened for each of us in detail. But up front, we can say that Richard Manning lost fifty pounds and became an ultramarathon trail runner. John Ratey lost some weight, too, and changed the way he eats every day — but the big change was a major expansion in what he thinks about. He is well-known for writing about exercise and the brain, but the compelling story that is emerging at the Center for Discovery has made him far more attentive to issues like sleep, food, nature, mindfulness, and — more important — how they work together to create well-being. But it's not just the Center for Discovery that has changed John's thinking. One chance meeting, and a remarkable, spontaneous, wrenching personal account, changed his life. We'll get to that, too.

1
Human 1.0

Why Evolution's Design Endures

Evolution has hard-wired health to happiness, which means happiness is not as hard to assess as we make it out to be — not if you approach it from the wild side. Ultimately, we don't need someone else (or a book, for that matter) to define our happiness. Our brains do that. Every single aspect of the way we are wired and evolved makes it our brain's job to tell us if we are okay. Our survival depends on it being so.

Think of what our lives would be like if this were not true, if the body operated on perverse feedback loops that would tell us we are okay when we are, in biological terms, doing badly: we are hungry, cold, exhausted, and broken, and the brain says we are fine. Imagine such a feedback system, and then imagine the prospects of survival for an animal that has it. Imagine it being encoded and passed on in genes. But no need to imagine. This is precisely the perverse system that prevails in a drug addict, a hijacked system that says he is doing well when everybody can see he is not. Survival prospects? We know this answer without further study.

What we need most to understand from this is that our happiness is greatly dependent on our biological well-being, and the conditions of that well-being have been laid down by the imperatives of survival, by evolution. All of this means we need to pay attention to the conditions of human evolution to ensure our happiness. But the problem is, we don't. The popular understanding of human evolution is more or less wrong. But more important, the way we live is a clear and long-standing set of violations of the rules of human well-being, and it's making us sick.

First, summon that image that invariably pops into mind when we begin to think about human evolution: the series of cartoon panels in progression—first ape, then caveman, then us, and then a punch line. These ubiquitous cartoons make great jokes, but the idea behind them is wrong in an important way. So is the concept of a "missing link." The cartoon supports the idea that evolution gradually produced modifications and changes in human design in one neat, clear progression from our ape ancestors to who we are today, that the change was progressive, and that the process continues. All of this is wrong.

Since the time of Darwin, there has been a running debate among evolutionists, with Darwin himself taking the view that evolution was and is built on gradual transition, shade to new shade, almost imperceptibly between generations. The opposing and minority view through most of this debate has been that evolution makes sudden radical shifts, a view the controversial evolutionary biologists Stephen Jay Gould and Niles Eldredge labeled "punctuated equilibrium." The consensus now in human evolution is with the latter point—punctuated equilibrium—and we agree.

In fact, the consensus view says the package we call human, *Homo sapiens*, emerged as a whole in Africa on the order of about fifty thousand years ago. Not much has happened since. This is Human 1.0 and there have been no significant upgrades.

The consensus view was laid out by Gould himself: "There's been no biological change in humans in 40,000 or 50,000 years. Everything we call culture and civilization we've built with the same body and brain."

Yet embedded in this same cartoon and in popular understanding is a second, wrong idea, the idea of a series of links and missing links. In fact, there was not a neat line of human ancestors, each shading to the next to become more and more human-like every step of the way. The human family tree is not a towering pine with a dominant central trunk. It is more of a bush than a tree, with a series of side branches and dead ends. The most obvious example of this is the case of the Neanderthal, long known from the fossil record in Europe, Asia, and North Africa. Neanderthals are the knuckle draggers in the middle panels of the cartoon; they're also a term of insult that we use for fellow humans we consider unrefined or "unevolved," to cite one of the more egregious readings of the fundamentals of evolution. The assumption in this is clear. Neanderthals were simply a step along the way to the pinnacle, to us.

But human evolution is not a linear progression. Rather, there evolved and existed for literally millions of years—much longer than we have existed—a handful of species of viable, big-brained, upright, tool-wielding, hunting, social primates, each successful in its own niche and place. Yet modern *Homo sapiens* appear on the scene only fifty thousand or so years ago, after 90 percent of hominid evolutionary time has already passed, and suddenly we become a breakout species. Suddenly, all of those other perfectly viable hominid species are extinct, every single one. We are the only remaining species in the genus *Homo*.

Interestingly enough, there was a corresponding decrease not just in species but in genetic diversity among *Homo sapiens*. All species of *Homo*, not just *Homo sapiens*, trace their lineage to Africa. There is no serious debate or disagreement about this. And there remains in Africa some genetic diversity among *Homo sapiens*, just as one might expect in a center of origin. But beyond Africa, there is very little genetic variation in humans. There's a good explanation for this. Separation of populations is the sponsor of diversity and speciation. That is, branches occur in an evolutionary tree when some sort of usual natural event — sea level rise makes an island; glaciers divide a home range — isolates subpopulations and they begin to diverge genetically. But for at least fifty thousand years, all humans have been connected to one another through travel, trade networks, and migration. The result is a genetically homogeneous population. As a practical matter, this means when we speak of human nature, we speak of all humans, both through the time span of fifty thousand years and across the planet. Our long-standing networks of connection mean there is no pressure to drift toward a new species, no pressure to evolve.

Nonetheless, there is some variation and even innovation. Much is made of these differences among populations for deep-seated reasons having nothing to do with genetics. Take, for instance, the relatively recent experiment in light skin and blond hair. Through most of human history, maybe 80 percent of it, humans were universally dark-skinned. The experiment in light skin began in Europe only about twenty thousand years ago, an adaptation to inhabiting places with little sun. Think of how much we humans make of this tiny and insignificant blip in the total genetic makeup of our species, how much of recent human history hinges on who has it and who doesn't, "it" being a subtle little tweak not even readable in the collective genome.

Other recent experiments include such genetic variations as lactose tolerance and resistance to malaria as evidenced in a tropical disposition toward sickle-cell anemia. In this sense, we humans are evolving, but over the course of fifty thousand years, the changes have been so slight as to border on inconsequential. At least by genetic predisposition, we are no taller, no faster or slower, no smarter than were the first *Homo sapiens*. We are to the core the same guys who somehow outcompeted, outsurvived a handful of very similar upright apes to do something no other species has done before or since: inhabit every square inch of land on our planet.

But no matter how it happened, it is clear that something unprecedented took place about fifty thousand years ago. This creature called "human" appeared all of a sudden and almost as suddenly was a breakout species. The evolutionary changes that powered this breakout are the core strengths of our species and the very characteristics that we ought to pay attention to. What are these traits?

BORN TO RUN?

Start with bipedalism and running. Our habit of walking on two legs is instructive in terms of what we might gain by reexamining the issue with a fresh set of eyes.

There's a beat-up pair of Inov-8 running shoes parked under David Carrier's desk in his office at the University of Utah, and the trained eye can spot these as every bit as telling as the shape of a thigh bone. This brand is British and happens to be favored by a subset of the tribe of minimalist runners who negotiate rough mountain trails. Carrier, a trim, genial middle-aged guy with oval metal-rimmed glasses, a brush of a mustache, and a frizz of curly hair, confirms for a visitor that he is indeed a mountain runner, but this is not his claim to fame, at least in the running world, and his claim to fame in the scientific world is different still. Runners know him as the guy who tried and failed to run an antelope to death in Wyoming but then eventually figured out how to get the job done with instruction from African bushmen. Turns out it wasn't about running; it was about empathy.

Carrier's work and that of his colleagues—his mentor Dennis Bramble, also of the University of Utah, and Daniel Lieberman of Harvard—is significant beyond dead antelope to those of us who run and those of us who should run. Their findings figure front and center in a way-too-common experience: a runner consults a doctor to complain of some injury and then hears the doctor intone the sober advice, "You know, the human body is just not made for running." Thanks to Carrier's work, the runner can confidently answer, "Nonsense." Humans are in fact the best endurance runners on the planet. The best. Might this have something to do with our dominance of the planet, that we are the lone surviving upright ape?

Much is made of the fact that apes are our closest relatives, that humans are the third species of chimpanzee, and this has produced the related and wrong assumption that humans are simply apes with somehow more refined apelike features, a tweak here, a tweak there—new shades, not new colors. Yet the evidence from endurance running makes a very different case. Humans are a radical departure from chimp design.

In their pivotal paper about this in the journal *Nature*, Bramble and Lieberman analyzed the whole issue in terms of running versus walking—a way of challenging the common assumption that humans are built to walk, not run. All apes can run, sort of, but not fast and not far, and certainly not gracefully. Humans can do all of this, and this simple fact can be clearly read in our anatomical structure, in the bones. The research detailed twenty-six adaptations of the human skeleton specific to running, not walking. Some of these are, as you might expect, in the legs and feet. For instance, running requires a springy arched foot, which humans have but no other apes do. Likewise mandatory are our elongated Achilles tendons and long legs relative to the rest of the body. Running, as opposed to walking, requires counterrotation, which is to say that the upper body rotates counter to the lower, negotiated by a pivot of the hips. So running requires a far greater commitment from the upper body than walking does, and a whole collection of features designed to cope with the shifting mass.

All of these features we share with other running species, even though all of the others are quadrupeds like horses and dogs (and the fact that these two elegant runners are our closest domesticated companions through time ought to serve as a hint to the basis of the relationship). We share none of these characteristics with other species of apes—that is, with the species one limb away on the family tree. To adapt humans to running, evolution reused some older adaptations from unrelated species, and all of this took place suddenly about two million years ago with the emergence of our genus, hominids. This means that not only are we adapted to run, but running defines us.

Science has known some of this for a long time, but it was Carrier who demonstrated why this sudden departure from the rest of the ape line was so important. His working hypothesis was something called persistence hunting. True enough, many mammals, especially mammals long recognized as important food sources for humans, are terribly fast runners. Evolution takes care of them as well. But those creatures—usually ungulates like deer and antelope—are sprinters, meaning all flash but no endurance. Carrier believed that if running was so important as to deliver a watershed in evolution, humans must have used the skill to get food, persistently running game animals until they tired and faltered, and then closing in for the kill.

He gave this a try in Wyoming, where there are plenty of antelope. He found he could indeed single out an animal from the herd and track it and chase it long distances, but just as the chosen animal was beginning to tire, it would circle back to the herd and get lost in the crowd, and Carrier would be stuck on the trail of a fresh animal ready to run. Finally, though (and by chance), Carrier learned of tribesmen in South Africa who still practiced this form of hunting. He went to Africa and learned the trick, and it did indeed involve endurance running, but it also involved a sublime knowledge of the prey species and its habits, a knowledge bordering on a supernatural ability to predict what the animal would do. The running itself was meaningless without a big brain. This connection is a track worth following, but the success of the bushmen in Africa at least allowed Carrier, Bramble, and Lieberman to close their case.

Humans are indeed *Born to Run*, to cite the title of Christopher McDougall's popular book, which summarized their work.

End of the trail? Not really. In our conversation, Carrier mentioned almost none of this, and in fact took issue with some work by Bramble and Lieberman that says the human gluteus maximus buttresses the case that we are born to run. He says that the muscle in question, the butt muscle, plays almost no role in running but does show up in a host of other activities, and it is those other activities that have his attention now. He launches into a line of thought drawn from a concept pivotal in the original research — an enigma, really: a notion called cost of transport.

It's a relatively simple concept that gets straight at the efficiency of locomotion. Imagine a graph, with one axis showing speed and the other axis graphing energy expended by the creature in motion. For most species this graph forms a U-shaped curve, and the bottom of the U is a sweet spot. At this speed, the animal in question covers the most distance with the least energy, just as a car might get its best gas mileage at, say, fifty-five miles per hour. It marks the point of maximum efficiency, the best speed in terms of units of energy expended. The very existence of the U shape says that most animals have bodies meant for a given speed, a point where energy use is minimized.

Humans match the rule, but only when walking. That is, human walkers lay out a curve with maximum energy efficiency of about 1.3 meters per second. That speed uses the least amount of energy to cover a given distance. But running, at least for humans, does not produce a similar curve with a defined sweet spot; it yields a flat one. We have no optimum speed in terms of energy spent. Meanwhile, all other running animals — horses, dogs, deer—do produce a U-shaped curve when running. So if humans are born to run, where's the sweet spot? Evolution likes nothing so much as energy efficiency. Species live and die on this issue alone, so why isn't human running tuned for maximum efficiency?

Further, the whole question offers a parallel line of inquiry, not among species but within the human body itself. That's where Carrier is headed with this, but he first notes that the flat cost-of-transport curve for human running appears only when you summarize data for a number of humans. On the other hand, looking at data for each individual does indeed produce a U-shaped curve, but the sweet spot is in a different place for each human. That's not true for other species, so right off, this suggests that there is far more variability in humans, and it has much to do with individual conditioning and experience.

But more interestingly, this whole line of reasoning can be and has been examined not just between species and among individual humans but among individual muscles within a given body. Muscle recruitment and efficiency vary according to activity, even with running. Running uphill requires one set of muscles, downhill another, on the flat or side hilling different ones still. So does running fast or running slow. But further still, so does jumping. And throwing, pushing, punching, lifting, and pressing.

Carrier says that the research on this shows no favoritism, no sweet spot according to any one activity, no real specialization, and this result is counter to what's found with any other species. For other species, one can make a categorical statement like "born to gallop," but for humans, no. Born to run? Yes indeed, but also born for doing other activities as well. Humans are the Swiss Army knives of motion.

"This is not a surprise to the vast majority of people who think about what humans do, but I think it is a surprise to the folks who are so focused on the running hypothesis. We are an animal that needs to do a variety of things with our locomotive system," Carrier says. "We do more than just walk economically and run long distances."

All of this movement dictates a couple of fundamental conditions of our existence: we need to take on enough nutrients (not just energy but *nutrients*) to power all of this motion, and we need outsize brains to control diverse types of locomotion. Thinking, creating, scheming, mating, coordinating—all those activities also require big brains, but locomotion alone is enough to seal the deal. The evolution of our unique brains was locked into the evolution of our wide range of movement. Mental and physical agility run on the same track.

FUEL

There is a paradox at the center of human nutrition. All the other parts of our body seem very good at what they do, are standouts in the animal kingdom, but we are truly lousy at digestion, which is limited and puny. Literally so, because we have to be lousy at it. First off, digestion is an energetically demanding process, so why burn the calories just to take on calories if there is a better solution? But second, if we are going to be able to move around rapidly upright, we need small guts, and small guts mean short intestines, less real estate for digestion. This bit of elemental engineering is a consequence of a number of design features, but the counterrotation we talked about with running is a good case in point. Unlike all the other apes, which are quadrupeds, we have a significant vertical gap between the bottom of our ribs and the top of our pelvis, the territory of the abdominal muscles. These muscles effect the leverage necessary to keep us reliably upright and control the twist of running, so we need a light, tight abdomen, or tight abs, which restricts room for intestines.

This anatomical adjustment explains much in human makeup and behavior, but start with a simple and profound fact: our short guts mean we can't eat grass, and this is no small thing, especially if you consider that two million years of evolutionary history occurred in savannas and grasslands. Grasslands are enormously productive in biological terms; that is, they efficiently convert solar energy into carbohydrates. But that energy is wrapped in the building block of all grasses, cellulose, and humans cannot digest it, not at all.

Our primary method for overcoming our inability to digest is to outsource the job. Our prey animals, the ungulates—grazers and browsers, largely—happen to be very good at digesting cellulose. These quadrupeds can handle such tasks as chewing cuds, patiently feeding and refeeding wads and tangles of grass into a labyrinth of intestines contained in a monumental bulge of a gut.

There is no ambiguity in the fossil record, in paleoanthropology or anthropology, in everything we know about the human condition, past and present. Humans are hunters and meat eaters. There is no such thing as a vegetarian society in all the record. Eating meat is a fundamental and defining fact of the human condition, at the gut level and bred in the bones.

Discussion about this has generally been cast in terms of

protein. Essential amino acids—proteins—are necessary building blocks for that highly adapted body. The only complete source of those amino acids is meat. True as that may be, it misses some essential points, as have anthropologists and nutritionists in trying to do the calculations that explain our continued existence. When we think of meat today, we think of, well, meat, defined as muscle tissue. We disregard the rest, all those other tissues of the animal body. It's not a new mistake.

In the nineteenth century, when Europeans were exploring North America, a few explorers and fur trappers made contact with the nomadic Indians of the northern plains, a people who, like many hunter-gatherers, lived almost exclusively off animals. The Europeans of necessity adopted that diet and soon found themselves quite ill, even to the point of sprouting open, running sores on their faces. They were like we are today and ate only muscle meat. But then the Indians showed them the choice parts, the bits of liver and spleen, bone marrow and brain and the fat, especially the fat. The Europeans ate as they were told and got better because the organ tissue contained some essential micronutrients lacking in the muscle meat.

The basic energetics of an animal diet involve not just protein but also and especially fat and micronutrients and minerals, a matter of bioaccumulation. Grazers store excess energy as fat, in and of itself a dense, rich source of calories to fuel our demanding bodies; but in doing so, they bioaccumulate a rich storehouse of elements like magnesium, iron, and iodine that the deep roots of grass pull from mineral soil. This is also an important factor. Certainly we could (and do) get many of these by eating plants directly, but they are far more concentrated in meat. To get everything we need from plants, we would have to eat far more than we literally have the stomach for. Further, these minerals and micronutrients tend to be unevenly distributed on the face of the planet, as any miner for magnesium, iron, or iodine will tell you. But the big grazers tend to be migratory and range over vast areas, thereby averaging out conditions and balancing geology's uneven hand. Over time, grazing animals accumulate a full range of nutrients as no stationary plant can, and we take advantage of that life history as stored and accumulated in an animal's body.

Yet our need for variety and diversity in diet also shows up in our omnivorous habit. Humans have for all human time eaten a wide array of plants and wandered far and wide to gather them, and this, too, is more than a simple matter of energetics. Diversity ensures the range of micronutrients to support the complexity of the human body, the importance of which will emerge in detail as we develop this story. All of this gets greatly aided by our cultural adaption involving the use of fire, which allows cooking and so further aids in concentration and digestion. Add to this our microbiomes, which are another way of outsourcing to compensate for our poor digestive abilities. Our guts are loaded with thousands of species of bacteria that break down food and add value — a lot more than we think.

By and large, though, these patterns — nomadism, bipedalism, and omnivory — are defining for our entire genus and have accrued over the course of two million years of hominid history. Yet there is a variation in this theme that illustrates its refinement and gets to our more central question: the difference between *Homo sapiens* and all other hominids, now extinct. The general approach to food outlined here is true of all the species of hominids, even Neanderthals; yet recall that our basic question is why the single species of humans, modern humans, beat out people like the Neanderthals.

Neanderthals were indeed hunters—in fact, highly skilled hunters—and, if anything, they were more selective to very large prey animals than *Homo sapiens* were, meaning that Neanderthals had the skills and social organization necessary to kill elephants with spears. They had big hunks of protein and fat, the very thing that gave all hominids the edge. Neanderthals had bodies that were as upright and graceful as ours. They had plenty big brains. What they did not have, compared with the *Homo sapiens* of their day, was fish. More to the point, they had not learned how to tap this source of nutrition that was all around them.

Their chief competitors, *Homo sapiens*, had. Evidence of fishing first appears in Africa, but only in *Homo sapiens*. When our species showed up in Europe and Asia about forty thousand years ago, fishing of marine and freshwater sources was widespread and important on both continents.

This is not to argue that fish gave *Homo sapiens* the edge that wiped out Neanderthals, Denisovans, and *Homo floresiensis*, the other hominid species already in Asia and Europe then—although it's possible. But it does signal something important to modern nutrition, especially in the case of salmon. Remember: we can prove that those ancient *Homo sapiens* ate fish because of chemical signatures, which is to say that some elements not present in terrestrial species were present in fish, and those elements accumulate in human bones, the fossil record. Further, anyone who has ever witnessed a salmon migration, even in today's relatively impoverished conditions, understands that collecting this protein took almost no effort, as it was an almost unimaginable abundance. Forget persistence hunting: salmon eaters need only sit at streamside and rake it in, literally tons of high-quality protein. But each of those salmon, one of the world's most peripatetic species, has ranged thousands on thousands of miles across diverse marine and aquatic environments during its short life cycle. That is, each fish has sampled and bioaccumulated a diverse collection of micronutrients lacking in a terrestrial diet. Remember the value of diversity realized by nomads hunting across diverse environments. Nomads eating a nomadic marine species takes that idea up a notch: nomadism squared.

EMPATHY

The message here is diversity, and we will hear it again. But this is a small element of the larger success of humans. The details remain somewhat in dispute, but from such evidence paleo-anthropologists have through the years assembled a list of traits they believe defined us as humans. In a recent book, the British scholar of humanity's roots Chris Stringer offered one such list, as good as any:

> Complex tools, the styles of which may change rapidly through time and space; formal artifacts shaped from bone, ivory, antler, shell, and similar materials; art, including abstract and figurative symbols; structures such as tents or huts for living or working that are organized for different activities (such as toolmaking, food preparation, sleeping, and for hearths); long-distance transport

of valued materials such as stone, shells, beads, amber; ceremonies or rituals, which may include art, structures, or complex treatment of the dead; increased cultural "buffering" to adapt to more extreme environments such as deserts or cold steppes; greater complexity of food-gathering and food-processing procedures, such as the use of nets, traps, fishing gear, and complex cooking; and higher population densities approaching those of modern hunter-gatherers.

It is a long list that accounts for much, but its elements, the traits, are derivative. They certainly derive from how we move, our athleticism, and what we eat and how we get it. But there are activities in here that do not derive from simple biological energetics, how we translate energy into life. Symbols (and remember: words are symbols, so this includes language)? Art? Music? Ritual? Clearly this list is telling us that something important and unprecedented has happened in our brains, something well beyond bipedalism, tight guts, voracious appetites, salmon, and the big brains that were characteristic of the hominid line for the preceding two million years.

The biologically unprecedented structures in the brain that enable these abilities don't leave much of an impression in the fossil record, so there is no hard evidence of when they appeared. We have come to know them only recently through neuroscience, an exploding field that continues almost daily with discoveries that illuminate the complexity of the brain. Yet a couple of structures, a class of cells or parts of the brain we've known about for some time, give us some hint as to why human abilities exploded on the scene fifty thousand years ago. For instance, since the 1920s, we've known about spindle neurons—a uniquely shaped set of cells that first showed up in ape brains, and to a lesser extent in dolphins, whales, and elephants, all animals known for having unique abilities. Humans have many more of them in very specific areas of the brain, and they are involved in complex reactions like trust, empathy, and guilt, but also in practical matters like planning. (You might ask why empathy and planning run together. Good question. Answer coming.)

Add to that a related and even more wondrous set of cells that neuroscientists call "mirror neurons," first discovered in the 1980s and '90s by a group of scientists in Italy. These get more to the point of empathy. The term "mirror" is apt. If we monitor a monkey's brain while the monkey is eating a peanut, the readout shows a set of firing neurons associated with activities like using a hand to pick up the peanut, chewing, and registering the satisfaction delivered by the food. But if a monkey watches another monkey eat a peanut, that same set of neurons—the mirror neurons—fire in his brain, as if he himself were the one eating the peanut. This is a major part of the circuitry of empathy, which is defined as a notch up from sympathy. More than simply realizing the feelings of another, we also literally feel them ourselves.

It would be hard to overstate the importance of this in social cohesion, but a bit of reflection shows how far this extends. It gives us some sense of another person's story, ascribing consciousness to other beings. It allows us to understand that they do not see the world as we see it, the importance of which is best understood by observing people who do not have this ability. For instance, people who have autism are notoriously altered in this very circuitry and these abilities, which is why they don't lie.

They don't see the point of lying, because they think everyone else knows exactly what they know.

This consciousness of another's point of view is exactly what enables the more elegant and refined form of lying so valuable to all humans: storytelling. It allows abstraction and conceptualization, which in turn allows language. It allows a concept of the future, which in turn opens the door to planning and scheming and is why planning is related to empathy. But it also gives us a sense that others see us, and hence body adornment shows up in the archaeological record. So does art, which is an extension of adornment but also a mode of storytelling, a symbolic representation of the world external to us.

All of this, on the other hand, comes at a great cost. As we have said, the brain is a costly organ in terms of the energy required to keep it humming along. Any additions simply increase that load, but these are more than simple additions, more than a few more cells tucked away in a discrete corner. The activities associated with spindle and mirror neurons are characterized not by the firing of a few cells but by the assembly of networks of cells all firing in concert, a glow of energy humming around the entire brain. These, unlike many of our more mundane tasks, are whole-brain activities, heavy calculation loads. This load translates into a requirement for even more calories to support it.

Yet there are more than these immediate costs involved, hinted at by one of the more intriguing and sobering bits of evidence in all the vast collection of bones: the case of a single individual, D3444. We know him only by his skull, but that's enough to tell us he was a Dmanisi man, which places his life in what is now the nation of Georgia about 1.8 million years ago. He is not even *Homo sapiens*; Dmanisi people were like Neanderthals, a separate species of hominids that left Africa long before *Homo sapiens* and eventually settled the grasslands east of what is now Europe. D3444 is a special case simply because his skull has no teeth, but, in fact, he had no teeth long before he died. Anthropologists believe this is evidence of infirmities that would have made him dependent on others for his survival. He needed help, and he got it, because hominids take care of those who can't take care of themselves and have done so since before they were humans. This generosity has real biological costs in terms of energy spent. All of this means that empathy must confer benefits greater than those costs, or it would not still be with us. This is axiomatic in evolutionary biology.

Yet any accounting of this matter can easily miss the even larger point in play. We need not look long and far for cases of humans caring for helpless humans, and this brings us to what is perhaps the most salient point of humanity, the fundamental fact of our existence largely overlooked in these discussions, because like many fundamental, important, and profound facts of life, it hides in plain sight. We take it for granted.

The biological term that we need now to move this discussion forward is "altricial," meaning simply "helpless young." Of course they are. Helpless is almost the very definition of the young of any species, from baby robins to newborn, sightless puppies. But this topic teases out probably the most significant difference between our species and all other animals now or ever. Our young are more or less helpless for a very long time, longer than any other species—fourteen, fifteen years. (Some present-day parents would insist that it's twenty-five or thirty years.) No other species is even remotely close to us in this regard. This, too, is a defining fact of the human condition.

And it is not happenstance but a predictable, derivative trait, given our big brains. Humans cannot be born with fully formed brains simply because the resulting head would not fit through the birth canal. Rather, our brains are built and formed after we are born, like a ship in a bottle, a process that takes fifteen, maybe twenty years.

Volumes of understanding and entire disciplines and sets of wisdom derive from this simple fact, but applying it to paleoanthropology offers a new lens on the human condition. In fact, some in the field now argue that this simple fact of life is the most salient characteristic of human nature, the founding fact of our life. Our young are so dependent that no parent is capable of the task of supporting and caring for that infant—not just the attention and protection, but the teaching and feeding. Hunters and gatherers must meet the energy demands of lactating mothers back in camp. Mothers simply cannot raise infants alone, and this dictates social bonding. The basic social contract has babies as its bottom line. Without this, the human species cannot go on as it is. All evolution hinges on successful reproduction of the next generation. In the case of humans, this is an enormous task. Through all human time, across all human cultures, there emerges a number associated with this task. It takes a ratio of four adults to one child to allow humans to go on. This is the real cost of our big brains.

This is why we must cooperate, and why tools like empathy and language evolved to enable that cooperation. All else of human nature is derivative of this single human condition.

Empathy and violence, tribalism and warfare, storytelling, dance, and music—all derivative. Our business as we go forward is to build the case for your well-being as it is built in humans: in mind, body, energetics, and motion, in the elements of life. But understand from the beginning that evolution—working in bone, muscle, neurons, fat, food, and fight—finally built a creature that is human. How are we different from all the rest of life? The paleoanthropologist Ian Tattersall offers a good summary. "To put this at its most elementary, humans care at least to some extent about each other's welfare; and chimpanzees—as well as probably all of our other primate relatives—do not."

Our other primate relatives did not—at least not to the extent that we do—and they are extinct.

2

What Ails Us

Not Disease but Afflictions

"Disease of civilization" is an old term that nonetheless has the power to unravel the most important questions of our time. The idea itself has been with us almost as long as the concept of evolution, yet it has taken nearly a couple of centuries for us to realize the power of linking the two ideas to explain our current disease.

But what exactly is it that ails us collectively and individually? It's not a simple or uncontroversial question, and it is one that engages a lot of scientific brainpower and serious money. There are a variety of ways to answer this, but they sort into a couple of piles, which are generally these: what kills us and what makes us sick while we are alive? The former is a problem because it runs up against the fact of our nature that we all die. Something has to kill us sooner or later, so if medical science triumphs over one cause of death, another steps in to do nature's job. We've worked around this issue with the concept of "premature death," whatever that might mean, but still, you've got to die of something. Thus we can get more traction by asking what makes us sick, what undermines our quality of life while we are alive.

It turns out that a recent and comprehensive effort to grapple with both of these aspects of the question is under way, and results will trickle out during the next few years—though the effort has already delivered some data we can use here. The Bill & Melinda Gates Foundation paid for a massive study carried out by the Seattle-based Institute for Health Metrics and Evaluation. Called "The Global Burden of Disease," it looks at causes of death but also debilitation and loss of quality of life for people suffering 291 diseases in 187 countries around the world. Further, it looks at changes in those patterns from 1990 to 2010, a snapshot of change. The first results, published in the journal *The Lancet* in late 2012, say that the world's top health problems today are, in order:

Ischemic heart disease
Lower respiratory infection
Stroke
Diarrhea
HIV
Low back pain
Malaria
Chronic obstructive pulmonary (lung) disease
Preterm birth
Road injury
Major depressive disorders
Neonatal encephalitis

More tellingly, though, these problems are related to causes, so the same study also details the top twelve risk factors for death and debilitation worldwide. Again, in order:

High blood pressure
Smoking
Alcohol
Household air pollution
Low fruit consumption
High body mass index (simply stated, obesity)
High blood sugar
Low body weight
Ambient particulate matter (air pollution)
Inactivity
High salt intake
Low nut and seed consumption

Both of these lists are telling if not surprising because of assumptions they shatter. Note the absence of cancer on the first list. Note that the list does not include, as we might expect, a litany of infectious diseases associated with poverty. The closest are malaria and neonatal encephalitis, and we can make a case that malaria is in fact a disease of civilization—just an old one. (The record shows that it only appeared with the cutting and clearing of forests associated with agriculture.) More revealing, though, is the second list: the risk factors. This is the list that undermines our concept of disease as some sort of genetic deficiency that needs to be corrected, or as simply infection by a microorganism. This list suggests that "disease" is the wrong word. What we really mean to say is "injury." Maybe it's time to abandon the time-honored phrase and begin calling diseases "afflictions of civilization."

These are not flaws or failings in the design of a person's body but, rather, self-inflicted damages brought on by the way we live. This is what ails us. Every single one of the twelve leading risk factors worldwide is a disease of civilization. But more to the business at hand: every one of these risk factors is a direct result of the foundational idea of this book. These injuries are a direct result of ignoring evolution's design of our body, a direct result of trying to force humans into conditions that the design was not meant to accommodate. And every one is easily and immediately correctable in every life. So what is the relevance of understanding nature's design of our body? Given this list, given a state-of-the-art assessment of the global burden of disease, we have a hard time imagining anything more relevant and urgent.

But you know this, or at least *can* know it. You can do your very own diagnostic of this issue without being bankrolled by Bill and Melinda Gates. Many places work well for doing this, but our personal favorite is an airport. Most any airport will do, but pick a crowded one and simply observe the stream of humanity. Obesity is what one sees first, because it is so painfully obvious; some are so obese as to require wheelchairs. Even the ambulatory are panting and sweating with the burden of a hundred-yard walk. But don't stop here. Look deeper and get some idea of everyone else's fitness, well-being, contentment (or lack), sallow sagging skin, downcast eyes. Now recall, if you're old enough to do so, the same scene in the same sort of place twenty years ago. Did it look the same? Both the numbers and your memory ought to suggest something very different. Something drastic and catastrophic is happening to our people and happening fast. We are getting worse.

Yet the irony of this fully emerges only in an airport, which is why we chose this space. What do you hear in an airport? Warnings trumpeted ad nauseam of the threat of a terrorist attack and the need for vigilance. And yet this imagined damage seems terribly meek in the face of the very real damage to our people on display before our eyes. Who did this to us? And can one imagine a greater threat to our future well-being, our future as a nation, indeed the future of our species than the condition of our people? Can you imagine an act of subversion or terrorism more powerful and more extensive than this profound injury we have inflicted on ourselves?

We can trace the concept of diseases of civilization to Stanislas Tanchou, a French physician who served with Napoleon — specifically, to some lectures he gave in the 1840s. Tanchou did not base his work on overweight people or high blood sugar; he was far more worried about cancer, as are we today. In fact, cancer was the original disease of civilization. Tanchou analyzed death registries of the day and noted that cancer was far more prevalent in cities like Paris than in rural areas, and it was on the rise throughout Europe.

By the beginning of the twentieth century, this idea had spread worldwide and had expanded to include a long list of diseases. Recall now that this was the age of imperialism, characterized by the spread of "civilization," at least as Europeans defined the term. Imperialism created a patchwork of frontiers across the globe that allowed the emerging science of the day to engage people living in the old ways, many of them hunters and gatherers. What the adventuring doctors noticed on virtually every one of those frontiers was that the so-called primitive people were in many ways healthier and more robust than Europeans. Cancer was absent in many populations around the world. For instance, a comprehensive report commissioned by America's National Museum of Natural History (part of the Smithsonian) in 1908 found cancer among Native Americans to be "extremely rare" then. One physician recorded only one case of cancer among two thousand Native Americans he examined in detail over the course of fifteen years. A population of 120,000 native people in Fiji yielded only two deaths from cancer. One physician practiced in Borneo for ten years and never saw a single case. At the same time, cancer deaths were common and well recognized (at a rate of thirty-two per thousand people) in places like New York.

Tanchou's original concept spawned a century and a half's worth of work in virtually every uncivilized corner of the globe, from Inuit, Aleut, and Apache of North America to Yanomami Indians in South America to various groups of Micronesians and Australian aborigines to !Kung San bushmen of Africa. Further, researchers began compiling a list of diseases absent in indigenous populations, no matter where they lived on the planet, including and especially cardiovascular disease, high blood pressure, type 2 diabetes, arthritis, psoriasis, dental cavities, and acne. Note that this list includes some of the very diseases that constitute our worst problems today.

Beginning as the research did in the nineteenth century, a period that made much of racial differences among people, an initial explanation for this phenomenon was, as you might expect, racist: these populations, the thinking went, were inherently resistant to these diseases by reason of what we would today call genetics. Not true. A host of studies looked at populations of these same people as they adopted Western diets and ways of living and found a coincident rise in diseases of civilization. Even the early studies showed that in those cases where indigenous people did fall prey to Western disease, it tended to occur among individuals who were living among whites. Likewise, immigration studies showed, and continue to show, that people who move from a disease-free to a disease-prone area — say from the Australian outback to Europe — quickly become as susceptible to the full range of problems as are people from that area. Diseases of civilization are not rooted in genetic differences.

A more persistent explanation emerged almost immediately in the nineteenth century and still surfaces today, a far more interesting idea tied directly to the notion that you have to die of something. In fact, some researchers signal their bias in this matter by preferring the term "diseases of longevity" to "diseases of civilization." Their argument is that the blessings of Western civilization, especially controlling communicable diseases, made people live longer and so gave them more time to develop heart disease, cancer, and type 2 diabetes. This argument stands despite a compelling counterargument: type 2 diabetes is emerging today in teenagers. So are we arguing that this is a disease of longevity caused by the fact that teenagers live longer as teenagers?

We'll be blunt, because this is vitally important to everything we will have to say, especially about nutrition: type 2 diabetes ought to be a screaming, wailing siren of a warning to our society that something is changing very fast, and we ought to do something about it. We are under attack. And while arguments and analysis may persist in complicating this problem, it is not at all complicated. Type 2 diabetes is a lifestyle disease that results from eating sugar and refined carbohydrates. It appeared among the earliest recorded diseases of civilization, coincident with sugar and flour appearing in people's diets in places as distinct as Africa and Arizona, and has been with us for more than a century. But this is not a static story.

A generation ago, doctors training in the United States would welcome the arrival of a case of type 2 diabetes, simply because it was so rare. Any walking, talking case presented an opportunity for hands-on experience. Among children, type 2 diabetes was then nonexistent. The problem began turning up more often in the general population, and then only after a lifetime of sugar eating had a chance to fully develop into the obesity that tends to run in tandem. Today, the disease is epidemic among American teenagers, especially poor American teenagers whose diet is dominated by nothing so much as sugar. To cite a news report from 2012:

> The percentage of U.S. teenagers with "pre-diabetes" or full-blown type 2 diabetes has more than doubled in recent years—though obesity and other heart risk factors have held steady, government researchers reported Monday.
>
> The good news, the researchers say, is that teen obesity rates leveled off between 1999 and 2008—hovering between 18 percent and 20 percent over the years.

The spread of diseases of civilization is a continuum that stretches into our time, an epidemic that took a couple of centuries to build. It began with imperialism but has exploded today.

Calling these diseases of longevity misses a crucial point, but longevity is indeed relevant in this context, and to explore this idea, we need a more refined picture of longevity among hunter-gatherers. The contention that they all died early is nothing more than an extension of the Hobbesian idea that life before civilization was nasty, mean, brutish, and short. Indeed, the average life expectancy of many hunter-gatherers was probably lower than ours. That's not to say that some of them did not live to a ripe old age; plenty of anthropologists' accounts record old people as valued and active members of tribes. They could live long, healthy lives. The average, nonetheless, was skewed by a number of factors, especially high mortality among infants and young people. In biology among all species in the wild, high mortality of young individuals is the norm, and humans were then living in the wild.

Still, there's an important extension of the record of this issue that speaks to the overall quality of life, longevity, and well-being of our ancestors. This inquiry into diseases of civilization is not at all restricted to the past couple of centuries. The imperialism and colonization of the nineteenth century was only the culmination of a process that began with the advent of civilization—by which we mean the advent of agriculture—about ten thousand years ago. That longer period produced a much longer record, and the evidence is clear. North America provides one of the best examples.

The general notion of pre-Columbian Native Americans is that all of them were hunter-gatherers like the archetypal bison hunters of the Great Plains. Yet by the time Columbus arrived in the New World, hunter-gatherers were as rare in North America as they were in, say, Eastern Europe at the same time. By and large, Native Americans of 1492 were farmers, settled agricultural people, but there were, at the same time, pockets of hunter-gatherers across the landscape. Paleoanthropologists have examined skeletal remains of both groups in detail and found general agreement with the record worldwide and through time. The hunter-gatherers were taller, less deformed, showed no evidence of diseases of civilization like dental cavities and no deformation of their bodies; but the skeletons of the contemporaneous Native American farmers revealed all of these problems. Native Americans showed evidence of suffering diseases of civilization long before Western civilization arrived, which is why we need to define civilization as the arrival of domestication, of agriculture. We are really talking about diseases of agriculture and adoption of the sedentary way of life.

Now we have arrived at the point in this argument that, according to established ritual, requires an insertion of a disclaimer, the "yeah, but...." These discussions generally become defensive, as if anyone raising these ideas is attacking the very core of civilization and advocating a return to living in caves. It is true enough that despite the costs, civilization came with considerable benefits: our kids don't die as often now, and we need not fear infection (as much) or a full load of body parasites. The disclaimer is indeed warranted but nonetheless misses the point. The costs associated with civilization, the diseases of civilization, are to some degree reversible. By paying close attention to what lies at the root of this series of problems, we can erase some of these costs. We can learn from our ancestors to steer our way to well-being. And it turns out that while these issues in all their layers are as complex as civilization itself, the root, the one central development that gets us to maybe 80 percent of what ails us, is simple: it is glucose and glucose alone, in all its permutations. In the end, this discussion will gather threads as diverse as violence, infant attachment, tribalism, meditation, and dance, but we must begin with glucose, because that's where civilization began.

IT'S THE GLUCOSE

In many ways, it took ten thousand years of gradual change to mold us in the shape we are in today. We like to fault modern industrial agriculture and everything that goes with it—overpopulation, a hyperindustrialized food chain, and sedentary living—as underlying the epidemic sweep of diseases of civilization. But the fact is, these all began millennia ago, when humans first domesticated grain. This is a bedrock belief among anthropologists. The effects of the Industrial Revolution and the Information Age pale in comparison with the effects of the advent of agriculture, the single greatest change in two million years of hominid history. So profound were its effects on humanity that it has been said it makes every bit as much sense to argue that wheat domesticated us as the more usual and opposite statement.

Yet it's wrong to say that humanity has been living under agriculture for ten thousand years and that it all traces to wheat. Wheat was simply the Western side of the story. True enough, agriculture did begin with the domestication of wheat about ten millennia ago, but early farming was far more integrated with hunting and gathering for several thousand years and did not do much to reorganize the human endeavor until maybe six thousand years ago in the areas that are now Iraq and Turkey. Further, agriculture also began with independent domestication of separate crops in a continuous process stretching to maybe five thousand years ago, with the domestication of rice in Asia and Africa, maize in Central America, and tubers like potatoes in South America. All spawned separate civilizations, but crucially, except for the South American case of potatoes, all were based in the taming and cultivation of a wild grass (yes, rice, wheat, and corn, or maize, as most of the world knows it, are grasses), and all, including the tubers, rested on plants that stored dense, durable packages of carbohydrates: starches. This is civilization. Civilization is starch, and by extension, diseases of civilization are diseases of starch, either directly or indirectly, and most of it is indeed direct: starches are complex carbohydrates, and they quickly break down, often even in a person's mouth, into simple carbohydrates, which are sugars. Further, much of that sugar is glucose or other forms that the liver converts into glucose.

The human body is perfectly capable of metabolizing glucose, which has been with us through the ages, especially in fruits and tubers. We convert it into glycogen, and any athlete will tell you that glycogen is what moves us forward. (It turns out that this is not nearly as true as we think, but for the moment, let's let this stand.) It is not that glucose is unprecedented or even that starch is new to us; hunter-gatherers have and had both. But not in abundance, not as a sole source, not in the tidal wave of starches that agriculture would begin yielding ten thousand years ago, a wave that has built exponentially in our time.

Today, those three wild grasses — rice, wheat, and corn — are the three most dominant forms of human nutrition, and the potatoes domesticated in South America are the fourth. About 75 percent of all human nutrition derives from those four sources alone. To oversimplify just a bit, this is what ails us, and we will unpack this idea in the next chapter, where we'll look at the diseases of civilization clustered around metabolic syndrome, the most important and most devastating of these ailments. Reversing this is where we can begin reversing the worst effects of the way we live. In effect, this is the reversal of domestication, which is to say the first step in going wild. Still, this issue does not end with glucose, obesity, and type 2 diabetes.

Dense packages of storable starch allowed sedentary lives. That is, we no longer needed to range far and wide as nomadic hunter-gatherer societies had done for a couple of million years; we could spend our lives in a single location — or, as this tendency has played out in modern times, in a single chair. Domestication allowed cities. Domestication created new sources of protein but also new sources of disease, because most of our infectious diseases come from domesticated animals, especially chickens and swine. Storage of grain, though, also allowed accumulation of wealth, almost immediately accruing preferentially to a few individuals. Evidence of disparate wealth is abundantly clear in the archaeological record in the very first agricultural cities, yet it's unknown in hunter-gatherer societies, both in the archaeological record and among contemporary wild people. By allowing wealth, civilization, by extension, created poverty.

Grain allows soft food for infants, and a sedentary life allows women to begin producing children earlier and more often, which is to say that grain greatly accelerated population growth.

These are the most cited and most obvious effects of domestication. The more subtle implications are just as interesting. For instance, remember that we began by talking about cancer, which develops from a complex set of circumstances through lifetimes. The story of cancer and civilization yields to no simple telling, but a quick look at one small example is illustrative and important in its own right, especially to women: the epidemic rates of breast and ovarian cancer in our time. But how does this relate to evolution and agriculture?

Evolution is profoundly attentive to a couple of issues: food and reproduction — how we survive day to day and through generations. Nothing is more important to evolution as a trait that speaks to *both* food and reproduction.

The human body has a long list of mechanisms for assessing well-being, and nowhere are these more important than in reproduction. Science has clearly demonstrated that the body's sensory systems have highly developed ways of ensuring that babies are born during times of plenty, during times of maximum well-being. The normal time of onset of a first menstrual period for a hunter-gatherer girl is about seventeen years old, which is somewhat surprising for anyone following the corresponding number among modern girls in postindustrial societies. Menarche for this latter group is more like twelve years old.

There is plenty of speculation as to why this is true. Genetic differences? Nope. There are many studies showing, for instance, that when Bangladeshi girls move to England as children, their first periods come at the normal time for English girls, not Bangladeshi girls. Can polluting chemicals and endocrine disruptors or food additives explain this phenomenon? There may well be an effect, but there is a simpler and well-researched explanation: body weight. The fatter a population, the more likely a girl is to menstruate early. Hunter-gatherer girls were and are lean and active and so develop according to nature's long-term plan. Carbohydrates and sedentary habits in domesticated populations circumvent that plan, simply because such girls are fatter and the body's sensors rightfully detect flush times. Time to reproduce.

The real downside of this (other than rampant teenage pregnancy, and we hope that you see in our reasoning that we think the coincidence of the epidemic of obesity and teen pregnancy among impoverished girls is more than a coincidence) comes at the end of life, though. Menarche launches girls into a regular cycle of hormones. The result is that any girl who starts early and has a lifetime of menstrual regularity with few pregnancies (lean, athletic girls and women often do not menstruate regularly) has approximately twice as many periods and so twice as many bouts of hormone cycling as hunter-gatherer girls. One of those hormones, progesterone, triggers cell division, and because both breasts and ovaries take strong doses twice as often, those become sites of tumors. This is how both breast and ovarian cancer appear as diseases of civilization. Researchers have examined this and suggested an interesting intervention for both forms of cancer: an exercise program for girls. We agree.

AUTOIMMUNE

The Tsimané people are a surviving population of hunter-gatherers in Brazil's Amazon rain forest. Doctors studied twelve thousand Tsimané extensively, a total of thirty-seven thousand examinations, and found what, by now, we might expect. No cancer of breast or ovary, but no colon or testicular cancer either. Cardiovascular disease? Absent. No asthma. Zero. One more fault of carbohydrates? Not really. Not directly. Asthma opens a new and fascinating door, and through it we enter a whole new area, a second wave, if you will, of diseases of civilization, one that ought to raise our appreciation of the intricacy of evolution to something approaching awe.

Asthma is an autoimmune disease, and the Tsimané people have about one-fortieth the rate of autoimmune disease as do the people of New York City.

An autoimmune disease is, in simplest terms, an example of the body attacking itself. Something relatively benign, a foreign body but not a real threat, triggers an immune response, and this powerful system suddenly launches the body's equivalent of all-out thermonuclear war, like a trigger-happy paranoid. This is our new epidemic, what the science writer Moises Velasquez-Manoff aptly labeled "an epidemic of absence."

First, the problem is indeed epidemic. Run-of-the-mill infectious diseases like rheumatic fever, hepatitis A, tuberculosis, mumps, and measles are all in decline worldwide, declining in some cases from universal in 1950 (everyone then got mumps and measles) to nearly zero today. In that same period, autoimmune diseases like multiple sclerosis, Crohn's disease, type 1 diabetes, and asthma have at least doubled, in some cases quadrupled.

Second, the epidemic is very new, appearing only in the last generation, and it followed an even more intricate but parallel path to that of diseases of civilization. All the autoimmune diseases showed up first and most markedly in people living at the very pinnacle of civilization, in cities, and in the best areas of cities at that. Penthouse dwellers on the Upper East Side got asthma. Alabama hog farmers did not.

The "absence" part of the characterization, however, is even more interesting. The standard explanation for the prevalence of autoimmune diseases is an idea dating to the 1980s. It suggests that autoimmune diseases are a direct result of our success in eradicating not only bacteria that cause infectious diseases, but also parasites like hookworms.

Velasquez-Manoff summarized the matter: "Immune-mediated disorders arise in direct proportion to affluence and Westernization. The more that one's surroundings resemble the environment in which we evolved—rife with infections and lots of what one scientist calls 'animals, faeces and mud'—the lower the prevalence of these diseases."

This is where the argument gets evolutionary or, more to the point, coevolutionary, a term coined by the conservation biologists Paul Ehrlich and Peter Raven. The hypothesis of coevolution says simply that when species evolve in the presence of each other, in a long-term relationship, removing one can damage the other, even if they are bitter enemies, like wolves and elk or infectious bacteria and humans. It is a rule that says even well-intentioned interventions in natural systems can have profound deleterious consequences. This idea, in fact, is getting some traction among researchers, and today consideration of the human microbiome—the population of microbes that inhabits every human body—is becoming one of the hottest pursuits of medicine. It's a truly positive development.

The mechanism that produces the epidemic of absence in the case of autoimmune diseases is fairly straightforward, and also evolutionary. Toward the end of the Paleolithic era, as glaciers advanced and pushed a growing human population into a more restricted area, even before farming began, there was an increase in a few infectious diseases like malaria. Over time, evolution adjusted and favored those humans with the most reactive immune systems, and there are specific, known genes for this. The most interesting case study was in Sardinia, an island off of Italy, which was in this period and until modern times plagued by malaria. Researchers found a prevalence of genetic fitness in the population of Sardinians. Selection pressure made them highly effective at defeating malaria. The phenomenon was so finely tuned that people in coastal areas had this fitness and people who had long lived a few miles away in the highlands (where there was no malaria) did not. But Sardinia, like many countries, wiped out malaria in the twentieth century, and then those hypertuned, aggressive immune systems went looking for a new enemy, like an overmuscled bully stewing for a fight. As is often the case, the new target was the body itself. Sardinia today has epidemic levels of the autoimmune disease multiple sclerosis. This is the very pathway that shows up in all the other autoimmune diseases that plague us today in ever-increasing numbers.

We have approached this whole topic as a separate front in the advance of diseases of civilization, but there are in fact interesting connections between the first and second waves, some cross talk between food and immune response. Know that this is not simply a matter of an oddball infectious microbe that we happen to encounter. Microbes are not at all incidental to our lives, an idea that we hope will give you a new way of thinking about yourself as not just yourself. The thing is, you have more microbes, mostly bacteria, inside of you right now than there are humans on earth. Bacterial cells inside you outnumber your own cells, and the genetic code of the raw information of the microbes that you contain dwarfs your own genetic code. Yours is a thumb drive to their terabytes of hard drive.

Do you think nature would use all of that information for nothing, or that those uses have nothing to do with your health and well-being?

Consider raw energetics, for instance. Remember: we humans need all the help we can get to boost our streamlined digestive system, and clearly we use microbes for this very reason. An argument we will make later on is that the often-cited dictum of traditional nutrition that says a calorie is a calorie is just plain wrong. Some research has shown that the calorie content made available to your body is, in fact, to some degree dependent on the type of bacteria in your digestive system, a population that varies wildly from person to person. But in a marvelous display of symbiosis, what happens typically is the bacteria in your digestive system live off your food — that is, they take the energy they need, and at the same time make some energy more available to you, increasing energy content by, on average, 10 percent. There is a species of bacteria found in obese mice that, when transplanted into other mice, makes them obese. Same diet. New bacteria, and they become obese. There is some evidence that certain bacteria give us vitamins we wouldn't normally extract from food. But even "good" bacteria can go bad in interesting ways.

For instance, in one experiment, researchers fed normally lean people a diet of junk food and noted a flourishing of a species of bacteria that caused the subjects to harvest even more calories from the junk food and in turn grow more obese. But because these are bacteria, they are of interest to our immune systems, and immune systems sometimes respond to invasions with inflammation. We will have a lot to say about inflammation as this book goes on, but know that many researchers now worry far more about inflammation than they do about cholesterol in the origins of heart disease, not to mention cancers. In the junk food experiment, those flourishing junk food bacteria produced a marked increase in both inflammation and insulin resistance, which is the indicator at the dead center of diseases of civilization.

Yet all of this merely scratches the surface of a largely unexplored universe. Our bodies contain thousands of species of bacteria, each with the potential to affect our well-being in direct ways; we know almost nothing about them, and yet we, for generations, have not hesitated to introduce tidal waves of upheaval into our internal biomes with routine doses of antibiotics.

Further, once this complex system has been so disturbed—and there is no doubt it has been in each of us—we still have not the foggiest clue as to how to put it back together.

A generation ago, scientists working in another field (literally a field) faced a similar problem, and it offers an informative analogy, perhaps even an exact parallel. The issue was simple enough that a few conservation biologists hatched plans to conduct what was then called restoration ecology: the idea of restoring intact ecosystems. That's the first step in connecting you to this analogy. You are not an individual so much as you are an ecosystem. Your health and well-being depend on the health of that ecosystem. You confront the exact same problem of restoration ecology in your internal biome.

These biologists faced a challenge, and prairie restoration, then and now popular in the American Midwest, was a good example. They encountered a plowed, fertilized, sprayed farm field and wondered how to restore the complex array of plants, animals, and microbes that once made it succeed so magically as prairie, with literally hundreds of species of plants working in concert.

They often would start out by simply cataloging the species of plants that they knew should be there; then they would get seeds and start planting the desired species, often discovering that target species would not grow. A prairie is a complex ecosystem and cannot be so straightforwardly engineered. What they got after planting, it turned out, was highly dependent on initial conditions and the unimaginably complex interplay of all the species in question. Often they found, for instance, that they needed fire, roaring, scorching fire, and often they found that they didn't need seeds. Once conditions were right, dormant seeds, some dormant for centuries in the soil, sprouted and flourished.

We face something like this in understanding how we restore our personal ecosystems, and, in fact, all the leading health-food stores are perfectly happy to offer you "probiotic" supplements, designed to replace this bacterium or that. There is no evidence that these work, that the species being sold is absent in you, or that this species will flourish, given existing conditions in your personal ecosystem, your microbiome. This is a more complex matter. Just as with prairie, it is not a simple matter of having the right seeds.

And yet we can't help but think that appreciating the complexity of the task at hand is itself enlightening, not just in matters of bacteria and autoimmune diseases but in everything we have to say about restoration of your body and mind. Above all, you are complex—too complex not to suffer some ill effects from all the tinkering civilization has wrought on your body. This nicely frames the task at hand.

3

Food

Follow the Carbs

These days George Armelagos can be found as often as not in a first-floor office of Emory University's Anthropology Building, although it does not look exactly like an office—more a wonderful mess. The place is strewn end to end with layers of books, papers, and generations' worth of academic accretion of near-archaeological proportions. A large, square plastic wall clock advertising Coca-Cola (we are in Atlanta, after all, corporate headquarters of the empire of sugar water)—the sort that one would expect to find hanging on the wall of a burger joint—stands on a desk. It doesn't work.

Armelagos's walker is parked to one side and the man himself has eased into a low chair behind the desk. He wears a weathered purple polo shirt two sizes too big, with no attention paid to the buttons. A pile of long black hair with strands headed in most directions rings his bald spot. He's seventy-eight and has a bit of a struggle getting around, but he carries a teaching load and commands the long view of the topic at hand. Years of thinking about what we ought to eat rests on some of the work he did in the

1970s, back when no one had really thought seriously about these matters, when no one challenged our most deeply seated prejudice about the manifest blessings of civilization. Back then, Armelagos thought civilization was a blessing, too.

Armelagos is an anthropologist but only deflected in that direction after signing on to the University of Michigan's medical school, a solid path for a Greek kid from Detroit in the 1950s. His academic pathway made him interested in bones, and he has been a bone guy ever since. Once he was in anthropology, med school gave him something of a leg up, in that there was bone work to be done. And, in fact, his colleagues were engaged in intriguing questions about mortuary practices, such as the detailed study of the angle of the head and the curl of the leg in ancient North American burial mounds. He had the notion, though, that bones might also offer some guidance on what were then viewed as less pertinent questions, such as about the health and well-being of the living.

In the late '70s, Armelagos set his sights on the Dickson Mounds, the leavings of a Native American culture that once lived along the Spoon River in Illinois. The mounds themselves were surviving evidence of a culture of about fifteen hundred years ago, in a period of transition. That is, they recorded a crucial event, the transition to agriculture—the corn and bean agriculture that was the mainstay of pre-Columbian North America, from Mexico northeast along a broad band stretching to the Atlantic coast and north into what is now Ontario. The Dickson Mounds held the bones of these people, but also nearby were remains of the hunters who had lived in the same area, the primitives who preceded the farmers. The working hypothesis of the day was that people around the world, not just in North

America, grew in numbers to the point of decimating game supplies, and so suffered famine, famine that sent them to agriculture and its greater productivity. And then they got healthy again, or so Armelagos and everyone else at the time thought. That assumption was also a testable hypothesis, given the bones at Dickson, so Armelagos set out to test it.

He began by looking at infectious diseases and expected those to be a negative effect of civilization. The more closely people live together, the more likely they are to become infected with disease, and even then, science acknowledged this as a cost of civilization.

"We expected to find an increase in infectious disease rates, but we didn't expect to find an increase in nutritional deficiencies. That was really counterintuitive," he said.

The evidence, though, was clear. The farmers were less well fed, more deformed, and shorter than the hunters who had preceded them.

To be fair, Dickson was probably an extreme case. Early farmers there probably had only corn, and later adopted the beans that provided some of the nutritional balance in this system of agriculture. Still, there has been a broad repetition of this line of inquiry ever since. Similar sites worldwide tell a story of the transition to agriculture that's consistent with the overall picture at Dickson. The record does indeed show that there were hunter-gatherers who suffered health problems from nutritional deficiencies, but these are exceptions. The overall record, the broad story, says civilization was a mixed blessing. It came with enormous costs to our health, and at the beginning, most of those costs were directly tied to a decline in nutrition. Agriculture brought malnourishment.

Armelagos started publishing his findings in the late '70s, leading to a couple of pivotal books, including *Paleopathology at the Origins of Agriculture* (coedited by Mark Nathan Cohen), long out of print but republished by popular demand in 2013. Colleagues of his at Emory University—Melvin Konner, Marjorie Shostak, and S. Boyd Eaton—cited Armelagos's work in *The Paleolithic Prescription* in 1988, which is the genesis of the current paleo diet trend, the line of thought that carries forward to today's popular diet books by authors like Loren Cordain. Along the way, the idea has become a movement of sorts, complete with schisms, disciples, true believers, and dogma. Today there are even "paleo" sections in supermarkets and a magazine dedicated to the whole business.

And to compound matters, paleo does not stand alone as the sole thread of this idea. A second strain follows the low-carbohydrate banner, beginning with the Atkins diet and extending through prescriptions like the Zone and fat flushing. The unifying idea of these two strains was to shun carbohydrates, especially the refined sort that arrived with agriculture.

Armelagos has watched all of this transpire with some bemused fascination and has commented in one paper: "A number of these studies follow rigorous scientific methods and have been highly influential in shaping what we know about variety, change, benefits, and costs of prehistoric diets. Unfortunately, these scholarly works have been used to create numerous popular publications that claim some degree of scientific validity."

He cites a reductio ad absurdum of this trend: a volume popular in some circles titled *What Would Jesus Eat?*

So what would Armelagos eat? He has a couple of ready answers to this, answers he believes properly reflect his original findings but also everything we have learned since. And his prescription is a lot simpler than you might think, boiling down to two crucial points. We cite them here because we agree. One is obvious, though it is not at all trivial: low carbs. The second is less talked about, but in Armelagos's thinking and ours, the second is even more important: variety. But understand first that these problems did not end with the demise of the people at the Dickson Mounds.

CASE STUDY

By the strangest of coincidences, our hunting and gathering for this book led us to a story of a young woman in Alpena, Michigan, who had suffered a remarkable string of health problems. And unremarkable in a way, because Mary Beth Stutzman, it turns out, had a lot in common with a lot of us—not just in her problems but in her encounter with our health-care system. So we tracked her down and let her tell her story in her own words. What follows is a transcript of a conversation recorded on May 29, 2013. It has been edited only for length. We wanted you to hear her story in her words, because of its relevance to the topic at hand, but also for the underlying themes that will recur throughout the book.

MARY BETH STUTZMAN

I am thirty-four right now, so going back to when I was about nineteen or twenty is when I first started noticing that I was having some issues. I was always a skinny kid. I never worried about weight. I could eat a whole bag of Hershey's Kisses and I did not gain an ounce. I grew up on a farm, so we would always eat good and fairly healthy.

I was getting ready to move away from home and go to school at Michigan State [University]. I started having bad stomach pain. It felt like my stomach was cramping. It lasted for weeks. It was really painful, like something inside was being twisted. I went to the doctors, and they said they were not sure what was happening. They said maybe you have an ulcer.

I started to not be able to sleep at night. I developed really bad acne. There were things that were unusual, but looking at them individually, I was a college student. I was very driven and ambitious. I was working while going to school. It is not uncommon that college kids have trouble sleeping, so I didn't think a whole lot about it.

I started having other problems with my stomach. I couldn't digest any food. I would start eating and feel bad. This was independent of the other stomach pain. All of a sudden, I would feel so bloated I couldn't take it anymore, and I would just vomit everything I had eaten the whole day fully undigested.

It was really hard to sleep at night, and some days I would just never fall asleep. I would have to go to work the next day, and it would make me feel like I had the flu for the whole day. After about five days of that, I would have to take a day off from work, go home, rest, and hope that I would fall asleep. It was getting to the point where one night Casey [her husband] and I were watching TV. A documentary came on about insomnia, and I started crying because I was so frustrated with myself [for] not being able to sleep.

I had tried all the home remedies, I had gone to a therapist, and people thought I was just a highly depressed person. I didn't think so, but that was what people were saying, so I thought, oh, I have to do something, so I tried meditation. I exercised regularly. I was running about three to four miles per day and lifting weights so I wasn't out of shape. It was really strange. So I went to the sleep clinic and I did the study. They said you don't have sleep apnea or anything like that. Your brain is hardwired to always be active.

After that, I tried maybe six different sleeping pills and an antidepressant to try to find something that would help me sleep, and nothing worked. This was over the course of another five years. I tried all these different things. I would try one for six months. It wouldn't work. I had bursitis in both of my hips. I was twenty-five when I went to the doctor about that. It is like an arthritic condition. What twenty-five-year-old gets arthritis?

So now we come up to the point where I'm pregnant. I had a whole lot of problems with pregnancy. I gained about seventy-five pounds. This was the first time in my life I gained any real substantial weight [in] more than a five-pound increment. I had postpartum depression. More problems with my stomach. I went in and had a CAT scan, and they said that parts of my intestines were becoming paralyzed. They put me on a liquid diet for three days, and then after that I could eat soft foods like mashed potatoes.

I struggled to take the weight off. I did boot camp after boot camp. I only lost two pounds. I cut back on crap in my diet. I hadn't eaten chips in forever. I didn't drink a lot of pop. I was following a very healthy diet. I had whole grains at every meal. I was eating vegetables and having meals plus snacks to keep my metabolism going. I was working out hard, at least an hour a day at least five days a week, and I was not losing a single pound.

Oh, and then the asthma. Asthma all of a sudden became a problem, and I had to carry an inhaler, and bursitis was still an issue.

No one suggested these things were connected, and no one suggested that I should look at my diet. No one ever mentioned it. I went to my family doctor, who had been seeing me since I was a kid. I went in with a list, and I had handwritten notes, both sides of pieces of paper covered with notes. I said I have been dealing with a lot of stuff, and I have been coming in individually for things, and they are not really getting any better. They are actually persisting, and I think all I am doing is learning how to cope with them.

I took in two pictures of myself. I said look at these two pictures. I know I look kind of the same [in each], but when you look at my face, right now my face looks bigger, and it looks like it's changing. I know your face changes as you get older, but mine looks longer, doesn't it? He looked at me, and he said, "Have you ever seen a therapist for your problems?" It was said with a tone that I am surprised I didn't start crying right there. But I was like, oh my God, I don't know who else to go to.

So he left the room to go and schedule an MRI with the nurse, and he didn't close the door all the way, and I heard the nurse say, "What? You want what? For heaven's sake, have you seen the list that girl has? It's two pages long. We are going to be here all night. I don't have time for this."

I was feeling like maybe I was making a big deal out of nothing. Maybe I'm too whiny. Maybe everybody feels this way, and

I'm not handling it well. It was just frustrating, and I kind of gave up a little bit for a little while.

I never felt rested. I started waking up, like, three times in the middle of the night having seizures, but with my whole body convulsing. I would wake up in the middle of them, and after a few minutes, they would go away, and I was conscious. It was very strange. I didn't go see the doctor about them because I was busy, and other stuff was happening, and I was so sleep-deprived, I was just trying to make it through every day. I had no energy to do anything, even though I was forcing myself to work out. I thought: Maybe if I could work out more. I'm not doing it enough. This is supposed to give you energy. Maybe I'm not doing it right. My husband is a personal trainer and he was helping me.

I remember sitting on the toilet one day, trying to have a bowel movement and nothing was happening, and this was after about five days. This was normal. I would go seven times in one day, and then I wouldn't go for a week. I remember I had the feeling it was growing [worse]. It was not anything that I noticed right away, but then it became really clear that something else was happening.

I made an appointment with a new doctor. I said stuff was going on, and I didn't really know why, and I talked with her about it. I said I would really like to start exhausting my possibilities. I told her, if you're willing to work with me, I want to have every test done because something is going on, and I don't know what, but I can't live like this anymore. She said, "Okay."

I started getting a migraine headache during the appointment, and within about ten minutes, I couldn't talk because the headache was so bad. It turned out it was just a normal migraine, and they sent me home with pain medication for the headache. After a day or two I recovered, and I just got back to my normal making-it-through-the-day routine.

A few days later, I have another migraine coming on. I get my daughter in the car, and I'm driving her, and it's getting worse and worse by the second. It had never come on so fast before. I'm starting to get worried. I go through the busiest intersection in town. The light is green, and I have to throw up. I couldn't stop. I didn't want to cause an accident, so I open my door and throw up on the street. I get through the light, and I have to stop and throw up again. I threw up all over my steering wheel, my seat, my lap, the floor, and the radio.

A couple of days after that, I'm not doing too bad, and we had plans to go on this cross-country ski trip. I hadn't been cross-country skiing since I was a kid, so I was excited. I was looking forward to it. We go skiing, and everyone leaves me in the dust. I was the slowest person there, despite the fact that I exercise regularly. I was behind everyone.

That night my stomach hurt like it had never hurt before. I just couldn't take it anymore. I had been getting up at night. I wasn't able to sleep, so I was getting up out of bed and trying to walk. I remembered growing up on the farm and having horses with colic. I couldn't walk without poking my fingers into my side where my colon was; it hurt so much.

Finally, about two or three in the morning, I woke Casey up, and I said, "I don't know what is going on but it never hurt this bad before. I have to go to the ER." I got there, and they put me in a room. They had me drink some stuff, gave me a CAT scan, and they took an X-ray. It comes back, and they said, "Your intestines are paralyzed in three different areas," and they showed me: here, here, and here. "Your colon is not working at all. We are not sure what is causing this, but you have stool backed up all the way to your small intestine." The doctor said, "You are one sandwich away from a ruptured bowel, which can be deadly. We need to get this out of you right now." In the X-ray, my colon was extended all the way up into my rib cage below my heart.

So that evening I had five enemas to try to clean out my system. I had never had one before. It was embarrassing. I felt completely humiliated, but at the same time, I was willing to do whatever it took to get me back home.

They put me on a liquid diet. I spent two, almost three weeks keeping myself alive with soup broth and Ensure shakes that old people drink. That was all I could handle. I couldn't eat real food. That would hurt too much. I remembered when I used to do marketing for the hospital, and I interviewed a cancer patient one time who had throat cancer and couldn't eat solid food. His wife said she had researched how many Ensure shakes he would need to drink each day in order to have enough calories and nutrients to stay alive, and that is what she did. This guy survived for a year drinking Ensure shakes. I thought to myself, no big deal. I can drink Ensure shakes and keep myself alive.

I went to a gastroenterologist and had more tests that basically said the same thing. They thought for sure that I had Crohn's disease, and the entire conversation centered on verifying that I had Crohn's disease. They did a colonoscopy of my lower intestine and bowel, and they found no evidence of Crohn's. There were no lesions. There was no scarring. Nothing. All they found was severe inflammation, which they said was not an issue.

My dad drove me to the appointment, and as I was coming out of the anesthesia, the doctor came in and said, "Good news. You don't have Crohn's disease," as if he had saved the day. At this point, I think I'd been almost two months on the Ensure shakes and eating lots of smoothies and soft foods like mashed potatoes, noodles, and rice. My dad said to this man, "She still can't eat real food." The doctor said, "Well, if that works, okay for her. She should just keep doing that." My dad said, "No, I don't think you understand. She can't handle eating regular food; it hurts." He said, "Well, if she can eat the potatoes, then she can just eat the potatoes." Then he walked out of the room.

I remember one morning, I woke up, and I was shaking because I needed to eat. I grabbed some leftover cooked chicken out of the Tupperware in the fridge. I sat on that kitchen floor because that was as far as I could get, and my daughter sat next to me. That was our breakfast. We shared a piece of chicken that we ate with our fingers out of the Tupperware dish. I sat there until it digested a little bit, and I stopped shaking, and I thought, this is ridiculous. I can't even get her a proper breakfast, let alone make myself anything. What is wrong with me?

I don't know what the turning point was. Maybe it was lying on the couch for two weeks and not being able to eat normal food, and drinking soup broth, and not being able to take care of my daughter. I finally decided: I am not ninety-five. These are things that happen to someone who is at the end of her life. What is happening to me? Am I slowly dying off? I remember, growing up on the farm, we had a pony. His name was Peanut, and he was getting old. Ponies live longer than horses. If they live to be thirty, they have lived a good life. This one was thirty-six, and he was starting to get sick. I remember the vet came over. The pony had one problem here, another problem there. Things were just one on top of the other. The vet said, "Well, he is old, and his systems were structured to shut down. That is what happens when you get old."

I thought, my systems are starting to shut down.

Mary Beth Stutzman's systems were not shutting down. Something more fundamental was in play, a disease of civilization that each of us suffers from in one way or another. What ailed her was a specific condition brought on by the way we eat and live. But knowing some basics helps us understand how she got better (she did get better—dramatically better) and what this story means for each of us. We'll come back to her story soon enough.

CARBS TO SUGAR

The diseases that ail us, that list of burdens on our health and the leading causes of premature death and debilitation worldwide, can appear like a tangle of threads suggesting complexity. But if one simply recalls two fundamental and crucial facts—that these are diseases of civilization and that civilization is by definition the domestication and resulting dependence on grain agriculture—then the tangle is really a Gordian knot, ready to be cut with one big satisfying whack of the sword. There is actually a better name for the Gordian knot, and it is metabolic syndrome. This is medicine's name for a series of problems that run together like type 2 diabetes, heart disease, and obesity, all related to the metabolism of sugar.

If one reads the succession of diet books, one might come away with the incorrect impression that much of this problem remains unsettled. There are a couple of reasons for this confusion. First, over the course of researching evolutionary nutrition, science's ideas and assumptions about what our ancestors actually ate, the diet that made them so healthy, have changed, and some of that change is interesting. We have always looked to the past with a set of cultural blinders that allowed us to see what we wanted to see. This is unavoidable and only partially correctable, over time, by doing more science: picking through bones, sorting DNA and arrowheads. But the thing is, we will never know for sure; there will be blanks, and our cultural preconceptions, prejudices, and imaginations will fill in those blanks.

But there is a more unsettling factor in much of the disagreement and confusion. The dirty little secret of the whole business is that diet books sell well, and so it is often in the best interests of authors to argue that their prescription is very different — new and improved, to borrow a phrase from marketers — from preceding prescriptions. Interests of commerce dictate an emphasis on differences and disagreements. We think a better approach here is to cut back to fundamentals and begin on the common ground, and the common ground is the indisputable fact that for millions of years, our ancestors thrived on a diet that did not include dense packages of carbohydrates. They had a low-carb diet for the very simple reason (and also indisputable fact) that dense packages of carbohydrates for the most part did not exist. When you consider that these very same foods constitute something like 80 percent of all human nutrition today, you get some idea of the significance of this revolution. This is the correlation that counts: high consumption of carbohydrates with high incidence of disease related to carbohydrates. But we have more than a coincidence here. We can explain the mechanism by which it works.

The world of carbohydrates subdivides pretty endlessly, but the first cut is two classifications: complex and simple carbohydrates. The complex carbohydrates are more intricate molecules better known as starches, and this is the stuff of our main agricultural crops: corn, rice, wheat, and all grains, as well as potatoes. Fruits and vegetables do indeed contain carbohydrates, but in far smaller amounts, meaning they're far less concentrated. Starch from grains and potatoes is to spinach what a glass of 180 proof rum is to beer—and that's more than an analogy, because the same substance is in play. Alcohol comes from fermented, broken-down carbohydrates.

So where does sugar figure in? Simple. Sugars are the simple carbohydrates. You eat both complex and simple carbohydrates, but your digestion breaks both complex and simple into simple and simpler. The process of digestion of carbohydrates is a disassembly of the larger, complex molecules of starches to yield sugars, and this elemental and straightforward process begins in your mouth. So simple is the process that some starches are rendered into sugars through chewing and saliva even before they hit your throat. The result is a long list of sugars, but these in turn reduce to two in the main: glucose and fructose. For instance, table sugar or cane sugar, known as sucrose, is really about half glucose and half fructose, the latter so named because it is the dominant sugar in fruits. (And it's present in most fruits in laughably small amounts, compared with the sugar in, say, a glass of Coke, or even apple juice. That's the issue.)

The dominant industrial food process of our day is, in fact, simply a replication of this reduction, breaking down the starches of corn into sugars as high-fructose corn syrup. And even high-fructose corn syrup is, like sucrose, a combination of glucose and fructose: it's about 55 percent fructose, which is what the manufacturers mean by "high." Next time you hear an argument that somehow cane sugar is better than high-fructose corn syrup, bear in mind you are arguing about 50 percent versus 55 percent fructose.

But like one big, long funnel, this whole process, both natural digestion and factory manufacture, aims at a single point, which is glucose. Glucose is a fuel, the dominant fuel of our muscles and especially our brain, especially in today's sugar-saturated world. The glucose you eat as glucose goes straightaway to the bloodstream and, in theory, at least, goes to work. Fructose goes to your digestive system, and a couple of hours later, enzymes have converted it into glucose and sent it to your bloodstream.

But here is the dark little secret in all of this, and it sounds very odd to say it: glucose is toxic. It is poison, and the body regards it just that way. We have spent generations now in a search for toxins that sponsor the diseases that ail us, the industrial chemicals, pesticides, and pollutants that may kill us, and yes, these may be killing us. But the supreme irony in all of this is that the obvious toxin hides in plain sight. It's difficult to accuse the very substance on which all of civilization depends. People who consider these matters often refer to the "omnivore's dilemma," but it gets more and more difficult to claim to be omnivores, creatures that eat both plants and animals. The prima facie case is we have become carbovores as a result of our domestication by grain. This is the carbovore's dilemma: we exist for the most part on a substance that our bloodstream treats as a toxin.

Now wait a minute. Carbohydrates in food are nothing new, and hunter-gatherers ate them all along, even fairly dense packages as one might find in the tubers that were the precursors of domestic potatoes or in the wild grass seeds that were precursors of grain. Further, haven't we argued that the hallmark of the species is our adaptability, our nimbleness, our bodies' ability to adjust to novel conditions and balance its systems through homeostasis? So what if we are eating more concentrated forms of carbohydrates? That hardly qualifies as turning what was a basic food group for millions of years — and not just for humans but for the whole animal kingdom — into something we call toxic. Why don't our bodies simply adjust and head right back for homeostasis? The answer is, our bodies do.

Glucose is a very specific toxin, toxic in large doses *in the bloodstream*. This is precisely why the more extreme carbovores among us make a big deal about blood sugar level, the highs and lows that come with the balancing act — because it is a balancing act. And our bodies are highly adapted to execute this balancing act with a series of reactions all regulated by the hormone insulin. When glucose arrives in the bloodstream, it immediately and reliably (in everyone but those with type 1 diabetes) triggers the pancreas to secrete insulin, which sends a series of signals through the body, all with the central purpose of removing glucose from our bloodstream. Fast. Insulin oversees the body's response to toxicity. Glucose is a three-alarm fire that demands immediate reaction, which is why your brain pays so much attention to it — the blood sugar rush.

The body has basically two choices for getting glucose out of the bloodstream. The first and best answer is to send it off to muscles and organs, where it converts into a derivative called glycogen, a readily burnable fuel for our muscles. The catch is, the body has a very limited capacity for storing glycogen in muscle fibers — maybe enough energy to keep a marathon runner going for an hour or so, the quantity of glycogen from a few ounces of sugar. Further, unless you are a marathon runner, the majority of this storage space in muscles is already pretty full most of the time. So the body deals by going straight for plan B, which is to convert the glucose into fat and store it in ever broader bands around the stomach, butt, and thighs, depending on gender. (Gender determines which other hormones are present and where they are in the body to interact with insulin and guide the process of storing fat.)

There's a side chain to this process of fat conversion, again related to the fact that the body considers glucose to be toxic in the bloodstream and so makes its removal a priority. It is this: muscles burn glycogen to do work, but they are also capable of burning fat in parallel, both what we eat and what is stored. No need to convert back into glucose; fat itself burns very well to fuel muscles. We are told over and over again, especially in the world of athletics, that carbohydrates are your fuel. But the fine print, even in mainstream advice on this issue, reveals that fat is your fuel, too. And for endurance athletes especially, but even in day-to-day movement, fat is the most important fuel, or it is unless you have a surplus of glucose from eating too many carbohydrates. Back to insulin: remember, it is a hormone and so sends a variety of signals designed to remove glucose from your bloodstream. One of the strongest and clearest of those messages is to tell your body to stop burning fat and burn glucose instead as a priority. Coincident to this is a signal to stop moving fat from storage. The priority is to remove the glucose from the bloodstream.

None of this is a real problem, as long as one eats carbohydrates at levels at which we were evolved to eat them—that is, few and mixed with a variety of foods. This is our adaptability: the system is designed to return our bodies to homeostasis, a built-in regulator that makes glucose useful and keeps it out of the bloodstream at toxic levels. The problem arises when we overwhelm that system, when we deliver far more glucose and deliver it far more directly than our bodies were designed for.

Mode of delivery is as relevant as quantity. Remember that through most of human evolution, the majority of our carbohydrates came as the complex variety embedded in a matrix of fiber, which is to say foods. The digestion of this food took time, and so our bodies metered out the glucose in dribs and drabs through the course of a day. Now, though, we deliver many of our carbohydrates in the simple form, much of it as glucose, and sometimes not even in food at all but dissolved in water, a practice that completely bypasses the leveling effect of the digestive system. Sugar dissolved in water is the worst-case scenario, which is why soft drinks are so insidious and loom so large in the problem of childhood obesity around the world. But this is equally true of more socially accepted forms of dissolved sugar, such as fruit juices. That all-organic, all-natural fizzy fruit drink from the health-food store (no high-fructose corn syrup, only natural cane sugar) is every bit as damaging as a Coke, at least with respect to glucose. If you come away from this book with one rule and one rule only, it is this: don't drink sugar water. In any form. Not a Big Gulp Coke. Not a Knudsen's 100 percent natural and organic fruit juice.

But even in food and even in the form of complex carbohydrates such as the bagel you picked up this morning at Starbucks, the effect is only slightly less corrosive and sets you up for the crash, which is a condition called insulin resistance. It means that like those who repeatedly heard the boy who cried wolf, your body slowly becomes calloused to the constant ringing of the three-bell alarm of insulin. Your signals become crossed and this sends you eventually into the full-on crisis that is metabolic syndrome. This is the Gordian knot, the cluster of nasty little maladies that run together: obesity, heart disease, high blood pressure, type 2 diabetes, and stroke—and, less directly, cancer. Each of these is rooted in metabolic syndrome. This is the core of the emerging argument that sugar is toxic and sugar is responsible for what ails us. Carbs are responsible, too, because—as we've just shown—carbohydrates reduce to sugar.

The argument remains controversial, especially among nutritionists, or at least in the public pronouncements of nutritionists, and there is an issue embedded here that has more to do with the sociology of science than with the science itself. We have heard nutritionists acknowledge in private that fat is not the problem but turn around in public and say it is, simply because they are reluctant to abandon a fifty-year-old message. Doing so, they say, might confuse the public. The result, though, is a mixed set of messages, made even more mixed by the big-money politics of food and sugar and industrial agriculture—some of which is sinister, and some of which is simply wound up in bureaucratic inertia and human nature. The problem is, we have been told for a couple of generations that we are fat because we eat too much fat, and that's a much more direct argument and easier sell than saying—as we have here—that we are fat because we eat too much sugar and complex carbohydrates. Some of us do indeed eat too much fat, and we'll get to that in a moment, but first let's challenge the fat-o-phobes straight on. Fat is good for you, and we ought to stop saying otherwise.

THE RISE OF FAT-O-PHOBIA

The history of blaming fat for the cluster of diseases around metabolic syndrome, it turns out, is short and focused. Science has been thinking about obesity for at least a couple of centuries, but for only about fifty years have the arguments focused on fat. We can blame Ancel Keys and Dwight Eisenhower for this. Keys was a researcher at the University of Minnesota who was first known for a series of intriguing studies during World War II on the effects of starvation. He used conscientious objectors as the volunteers in his experiments and demonstrated that the psychological effects of starvation were extreme and included lifelong psychological debilitation, even after full nutrition returned. But he was better known for focusing on fat in general and cholesterol in particular. Keys is the reason most of us now know our cholesterol numbers.

Eisenhower's contribution to all of this was the heart attack he had while still serving as president, which greatly drew national attention to what was then, as now, a widespread health problem. And true enough, Eisenhower had by then given up his four-pack-a-day Camel habit, but he also had a high cholesterol number at about the time Keys, a messianic character, was trumpeting the evils of cholesterol to public health officials.

This case emerges in intriguing detail in the work of Gary Taubes, a science writer and historian. We recommend his book *Good Calories, Bad Calories*, which is far more comprehensive and important than the diet-book title might suggest. It is an exhaustive summary and builds a broad case about cholesterol, fat, and carbohydrates, but the story is best summarized by an old, peer-reviewed joke that Taubes uses and we repeat here. A guy walking down the street one night notices a drunk hunched over in a determined search under a lamppost. "What are you looking for?" "I lost my car keys." "Well, I'll help you look. Are you sure you dropped them here?" "Nah. I dropped 'em over there a ways, but the light's better over here."

The light that has focused our search on this matter for a couple of generations is the fact that doctors can easily measure cholesterol—which is one of hundreds of biochemicals vital to our system and yet somehow the one believed to reveal everything there is to know about heart disease.

The common understanding is that cholesterol is a fat. It is an essential fat, meaning every single cell in your body needs it. But when we talk about cholesterol, we generally talk about lipoproteins, which are specialized structures the body makes to transport fats (including cholesterol) and proteins in the bloodstream. There are a variety of lipoproteins, and cholesterol is contained and freighted in each. There is no good way to measure cholesterol itself, so we measure lipoproteins as a proxy.

The first cut of classification gives us low-density lipoproteins (LDL) and high-density lipoproteins (HDL), the "bad" and "good" cholesterol, respectively. Those two and a third, triglycerides, make up the three common numbers of the garden-variety lipid profile. The focus is mostly on LDL, the so-called bad cholesterol. But not so fast. LDL itself subdivides into two distinct structures, according to size, and only the very small ones are thought to lead to damage. When your doctor uses your lipid profile to prescribe a lifetime of statin drugs and possibly a lifetime of the muscle cramping that is the known side effect, she often hasn't a clue which type of LDL particles dominate in your profile, despite evidence that says only one of these is associated with heart disease. Further, we have known about the two sizes of particles and their relative importance since cholesterol was first discovered early in the twentieth century, but mostly we ignore the distinction.

And further still, there is plenty of evidence that says heart disease is better predicted by triglyceride levels, and this number ramps up according to how much sugar you eat, not fat. And even further, a lipid profile that shows high triglycerides and low HDL is neatly predictive of the bad kind of LDL. This profile, and not high cholesterol or even high LDL, is far more strongly associated with heart disease.

The whole issue has become layered in misinformation and mythologies. For instance, there is the widespread belief that eating foods high in cholesterol will yield elevated cholesterol in your bloodstream. This is a straightforward enough assumption, but it's probably wrong. Taubes reviewed the evidence through the years and concluded, "Dietary cholesterol, for instance, has an insignificant effect on blood cholesterol. It *might* elevate cholesterol levels in a small percentage of highly sensitive individuals, but for most of us, it's clinically meaningless."

At the same time, a diet high in *carbohydrates* is strongly associated with high triglycerides, low HDL, and the damaging particles of LDL, which is the killer profile. And none of this is new, although it has been borne out by new studies. Even before Keys began his mission, there was plenty of evidence to contradict his views. A whole generation of nutritionists have rested arguments on Keys's famous Seven Countries Study, a piece of work he said proved his hypothesis about the connection between dietary fat and heart disease. The problem is, Keys analyzed data from twenty-two countries and deliberately assembled a list of the first seven that made his point and ignored the longer list of countries that contradicted it.

The irony here is that the misguided attack on all fats and cholesterol targeted high-cholesterol foods like eggs and butter and argued that we would be better off eating highly processed substitutes like Egg Beaters and margarine. Which brings us to the fats, and the refinement of the argument about fats. Those substitutes had in common a type of fat that is manufactured and has no precedent in evolutionary history: what we call "trans fats," which is a truncation of their technical chemical name, trans-isomer fatty acids. These are also labeled "unsaturated fats," but the better way to think of them is as not existing in nature. These are the fats that harm you, and together with sugar they are the foundation of the industrial foods system.

The damage began with Crisco. Procter & Gamble used a process called hydrogenization—a way to turn oils into solid fats—to invent and introduce Crisco, billed as a lard substitute, in 1911. The same process has since spawned a string of fat substitutes, all based in vegetable oil—especially oil that derives from processing corn and soybeans. It was, for the food industry, a way to spin what was then a waste product of our farm surplus production into a marketable product, and marketing was the key. The early campaigns to sell the public on shortening and margarine were the prototypes for today's sea of hype and cynicism that is the processed foods system. These are the roots of fast food.

The problem with trans fats is that hydrogenation created a set of fatty acid molecules unprecedented in our digestive systems. We are not evolved to handle them. As often as not, foreign molecules in the body rightly trigger an immune response, including inflammation. Inflammation, in turn, is every bit as important as, if not more important than, cholesterol in the genesis of arteriosclerosis and the resulting heart disease. That is, there is a pretty direct and logical link between heart disease and the margarine once marketed as the heart-healthy substitute for butter. By the 1950s, nutritionists were beginning to suspect that link. Epidemiologists now estimate that every 2 percent increase in consumption of trans fats increases the collective risk of heart disease by 23 percent. The National Academy of Sciences says that no level of trans fats in our food is safe. None. Because they are so tied up with heart disease, this, of course, strikes straight at the core of one of our most important diseases of civilization—but there are also linkages here that one might not expect. For instance, a study in 2011 showed that eating trans fats greatly increases the risk of clinical depression, which—as you will recall—is identified as a rapidly growing problem worldwide and, we argue, a disease of civilization.

In the case of trans fats, a measured dose of fat-o-phobia may well be in order, and one should avoid them like the plague. Unfortunately, the bad advice on other fats that began with Ancel

Keys tarred some of our healthiest foods with the same brush, and this needs to be corrected, especially in the case of omega-3s. That's a term you have heard and may well have heard in nutritional advice like this. Step one: Avoid fats. Step two: Be sure to get a good supply of omega-3s. This is not so much advice as it is a hangover of fat-o-phobia. Omega-3s are fats—fats that are in critically short supply in our diets. This shortage may well be a factor in widespread depression but also in high cholesterol, heart disease, inflammation, and compromised brain development.

The clue to the importance of all of this is the name of the category that includes omega-3s, which is essential fatty acids. They are labeled "essential" because without them we could not survive. Literally. We get omega-3s from a variety of sources, but mostly from free-range meats, especially cold-water fish. Vegetarians get them from the few plant sources that contain them, such as walnuts or flax oil.

Their counterparts are omega-6 fats, also present in meat, and although omega-6s are seeing some bad press lately, they are also essential fatty acids. The problem is one of balance—and again, this is rooted in our industrial system of agriculture. Cows evolved to eat grass, but mostly we no longer feed them grass; we feed them the corn and soybeans that are the prime products of our industrial agriculture system. The practice creates beef high in omega-6 fats and low in omega-3s. The practice of fattening beef in feedlots and the preponderance of factory beef in the fast-food system passes this omega-3 shortage into our bodies.

But this is also why eating red meat itself has gotten a bad rap, with endless strings of studies linking it to heart disease and a variety of other issues. The beef that is the basis of these conclusions is factory beef, and no wonder.

Meanwhile, the shortage of omega-3s undoubtedly shows up in areas we might not suspect, and one example from the literature demonstrates just how far-reaching this effect might be. One researcher in education — not in nutrition — performed a meta-analysis of all peer-reviewed research on proven methods to increase a child's intelligence (that is, boost academic performance). The conclusion: "Supplementing infants with long-chain polyunsaturated fatty acids [specifically omega-3s], enrolling children in early educational interventions, reading to children in an interactive manner, and sending children to preschool all raise the intelligence of young children."

(We think there is enough evidence to add exercise to the list, but the point stands.)

And it is a problem that can be easily solved by eating grass-finished beef, now widely available thanks to increased awareness and demand, but also wild-caught fish, free-range eggs, and even walnuts. This is a corrective to generations' worth of bad assumptions about fats. And yes, our bloodstreams are full of fat as a result of the industrial diet and processed food, but this is not all fat's fault. Remember the insulin response and the insulin resistance generated by excess carbohydrate consumption. Remember that insulin immediately shuts off the body's use of fat; it sends signals to keep it in storage and at the same time signals muscles to cease burning fat and start burning glucose. This alone goes a long way toward explaining why fatty acids jam up in our bloodstream, especially as triglycerides. It's not because we are eating fats; people always have. It is because excessive carbohydrates, especially sugar, are preventing us from burning them. Cut out the carbs, and the fat problem takes care of itself, as long as you eat the right kinds of fats.

But in his book, Taubes takes on this issue from another direction, a convincing capstone of an argument. There is no doubt that obesity is increasing in a number of countries around the world. In the United States, we can plot that increase on a graph over the last fifty or so years. And we can plot, alongside that, three other graphs, for per capita consumption of protein, fats, and carbohydrates (including sugars). The first two graphs show flat lines with no real increase in per capita consumption of either protein or fats. In sharp distinction, per capita consumption of carbohydrates in the United States has risen steadily in marked and obvious parallel to obesity.

This is not a new trend. Annual per capita sugar consumption in the United States was 5 pounds per person in 1700, 23 pounds in 1800, 70 pounds in 1900, and 152 pounds today. This is why we talk about sugar when we begin talking about what ails us. Want to go wild? Here's how. Don't eat sugar, not in any form. Not sucrose, not pure cane sugar, not high-fructose corn syrup, not honey, not in all those other polysyllabic chemical names that reveal industrial processes rooted in corn: maltodextrin, dextrose, sorbitol, mannitol. Not apple juice. John thinks this is one of the hidden causes of childhood obesity, even in households where there is very good parenting.

Don't eat dense packages of carbohydrates, particularly refined flour. No bread, no pasta, no bagels, certainly no cookies. No grain, period, not even whole grain. Don't eat trans fats. Period. And you may have figured out the derivative rule by now. Trans fats and sugars are the foundation of processed food. Do not eat processed food.

You will notice that in this prescription, we have remained silent on the topic of dairy products, and not because the topic is irrelevant. Dairy is, in fact, interesting both for what it tells us about evolution and also in the ways it resonates through your health and well-being.

To begin with, dairy is one of the more outstanding—if not *the* outstanding—exceptions to the rule that the basic human design has not changed in fifty thousand years. The fact is, about a third of humanity has evolved the ability to digest lactose, the sugar in milk, as adults. All children make the enzyme lactase (the gene product that digests lactose) for the obvious reason that baby mammals have to digest milk to survive. But in deep evolutionary time, all adults lost that ability as we matured, which was not a problem in our ancestral homeland in Africa, near the equator, with ample sunlight. But as humans migrated north, winters brought shorter days, less sun, and a vitamin D deficiency, which was a serious problem. (And as we shall see, it still is a serious problem.) We get vitamin D from the sun, but also from milk.

In evolution, necessity does indeed mother invention, and it was in Eurasia that a mutation occurred that allowed adults to digest lactose. To this day, that ability tracks in populations with roots in Eurasia, the third of us who can tolerate lactose into adulthood.

But interestingly, there was a parallel step in cultural, not biological, evolution that solved the same problem. Around the Mediterranean and on the Asian steppes, there is widespread lactose intolerance in the populations, yet these people eat dairy products like cheeses and yogurt and have for a very long time. They have adopted a cultural practice that outsources the job of digesting lactose: fermentation. Fermentation uses bacteria to digest lactose, meaning that people with lactose intolerance can still get nutrition and vitamin D from fermented dairy products. They are using an external microbiome, an ingenious bit of outsourcing.

We have remained silent on dairy in our prescription because this evolutionary history outlines some individual solutions. Do what works for you.

WHY VARIETY

Close readers will notice by now that our argument appears to have painted us into a corner, and it is precisely the same predicament that traps most diet nags, an argument that we become ill and fat by eating this or that food. Because we are not just talking about quantity here; we are talking about restricting a whole class of foods, and humanity's most important foods at that. This contention runs smack up against the evolutionary foundation of humanity that we laid out in the beginning: we humans are the ultimate generalists, the Swiss Army knives of not just movement but nutrition, too. The foundation of our success as a species is our ability to adapt to a wide range of conditions, environments, and foods—the very ability that allowed us to occupy the entire planet, unlike any other species. In fact, we are not going to shy away from this apparent contradiction. Not only did evolution equip us so we can eat a wide variety of foods, but it made variety a necessary condition of our well-being. We not only can but must have variety to be healthy. Remember, this was George Armelagos's second and more important rule, a fact so often missed in books that attempt to adapt evolutionary understanding to prescriptions.

"I think variety is the key to all of it," he says.

Even our argument that you should not eat sugar does not violate this rule; restricting sugar enables the body's responses that support variety. Remember homeostasis, the complex array of thermostats that allow our bodies to roll with the punches? Homeostasis underscores much of what we have to say. These thermostats let us weather variation and return to a sustainable state. Insulin's response to sugar in the bloodstream is homeostasis at work. But insulin resistance is the signal that we have swamped that system, so much so that our internal thermostats cease to function and therefore cease to enable us to navigate the world of diversity and variety.

This is the negative side of the argument, and the positive side is more intriguing still. The enormous energetic demands of our brains mean, as we have seen, that we could not be at all casual about nutrition. The demand for energetically dense foods dictated that we eat meat, which meant hunting, which in turn required a great deal of intelligence. But it also meant gathering plants, which in turn required detailed knowledge of plants, seasons, and even subtle clues like what sort of leaf pattern in what sort of state of wilt signaled that a succulent tuber was hidden a few feet under the ground, ready for harvest. Our attention to color, our empathy for animals, our recognition of patterns, even our ability to communicate with one another—all are rooted in this fundamental need to feed our brains, and at the same time, our brains return the favor by allowing it all, a sort of positive feedback loop that drives development. We revel in all of this and take pleasure in it, still enjoying a primal rush of pleasure on walking through a bustling farmer's market on a sunny afternoon.

But the whole array of demands gets ratcheted up to another

level still when we add to this what has come to be called the omnivore's dilemma, a dilemma caused by conflicting interests. Because we are omnivores and because we range over the entire planet, it is in our interests to exploit as many food sources as possible. This means that an important characteristic of omnivores is bred to the bone in humans: we are neophiliacs. We have to be. We have an innate love of novelty, of variety, a need to sample new things. And at the same time, some of those bright and shiny new things, some of those foods on offer in the wild, are poisonous—a lot more than you might think. Not acutely so, like sugar, but lethal poisons that drop you dead on the spot. Thus, it is equally in our interests to be neophobes, to fear new things, thereby causing a conflict at the center of the human condition.

Throughout the course of our evolutionary history, we have negotiated this dilemma with cuisine, sharing cultural information about what is good to eat and not good to eat. We depend on others—elders, mothers, and fathers—to hold this information specific to place and teach it to those who need it. It is the very essence of culture, one more way in which we depend on one another for survival. And there is nothing perfect about this solution; if it were perfect, a given culture long adapted to a given place would make use of all the nutritious plants and animals and leave all the poisonous ones alone. Not the case. For instance, in one of his papers on this topic, Armelagos reports that the !Kung people of the Kalahari Desert eat a total of 105 species of plants and 260 species of animals from the desert savanna environment—a total of 365 species of plants and animals. But modern biologists have determined that the same place holds at least 500 edible species. The gap is a measure of the cultural negotiation of the omnivore's dilemma on the safe side. Still, the undeniable push in humanity is toward variety.

Tyler Graham and Drew Ramsey are not evolutionary biologists but a science writer and a medical doctor, respectively, and their argument, summarized in their book *The Happiness Diet*, does not derive from !Kung practices but from modern humans. They argue as we do that our happiness and mental well-being are rooted in what we eat, and this is more than a matter of depression. For instance, trace brain-derived neurotrophic factor, or BDNF. In *Spark*, John called this chemical "Miracle-Gro for the brain." It is the important link that explains why simple exercise can have such a profound effect on cognition and well-being, and we'll have more to say about it in the next chapter, when we address movement. But nutrition affects BDNF, too. Eating a diet high in sugar decreases BDNF. Eating foods with folate, vitamin B12, and omega-3 fats increases BDNF in the brain, just as exercise does.

Graham and Ramsey examine a list of twelve micronutrients and vitamins: vitamin B12, iodine, magnesium, cholesterol, vitamin D, calcium, fiber, folate, vitamin A, omega-3s, vitamin E, and iron; each is plentiful in the very foods, like fresh fruits and vegetables, that we have eliminated from the modern industrial diet, and each is vital to brain health and well-being on very specific pathways. But this is just the beginning. We are starting to understand the phenomenon of bioavailability, which says that addressing the lack of a given vitamin or micronutrient is not simply a matter of adding a given amount back through a supplement. The body's ability to absorb those nutrients is greatly influenced by the presence or absence of other nutrients. For instance, eating spinach with lemon helps the body absorb much more of the iron in the spinach. Eating eggs and cheese together delivers a better uptake of vitamin D and calcium.

What emerges is the rough outline of a picture far too complex to detail in a prescriptive diet, and in the end, that's the point. Yes, we can keep track of some of this in the cultural wisdom that has evolved through the millennia, but in the end, we're simply not able, as individuals, to account for all of it, to count the calories, read the labels, and total the RDAs for a long list of necessary nutrients. The case that emerges, then, is precisely the situation evolution prepared us for. We can only begin to satisfy the complex and highly evolved requirements of our bodies, especially our brains, through variety. That's why evolution hard-wired us to value it so greatly.

And the fact is, no one understands this fundamental, innate drive for variety more than the modern-day marketers of industrial and processed food. Walk through the aisle of any convenience store or thumb through ads for fast-food chains, soft drinks, and box cereals. Note the variety, exotic names, every shape, color, and texture imaginable. This is what we crave. Then begin reading labels and note the predominance of the suffixes "-trose" and "-crose," i.e., sugar, and of corn and corn derivatives, processed soybeans, trans fats, and flour. The variety is an illusion. Under the label and chemical colorings and aromas, it is the same deadly industrial blend.

All of this forms the outline of our prescription, and the first half we've already given you is indeed negative: to not eat sugar, dense carbohydrates like grains, and trans fats, which is to say processed foods. But this is really advice to reject the monotony of the modern industrial diet. We are not urging a diet or even calorie restriction; we are outlining a sustainable way of life, and it rests on variety: the profusion and explosion of flavors, colors, and textures that evolution tuned our senses to pursue. Nuts, root vegetables, leafy greens, fruits, fish, wild game, clean, cool water. Range far and wide. Eat well.

BACK TO MARY BETH STUTZMAN

We caught up again with Mary Beth Stutzman during a quiet summer's evening in 2013 over dinner in a pleasant little restaurant at the mouth of northern Michigan's Thunder Bay River. She was well. We ordered, and she decided to pass on the local lake-caught fish fillets, which on the surface may seem a bit odd, because she is an active booster of the local sport fishery and even has her own television show dedicated to the topic. It's how she supports her community, and that's part of what she is about and glad to do now that she is well.

But the restaurant's fillets came breaded. No bread—no way. That's the rule that made her well. That was the key she was looking for in all those years of traipsing to specialists and emergency rooms doubled over in pain. She found the solution not from any advice from an MD but by accident. Just about the time she thought she was going to die, a friend happened to bring her some cupcakes to cheer her up. The irony is, the friend himself knew better than to eat cupcakes, but he thought Mary Beth might like them. He also brought her a book on the paleo diet, which he himself had adopted and which was why he didn't eat cupcakes. She read the book, particularly the section about a problem called leaky gut, which sounded terribly, achingly, shockingly familiar. Leaky gut is caused by eating dense, refined carbs and sugar. In all those years of seeing doctors and delivering long lists of symptoms, no one suggested this to her, let alone asked what she was eating. No one asked about her nutrition. She adopted the diet and got immediately and noticeably better. And better. And better. Food healed her. It's as simple as that.

Now she is vibrant and alive, an exercise enthusiast, actively promoting fitness as fun. She is engaged with her family and happy.

"I can't even describe how great I felt. It was like being born again. It was a feeling of how great it is to be alive. It was out of this world," she told us.

And no, she is not a food fanatic; in fact, she loathes the term "paleo." If you press her on this matter, she'll simply label her diet "trending toward paleo." She even allows herself occasional tastes of selected whole grains, and now and again a little ice cream with its sugar. She's okay with a little lactose. And maybe this variation and experimentation, even more than her diet and recovery, are the lessons we'd like you to carry with you as we develop our story. Here, though, are some key points: First, her path to well-being began with diet, specifically with recognizing the basic fact that civilization's grain and sugar were making her ill, and even — as a young woman — close to death. All she had to do to fix it was pay some reasonable attention to diet — nothing extreme, but simply head in the direction of eating the way humans were evolved to eat. Second, she used that knowledge to devise her own path through the pitfalls. But most important, once she started to get better, her path to well-being led beyond diet, through other areas like fitness, family, and community. You will see this happen to others as we go on. Not every pathway begins with diet and nutrition, although many do, and it's hard to imagine getting better if nutrition is wrong. But in some way or another, we think every pathway begins with a lesson from evolution.

CAUTION: EVOLUTION RUNS BOTH WAYS

There is a popular myth about evolution: that it is progressive and leads only one way, to bigger, better, and smarter, to more complex. It can lead that way, because complexity takes time to assemble, so complex comes later. But so does simpler, and the koala bear, that cuddly icon of cute, is our favorite example. Koalas are interesting to biologists because they eat only one thing, eucalyptus leaves, so they inhabit these trees ubiquitous in Australia. As a result, they really never have to leave the trees; they can just sit and watch the world go by, day in, day out.

It wasn't always so. Koalas once had a more diverse diet in their evolutionary history. The mark of this is inside their head, as their brain does not fill the entire space allotted for it in their skull. That's because, coincident with adopting the narrower diet, their brain shrank, and evolution has not yet had time to make skull size compensate, so the tiny little brain rattles around in a too-big case. One single source of food. That, and they are sedentary. If the koalas wanted to retain the bigger brain that evolution gave them, they also needed to move, and this is the lesson we turn to next.

4

Nimble

Building and Rebuilding the
Brain Through Movement

No one can be blamed for being confused about this matter, particularly those who follow health news in the popular press. Dueling headlines appear almost daily summarizing the latest published results and fronting pronouncements such as this one from a recent paragraph in the *New York Times*' health section: "And in a just world, frequent physical activity should make us slim. But repeated studies have shown that many people who begin an exercise program lose little or no weight. Some gain."

The fact is, we don't care whether the studies like the ones reported here are the final word on the matter. (We don't think they are.) The larger issue is far more important: these sorts of conclusions are irrelevant. Physical exercise is not about weight loss; it is about your well-being.

The British scientist Daniel Wolpert likes to begin his case with the sort of fundamental and vexing question that seriously shakes up our thinking: why do we have a brain? He expects the obvious answer: to think.

"But this is completely wrong," he says. "We have a brain for one reason only: to produce adaptable and complex movements. There is no other plausible explanation." He is saying that our brains are literally built on and inextricably tied to movement of our bodies. Movement builds our brain because movement requires a brain.

Wolpert's career of researching this traces the same argument that people often use about basic intelligence: that computers can't do what we do. After generations of trying, the best and brightest of computer science still have been unable to approach something like artificial intelligence, and what we mean by that is that we can't program computers to perform music, exercise judgment, or write books. Wolpert thinks something is missing in this familiar argument: "While computers can now beat grand masters at chess, no computer can yet control a robot to manipulate a chess piece with the dexterity of a six-year-old child."

This is because even the simplest of motions—a flick of a finger or a turn of the hand to pick up a pencil—is maddeningly complex and requires coordination and computational power beyond electronic abilities. For this you need a brain. One of our favorite quotes on this matter comes from the neuroscientist Rodolfo Llinás: "That which we call thinking is the evolutionary internalization of movement."

The telling encapsulation of this argument is the case of the sea squirt, a primitive sea animal with a rudimentary nervous system. For part of its life, the squirt spends time moving but only to look for a spot where it can anchor itself in the path of a ready source of food. On doing so, its first act is to eat and digest its own brain; it doesn't need one anymore because it no longer needs to move.

Yet this is the sort of linkage between brain and movement that holds up from sea squirt to human along the long evolutionary chain. The association is clear: the more a species needs to move, the bigger its brain—a relationship particularly pronounced in mammals. And although we don't often think of it this way, the argument gets its clincher with the great ape that (a) has the very largest of brains (we humans) and (b) happens to be the champion of movement. Coincidence, you think? One of our greatest and enduring fascinations as humans is with movement. Sedentary as we may be, we still pay enormous amounts of money and invest enormous amounts of cultural capital in watching people move, obviously so with sports but consider, too, movement like ballet. What other species could accomplish this level of variation and control in pure movement? Our attraction to ballet and dance is not coincidence, just as our deep appreciation for a naked human body of the gender that attracts us is not coincidence. This attraction is evolution's way of making us pay attention to what matters, and movement matters. Evolution has made us think that graceful movement is beautiful.

BRAIN BUILDING

Neuroscience in the '90s delivered a game-changing set of realizations that shone a couple of bright lights in new directions on the concepts of neuroplasticity and neurogenesis. The first says your brain is plastic in the prechemical sense of the word, malleable, shape-shifting, moldable. It is not the hardwired, compartmentalized organ we once thought it to be; it's not true that given cells and networks of cells and given areas and structures of the brain are assigned a task and that's that. Lose a set of cells to, say, a stroke, and you lose the ability to perform that task. Or, more to the point, get dealt a weak spot by genetics, say for language, and you will always have a struggle with language. But the brain can, in fact, rewire itself, repurpose bits and pieces. It can adapt. It grows. This is neuroplasticity.

Neurogenesis says something similar but even more revolutionary. New cells and networks of the brain grow as needed, very much as muscles grow with exercise. In fact, new-era neuroscience says that the brain is a muscle. This is more than an analogy. As science began to understand these phenomena, it began to tease out mechanisms, the cascades of signals and biochemicals that triggered this exquisite set of responses. This line of inquiry greatly illuminated what evolutionary biologists had already realized: that big brains and intricate physical movement went together, that evolution had in fact used some of the same principles to signal brain growth that it had used to signal muscle growth. Through time, evolution used biochemistry to enhance muscles, movement, and brains.

So far in our story, we have relied often on the concept of homeostasis, which is an array of signaling mechanisms within the body that responds to shocks or changes in the environment to return systems to a normal operating state. We'll see it again and again to the point of ramping up to a new level of complexity and a new idea as our argument develops. All in time. But at this point in the discussion we need another related idea: hormesis. Hormesis is a biological response to low doses of a stressor, such as a toxin, that improves the ability of the body to handle that toxin. It can be applied to exercise. Unlike homeostasis, hormesis does not return the body to a normal state. It returns it to a better-than-normal state. When a bodybuilder lifts weights, he is placing heavy stress on a given set of muscles, a process that damages them by overload. The body reacts with an immune response and inflammation. And now notice that we have introduced two troubling words into the discussion, at least troubling in terms of the popular understanding: inflammation and stress. The fact is, the body uses both to rebuild, and we'll argue later for a more refined appreciation of these forces.

But for now, the important point is that rebuilding the body does not simply build back what was torn down: it builds bigger and better, an adaptive response. Your muscles face a new challenge in the form of heavier weights, so the body responds by building infrastructure to meet that challenge. It grows and makes the body more resilient. Take the challenge away, and the body heads in the other direction: once again, use it or lose it.

And now we come back to BDNF, brain-derived neurotrophic factor, the Miracle-Gro of the brain. Movement places demands on the brain, just as it does on muscle, and so the brain releases BDNF, which triggers the growth of cells to meet the increased mental demands of movement. But BDNF floods throughout the brain, not just to the parts engaged in movement. Thus, the whole brain flourishes as a result of movement. It provides the environment that brain cells need to grow and function well.

Chemically, there is more to this story—lots more. For instance, exercise also triggers responses in the important neurotransmitters long studied in connection with issues like addiction and depression, chemicals like serotonin, dopamine, and norepinephrine. These are parallel processes. It all hangs together. But in the end, cells are cells. The brain is an energy-burning network of specially adapted cells like any other organ and is wrapped up in the health of the rest of the system. This ought to follow logically from the connection between the brain and movement: if the body needs stronger or more refined movement to meet a given challenge, it will need more brain circuitry to guide that movement. It would make no sense adaptively to build one without the other, so we need the biochemical provisions to do both.

This is no longer conjecture or theoretical construct. We may be a sedentary culture, but while we've been couch-bound in front of video games and computer monitors, science has been busy assembling a massive pile of evidence that says the quickest, surest path to the health and well-being of the brain and body is movement, or vigorous aerobic exercise.

Begin by considering a formal review of the literature, now more than a decade old but with conclusions that have even more support today. Writing in the *Journal of Applied Physiology*, researchers including Frank W. Booth laid out the case that inactivity was a looming factor in at least twenty "of the most chronic disorders." Yes, it does include obesity, but it extends far beyond to other afflictions of civilization, including congestive heart failure, coronary artery disease, angina and myocardial infarction, hypertension, stroke, type 2 diabetes, dyslipidemia, gallstones, breast cancer, colon cancer, prostate cancer, pancreatic cancer, asthma, chronic obstructive pulmonary disease, immune dysfunction, osteoarthritis, rheumatoid arthritis, osteoporosis, and a range of neurological dysfunctions, a subcategory of particular interest here and one we will unpack in a moment.

In almost all of these cases, the causes of the disease are directly linked to inactivity, but not all. For instance, Booth concludes that there is no evidence saying inactivity *causes* chronic obstructive pulmonary disease. That is, exercise may not prevent it but can heal it once it does occur—an important distinction. This is the realization that ought to ring through public discourse like a loud pealing bell, given that the list cited above is hugely responsible for the crushing burden of health-care costs in our society—and yet almost nowhere in the wide-spread discussion of reducing those costs do we mention how much of that bill is traceable to our sedentary ways.

In Booth's analysis of all of this, there is a simple sentence that greatly adds to the urgency. We are not just talking about sick people or physical debilitation. He writes: "Sedentary life-style is associated with lower cognitive skills." Stated more bluntly still, our inactivity is making us dumber. If anything, this conclusion can now be stated even more confidently, given the wealth of research in the decade since Booth made it. Both epi-demiology and neuroscience have described the biochemistry that makes it so.

The definitive statement about this comes from a group of researchers headed by J. Eric Ahlskog from the Department of Neurology at the Mayo Clinic. Prompted by some inconclusive work by the National Institutes of Health, Ahlskog and his group undertook a comprehensive review of all the research they could find on the relationship between cognition and exercise. They used the keywords "cognition" and "exercise" to search the massive PubMed database of medical research. The search returned 1,603 published research papers on the topic, a number that in itself gives us some idea of how thoroughly this issue has been examined. And the researchers read every one of those papers and compiled conclusions in a paper of their own published in 2011.

Their emphasis was on dementia, in its severe form as Alzheimer's disease but also as evidenced in problems like the memory loss and decline of mental acuity that we think of as a sign of aging. Their results are sweeping and speak to all of us, not just the elderly. First, the preponderance of those 1,603 studies showed that exercise delivered marked improvements for people suffering all the cognitive impairments examined, from minor memory loss to full-on Alzheimer's. Further, the studies that examined middle-aged people who exercised regularly found a substantial preventive effect of all forms of impairment later in life. Exercise helps the afflicted but also prevents the affliction. Cognitive impairment is not so much a consequence of aging as it is a consequence of our sedentary lives.

Yet the consequences of dementia in our society are huge and getting much worse. A 2013 study by the Rand Corporation showed that now about 15 percent of people older than 71 — 3.8 million people — suffer from dementia. But the aging of baby boomers along with the way we live will nearly triple that number by 2040, to 9.1 million people. In addition, another 5.4 million people, 22 percent of those older than 71, suffer mild cognitive impairment, as opposed to full-on dementia. Current social costs of treating dementia alone in the United States are $109 billion, more than we spend treating either heart disease or cancer.

One might think the reason for this decline during old age is obvious. We have long thought that many of the late-life neuro-logical problems of aging stem directly from the decline of the cardiovascular system, that poor circulation robs the brain of oxygen. The group at the Mayo Clinic did indeed follow this trail and did indeed find what they called a "vascular" effect. But interestingly, the weight of the evidence caused them to con-clude this was secondary. The main benefit of exercise, they wrote, was improved neuroplasticity and neurogenesis. Specifi-cally, they traced this to the key neurotrophic factors of exercise, the Miracle-Gro effect with BDNF that we have talked about, but also to a group of parallel biochemicals, especially IGF-1, or insulin-like growth factor.

To take this line of reasoning one step further, the research-ers were able to find a number of papers in the pool that looked at brain growth — actual, physical, measurable brain growth — as a result of exercise and found that seniors who exercised devel-oped "significantly larger hippocampal volumes," and because the hippocampus participates in memory processing, they had improved memory as a result. They found that exercise also pre-vented a loss of gray matter overall (a loss common in aging) and, additionally, improved brain function as measured by func-tional magnetic resonance imaging, showing better and more robust connections throughout.

But now consider the word "aging," which doesn't just refer to old people. We are all aging, and as is the case with gravity on the rest of our bodies, the downward forces on our brains begin early and extend through life. This research is therefore relevant to all of life. We may well notice the loss of memory at age seventy-one, but it began a lot earlier. Which means there is every reason to start looking at this issue at the other end of life.

ALL EDUCATION IS PHYSICAL EDUCATION

There is an emerging and every-bit-as-robust body of research on the effects of exercise on young brains. Maybe the best example is not a research paper (although the project certainly has spawned its share of publications) but the long-running educational experiment that was the centerpiece of John Ratey's book *Spark*. If you haven't read the details of that case or the rest of the evidence presented in *Spark,* it's worth doing so to see this issue unfold. But we can encapsulate it here by citing the experiment in the Naperville school district, which demonstrates unequivocally how exercise builds brains at the beginning of life. The Naperville school district became the national leader in recognizing this by integrating a comprehensive program of aerobic workouts into the daily routine for its students. The program has paid off handsomely in stunning improvements in academic performance, improvement at the level that would in and of itself benchmark the sort of education reform that the nation needs and never seems able to accomplish.

But as is the case with research on aging, the body of evidence regarding exercise has only grown since. To date, no one we know of has gone so far as to compile in meta-analysis all the research on exercise and young people, as was done with the Mayo Clinic study. Nonetheless, there are some large and compelling data sets that prove the point. One of our favorites is a result in California, where state officials looked at eight hundred thousand fifth-, seventh-, and ninth-grade students, ranking their performance on a series of six physical fitness standards against their scores on standardized math and language tests.

The result was a clean, stair-stepped relationship: the more fitness standards a student met, the better the test scores.

Meanwhile, Sweden has assembled a massive database looking at 1.2 million boys who entered military service between 1950 and 1976, measuring both cardiovascular fitness and muscle strength against IQ and cognitive abilities when all the subjects were fifteen years old and again at eighteen. Cardiovascular fitness did indeed demonstrate the same positive relationship with both intellectual measurements. This study, however, went further and tracked the subjects into adulthood, finding that those with better fitness scores wound up with better education, more life satisfaction, and higher socioeconomic standing.

But there is an even more intriguing pattern in the Swedish case. The data set included 270,000 brothers and 1,300 identical twins and showed that cardio fitness and not familial relationship turned out to be the better predictor of both cognitive ability and IQ. That is, despite the popular assumption that IQ is genetically determined, fitness and not genes held the greater sway over these tests of intellect.

All of this traces to a thread of this idea that John has been following since the 1970s, when he first noticed that marathon runners suffered depression when they quit running. Stopping running was like stopping effective medication. This phenomenon goes beyond cognition to tie in the element of mental health.

Lately, and since John detailed these issues in *Spark,* there continues to be an ever-widening use of exercise in treating mental issues. We are seeing paper after paper showing positive results in treating anxiety, addictions, attention deficit disorder, obsessive-compulsive disorder, schizophrenia, and, lately, bipolar disorder, but nowhere has there been as much work done as with depression. In 2010, the American Psychiatric Association issued new guidelines for treating depression, and for the first time, exercise was listed as a proven treatment. Thus, the APA finally caught up with Hippocrates, who recommended that all people in a bad mood should go for a walk—and if it did not improve, walk again. The APA's change of heart was fostered by a lot of this convincing new evidence.

Psychologist James Blumenthal of Duke University has been leading the charge. He conducted trials looking at the effects of exercise on sedentary patients with anxiety or depression, and his research culminated in a seminal report in 1999. In this study, 156 sedentary depressed patients were assigned to one of three groups. One used increasing doses of sertraline, or Zoloft (a popular antidepressant), another began exercising three times a week for forty minutes each day, and the third received both the drug and the exercise regimen. At sixteen weeks there was no difference in their depression scores, but at the end of a ten-month follow-up, those still exercising were better off than those on pills alone.

Blumenthal was criticized by prominent psychopharmacologists for not having a placebo group, and so he completed another study, published in 2007, with 202 patients, showing similar positive results for those doing exercise. Since then there have been many other studies looking at both aerobic exercise and strength training, and both interventions show positive effects. Movement regimens such as yoga and tai chi also help, but not as much.

But looking at this impressive body of evidence—evidence largely absent in the public discussion of issues like education and health care—it's easy enough to miss the most significant accomplishment of the research. The evidence begins with what we will call the epidemiological case, that is, a statistical examination of outcomes for people who exercise. This can take us only so far; it steers us toward the pitfall that scientists understand when they warn us that correlation is not cause. This is the very pitfall that allowed, say, tobacco companies to wriggle out of responsibility when early epidemiological studies showed that smoking was associated with lung cancer. But years later, science was able to delineate and prove the biochemical linkages that made this so. They described *how* smoking caused lung cancer, and now there is no doubt. Not many people have noticed, but we are well past that point now with brain health and exercise. Sedentary behavior causes brain impairment, and we know how: by depriving your brain of the flood of neurochemistry that evolution developed in order to grow brains and keep them healthy.

WILD MOTION

So we've made the case and now you see the next step coming, the directive to pay up the gym membership, squeeze into the Lycra, load yourself onto a treadmill or stationary bike six days a week, set the timer for thirty minutes, punch up the iPod workout playlist, and slog your way to health. You know the drill, but if you think this is it, then you haven't been paying attention. The regimen described above is to movement what processed fast food is to a full-on feast. The gym drill may get you by—and we're not against it—but this is about going wild, about getting better, being as good as you can be. There is a better way to move.

We hope to entice you out of the gym and, toward that end, invite you on a run with us, a late spring day of the sort that pulls you outdoors, the first day this year without gloves and a jacket, cold at first, but sun and a few hundred yards of warm-up make light dress just right. We're in the Rocky Mountains. The path winds out from the trailhead through a short stretch of flat ground, a gentle warm-up, and then the climb begins, a short uphill that catches you pushing a bit too hard and then your clean, aerobic heart rate spikes past the red line. You hold your pace for as long as you can, pitting will against slope, and then you're light-headed and winded and the quadriceps signal fatigue. Too soon for this. You're busted, and you walk. Heart rate recovers as you climb, head clears in a few hundred yards, and then you notice the hill has flattened at ridgetop to deliver a sweeping vantage of the valley below. You take it in, recover, and now trot. You measure your pace, tune it to the incline, and then again you are running. You don't let up but aim a steady climb for the first little summit you spot a hundred yards on. Now there's mud, and the trail becomes a trench, catching the melt of a winter's retreating snowdrift just above. More distress messages from quads and lungs, but you've got the pace right and hold it, light head be damned. And then you make that bit of a summit in a rush and a slight little giggle of triumph — first of the day — and then almost immediately sweep down the back side of the hill, shift gears, take it a bit too fast in skippy, quick steps, but it feels right, hopping rocks and roots, rocking off banked turns with a quick roll of the foot, vaulting puddles and little stubborn slicks of ice. The trail steepens and winds to a bend. You careen around the curve, bracing off rocks, and then spot a quick four-foot stair-step drop through a wall of rocks, step it, tick, tick, tick, splash in the mud below, then another bend and just beyond, the light signals the trail's bend into tree cover, where sun does not pene-trate this early in the year. Now you're moving a bit too fast for control, and the next step places you on the high end of a foot-wide luge course of ice that ends in a bend above a rock-face cliff. Your feet look for grit and gravel of any kind, anything to slow your mad sliding scramble down. By all means do not panic now. Do not lock up and brake. Easy does it. Balance. Control. And just then your dog, who has been following you in all of this, decides, as she always does, that being behind you is not good enough, and she goes in for a quick pass on your cliff side by ducking between your feet, a canine foul of clipping. You get a half second to debate whether she goes over the cliff or you do, but then you notice you have bent one leg 90 degrees from the knee, just right, and the dog makes a quick move to expertly snake her way around your other leg, no foul. (Every animal knows way more than you do.) And you carry on, another grin, another little victory over the trail. And so on.

We've just given you a little slice of life, a description of maybe ten minutes of running on a mountain trail. In contrast, consider how we might describe ten minutes of running on a treadmill: Get on the treadmill, take a step, left foot, right foot. Repeat. Even the vicarious experience on the mountain trail, even reading along, invited more of your brain to come for the ride. With luck, our description of the mountain run engaged some of your mirror neurons, your sense of empathy. Even in the telling, it is information-rich and, as a result, engaging. So it is with the real thing.

This is not to say we are writing a prescription for mountain running as the single true and only heaven. Nonetheless, mountain running provides a great path to understanding an important element of productive exercise, and it may, in fact, be time to do away with the idea of an exercise routine. The term "exercise" is an artifact of our industrialized, regimented, domesticated lives. If the brain is to take full advantage of what we now understand about the importance of movement, then you don't have to exercise; you've got to move. You've got to be nimble.

SMARTER MOVES

The argument that humans were born to run in many ways makes running the ideal subject to serve as a doorway into a better understanding of motion and brain development in general. Running lies at the core of the human experience, but that deep connection has also, in recent years, produced a flurry of investigation and research across disciplines that give this topic a better platform than most for launching the broader discussion of the importance of movement. This is especially true because the general line of thinking got a huge leg up into the popular discussion with the work of Christopher McDougall and his groundbreaking book, *Born to Run*, which encourages barefoot running on evolutionary grounds.

Ask any physical therapist who practices in a running town, and you'll hear about McDougall's influence. Such clinicians are fond of claiming a real affinity for his work, simply because barefoot running has delivered so many injuries and thus ensured a steady flow of income. Barefoot running is their business model.

Press them further, though, as we have, and you will find out this is not so much a critique of McDougall's work or the idea behind it. The injuries accrue from a narrow reading of that research, particularly the assumption that barefoot running is all about, well, bare feet. It's not. But more tellingly, some physical therapists report that the injuries are accruing disproportionately to road runners, people who adopt minimalist shoes and then run serious mileage on consistent, flat, even terrain, the same surface and motion, step after step. Further, many people make the change too quickly and do not give their feet time to overcome a lifetime of bad form. The resulting injuries, then, are not a contradiction of the whole idea; they are a confirmation.

The rationale behind minimalist or barefoot running is this: humans evolved without shoes but also evolved running. A lot of it, on the order of a 10K every day. This dictated a body and movement built around what is called a midfoot or forefoot strike. The foot does not reach out ahead of one's body to land on its heel but, rather, tucks in under the body in a shorter, gentler stride. The long, heel-striking stride prevalent in competitive running became possible only with the introduction of heavily cushioned shoes. More important, that change in stride and shoes, while protecting the heel, shifted forces through ankles, knees, and hips, places not meant to take those forces, and as a consequence, runners become more, not less, injured in the long term—injuries that result from the shift in form allowed by artificially padded shoes.

This is an important principle that goes straight to the core and founding idea of this book: that shortsighted, simplistic, single-factor fixes—especially those that ignore the evolutionary design of our bodies—often create more problems than they solve. To some, this was the end of the story. Shoe companies, even the very ones that developed the heavily padded clunkers of the late twentieth century, got into the business of offering minimalist shoes: lightly padded, low-to-the-ground, slinky, lightweight bedroom slippers. Our culture, being what it is, thought this was the answer, that you fix a problem by buying a single product, be it shoe or pill, and people did buy them and made minimalist running shoes the fastest-growing category in the industry. And then many of these runners did nothing to change their running stride, but went straight out and started pounding pavement and treadmills and then lined up for physical therapists to fix a new set of problems. This is a cautionary tale for all of us, not just runners. A deeper reading of this idea is in order, and therein we might find some exquisite and marvelous detail to guide us through subjects beyond running.

Take, for instance, proprioception, to begin simply. It's a concept well within anyone's grasp, quite literally, and it's a good way to begin. Imagine yourself forced to navigate a dark room crowded with the usual obstacles, like furniture, tight turns, and a light switch across the room. First, you reach out and use proprioception to know where your hand is without seeing it, but you also use your sense of touch to gather information that feeds your brain, taps memories, and reconstructs a map of the room in order to steer your body toward the switch. Part of what is going on here is proprioception, the brain's ability to use signals from your hand to tell you where you are in space and where you should go. Proprioception is your brain's ability to know where your body parts are relative to one another at any given moment.

Also at work are the extraordinary abilities of the hands to gather information, the sense of touch and perception through touch that we rely on in activities like writing with a pencil, manipulating tools, playing the guitar, and foreplay. All of this feeds the brain in a sort of map, and not just of the hand. The surface of the brain contains almost literally a map of various points on our body, a diagram that the brain uses to build the sense of where we are in space. This map even speaks to priorities: our hands, our most important instruments for command of the sensory world, map out on the brain right next to our genitals, areas of maximum sensitivity staked out by evolution for good reason, and so the example of foreplay above is not nearly as frivolous as it might have seemed at first. Likewise, our feet are mapped next to our hands, signaling their importance in guiding us through space, in coordinating with the brain to maintain our sense of order, direction, and balance. The extraordinary sensitivity of our hands to guide us through a dark room ought to be equaled by the ability of our feet to guide us through the world—but, as with many of our evolutionary endowments, civilization has short-circuited the relationship, in this case with shoes. While it may not have been the intent, all that foam and gadgetry and those stiff soles robbed the feet of proprioception, and robbed our brains, our neural circuitry, of the refined information and information processing that directed us for millions of years.

With aging, we worry about matters such as cancer and heart disease or maybe even Alzheimer's taking us out or leaving us debilitated in a nursing home, but gerontologists say that a far more prosaic problem is a bigger one. The simple act of falling often breaks hips and legs and robs people of independence and mobility prematurely. We fall because we have lost our sense of balance, literally lost our way in the world, or, more to the point, have given it up by allowing the neural circuitry that oriented us to atrophy.

This is not to argue that we will solve all our problems simply by getting rid of shoes, or by wearing minimalist shoes. Rather, we offer this as simply one more case study in unintentional damage done by insulating ourselves from the real world. But this is just the beginning. We didn't tell you this, but we had you in minimalist shoes along that mountain trail, so at every twist and turn, your feet were playing a symphony of muscles and nerves to roll off rocks, bank off curves, accelerate, and brake. But this was about far more than feet. Each time you shifted gears from uphill to down or from straight to curve or to hop a rock, a new set of muscles came into play, or the same set of muscles shifted from push to pull, from expand to contract. Quads, calves, and hamstrings, sure enough, but also hips if your stride was right and the full girdle of muscles that wrap your abdomen—all engaged in not just the running but the breathing, the twisting and turning. And you didn't just run. On the uphills you pushed your heart well beyond its aerobic rate, held this as long as you could, then you walked, and suddenly a whole new set of muscles came on line.

Simply by engaging the real, rocky, rolling world and its variety of stresses and varied challenges, you have engaged the full range of muscular and neurological activity that evolved in places just like this. And more than muscles and neurons. Take, for instance, that little giggle you had after that long uphill slog, the summit experience, that little triumph over adversity and challenge. What lay behind that rush of elation was a squirt of biochemistry stimulated by the muscle activity but crucial to your sense of well-being and your brain. Doubtless dopamine was a part of this little reward, the rush that we try to replace with drugs and stimulants or try to re-create with prescription antidepressants. Here it is free for the taking. But here we can see the evolutionary logic behind it: these little rewards are evolution's way of keeping us going, of making us survive. Evolution has made provisions for our happiness, but to take advantage of them you've got to move.

DISCOVERING A NEW WAY TO MOVE

Matt O'Toole has always made his living on health and fitness, enjoying a twenty-five-year career that has, when we talked to him, taken him to the head of the international sports gear manufacturer Reebok. He is buff and tough, as you might expect, and he dresses in the athletic casual code common in the Reebok offices just outside Boston. Like Reebok itself, O'Toole has recently undergone something of a personal transformation.

"I had started a streak about nine years before [my transformation]. I was running every day and I decided to make that my form of exercise, because I was always finding that when I had a different routine I could easily break it. I would miss two or three days because of traveling. So I started this thing where I ran every day, so if I got a streak going, I would not break it. But what happened at the end of nine years, my body was actually a wreck. I had all kinds of back problems, knee problems. My back problem got so severe that my doctor told me I couldn't run anymore." It was an odd admission for a guy in the business of selling running shoes.

Running was probably not O'Toole's problem as much as was

the fact that he did it every day and did it in that flat, monotonous pattern of a street runner, a treadmill runner—but that's not our point here. The point is where O'Toole and Reebok went. He joined CrossFit, a worldwide formalized form of exercise that stresses a variety of movements: weight training, jumping, running, throwing, push-ups, pull-ups—all designed to involve the entire body, recruit all muscles, just as it recruits heart, lungs, and mind. Further, it is done in groups of people and is competitive, but not in the sense of team against team. Rather, there is a group ethic. You compete against yourself first and the group cheers you along, marks progress, forms a sort of community. We'll have lots more to say about the element of community in a later chapter, but for the moment, let's be reductionist and stick with the physical.

O'Toole's back problems simply went away with CrossFit. His new routine was so transforming that it has transformed Reebok itself. The corporation has consciously and explicitly moved away from the model that tied sales and promotion to professional athletic superstars in football, soccer, hockey, and basketball (sports in which most participation involves a couch and a flat-screen television). Instead, Reebok has specifically endorsed CrossFit and is basing its corporate direction on getting people off couches and into gyms.

But there needs to be a bit of disclosure here, especially because one of the authors' direct involvement with Reebok is part of this story. John is a paid consultant to Reebok, hired to help shape this transition and to guide a comprehensive program of exercise based in schools. O'Toole says that reading John's book *Spark* was every bit as important as CrossFit in shaping a new direction for Reebok.

Again, we're not offering CrossFit here as a prescription so much as it is an illustration. We hope you hear in our brief description of CrossFit an echo of our earlier conversation with David Carrier, the University of Utah biologist who has spent a career looking at topics like persistence hunting and movement. Remember, Carrier's ultimate point was that the human body is unique among the bodies of our close relatives, our fellow mammals, in not having a sweet spot, in having muscles and a supporting skeletal system designed for a whole variety of movements. We are, as we've said, the Swiss Army knives of movement, and CrossFit is one exercise program consciously designed to reflect that fact. There are others, specifically some forms of martial arts and even dance that are evolving to grasp this awareness of the human body. Our prescription does not necessarily lock you into a gym. It certainly doesn't lock you on a treadmill in front of a flat-screen.

In our conversation with O'Toole, another echo emerged in his description. Repeatedly, he cited the variety of activities as being among CrossFit's greatest attraction. This word "variety," if you recall, was also pivotal in our earlier discussions of food and nutrition, pivotal in our consideration of human evolution. A standout feature of humanity in evolutionary terms was the ability to adapt and thrive in a variety of environments facing a wide variety of challenges. Evolution tells us that this overarching condition of our deep ancestral past is also the foundation of our present well-being and happiness.

And, in fact, this idea can steer us toward a metric of sorts. Yes, we have shied away from a specific prescription in our arguments, preferring to lay out some general ideas like variety to guide you toward a personal program. We are not saying you must go to a gym and do so many reps of these and a half hour of those at this heart rate at that frequency wearing this brand of shoe and fueling on this sports drink and supplement. All well and good, but how do you know you're on the right track? Weight loss? Tighter abs and butt? Posture? IQ test? None of these. We've got a better one, and, in fact, O'Toole brought it up on his own, unprompted, during our conversation.

"With CrossFit I realized right away the reason I wanted to keep coming back was it was a lot of fun to be around these people and do things that I hadn't been doing and really challenge myself," he said. "The experience became a lot more positive, where with running it was, check the box, I have to do it. CrossFit was, hey, I might actually want to do this."

That's it. That you actually begin to look forward to that point in the day when you get to cut loose and move, that you want to do this. That's when you know you are on the right track, and don't give up until you are. We're telling you that whatever form of movement you do to stay healthy is not right until it gets to be fun. Enjoyable. Nor is this as squishy and nebulous as it might seem. Remember the pathways of biochemistry between muscles and brain. Much of that chemistry is wound up in building a better brain, but much of it is also wound up in rewards, in feeling better, in being attuned to your body's signals that tell you that you are okay, on the right path, and moving forward.

And then one thing leads to another; for O'Toole, it leads to a mountaintop. Although he described himself as "not an outdoor person," he nonetheless decided to mark his fiftieth birthday and the changes in his life by climbing Africa's Mount Kilimanjaro.

DEEPER LAYERS

Our description of the mountain run was, we argued, information-rich, but now is where we admit to rigging the argument a bit more than you may have noticed. As we said, the information contained in the actual run was at least several orders of magnitude greater than would fit on a page, a flood of data to the runner's brain. Nonetheless, there were a couple of simple facts embedded in our description that freighted far more meaning than you probably realized. Remember the dog? Remember how the dog almost knocked you off a cliff at a critical juncture and that this apparent conflict resolved itself by a quick movement instinctive to both dog and runner? In this nanosecond, the runner's brain was presented with a whole set of information way outside the box of the usual exercise routine; at bottom, there was a calculation and evaluation of the well-being of something outside himself, an animal he cared about and even loved. He first faced a moment of peril and then shared that peril with another being in a burst of empathy. Do I kick the dog off the edge of this cliff, or do I go off myself? Then a decision, and then survival. How important was this moment in enriching the experience? This question deserves examination in detail, and we will do just that in a subsequent chapter about empathy and caring and our brains. But first, we need to point out a few more elements of this run that foreshadow larger considerations. It was a mountain run, an experience in the real world. It included ice, rock, mountains, wind, sun, and sweeping vistas of grassy slopes and valleys. It was grounded in nature, which is our ancestral home, the context of human evolution. How much of the value the runner gained from this experience derived from that context? This question deserves its own chapter and will get one.

But this context raises another idea, and we will turn to this idea next. Nature is a valuable setting for our challenges because it just doesn't care about us and is all-powerful. The day that we described was relatively benign. There was sun and blue sky to soften the edges of ice and rock, but every mountain runner and trail runner knows that it could just as easily have been otherwise (and often is), that winds at ridges can summon blasts strong enough to knock you off your feet, or a weather front can blow in whiteout blizzards and temperatures plunging to subzero in a matter of minutes. What do you do about your run on such days? Do you gear up in the latest wonder fabric and press on? Some days, sure you do. There is value in facing a challenge that is real and has real consequences.

But think about our ancestors who faced such conditions routinely and without benefit of wonder fabric. Sometimes the right thing to do is press on, and sometimes it's better to hunker down, to retreat downslope to the cave and the fire and a circle of family, friends, children, and dogs curled in the corner in tight, heat-holding balls. And then it is time to sleep. You've got to move, and then you've got to rest.

5

Bodies at Rest

Why Sleep Makes Us Better

The writer Elizabeth Marshall Thomas may have the most privileged window into the wild life. As a child in the early 1950s, she accompanied her eccentric, wealthy parents on an expedition into a then-unexplored and unroaded region of southwestern Africa, the Kalahari, in what was among the first contacts by civilized people with the hunter-gatherers she calls Ju/wasi, otherwise known as the !Kung or San. These are the guys in the photo we showed you in our introduction. She lived among them for long periods and in a 2006 book, *The Old Way*, recorded her memories in exquisite detail, some of it greatly illustrative of the case we make, some of it enigmatic, puzzling, and even contradictory, as any account of the human condition must be. But at the moment, we focus on this recollection because of what it tells of the subject we now turn to: sleep.

A further safety measure is that everyone sleeps lightly and not at the same time. In the Ju/wa camp at night, someone always seemed to be awake, getting warm by a fire or having a sip of water from an ostrich eggshell.... The arrangement was very informal, not like a soldier's guard duty or a sailor's watch. It just seemed to happen, part of the normal way of life.

Normal for them, maybe: they were guarding against lions. But what has this to do with us? Ultimately, this account steers us to the context of the wild life, and how the wild taught us how to sleep.

Probably the best place, though, to begin asking about sleep is in the noontime basement cafeteria of Boston's Beth Israel Deaconess Medical Center. Lions are not an obvious presence in the lunchtime rumble and chatter of a research hospital cafeteria, crowded with mostly scrubs-clad medical stars and up-and-coming stars, as harried, caffeinated, and sleep-deprived as the rest of us. No one knows more about this than our host at this lunch, Robert Stickgold, one of the world's leading researchers on sleep, who works out of a lab based at Beth Israel. Mostly people call him Bob, which fits his informality and directness. He is the sort of scientist who knows the data, and knows what the data can and can't tell us, and what it can't tell us is the answer to the most fundamental question: Why do we sleep?

"We understood the biological functions of the sex drive, hunger, and thirst two thousand years ago, and for sleep we didn't know it a dozen years ago, so the first thing I would suggest is, it is subtle," he says. Nonetheless: "If you don't sleep, you die. The rat work is very clear, but after twenty years [of studying this], we don't know why the rats die. Cause of death unknown."

That's not the same as saying we don't know what will go wrong if we don't sleep, just that it's not at all clear what it is about this state of apparent mental and physical retreat, this little death each of us must go through each day that serves our well-being. And what can go wrong for the sleep-deprived— we'll bet most of us are—ought to be front and center in the broader conversation. Here's a snippet from our conversation.

Stickgold: If you don't get enough sleep, you are going to end up fat, sick, and stupid.
Ratey: Which is the way the world is going anyway.
Stickgold: And that may be why.

Fat: Stickgold says the Iraq War, which consumed multi-trillions of dollars across the decade of American involvement, really ran on Snickers bars. As wars go, Iraq was a standout for a variety of reasons, but mostly it was an air war and mostly it was fought at night when American technology granted complete command of the dark. As a result, a lot of sleep was lost, which has prompted a great deal of research, especially by the military. Now we understand that one of the consequences of sleep deprivation is craving the very dense carbohydrates and sugars that featured so prominently in our discussion of nutrition. Researchers have since duplicated the phenomenon with studies that deprived volunteers of sleep.

"Put college students on four hours of sleep a night, and then give them a glucose tolerance test, and they look prediabetic. Food consumption goes up." This is insulin resistance, provoked solely by lack of sleep. Obesity and sleep loss have long been associated, but the research has zeroed in on the reasons why. For instance, in a study published after our conversation with Stickgold, researchers based at the University of Colorado found that sleep deprivation did indeed show a marked increase in weight gain, even with no measurable decline in activity or in energy expenditure. Instead, the experience disrupted the body's signaling pathways associated with the insulin response, particularly a set of hormones that signal satiety: ghrelin, leptin, and peptide YY. As a result, people ate more—especially women, especially in the evening.

Sick: Sleep deprivation seems to wreak havoc with the immune system, and this is not especially difficult to prove. Again, volunteers are sleep-deprived for just a few days, and then researchers give them and a control group a hepatitis C vaccination. The sleep-deprived people produce fully 50 percent fewer antibodies in response to the vaccine, a measure that says their immune systems are about half as effective.

This is what Stickgold means by subtle, in that most of us would never notice a compromised immune system, and most of us would never associate that cold with a lack of sleep.

"Is that going to kill you? Maybe. If it does, you are never going to connect the dots," he says.

Stupid: Well, yes, and just that directly. Reams of research and a variety of related ideas demonstrate this conclusively: Sleep-deprived people generally perform more poorly on straightforward skills tests, such as the ability to recall a list of facts. Subjects allowed to nap between learning the facts and taking the recall test do better. And this area of inquiry is what has made sleep science something of a growth industry. As the Snickers bars suggested, the military paved the way, but the front of this effort now is centered in the dollars-and-cents world of business. Sleep is just good business.

For instance, companies like Google, Nike, Procter & Gamble, and Cisco Systems have begun allowing employees to take naps at work as a way to enhance both productivity and creativity. Business consulting firms have capitalized on the research to show that sleep is essential to success.

On a simple and important level, all of this is a matter of competence, of simple ability to recall facts and solve problems, and indeed the work began aimed at those sorts of skills. Stickgold, for instance, is known for running labs full of subjects playing the popular video game Tetris and demonstrating that various combinations of sleep made them better at it. This is enough to fly straight in the face of the popular archetype of our culture drawn from Silicon Valley, where, legend tells us, fortunes were made by amped-up engineers writing code around the clock, never leaving the office and never taking a break. It is a dangerous stereotype. Still, it persists, and Stickgold has a way of challenging it directly. Students he knows who still buy into this idea of the caffeinated overachiever often boast of their ability to function on four or five hours of sleep each night. He suggests to them that they account for their time and performance, and they quickly figure out that the reason they need to work twenty hours a day is they are doing everything twice. They have to, because sleep loss is making them work inefficiently.

John encounters this problem in schools, especially when he is working in Asia. Kids are extremely sleep-deprived from staying up all night playing video games. They come to school and perform poorly, then are sent to special study halls at night, lose more sleep, then play more video games, and the downward spiral continues.

In fact, the research suggests that sleep has far more effect on far more complex skills, that it almost serves as a sort of retreat for our brains, a time to shut out extraneous noise and the rush of new information and, instead, sort through information to make sense of it. Seen in this light, sleep is a time for forgetting, for putting away what is not relevant, for pruning and sorting to allow the remaining information to form patterns and assist your brain in recognizing those patterns. This helps explain the almost legendary anecdotes about creative bursts and elegant solutions to complex problems that emerged spontaneously after a good night's sleep, the sort of thing that wins someone a Nobel Prize.

In our conversation, though, Stickgold raised a more mundane example of a common decision someone must make when offered a new and better job in a new town.

"The anal-compulsive person draws a chart: stay, go, pluses and minuses. It never helps. But then they wake up the next morning and say they can't take the job. And when friends say 'Why?,' they say, 'It's just not right for me,' and they can't tell you why."

The chart doesn't help because it can't include all the costs and benefits to the person and the spouse and the children and the weight of severed relationships and distance from family and the upheaval of disrupting a life. Not all of these can be neatly categorized and quantified, and even to the degree that they can, the calculation load becomes literally mind-boggling. The important judgments we make in our lives do not yield to lists of pluses and minuses and calculations. We settle these issues during sleep because that is when the brain seems best able to tackle the incalculable problems by pruning, consolidating, and synthesizing.

"One of Bob's aphorisms," says Stickgold, "is that for every two hours your brain spends taking in information during the day, it needs an hour of sleep to figure out what it means. If you don't get that hour, you don't figure it out. The difference between smart and wise is two hours more sleep a night."

This idea takes on a new dimension in the results of further research that appears at first to be a simple test of recall. Researchers showed subjects lists of images and then tested both people who were sleep-deprived and those who weren't on recall of the images. But these were images with clear emotional content, like a soft little puppy or an image of war, images sortable as negative, positive, or neutral emotionally. Of course, as we've already discussed, sleep-deprived people had some difficulty with recall, true enough, but not with the negative images. Those they could remember.

This finding is a slam-dunk link to depression. Almost by definition, depressed people are those who can remember only the negative aspects of their lives. The link goes further. For instance, people who suffer from sleep apnea, a common breathing malfunction that causes them to lose sleep, often also suffer from depression. But Stickgold says that one study, in which the apnea was successfully medicated and the depression was not, revealed that the depression corrected itself—showing that ensuring a good night's sleep cured the depression.

This phenomenon is especially pronounced in a particular area of emotional memory processing in those who suffer from post-traumatic stress disorder, a problem much larger than a Snickers bar habit for Iraq War veterans. One line of research demonstrated that people who were truck drivers during the war did not suffer nearly the levels of PTSD that other veterans did. This was because the military had a rule that truck drivers had to sleep eight hours in every twenty-four, and the rule was enforced.

We know now that PTSD is a creature of memory, a disease of memory. Sufferers are unable to process and assign their traumatic events to the past and so are condemned to relive these terrifying scenes day after day as real and present threats. Sleep's power over memory, however, can allow soldiers who have been through frightening and wrenching experiences to relegate them to their proper place in memory, where the events become just bad memories, not present threats.

So what do we do about all of this? Stickgold has a prescription and is, in fact, rather blunt about it: everyone needs eight and a half hours of sleep out of every twenty-four. Everybody. Further, it is more or less impossible to oversleep. That is, if you need an alarm clock to wake up every day, if you can't get rolling until after the third or fourth shot of espresso, and you find that you sleep long and hard on weekends, then you are probably not getting enough sleep. In this regard, the body is wonderfully homeostatic; that is, it has strong measures and mechanisms to enforce its need for sleep. It's almost as simple as this: if you are sleepy, sleep.

BEVERLY TATUM'S STORY

We met Beverly Daniel Tatum at Rancho La Puerta, a wellness retreat near San Diego that centers its methods on getting people back in touch with their better nature by putting them in contact with nature. But the path that brought her there began with a good night's sleep, and ultimately that path leads to the well-being of thousands of young women, because she is president of Spelman College. Tatum was taking one of her regular fitness breaks at Rancho La Puerta, part of her program to take care of herself so she can better do her job and take care of others, which she learned to do through direct experience.

Before she came to Spelman, Tatum was a dean at Mount Holyoke College, and that job placed some heavy demands on her time that she met by spending, as many of us do, too many late-night hours in front of a computer answering email. The emails multiplied when she became president of Spelman, a four-year college historically for African American women that's located in Atlanta, Georgia. So did the requisite official breakfasts, lunches, and dinners, which she calls "state dinners." So she was getting four or five hours of sleep a night, cutting back on her exercise, and she put on what she calls the "presidential twenty," not just the freshman fifteen familiar to many college students.

Tatum took a vacation in 2005 and realized that her weight gain was somehow tied to the long hours, just as Stickgold says—and she decided that she needed to take control. She set for herself a hard, fast rule to shut off her computer at 10 p.m. and go to bed. She slept at least seven to eight hours per night, regained her exercise habits, and soon began to lose some weight. She had more energy, felt better still, and saw that a lot of her students had the same problem she had had.

"I told them we're investing a lot in your education here," she said. "We want you to live long enough to get a return on our investment." Her dire warning was not conjecture. She had already learned that the obesity problem left her student body with high rates of diabetes and heart disease, to the point where she was going to the funerals of alumnae in their thirties.

So Tatum went ahead with a controversial decision to end Spelman's participation in the NCAA and organized collegiate sports, a move that made national news. Instead, she launched a comprehensive program of fitness and nutrition awareness campus-wide, designed to get students moving and eating well. And so twenty-one hundred students, future leaders, get the message and a better life, and this is how it builds. This is how change happens.

That path for change for Tatum began with a single step, which she calls a "lever." She pulled a single lever, and in her case, it happened to be sleep—but that gave her the foundation to embrace better nutrition and exercise. It all hangs together. And ultimately, her improved well-being manifested itself as service to the well-being of others. This is our model, and its context is nature, the wild.

THE SOCIAL CONTEXT

So sleep is good, but sleep how? In what environment? It turns out that the question of how is as relevant as how much. Much of the research has illuminated the complexity of sleep. We sleep in discrete stages, each marked by clear and distinctive patterns of brain activity. Further, some of these stages correlate with specific benefits. This means that a particular stage is necessary for learning or for memory consolidation, for instance, and if you disrupt sleep in ways that deprive a person of that specific stage, the benefits linked to that stage do not accrue, even if the total sleep is at the golden average of eight and a half hours per night. This shows that there is a quality issue at work here, and this is where we are left in the dark. We really don't know what normal sleep is, but we have some strong signals that the way we do it, a single, solitary, silent stretch, eleven until seven thirty, entombed in retreat from all others, is downright freakish behavior in terms of the human condition and human evolution. Might this habit of ours cause troubles? Maybe our dreams can tell us something about this.

At least when considered in one aspect, sleep is not a peaceful proposition. We dream about bad things. And the research on this matter is interesting: acts of aggression and threats and violence are overrepresented on our list of dream topics. We are more likely to dream about a thug threatening us with violence than a sunny day in a meadow with bunnies and butterflies. For instance, one study found that acts of aggression constituted about 45 percent of the dream content of one sample of people — by far the dominant dream category. In those cases, the dreamer was directly involved in the aggression about 80 percent of the time and was more often than not the victim. However, this burden of fright is not equally shared among all humans, although there are some common elements between genders and among adults. With both genders, the attacker in a violent dream tends to be a male or group of males or an animal, with animals in the minority, at least among modern adults.

This analysis gets far more interesting in the case of children, for whom the scary element tends to be overrepresented as animals. Further, the animal content of younger people's dreams tends to be skewed to the violent and threatening. Dogs, horses, and cats are underrepresented, while snakes, spiders, gorillas, lions, tigers, and bears make far more frequent appearances. More telling still, there is an age gradation to both of these factors. That is, dreams of situations involving threats from animals are more common among the very youngest children and taper gradually as children move toward adulthood. In effect, children—and this is true across cultures—slowly adjust their dream content to the realities of their world. It seems as if they are born afraid of attacks from aggressive animals and gradually substitute bad guys with sticks and guns for lions. But still, threatening situations are overrepresented.

That this is true, even of children who have never seen a wild animal and have no reason to fear an attack, suggests something quite innate, a hardwired memory of conditions more realistic in evolutionary time, when children and adults both had every reason to fear animal attacks. This can seem a bit preposterous to the modern, rational mind, but probably only because we are talking about dreams. There is plenty of nonsense, superstition, and speculation involved in the topic of dreams through the years, and so there's every reason to be suspicious. Nonetheless, there is a parallel and well-established phenomenon among the waking, and not just among humans but among other primates as well. Take a city-bred, born-and-raised denizen of concrete for his first walk through the desert, and then surreptitiously toss a live snake in his path. The reaction will be quick and predictable, regardless of whether your subject has ever seen a snake before. Same is true of chimps raised in cages. We have instincts, animal instincts, and this is demonstrable.

Yet even more interesting is the maintenance and sharpening of these very instincts among people living where the instincts come in handy, and this is borne out in the dreaming research as well. The closest we can possibly come to knowing about how our ancestors dreamed is through studies of contemporary hunters and gatherers, and it turns out that this has been done at least twice: once with aboriginals in Australia and once with the Mehinaku Indians of central Brazil, before there had been significant contact with the outside world. The latter case proved especially informative because these people actually valued dreams, so they were careful to note content and often talked about dreams with one another. In both Brazil and Australia, animals and aggression were overrepresented in dream content. In both countries, people dreamed about animals far more often than similar samples of civilized humans did, but at about the same rate as civilized children did, indicating that the decline of animals in dreams as we age is indeed an adjustment to our civilized, tamed world. We enter the world programmed to dream of the wild, but civilization takes those dreams away.

But just as important, the gender differences are alike among both hunter-gatherers and the civilized. In both cases, aggression and animals loom larger in the dreams of men.

Antti Revonsuo, who compiled and analyzed this large body of research in an important paper, concludes that this is really about something other than fear and trauma. Rather, it is far more in line with the main body of research on sleep in general. In his view, sleep is not a retreat to helplessness, but rather a functioning part of our learning process when the brain works through problems and devises solutions. Humans evolved among predators. Our formative years were not spent at the top of the food chain, a factor we think is too often glossed over in formulating the just-so stories about human evolution. Modern humans have forgotten what it is like to be meat, and being prey must have entailed terrors beyond imagination, particularly for the young and helpless and for the people who cared about them most.

We can begin to imagine this state of being through extrapolation, especially those of us who have seen lions or grizzly bears or Siberian tigers in the wild (all, in fact, still posing a significant threat to some humans). And yet these animals were far more numerous during humanity's history than they are now, and they were joined or preceded by even more formidable predators, now extinct. For instance, modern-day !Kung people fall prey more often to leopards than to lions, but ancestor leopards of that place were in fact much larger, giant leopards, with every bit the speed and prowess of the more compact variety that still kills people. Even North American native people encountered saber-toothed tigers and short-faced bears, which were larger and faster than modern grizzly bears.

In such an environment, skills for dealing with predators would have been highly adaptive, to say the least, and that is exactly what determined the content of our dreams. Revonsuo believes that dreams served as a rehearsal of challenging events, to allow our brains to work at night on the reactions and skills necessary to deal with our most important threats. He concludes:

Any behavioral advantage in dealing with highly dangerous events would have increased the probability of reproductive success. A dream-production mechanism that tends to select threatening waking events and simulate them over and over again in various combinations would have been valuable for the development and maintenance of threat-avoidance skills. Empirical evidence from normative dream content, children's dreams, recurrent dreams, nightmares, post-traumatic dreams, and the dreams of hunter-gatherers indicates that our dream-production mechanisms are in fact specialized in the simulation of threatening events, and thus provides support to the threat simulation hypothesis of the function of dreaming.

Carol Worthman, meanwhile, believes that the presence of predators also formed our habits of sleeping, which steers us in another direction, toward the flip side of fear. If we look closely, we can find ample evidence that sleep is not retreat but an act of social engagement, and this, too, can be derived from wondering where the lions are.

Worthman is an anthropologist and probably the only one in captivity who specializes in sleep. We caught up with her at Emory University; she's a polite and engaging woman in a neat and fully organized office. She had just returned from a stint in India teaching the scientific method to Buddhist nuns and a stop in Vietnam to check on research in a remote village where television had been introduced for the first time.

Years ago, Worthman tackled the topic of sleep, mostly out of curiosity and her wonder as to why there was not more on the subject in the anthropological literature, given the importance of sleep in our lives. She did a survey of cross-cultural research on sleep habits and found, much as Stickgold found in research on the reasons for sleep, that we know almost nothing. There is some excuse for this. People sleep in private, or at least we once assumed so. Further, unlike spear tips and hand axes in hunting and fire smudges in cooking, sleep leaves no trace in the archaeo-logical record, not much in stories, and not much in our bones— and so there is precious little to go on if we need to ask the very question about sleep that we have been asking in this book about other endeavors, like food and movement: what is the evolutionary history of this fundamental human activity?

It turns out that the anthropological perspective does noth-ing to contradict Stickgold's conclusions from studies of modern-day sleepers, but it does provide a different emphasis, especially on the prescription. There is nothing in the cross-cultural studies that disagrees with the idea of the need for a baseline of sleep of about eight hours out of every twenty-four, but Worthman says her real concern is with quality, not quantity. For instance, she says people who complain about insomnia—the torturous variety that has one lying in bed awake, tossing and turning through the night—often sleep far more than they report, but they get only low-quality sleep. They believe they are awake—and, more to the point, the sleep they do get doesn't do them a lot of good.

"The question is how do you get good sleep, and that draws attention to context, and that's where the evolutionary context can be helpful," Worthman says.

What we know about evolutionary context is extrapolation from what we know from cross-cultural sleeping habits. But nonetheless, the studies contain some clear evidence that we are missing something important about context, at least we who practice what Worthman calls the "lie down and die" model of sleep: to bed at ten, lights out, silence, set the alarm, and await resurrection. The simple fact is, across the world and across time as far as we know, few cultures sleep this way.

"In virtually all societies there is a sense of the social organization of sleep, and in many, many societies the provision of an appropriate sleep context is viewed as extremely powerful," she says.

And what does an appropriate context look like? To begin with, it includes other people. Few other cultures view sleep as a retreat, even a private act. Just the opposite.

Back to the lions for a moment, to see where that comes from. Thomas described a scene as much about being awake as it was about being asleep, which makes perfect sense if you happen to be a !Kung sleeping outside among lions, and through most of evolutionary time, humans did indeed sleep outdoors among predators. But there is actually some math at the root of this casual observation, calculations that Worthman has done. This is based on well-known and established variations in sleep patterns that remain fixed in modern humans, according to age. Babies can be and often are awake at seemingly random periods around the clock, but once they are a bit older, they lock onto a circadian rhythm much like that of adults. Adolescents, however, have a rhythm of their own, worldwide and across cultures: they go to bed late and get up late, compared with adults. Older people, meanwhile, are often awake longer and for periods in the night. This age segregation is consistent across cultures but begins to make sense when one superimposes those various patterns on one another. Worthman says that doing so allows a calculation that, given a band size of about thirty-five people with usual age distributions, yields a group pattern in which at least one person is awake at any given time.

Yet there is more to this than simply being awake. Many cultures, for instance, cultivate a form of light sleep, a watchful doze that is instantly reversible. In the studies of modern sleepers, this corresponds with a stage of sleep that confers a distinct set of benefits. Everyone performs this sort of light sleep without realizing it, but each of us also needs periods of very deep sleep, a stage vital to brain benefits and at the same time deeply threatening to people who live among lions. Researchers generally divide sleep into two categories by eye movement: rapid eye movement, or REM, sleep and non-REM sleep. The latter category has four distinct stages. Both REM sleep and the deepest stage of non-REM sleep are marked by a near complete lack of muscle tone and awareness; it's like being in a coma, helpless against threats like predators.

In REM sleep, debilitation is nearly complete. Two pathways of brain chemistry work together to induce paralysis in all muscles but the eyes. Researchers don't know the function of this paralysis but speculate that it prevents injury caused by muscles acting out our dreams, which also mostly occur in the REM state. People with disorders that prevent this paralysis often suffer such injuries.

Worthman says these stages, more than even the threat of lions, are why the social context of sleep is vitally important. We are not checked out or mentally absent during sleep, at least not all the time. On the contrary, as the research has shown, our brains are doing some of their heaviest lifting during sleep. But doing that requires modulation, a shifting of gears from one stage of sleep to another, which in turn requires some attention to context, reading of the signals that tell us when it is safe to check out and become helpless against external threats. In order to sleep properly, we need to pay attention to what is going on around us, using that awareness to guide us through the necessary stages of sleep. Isolating ourselves in soundproof rooms may be about the worst way there is to go about this—but, more to the point, so is isolating ourselves from other people.

This conclusion is not speculation. Worthman carried out one research project in Egypt, which gave her access to subjects who have been settled in cities for millennia. The choice was deliberate: she wanted to look at the persistence of hunter-gatherer sleep patterns, despite civilization. Egyptians, in both city and countryside, sleep the way most of the world does, which is to say together—what she calls "consolidated sleeping." Typically, whole extended families sleep in great rooms, with almost no isolation. There are exceptions, though, and those proved to be the most telling. Egyptians and others typically segregate post-pubescent girls from boys. Not always. Sometimes there is an aunt or grandmother and the teenage girl bunks with her. But some end up sleeping alone, and it was those people, both boys and girls, who had the insomnia and other forms of dysregulation. The people who slept alone had the emotional problems.

This same pattern has emerged in a variety of studies to the point that we begin to understand why social sleeping seems to be a nearly universal characteristic of cultures, as are the staggered patterns of wakefulness of the group. While we are sleeping, we continue to monitor our surroundings for cues of safety: relaxed conversation, relaxed movement of others, popping fire. Those cues, subtle sounds signaling safety, tell us we can retreat to our deepest sleep.

Many cultures are, in fact, conscious of all of this and the importance of these arrangements, and no place is the importance more pronounced than in the case of infants. (We need not necessarily bring lions into the picture to underscore this, although predators like hyenas and leopards are certainly preferential to the young of our species, undoubtedly one of the reasons infant mortality was high among our ancestors. Thomas, for instance, records one example of great injury to a toddler who stumbled into a campfire while others were sleeping, and this was probably a common occurrence through time.) One of the biggest reasons for modulated sleep is to protect infants.

But the research suggests that this works in both directions — that is, infants' bodies are instinctively aware of their vulnerability and so do things like dream about frightening animals. They are even more dependent than adults on signals of safety. All of this helps explain what Worthman characterizes as an almost universal perplexed response among most other cultures upon hearing of the Western practice of making babies sleep alone.

"They think of this as child abuse. They literally do," she says.

The evolutionary context of sleep, however, extends well beyond the people around us, and this may begin to suggest some antidotes to our present isolation, some practical steps one might take to reintroduce evolutionary context to our rest. Anthropological studies have shown that almost all cultures pay a great deal of attention to the sound of a fire, and not just as a threat to babies. Changes in the crackle and pop might, for instance, signal that a fire is dying and trigger a new level of alert sleeping, just as the sounds of a fire settling into a sustained glow might signal that it's okay to sleep deeply. This doesn't mean you need to sleep next to a fire (although it's nice if you can). But you can look for similar patterns of sound that may help, even recordings.

Likewise with animals. Herders in particular sleep with such sounds as cud chewing and gentle bovine breathing, signals from sentinel animals of peace that transpires when no predators are around. Our favorite sentinels through evolutionary time were once predators: wolves slowly tamed by food to be dogs. Any suburban dweller can attest how the sound of an incessantly barking dog can be profoundly disturbing to sleep, more than decibels and persistence alone can account for. Yet we forget how the reverse is certainly true: that many of us tune our degree of peace and relaxation to the rhythms of a snoring dog. If something were wrong, the dog would say so.

All of this may be enough to explain the finding of epidemiology that people who are married and people who have pets live longer. It may be because they sleep better.

AGAIN, VARIABILITY

In one of her papers, Worthman wrote something that circles this whole idea back to fat, sick, and stupid. Like Stickgold, Worthman is deeply impressed with the homeostatic nature of sleep, that the body has an overwhelming sense of needing it and, left to its own devices, will do what must be done to ensure adequate sleep.

It's a wonderfully fluid phenomenon, she says, which is why most cultures don't worry about sleep or even losing sleep. If you're awake tending the fire or sheep one night, no big deal: doze through the afternoon and catch up.

She's seen conversations like a business negotiation among, say, a group of men in Egypt that conclude when one guy simply falls asleep.

"Literally, a guy will just pull a cloth over his head and go to sleep," she says. "And that's no biggie. It's not like a guy just slid under his chair in the boardroom. It's not asocial. If you view sleep as a social behavior, then it is just integrated in life."

But this is only true if our bodies are left to their own devices, and our rushing, wired world has all sorts of devious mechanisms for overriding those controls. That's the dilemma. How do we get away with this, this deficit that accrues not just for a couple of days but day in and day out, through whole careers? Where is homeostasis? How do our bodies balance this behavior?

Worthman's answer is this: we pay for sleep deficit in the currency of stress.

"Sleep deprivation looks like stress. It increases cortisol, it increases appetite, decreases satiety, increases blood glucose levels," she says. "This is straight out of the stress literature. If you curtail sleep just now and then, you can manage the hit, but if you do it too much, it erodes the health of the organism, the person, and her ability to cope."

This, too, is a case for modulation and adaption. On the one hand, sleep is far more elastic than we make it out to be. Indeed, it is wrong to characterize it as inactive or in retreat. Rather, it is a dynamic state important to brain function and some of our most important work. More to the point, sleep is when we *do* some of our most important work, both in processing information and, as the cultural studies show, in engaging others and building social bonds of trust. And because it is so important, it is adaptable and fluid. That is, our bodies are hardwired with a series of circuits to allow sleep to flow with the needs and demands of our day, what Worthman means when she calls it "fluid." And as with most other cases of our adaptability, we need to practice adapting to strengthen that skill, to modulate, to read the signals and cues that attach us to our physical and social environment, flexing the adaptive tools like muscles.

This is just like the response to stress that makes us stronger in exercise, that is unless that stress becomes chronic and unremitting, day in and day out, and then we pay in the currency of cortisol and inflammation: fat, sick, and stupid. Complete recovery of the evolutionary context of sleeping is probably lost to us, but we have the basics. We probably don't know enough and have lost the proper environments to make sleep perfect, but at least we have some clues as to how to make it better. That and ample evidence that we ought to do so.

For many of us, this is a simple matter of ensuring sufficient sleep, the fundamental issue in our overstimulated, overcaffeinated lives. It is true that much about sleep and sleep disorders remains a mystery, especially when we begin considering the evolutionary rules, as we have here. But one important fact we know for sure is that you must get sufficient sleep, and way too many of us don't.

Beyond this, evolution provides some hints about the proper context of sleep: Irregularity is okay. So are naps. A sense of safety is critical. If you can, sleep around others, and this may include traditional sentry animals like dogs. Some people have even found that the relaxed sounds of conversation typical of all-night radio do the trick. Avoid alarming sounds like sirens. Look for safe sounds like the lapping of gentle waves (a signal of safe weather, no storms) or a settling wood fire. Try recordings if you can't be near the real thing.

And then there is light, and in this there is an intriguing clue that suggests we have so much to learn. Much has been made of this issue of light as it affects our sleep, and the advent of artificial light is right up there with agriculture as one of the more profound shifts in the conditions of our existence, particularly for those humans who ventured north and south to where day's and night's lengths vary widely.

Of course, we can argue that artificial light has been with us a very long time; we've already talked about the importance of fire. The famous cave painters at places like Lascaux and Chauvet had fat-fueled lamps that they used to execute their artwork as long as forty thousand years ago. But fire and fat produce light of very different wavelengths than electric lights do and, more to the point, much dimmer light. This is key. The real problem is light bright enough to mimic the sun. Virtually all living organisms, even plants, are finely tuned to cycles of light and dark, to the passing of days, but also of seasons, patterns of life called circadian rhythms. Evolution has embedded layers on layers of mechanisms in humans to honor these cycles, and there has been plenty of research into at least one of these layers to tell us light is pivotal, not just to sleep but to our health and longevity in general.

The mechanism is pretty simple. Sunlight strikes a tiny gland behind the eye called the pineal gland, which in turn regulates the production of melatonin, the hormone that governs sleep and our circadian rhythms. Any artificial light that approaches the brightness of the sun is enough to trigger this same process, and the research shows that the everyday, garden-variety 100-watt lightbulb is enough. The average office is about three times as bright as the threshold. The effect ratchets up with certain wavelengths, especially those that produce blue light, which takes us to electronic devices and televisions, all of which mess with melatonin. The blue wavelengths are accented in these devices, as they are in any light-emitting diodes (LEDs), such as those in super-energy-efficient lightbulbs. Research has already demonstrated a clear effect of computer monitors on melatonin, largely because of the specific wavelengths emitted.

Yet the effect of even the simple lightbulb goes a lot farther. Electric light conquered the night and made things like shift work possible, allowing people to work around the clock. Even those not working are more active than our ancestors, creating cities that never sleep and a regimen of noise that is unavoidable and takes a toll on our rest. Thus it gets hard to sort out the root cause of the damage—noise or light—but also the answer to this question: is the damage caused by lack of sleep or by disruption of the powerful circadian rhythm?

Nonetheless, the damage is there, and the studies bear this out. Nurses who work night shifts, for instance, are more likely to develop breast cancer. That same group had a 35 percent greater chance of suffering colon cancer. Studies have linked the disruptive effects of artificial light at night to depression, cardiovascular diseases, diabetes, and obesity. We believe that light is an enormous factor in problems like attention deficit disorder. And while it may be difficult to control the social conditions of sleeping for some people in some situations, most of us have much more control over light. An effective intervention here might be as simple as dimming all the lights and shutting down the television and computer monitor a few hours before bedtime. Another might be as drastic as finding a different job if the current one makes you work at night. But when weighed against issues like an elevated risk of colon cancer, such measures seem less drastic.

It's important to stress here that we are not arguing against exposure to light that mimics the sun, which would be like arguing against the sun. The problem here is timing, not exposure. Thus, the goal is to control the timing of our exposure to light to mimic the natural cycle of day and night and of seasons. This prescription, then, links with ideas we will raise later about the benefits of exposure to nature. Spending time outdoors in sunlight is as important as turning off lights at night to harmonize your body's circadian rhythms with the earth. This helps not just with sleep but with the full range of your body's finely tuned systems.

But go back for a moment to the idea of the second sleep for yet another link to other matters. Interestingly enough, some

experiments in removing subjects from the influences of all artificial light have been done, just to see what would happen. In a
matter of days, a pattern emerged in many subjects. They could
sleep when they wished, and many adopted a habit of going to
sleep early, say at eight o'clock, then would awake around midnight or so for a few hours, and then would go back to sleep—a
bifurcated pattern of sleep. But what was intriguing about this
was a parallel pattern that appears in writings from preindustrial
Europe, a pattern of this "second sleep." Historically, people
would use that interim period as quiet, thoughtful time, or for
having sex, or even for going to visit neighbors. It was social time
and it appeared naturally on body clocks set by the absence of
artificial light. Researchers have also found similar patterns in
various cultures.

There are a couple of key lessons in this intriguing fact. First,
it tells us that our bodies are strongly hardwired for a specific and
important behavior, and if we remove the artificial meddling of
industrialism like electric lights, our systems will self-correct. We
think this principle applies to a lot more than just sleep.

But there is a second clue here. That interim period between
first and second sleep has a biochemical signature: elevated levels of the hormone prolactin. Prolactin shares a common etymo-
logical root with lactation and lactose because it was first identified,
along with oxytocin, as a dominant hormone of breastfeeding,
of lactation in mammals. Oxytocin especially has since gotten a
reputation as the social hormone, as we shall see in a later
chapter.

But prolactin shows up prominently in another context,
among people who practice meditation—the topic we engage
next.

6

Aware

What Is Revealed in the Wild Mind

A couple of decades ago, the anthropologist Richard Nelson told us an anecdote that seemed to say a lot then—and even more now, knowing, as we do, so much more about the mind. Nelson is one of those maverick researchers who became an anthropologist not because he was attracted to academia but because he'd rather live in remote places among wild people. His particular chosen station early on was living among Koyukon people, caribou hunters of the frigid interior of Alaska. Later, though, he chose to live in the very different environment along the coast, the warmer maritime archipelago of islands that Alaskans call "Southeast." This is a place of rain, cedars, seals, and salmon, the interior a place of Arctic winters, fur, wolves, and ice.

Several of the Koyukon became Nelson's friends, and after he had lived some time in Southeast, he decided to invite a few of them to visit him at his new home. He expected a reunion—swapping stories, laughs, and endless rounds of warm conversation. But when they arrived on the island where he lived—a place wholly unfamiliar to them—they gave him only silence.

They were struck near dumb by the overwhelming detail in the strangeness all around them, and they wandered the island absorbing every sodden green inch of the place. After days of this, they could at last speak, and they proceeded to describe to Nelson his own island home in far more detail and with far more insight than he could after years of living there.

This is the hunter-gatherer state of mind, a hyperawareness, a presence, a capacity for observation we can only begin to imagine. The authors have some inkling of what it means and where it comes from as a result of deep personal experience. Richard Manning is a lifelong hunter, with almost fifty years' experience stalking game in the woods. Most of his household meat supply is hunted game. Even after a year at a desk, tethered to a computer and a cell phone, Richard finds that the hunting experience can summon forth a state of mind like no other. We had one watershed conversation about this, and oddly, although John has never hunted, the concept snapped into focus much of John's thinking about noise—mental noise—and mindfulness. Yet we think this modern experience of hunting is the merest approximation of the heightened powers of observation and awareness that were a fact of everyday life for the Koyukon and for all wild people. Generally, this mindful state is regarded as an ephemeral phenomenon that will not yield to hard-science, data-based analysis. Yet we think that mindfulness plays a large role in forming this common and wistful assessment by field researchers who have spent time among wild people: there is an other-worldliness and peacefulness to their lives we can but begin to imagine.

Through time, we have come to think there is a rough draft parallel to the hunter-gatherer mind-set that can be found in a modern-day practice—a practice that is in fact readily available to us and has been studied in detail, especially in recent years with the emerging tools of neuroscience. We are going to have a look at the formal practice of meditation as it emerged from Buddhist tradition. The thing is, the Koyukon hunters in our anecdote were not practicing meditators, as far as we know, and in this chapter, we are far more interested in the Koyukon state of mind than in meditation. We are, however, going to talk some here about formal meditation and the research behind it because we believe it illuminates the more general mind-set of hunter-gatherers. Later, we will link back to this general state of mind in ways applicable to modern people, meditators or not.

THE SCIENCE DEVELOPS

Richard Davidson began meditation quietly in the 1970s, when people training in serious disciplines like psychology at serious universities like Harvard didn't go in for this sort of idea. To complicate matters, serious psychologists also did not talk about emotion back then, and that's what happened to capture Davidson's interest.

"Overall, though, there just wasn't much room for emotions in the cold, hard calculus of cognitive psychology, which considered them downright suspect," Davidson wrote in his book *The Emotional Life of Your Brain*. "The attitude was basically one of haughty disdain that this riffraff occupied the same brain that gave rise to cognition."

Davidson latched onto an emerging tool then absent in psychology departments: the electroencephalogram, or EEG, which measures activity in various parts of the brain. He wanted to track the physical manifestations of emotion in the brain, but also other measures like heart rate and respiration. The concept was to link human behavior to a real, physical set of responses in the body. This was the line of thought that would lead to mapping the neural pathways of emotion.

During this period, Davidson was mostly mum about meditation in his professional life but was nonetheless pursuing the idea in some interesting social circles, arguably in the very house in Boston that served as a focal point for science's distrust of practices like meditation. Davidson's original contact at Harvard was the psychology professor David McClelland, who a decade earlier had run the research center that supported two faculty members, Richard Alpert and his coinvestigator, Timothy Leary, of LSD fame. When Davidson joined this circle in 1972, Alpert was by then known as Ram Dass and was living in the carriage house behind McClelland's house and teaching meditation. Davidson began a meditation practice then and followed that thread to India for formal training while he was still in graduate school.

Still, he kept that practice out of his work and instead chose to study emotions like fear, anxiety, and depression. He gained some new ground there, publishing some of the original work that tied those emotions to specific, identifiable parts of the brain, using tools like the EEG. But Davidson says that part of the reason he did not pursue research in meditation was because the tools of neuroscience were then not up to the task. And part of his reluctance was undoubtedly encapsulated in the phrase he uses for finally reversing that decision and beginning specific lab work on meditation. In his book, he labels this reversal "coming out of the closet."

It was indeed a dramatic exit from that closet, involving trunk loads of computer gear, electrodes, generators, and battery packs that had to be lugged by literal Sherpa guides on foot for days on end on treacherous, cliff-edge mountain passes; he was seeking out swamis, mystics, and gurus. No, really. Davidson launched an expedition near Dharamsala, India, attempting to find and wire the brains of some of the most experienced meditators on earth, those associated with Tibetan Buddhism. These were, Davidson allows, truly odd people, like Olympic athletes of the mind, in his analogy. They were far removed from the common experience, which is precisely why he sought them out. They are outliers, and it is interesting to consider how their extreme example might inform the rest of us.

Davidson, however, failed in this mission—but it led to nothing less than a challenge in 1992 from the current Dalai Lama, Tenzin Gyatso himself, who had become engaged in the process. Tenzin Gyatso challenged Davidson to bring to bear on meditation the same rigorous elucidation his EEGs had brought to his study of emotions.

Davidson was by then at the University of Wisconsin–Madison, where he remains, as a professor of psychiatry and psychology and the director of the Center for Investigating Healthy Minds at the Waisman Laboratory for Brain Imaging and Behavior. He used the challenge and the network of Tibetans he had come to know to eventually entice a handful of meditators, all of them experienced in the Tibetan Buddhist tradition, to his lab to have their brains wired. And they were indeed Olympic athletes of the practice. Each had logged at least ten thousand hours of meditation. Each had lived at least one three-year period in retreat, which means doing nothing but meditation every day, eight hours a day, for three years, never leaving the retreat site. One monk had spent more than fifty thousand hours in meditation. If meditation does indeed change the brain, then it ought to be obvious in these people. And it was.

By then, the more advanced brain imaging tools available through functional magnetic resonance imaging had come into play, so Davidson's lab could be a lot more specific about brain activation than he could have been with EEGs, which measure only surface activity of the brain. The researchers loaded the monks in fMRI tubes and had them meditate, not meditate, and meditate in various ways. They also played distressing sounds (like a woman screaming) for the monks at various unannounced intervals to record reactions. Researchers used similar routines for control subjects.

What they found was that the monks reacted much more to the screams than the control subjects did, and in a particular area of the brain—at the temporal parietal junction, which is strongly associated with empathy and the ability to take the perspective of another. This result occurred when monks were both meditating and not meditating. Davidson says the differences between the monks and the controls were not subtle, and the researchers had not expected such emphatic results, having long experienced the delicacy of brain waves and the difficulty of reading them. Normally, differences—even significant differences—are barely readable, or readable only with computer enhancement and amplification.

"We were absolutely stunned because the changes were so

robust and so dramatic that we were able to observe them with the naked eye, which is almost never the case in this kind of research," Davidson said in one interview about the work. "We can literally see the signal in front of us."

The problem was, the results really didn't answer the fundamental question: does meditation indeed change the brain? There's a perfectly good alternative explanation, which is that these people were somewhat freakish to begin with, given their long history of behavior that most of us would not even consider. Further, even if meditation can make a brain better and more empathetic, who has ten thousand hours to spend in a cliffside cave?

The monks' results only suggested a direction for research; the more interesting results have come in the twenty years since, as Davidson's lab has recruited and randomized samples of volunteers, taught them meditation in short courses, and loaded them in the fMRI tubes as well. Among the findings were clear and readable patterns in brain activation and reduction in anxiety and depression, but also some results you might not expect. During one experiment, researchers gave both meditators and control groups a flu vaccine and found a better immune response among the meditators, even the novices. Davidson's lab has subsequently shown a marked improvement among meditators who are undergoing a standard treatment for psoriasis, further establishing the brain-body connection. Specifically, meditators healed at about four times the rate that controls did.

"We did the study twice because we didn't believe the results," Davidson says.

Yet in all of this, there are some intriguing results that point toward the idea that brings us to this topic: meditation in some way mirrors the state of mind among hunter-gatherers. The common perception is that meditation is a state of retreat or withdrawal, much like the common perception about sleep that Carol Worthman's work contradicts. With meditation, the misinformed assumption is that the practice is aimed at relaxation and bliss. It is not. It is about attention and awareness of the here and now, which is precisely what wild people need in order to survive in a state of nature.

And, in fact, Davidson has done experiments that begin to illuminate this point. For instance, there is the matter of what is called the attentional blink. Each of us, no matter how we live, is perpetually immersed in a fast-moving stream of information, and it is up to us to pick out what is relevant from the stream to function, to recognize a threat or an opportunity or a clue that a game animal lies ahead or a child might fall or a potential client just walked in the door. Psychologists have a standard test for this: they read off a stream of letters and numbers in random order and ask people to respond whenever they hear a number but not a letter. It turns out that people are good at this simple task most of the time, but not when a number follows another number closely. The assumption is that the mental energy reserve they expend identifying the one target needs time to recharge, like a camera flash with rapid-fire photos. Those with weaker "batteries" miss the number that follows closely, causing an attentional blink.

In Davidson's experiments, meditators performed better, with less attentional blink, showing that this is not a matter of bliss or relaxation but of awareness and competence.

The improved perception is a benchmark of meditation; the benchmark is known from some of the earliest experiments, and the results are robust enough to become recognized as a neuro-logical signature of meditation. The meditative state is character-ized by synchronized gamma waves throughout the brain. "Gamma" simply means that they are of high frequency compared with other brain waves, but it is their synchrony that is more interesting. As you can imagine, the brain is driven by a cacopho-nous mix of waves and signals blasting away at all frequencies and in all directions, the exact picture presented by an EEG of an active mind. It looks like a sound wave pattern of street noise, and a chaotic street at that. But there is understandably a profound effect when those waves settle into a common, synchronous pat-tern, analogous to an orchestra's transition from the chaos of tun-ing to playing a root, third, and fifth of a chord in unison.

The term "neural pathways" makes us think of our brain as a sort of circuit board, where miniature wires connect one cell to another to make that path. An even more apt analogy for this profound effect is to imagine each neuron or cell as a radio that can be tuned to receive certain frequencies, to respond to a cer-tain wavelength generated somewhere else in the brain. Synchro-nous waves recruit bigger neural networks because more cells are tuned to that "station." Davidson calls it "phase-locking."

When a brain is wandering in noise, unsynchronized, "the response to an external stimulus is as difficult to pick out against this background cacophony as the ripples from a rock splashing into a turbulent sea. There are so many other waves and distur-bances that any ripples from the thrown rock are almost imper-ceptible. But if the rock lands in a perfectly still lake, the ripples stand out like a walrus in a desert. A calm brain is like a still lake," he writes in *The Emotional Life of Your Brain*.

This is not a matter for meditation alone but a concept

rooted in much thinking about mental well-being and mental illness. Think of it as noise, as we long have—not literal noise but analogous: meaningless rumble, chatter, and static in the backdrop of the brain like the conversation-killing roar of a busy restaurant. It is implicated in problems including schizophrenia, manic-depressive disorder, autism, mental retardation, and brain damage. People afflicted with these problems are often unable to control the rush of stimuli, to still the lake. What they suffer from is just the opposite. The noise arrives in a sort of mental echo chamber that ratchets up the racket to an unbearable level and provokes behaviors we call pathological. These behaviors are an attempt to cope with the noise. Some of John's early work on this idea found that calming the body in various ways served to calm this storm, a connection of physical to mental. But meditation also stands as a more direct attempt to calm the background of the mind—not to retreat, but as a way to allow the mind to more directly attend.

It is this state of awareness that brought us to the evolutionary roots of this matter in this discussion, but the question is, what has this to do with our present world? What is the importance of this awareness? We've already cited increased competence, and that is certainly enough to merit our attention, but there's a great deal more going on here.

LINKS TO STRESS

There was a remarkable gathering of minds in 2005, an interdisciplinary conference, and the conversation was recorded in a book edited by Jon Kabat-Zinn and Davidson called *The Mind's*

Own Physician: A Scientific Dialogue with the Dalai Lama on the Healing Power of Meditation. We recommend it as an interesting rundown of the confluence between neuroscience and mindfulness, summarizing what we know and speculating where we might go with this idea. It offers many remarkable insights—and not just into meditation but also into the more general and all-encompassing idea of mindfulness. For instance, at the conference, Helen Mayberg, a professor of psychiatry at Emory University, traced depression to detailed neural pathways, and she showed how those pathways changed through not meditation but cognitive behavior therapy—another way in which the mind reshapes the brain.

But the discussion was expanded significantly by the inclusion of Robert Sapolsky, the Stanford neurologist who has made a name for himself as the go-to guy on stress. The foundation of his work is tracking stress through the hormone cortisol, which has emerged as the accepted biomarker of stress. Sapolsky's most famous subjects were baboons living in the wild in Africa. He captured them periodically to measure cortisol in blood samples and discovered that the life of a wild animal could indeed be loaded with stress, the very factor we associate with the noise and rigors of civilized, human life. Sapolsky concluded that baboons suffered this same problem for much the same reason we do, and it had little to do with scarcity or predation. It actually arose from hierarchy. Baboon society is dominated by aggressive males who enforce dominance with violence and more or less constant harassment of subordinates. (Both leaders and subordinates wind up suffering from chronic stress, but in different ways.) One need not get very far into Sapolsky's research to realize that an alpha male baboon in a suit and tie could probably do a passable job of running a Wall Street firm or, in a black turtleneck, a Silicon Valley start-up. In fact, parallel research showed a parallel distribution of cortisol among British civil servants.

There are a couple of keys to this, and one is that stress is about control and the attempt of dominant players to exert control. But there is also a key point about chronic stress. In baboon society, aggressive behavior and punishment are an unrelenting way of life, or at least it was for these baboons. For a time. Sapolsky's research in Africa tracked a disease outbreak among the baboons that happened to be selective in its lethality to dominant males. After a critical mass of them died off, the surviving baboons reorganized without the violence and resulting cascade of cortisol. Peace prevailed. That is not to say that stress was removed from their lives—just that it was no longer the dominant force of their lives, and this is the refining point that brings us to Sapolsky's contribution at the 2005 conference.

Stress is one of those concepts that has been beaten to death in popular understanding, but the general discussion misses something important. The very mention of the word provokes something like the universal response to the mention of vampires in old horror movies: zero tolerance, and a sign of the cross to ward them off. The fact is, a complete absence of stress in your life is not an ideal state.

"For a short time, one or two hours, stress does wonderful things for the brain," Sapolsky told the conference. "More oxygen and glucose are delivered to the brain. The hippocampus, which is involved in memory, works better when you are stressed for a little while. Your brain releases more dopamine, which plays a role in the experience of pleasure, early on during stress; it feels wonderful, and your brain works better."

Dopamine is the big indicator here; it's the neurotransmitter wound up in our primary reward system, the big player in making us feel better and keeping us focused. The presence of dopamine signals something quite remarkable about stress. Sapolsky cited a bit of monkey research, simple and straightforward: researchers tracked dopamine when a monkey was given a reward each time it pressed a lever, and they compared the results with those when a monkey randomly got a reward only about half the time it pressed the lever. The results showed that the monkey released more dopamine in the latter case. More pleasure for half the number of rewards, but also when rewards are irregular or unexpected.

Sapolsky: "I said that lack of control is very stressful. Here a lack of control feels wonderful and your dopamine goes way up. What's the difference? As I mentioned earlier, the research shows that if your lack of control occurs in a setting that you perceive as malevolent and threatening, lack of control is a terrible stressor. If the lack of control occurs in a setting perceived as benign and safe, lack of control feels wonderful."

All of this is to say that our pleasure circuits are attuned to awareness and unexpected rewards, and stress is in this mix — not chronic unremitting stress that characterizes day-to-day life for many of us, but the ups and downs that flow from normal life. The pleasurable life is not stress-free, and Sapolsky argues that this realization provides a precise analogue for meditation:

People think that you secrete stress hormones when there is stress, and when there is no stress, you don't secrete them or secrete just a little bit. You are at baseline. It was a long-standing tradition in the field to consider the baseline to be extremely boring. What's now clear instead is that the baseline is a very active, focused, metaphorically muscular process of preparation for stress. The jargon used in the field is that it has permissible effect, allowing the stress response to be as optimal as possible. That's a wonderful endocrine analogue to the notion of meditation. A state of peace is not the absence of challenge. It is not the absence of alertness and energetic expenditure. If anything, it is a focusing of alertness in preparation. It absolutely matches the endocrine picture.

We think "alertness in preparation" is an exact summary of the hunter-gatherer state of mind, and now it appears that evolution has wired us to be rewarded by achieving it. Of course it has. The ideal state is not noise or absence of noise, stressed or relaxed, feast or famine, awake or asleep. This is more the case of defining one more edge between two states and then noting how our bodies are attuned to walking that line.

Cortisol can track this matter with stress, but there is a more interesting way that's emerging to gauge our undoing, our literal unraveling. Remember that confounding the issue of diseases of civilization was the unavoidable fact of nature that we all must die of something. Obviously, though, most of us would rather there be nothing more precise than "old age" written on the certificate under "cause of death." The process we'd all like to see in play (given the alternatives) is senescence, the unwinding of the biological clock spring.

The study of our DNA, though, has turned up an interesting measure of this process, structures called telomeres that serve as protective caps on the ends of strands of DNA. Telomeres seem to have some clear role in preserving the integrity of DNA through the countless divisions and recombinations that occur with cellular growth and reconstruction. They keep the code intact—but as we age, they seem to wear out, which is part of the reason the process of cellular growth becomes less reliable. And then we sag, sink, and wrinkle. Senescence.

Yet the decay of telomeres is not simply a chronological process, a measure of time, of old age. Besides time alone, conditions of our life can damage telomeres. And those conditions happen to be the ones we have been talking about throughout this book: bad nutrition, lack of sleep, flawed relationships, obesity, sedentary lives. All of this causes us to wear out before our time. Stress itself is now being tracked by telomere decay, just as it is with cortisol. So is lack of sleep, which brings real meaning to Worthman's contention that we pay for a lack of sleep in the currency of stress, as reported earlier.

This currency is denominated in telomerase, which is an enzyme the body secretes to protect telomeres. Dopamine may signal our sense of pleasure and well-being, but the presence of telomerase signals that we are not rushing our body's clock toward senescence. In 2010, one group of researchers published results that showed a significant increase in telomerase among participants in a meditation retreat.

BUILDING YOUR BRAIN

On this topic of meditation there is an interesting gap that pulls us back to the discussion of human evolution. But first, consider what is not going on in most forms of meditation. It is not about thinking; it's not what you think.

As you might imagine, years of tradition funneled through diverse cultures and personalities have created variations in the practice of meditation. The details differ, and in some traditions, practice actually does involve a sort of religious fixation on a specific object or person, like the Buddha. But more often than not, especially as the practice has been interpreted in Western tradition, in the austere forms of Zen Buddhism and in research labs, the actual focus of the mind during meditation involves pretty much nothing at all. One common approach is to simply sit and not try to control thoughts or sounds or the flow of events, but to observe and note the various streams that enter one's mind.

Another form of practice is more focused on a single set of sensations—more often than not the breath, or simply intense concentration on an imaginary point inside one's head, directly behind the eyes. Yet notice what is *not* happening in all of these practices. The practice itself is directed toward no particular goal or personality trait. Practitioners are not exercising the mind in mental acrobatics like memory drills, conundrums, or puzzle solving. They are certainly not instructing the center of self to become more moral, pious, or upright. One simply tries to quiet the background substrate in which thoughts flow.

In light of this, it seems somewhat odd that what we have reported does occur, that memory or performance or cognition or even physical health get better as a direct result of training the mind to do nothing. A demonstrated improvement in immune response from simply quieting the mind? Yes indeed. Or, more profound still, recent results from one research project show a link between meditation and increased brain mass, including increased gray matter in regions of the brain associated with learning, memory, and emotional regulation — the last linked to specific physical changes in the hippocampus and posterior cingulate regions of the brain.

What this is saying is that the brain responds to meditation as a muscle does to exercise, and of course it does. That was the implication from neuroscience's realization about neuroplasticity and neurogenesis. Yet it is wrong to say that meditation alone accomplishes a reshaping of the brain. The fact is, everything effects a reshaping of the brain, especially our relationships with one another. The tangible, weighable, measurable, energy-sucking organ is being built from the ground up, beginning even before we are born, and the whole stream of information we call life is doing the building work. The degree to which those relationships are healthy, especially when we are children, is the degree to which our brains are healthy.

What is different about meditation and a number of other practices like talk therapy or exercise or sound nutrition is that we are *deliberately* shaping our brains, intervening in the building process. Someone once argued that there is no choice about whether to train your dog. You either train your dog or your dog trains you. Something similar happens with our brains.

The new and urgent message, not just from meditation research but from neuroscience in general, is that we know now that directed forms of mental exercise begin shaping our brains in ways we want them to go. Davidson said in an online interview that what he has produced in his lab at Madison is really "the invitation to take more responsibility for our own brains. When we intentionally direct our minds in certain ways, that is literally sculpting the brain."

Yet this process is not completely independent from human design, which is to say what natural selection delivered us. Remember, meditation has no goal, but it is a sort of tune-up of the components. And yet from the process, a common thread emerges—a common end that is wholly in tune with our evolutionary history and hallmarks as a species.

Psychologists have devised a simple way of measuring this, a game that begins with giving volunteers real money, fifty bucks or so, and then placing them in a three-way relationship in which they dole out that money according to what other players do. And then, without the subjects knowing it, the testers rig the game so it appears as if one of the other players is stingy and is in fact punishing the third player by not doling out a fair share. The choice for the volunteer is whether to part with some of her own money to effect a more equitable distribution of the cash, and the test is real enough in that the volunteer, usually a broke undergrad, gets to keep whatever cash she has left after the game ends.

Davidson's lab has run this game on randomly selected subjects who undergo a short training in meditation, and after they do so, they give away more money. Researchers regard this as a measure of empathy. The meditative practice does not tell the subjects they should be more empathetic or equitable or compassionate or just. It does not offer skills for doing so. It simply quiets and tunes the mind. Once cleared of clutter, the mind reverts to its default mode set by evolution, which is empathy.

MINDFULNESS FOR EVERYONE

In psychological circles, Ellen Langer, a professor of psychology at Harvard, is known for bringing the term "mindfulness" into play. The term, of course, is much older in the English language, but Langer has secularized it, employed it as we have above in the more general hunter-gatherer state of mind. She is in fact known for a couple of experiments that bring this whole idea into common, general, no-nonsense experience. The first is the chambermaid experiment. She selected a sample of hotel chambermaids and asked them all whether they exercised. Most said they did not, although their work routines kept them active enough to meet the surgeon general's guidelines for healthy physical activity. Nonetheless, Langer recorded their body fat, waist-to-hip ratios, blood pressure, weight, and body mass index and then split the subjects into two groups. She followed around the members of one group through their daily routines and pointed out to them how the specific motions of their work looked like gym exercises. A month later, she interviewed everybody to make sure they had not changed behavior (like diet or exercise) and then redid the measurements. The group that had been told that their work resembled gym exercises in fact physically looked as though they had been exercising: they decreased their systolic blood pressure, weight, and waist-to-hip ratio, and they showed a 10 percent drop in blood pressure. The control group stayed the same. It appears that the mind literally can shape the body.

In a second famous experiment called "Counterclockwise,"

Langer rounded up a group of old men and housed them in quar-
ters decorated and furnished as if it were twenty years earlier.
The men began to look and act as if they were twenty years
younger.

Langer has also recruited professional musicians and divided
them into two groups, telling one to perform a piece to match
their best-ever performance of that same piece. She told the
other group to play a familiar piece in a new way, with subtle
variations that only they would know. Then she had audiences
evaluate the performances. The latter group of performers got
higher marks from the audience. She then told salesmen to vary
their pitch every time they gave it, instead of giving a rote presentation. They logged more sales as a result.

This last experiment steers us toward Langer's definition of
mindfulness, and it is every bit as simple as "awareness." She
doesn't teach subjects in her experiments how to meditate, but
she does teach them how to "notice new things." That's all:
notice new things. This is the same instruction that evolution
issued to hunter-gatherers to ensure their survival.

Our favorite experiment in this vein was conducted not by
Langer but by Daniel Simons of the University of Illinois at
Urbana-Champaign and Christopher Chabris, at Harvard at the
time of the research. In it they showed subjects an impromptu
game of two teams passing a basketball back and forth. Subjects
were asked to note how many times the basketball changed
hands, meaning they were asked to pay attention to a single
detail and account. Then, during the game, a guy in a gorilla suit
walked onto the field of play and weaved among the players.

Remarkably, the participants in the experiment did not see

the gorilla. Not at all. They were too engaged in the counting, in the narrow task at hand.

Maybe Langer's instructions to be prepared for something new, for an anomaly, would have helped them see the gorilla in the room — but we think that any hunter-gatherer would have seen it, no problem.

7

Biophilia

Finding Our Better Nature in Nature

Now we need the great biologist E. O. Wilson and the idea of biophilia. (The term is widely attributed to Wilson but in fact traces to the German socialist philosopher and social psychologist Erich Fromm. He uses it much as Wilson does in the 1964 book *The Heart of Man*.) Wilson lays out the idea in deceptively simple terms: "Biophilia, if it exists, and I believe it exists, is the innately emotional affiliation of human beings to other living organisms. Innate means hereditary and hence part of ultimate human nature."

The real power of this idea is rooted in the implications of "innate." It means that it is encoded in us by evolution—and if it is programmed, then heeding that innate attraction has the power to ensure our well-being. There is something about the deep attachment to nature as opposed to attachment to the artificial world that confers fitness, or at least did confer fitness during most of the course of human evolution.

The logic of this is as follows: Humans, and all species, for that matter, succeed as a species only to the degree they are able to adapt to their environments. Humans, though, did this in part with big brains, by exercising a knowledge of the natural world—a task made more complex for our species by our varied habits and habitats and variety of diet, as we have already explored. Imagine for a moment how simple attentiveness to one's surroundings becomes when amplified with a bit of obsessiveness, of fascination, of real attachment—not merely observing but reveling in the conditions of nature. People with this trait would be more likely to survive. This is not to argue that there is a gene or a hormone for biophilia. Like most interesting traits in humans, this is far more likely a number of traits working together in a networked system. But it's easy enough to see how evolution might reward and amplify those traits. For example, an attraction to the color red causes one to notice it more, and in nature, red often equals ripe fruit.

And so it follows, as was the case with motion and running, protein and fats and sleep, that elements of our sense of well-being and happiness are wrapped up in this trait. This is a hypothesis we can take to the lab (and we will), but our first preferred venue for testing this idea is an ordinary scene. Most of us who have wandered forest trails, or even strolled urban parks, or even driven a scenic highway, can conjure this thought experiment. Think of the place in such a hike or drive where you stop to take it all in. On the highway, there will be a sign marking the "scenic turnout," a sign erected not because some highway engineer thought this was an opportune place to pull over but because so many people actually did pull over and the engineers needed to accommodate the demand. This tells us something in and of itself—but the parallel scene on a mountain trail tells us more. It often comes miles up the trail after winding through rock, scree, and trees, to a ridgetop and a grassy park with a sweeping view of a valley below, when a broad expanse of territory reveals itself—and then comes your urge to stop and take it in, to rest and settle with the peace of the place.

We brought you to this ordinary scene in the mountains for a reason. Look around for a moment—not to the panorama, but at your feet, on the ground. If you are in a place where mule deer or elk live, you will notice that this particular spot is littered with droppings. And just this spot. Everything you crossed en route was not so littered, despite the fact that the rest of your hike was an elk and deer habitat as well. This means simply that the elk bed here, spending sunny afternoons lounging and taking in the day. Those elk feces are hard evidence of our thesis, a deep kinship between you and those strange majestic animals, the sense that both of you have an innate preference for places like this because the vista makes you safe from predators and gives you vital knowledge of your surroundings. You can see, and you are safe. Evolution has written this in your programming for the same reasons it has written the same instructions in the program of elk. And for a moment in this place, animals do not know way more than you do. You read the signs the same as a wild elk does, and the signs say you are home.

This simple idea can translate into hard dollars and cents. Rooms with a view or houses fronted by a lake or stream replicate conditions important to us throughout evolution. Anthropologists who have studied bushmen invariably note that the nomadic wanderings of hunting and gathering are governed by daily cycles that place people in safe camps at night, always with access to water and with an unobstructed view of the surroundings. There is no reason for that preference to hold up millennia later other than a genetic memory—but an apartment with a commanding view of Central Park or waterfront property costs more. This is a measure of biophilia, the price tag on our genetically programmed preference for certain places.

The idea of biophilia has undergone rigorous testing, specifically the idea that we humans, just like any creature with a long history of serving as meat for predators, still seem to prefer vistas and fear enclosed spaces. There is, however, a flip side to this phenomenon that turns out to be just as telling: along with biophilia, there is a balancing set of predispositions tuned to our ancestral enemies. Besides preferences, we ought to have fears that are genetically encoded, biophobias, confirmed in a number of cross-cultural, controlled studies that show an innate aversion to creatures like spiders and snakes (especially snakes). These details are even more illuminating.

Some experiments do indeed show an innate fear of snakes, but in others researchers instead found what psychologists call "biologically prepared learning." That is, we seem to have pre-wired circuitry for learning some things better than others. We learn to fear spiders and snakes very quickly and retain the learning better than we retain other sorts of conditioning; this difference is most telling when compared with our learning about real hazards in the modern world.

Most of us today have far more reason to fear bare electrical wires or traffic than snakes, and yet researchers have found no innate aversion to or prepared learning about these, nor abilities to retain conditioned responses or learned experiences. This is in sharp contrast to the same sorts of experiences with spiders and snakes and fear of heights. Our modern world is full of hazards and pitfalls, and almost none of them are natural or anything like what our ancestors feared—and yet our minds dwell on the same fears that our ancestors had. A highway fatality now barely makes a headline, but a lethal grizzly bear attack gets page one play and is all the buzz on Twitter and Facebook the following day. All of which steers us toward an interesting conclusion.

"It suggests that when human beings remove themselves from the natural environment, the biophilic learning rules are not replaced by modern versions equally well adapted to artifacts," writes Wilson. "The brain evolved in a biocentric world, not a machine-regulated world. It would be therefore quite extraordinary to find that all learning rules related to that world have been erased in a few thousand years, even in the tiny minority of peoples who have existed for more than one or two generations in wholly urban environments."

Yet as a practical matter this offers enormous opportunity. Our attention to this topic is drawn not so much by vestigial fears of spiders and snakes; we are pursuing this idea because it points to some easily reachable antidotes and pathways, even literal pathways, and to our well-being in everyday life, urban and otherwise.

It's easy to see how society might have missed the importance of maintaining our ties to natural surroundings, and in fact there is research on this very issue. One study in particular demonstrates not only that contact with nature, something as simple as a walk in the park, makes us measurably better and a bit smarter but that the participants in the study underestimated the benefits. That is, the subjects tested better on some mental performance measures than they thought they would and didn't credit their walk in the park for the improvement.

The research was the work of the Canadian psychologists

Elizabeth K. Nisbet and John M. Zelenski, who wrote: "Modern lifestyles disconnect people from nature, and this may have adverse consequences for the well-being of both humans and the environment."

Their work fits within a larger body of research from around the world, and the net result of all of this is that we probably can remove the qualifier "may" from the above statement.

When we deny these preferences, these innate attachments to nature, we suffer, and this is a big part of what ails us in a high-tech world of artifice that's increasingly disconnected from nature. The author Richard Louv has argued that this is a key affliction of civilization, even going so far as to give it a name: nature deficit disorder. Louv built his case on ten years' worth of interviews with parents in the United States and concluded that the glitzy attractions of the virtual world, coupled with what he cites as oversensationalized media coverage about the dangers of the outdoors, have created an epidemic of detachment from nature among modern children and, by extension, adults.

This is troubling enough, even on the obvious level that nature contains all of biological life, and children ought to gain the knowledge and appreciation on offer in the wild. But Louv and others point out that there are more subtle issues, and those parallel some we have already talked about in detailing the afflictions of civilization. To cite a few, play in nature exposes kids (and everyone else) to a full range of microbes to support their internal microbiomes and challenge and tune their immune systems; these microbes also fight autoimmune disease, the epidemic of absence. Also, play outdoors exposes people to the full spectrum of light, with a variety of benefits, not the least among them regulating melatonin and sleep cycles but also making for healthy levels of vitamin D. Shortage of vitamin D is an epidemic in its own right, but in this light, it is also a subset of the epidemic of nature deficit disorder.

All of this goes a long way to explain why we are evolved to be in nature, and therefore to value it. All of this supports the hypothesis of biophilia.

Much of this line of thought began in the late 1970s in Ann Arbor, an appropriate center of origin given that its very name includes a reference to trees. While working on his PhD in geography, Roger S. Ulrich happened to notice that Ann Arborites on their way to a mall had a habit of driving out of their way to avoid a freeway and instead took a tree-lined route. That began a series of research projects to demonstrate that these people were in fact deriving some benefit from the eccentric (and more costly) route. Ulrich used an EEG to measure alpha wave activity in research subjects. Alpha waves are associated with serotonin production, and serotonin counters depression. Natural scenes and association with nature did indeed show positive results with alpha waves, and both also had a positive effect against anxiety, anger, and aggression.

In their 2012 book, *Your Brain on Nature: The Science of Nature's Influence on Your Health, Happiness, and Vitality*, the authors Eva M. Selhub, a medical doctor, and Alan C. Logan, a naturopath, summarize Ulrich's work along with examples from around the world. Among them: subjects in an adult care center in Texas showed decreased cortisol levels (the stress hormone) when in a garden setting; a study in Kansas using EEG showed less stress in subjects when plants were in the room; researchers in Taiwan, using measures like EEGs and skin conductance, noted therapeutic effects in subjects viewing streams, valleys, rivers, terraces, water, orchards, and farms; 119 research subjects in Japan showed less stress response when transplanting plants in pots than they did when simply filling pots with soil; and another group of subjects in Japan had lower heart rates after viewing natural scenes for twenty minutes.

Japan, in fact, is the center of some of the most interesting and innovative thinking about this issue; the research has been formalized through the Japanese Society of Forest Medicine and a national movement called *shinrin-yoku,* which translates poorly into English but means something like bathing or basking in the forest. The movement has spawned a series of studies that use objective markers like cortisol, heart rate, and blood pressure to demonstrate that there are real and measurable benefits to well-being and mental performance through simple contact with nature. For instance, a number of studies have shown that people in hospitals get better measurably faster if they are in a room with a window or have a bit of green as simple as a potted plant. Placing potted plants in view of workers at one factory reduced time lost to sick leave by 40 percent.

One of the more interesting findings in the Japanese research is a sort of Goldilocks effect that shows up with trees and potted plants, and results have been replicated elsewhere. It seems there is a sweet spot. Up until that point, benefits to one's well-being increase when more plants or trees are introduced to a room— but beyond the sweet spot, subjects begin to feel worse. Too many plants or trees, and we begin to feel uneasy. The herd of elk we visited earlier could predict this response. It replicates our ease with open views but relative unease in overdense forests, where we and elk were more vulnerable to predators in evolutionary times. The dense forest, as Dorothy and her friends understood, was the habitat of lions and tigers and bears—even in Oz.

Taken together, these findings begin to offer some advice for public policy and design. That is, greenways, open space, landscaping, and even potted plants ought to be integrated into any efficient design of urban space as a simple, cost-effective investment in public health and tranquility. Research in both schools and workplaces has demonstrated clearly that performance of students and workers increases as a result of these simple, low-cost, and uncontroversial measures.

Japan leads not only in research into the tangible benefits of exposure to nature but also in the commitment to making it happen. The government has already invested $4 million in research and over the past ten years has launched one hundred forest therapy centers around the country. The movement is taking root throughout Asia, with active research in Taiwan and Korea. The government of South Korea is spending $140 million on a forest therapy center.

But where this becomes really interesting is in more costly matters like health care, and indeed some of the more sophisticated research has demonstrated that death rates from diseases like cancer decline in areas with more forest cover. Researchers used GIS (geographic information system) mapping tools to control for all other factors, like smoking and socioeconomic status, and found that the dominance of forests alone decreased death rates from cancer. This macro-level series of investigations gets support from individual research that demonstrates a positive immune response from natural settings. Demonstrably and measurably, simple exposure to nature makes you more resistant to disease.

A study in the Netherlands examined the records of 195 doctors who served a total of 345,143 patients. Researchers were looking for a correlation between living near green space and the rate of morbidity, or being sick. They found rates lower for fifteen of twenty-four diseases examined for those people living within a kilometer of green space, and the relationship was especially important for poorer people. The benefits of green space were strongest for those with anxiety disorders and depression.

Yet as Nisbet noted in individual subjects—even subjects getting the direct benefit of this exposure—people fail to appreciate the value of green space, which is likely an enormous factor in why this is also underappreciated in public policy. But the fine details of our cluelessness on this topic become even more interesting and suggest that there is far more to this than we might think. Some of the research with biophobia of spiders and snakes, for instance, used subliminal exposure to pictures of the creepy crawlers. Participants were shown video of some innocuous scenes, and researchers slipped in a picture of a snake that was not really visible—it was present for only a few milliseconds, passing too fast to be comprehended. Yet there was still a fear response. And there wasn't a parallel response to subliminal exposure to more modern hazards like bare electrical wires. At least in this experiment, nature was having a measurable effect on subjects' emotional states, and the subjects had no idea why.

This lack of perception is even more interesting as seen in some work done with *shinrin-yoku* in Japan that looked at aromas in the forests. Trees and other plants exude literally scores of phytochemicals that make their way to our olfactory system, which provides a direct pathway to the brain. The class of chemicals involved are called phytoncides, and many of them have profound effects on the brain, such as lowering stress hormones, regulating pain, and reducing anxiety. Notably, some of them up-regulate powerful tools in our immune systems called natural killer cells, first-line defensive weapons against infections like influenza and common colds. Yet many of these phytoncides are undetectable as aromas. We have no idea that a natural setting is chemically stimulating our immune systems as we simply inhale the open air.

Interestingly, the Japanese research showed that this increased immune response endured. A group of Japanese businessmen who were the research subjects showed a 40 percent increase in natural killer cells after a walk in the woods, but follow-up research showed that their killer cells were still elevated by 15 percent over baseline a month later.

Yet by now, you may be noticing that there's something else in the air, that the pathways and effects of nature parallel those we talked about with sleep, exercise, nutrition, and even meditation. There's more to this. As with these other topics, researchers have begun to use fMRIs in their research; as a result, they have found where exactly it is that nature works in our brains, even pinpointing it as specifically as the parahippocampal gyrus, which is an area rich in opioid receptors (special cells for attaching to opioids, a family of chemicals that includes drugs like morphine and has powerful effects on the brain).

"This was an incredible finding, revealing that nature is like a little drop of morphine for the brain," write Selhub and Logan.

Korean researchers took this a step further and found that urban settings activated a brain area associated with anger and depression, but that natural scenes produced a pronounced effect in the anterior cingulate and insula. This is an important center for empathy, and the effect was confirmed through psychological tests in which people are asked to give away money to other people, exactly as was the case with the meditation studies we cited. And just as with meditation, there was no goal or described pathway for becoming a more empathetic person. Just as the simple act of calming one's brain made one more empathetic, so did a simple walk in the woods.

All of this research seems to be steering us to an almost mystical aspect of biophilia because we are dealing with the unseen and unperceived. Yet it is not mystical or supernatural—just real physical forces we have no ability to perceive (or maybe our urban ways have deprived us of the ability to perceive them). Maybe this is what so fascinates and engages hunter-gatherers or the Koyukon people we spoke of in the last chapter. Maybe they are so engaged with the natural world because the conditions of their lives have trained their minds to see and comprehend the gorilla in the room, a real presence that pulls them in and makes them happy. We mean to leave this possibility open for you to explore.

But at the same time, know that there is plenty of hard evidence that these unseen forces make a real and measurable difference in our lives, and we need not go as far afield as invisible, unsmellable phytochemicals to make the point. We also don't perceive the ultraviolet B wavelengths of light that cause our skin to manufacture vitamin D. But it is nonetheless a fact that full body exposure to sunlight for thirty minutes causes your skin to manufacture ten thousand to twenty thousand IUs of vitamin D, and it is an understatement to say that your body needs vitamin D. Your body *must* have it or you will get sick.

As we said, vitamin D deficiency is a growing problem among modern people. One nutritionist we interviewed was performing blood tests on poor inner-city children in Boston, and we thought that conversation would steer us toward talk of blood glucose and diabetes. It did. But the same nutritionist was equally alarmed by the vitamin D deficiency she found in these children. Michael Holick, an expert on vitamin D at Boston University School of Medicine, told the *New York Times* that on average, Caucasian Americans are short of ideal levels of vitamin D by about a third, and African Americans by about half. And many individuals are much worse off.

In severe cases in children, this deficiency can lead to the disease rickets. But in both children and adults, lack of vitamin D can lead to increased risk of colon, breast, and prostate cancer; high blood pressure and heart disease; osteoarthritis; and autoimmune disorders. We think all of this can be headed off by simply spending more time outdoors, in the sun, which is by far the most direct way to solve this deficiency.

Yet what is intriguing about this topic of nature is the way it seems to double back on all else we have talked about so far, so that we begin talking about our place in nature and then high blood pressure, lack of movement, autoimmune disorders, and depression all come into play. We can take this a couple of steps further. The researchers S. C. Gominak and W. E. Stumpf published a paper detailing the results of treating insomnia with vitamin D after sleep doctors noticed that some of their patients who just happened to be taking vitamin D supplements saw improvement in their sleep patterns. That led to a two-year study of fifteen hundred patients with all sorts of sleep disorders, which showed that areas of the brain with important vitamin D receptors also happened to be areas involved in allowing a positive result for the patients in the trial: sleep.

The researchers concluded: "We propose the hypothesis that sleep disorders have become epidemic because of widespread vitamin D deficiency."

Here's another crossover: remember the hygiene hypothesis — that modern people, especially urban people, are showing a rapid increase in autoimmune diseases simply because they live in a sanitized, built environment and so have removed their immune systems from the challenges of the real world? We evolved living in contact with and dealing with the full complement of microbes, and when removed from that contact, we suffer the results, especially in our internal biome. To be healthy, our internal ecosystems need to be connected to external ecosystems. We connect them by spending time outdoors, in nature, away from sterile, artificial environments.

To be sure, there are layers and complexities to this issue beyond most of our understanding (we think some even beyond all of our comprehension), but the prescription here need not be complicated. For instance, we have long been advocates of connecting children with the natural world by ensuring that they get outdoors, dig in the dirt, and bask in the sun. The research bears out this prescription, and besides that, it sounds like fun.

ANOTHER LEVER

At the very least, these findings suggest some direction for public policy on such matters as greenways, trail systems, and open space, but we hope they also suggest possibilities for your own life. If a simple walk in the woods accomplishes this much alone, what about combining these benefits? What about meditation in a natural setting, or attending to nutrition and taking daily walks along the stream—and adding an adequate amount of high-quality sleep to the mix? All along, we have built the case for re-wilding your life. It almost goes without saying that part of the process ought to be some real, physical contact with things wild.

And if a potted plant helps us inside, are trees better help outside? How far up the mountain can one go? Do I really want to run on a treadmill in the middle of a gym lined with television monitors and smelling of, well, not trees and flowers? And might there be an advantage to running instead in the mountains, to movement in nature, which Selhub and Logan call "exercise squared"?

As we progress in our story, the lever effect is going to come increasingly into play. Remember the lever? Beverly Tatum gave it that name when she talked about sleep, that the simple act of getting more sleep made her attentive to other matters, like nutrition and exercise. One thing led to another. In the authors' lives, this matter of contact with nature is also a lever, and one with a profound effect. A lot of this comes together at Rancho La Puerta. That's where we met Tatum, but also the remarkable Deborah Szekely, now in her nineties, who cofounded the ranch in the 1940s. She also founded and is pressing forth with her project Wellness Warrior, to do the sort of grassroots change necessary to fundamentally rework society. The message is fitness and nutrition, but the lever that works these is contact with nature, a conscious goal of re-wilding the people, sometimes rich and famous, who are the ranch's clients. Szekely says everything begins with the mountain at Rancho La Puerta, which is another way of saying everything begins with nature. Szekely and the ranch loom large in John Ratey's own story, and we will get to that in time.

THE JOYS OF ADVERSITY

You might be thinking that nature can be capricious and cruel, and that maybe it's better to stick to the gym. But we think this capriciousness is a part of the real benefit of living as much of your life as you can in wild settings.

The romanticism of nature means that it conjures birds singing and warm rays of sunshine shafting through trees on a sunny afternoon—a Disney version ready to embrace us with warm, open arms. This is not nature, but, more to the point, we would not reap all of these rewards from our contact with nature if it were. And this realization brings us again to the slippery slope of evolutionary arguments that cohere too tightly to our assumptions about the crown of creation, when we think that nature somehow had us in mind through its billions of years of unfathomable motion, or that nature has our best interests at heart and will mother us. To quote the evolutionary biologist Richard Dawkins, "Nature is not cruel, only pitilessly indifferent. This is one of the hardest lessons for humans to learn. We cannot admit that things might be neither good nor evil, neither cruel nor kind but simply callous—indifferent to all suffering, lacking all purpose."

And this is indifference we need. Robert Sapolsky's baboons headed us in exactly this direction when we first met them a chapter ago, with the vital and unexpected realization that predictable rewards failed to fully stimulate the brain's circuitry of rewards, and that it was only when researchers removed the regularity that the brains lit up in happiness. Nature does not rig the game in our favor, and so it would follow that our brains and our happiness had to evolve to match an unrigged game.

At the same time, this lack of regularity demands our awareness. Our attention makes our lives better by stimulating mindfulness. And we have seen this in action, even before the monkeys. Remember when we went for a run with our dog along a mountain path? You probably realized then and should realize now that the natural setting was in fact the key element of that activity, the major player — that and the full engagement of your brain in complex and varied motion. When we first introduced the scene, we were making a point about variability and the simple physical mechanics of motion. That is, the undulating terrain and capricious weather of a mountain run deliver the random ups and downs, obstacles and challenges to recruit a wide variety of muscles and motions. This is what the body evolved to expect and what best stimulates the brain as it coordinates the body's physical motions. But there is not a clear line between the variability provided by nature and the larger connections we are making now. The environment randomly dealt out a set of mental challenges, some of them with real consequences, like a stumble, a broken ankle, a cliff, a snow squall, or a bear.

Trail running is an odd sport, and we are not arguing that everybody ought to do it — but we come back to it because it illustrates some of the seminal ideas of the book. We have every reason to expect these runners to be just another bunch of jocks, with opinions and sentiments much like those of Olympic marathoners, bikers, weight lifters, or soccer players. But there are some intriguing differences in behavior that we think are relevant to our larger points. We think these differences stem in part from the natural context and evolutionary precedent of this activity.

First, the sport is growing faster than probably any other. *UltraRunning* magazine reports that 63,530 runners finished ultramarathons in 2012, ultramarathons defined as any distance greater than the 26.2 miles of a marathon but almost exclusively run on trails on mountains and in deserts and forests. That number represents a 22 percent increase over the year before but a more than twentyfold increase over 1980. But further, this is not just a sport for young studs bursting with testosterone. The sport is reasonably gender-balanced, and some races are won by women. And there are big-time major event winners in their forties and active participants in their sixties and seventies, senior citizens finishing hundred-mile events. We think all of this enthusiasm stems from the fact that the sport seems to closely resemble what we did in our evolutionary past. The basic elements of mountain running appeal to those deeply seated urges encoded in us by evolution.

All of this, it turns out, has produced an interesting internal conversation, and it is worth eavesdropping on the blogs and websites. For example, take this post from Willie McBride from the popular website for trail runners iRunFar, built, remarkably, from ideas from Erich Fromm, the German philosopher we credited at the start of the chapter with the term "biophilia." McBride was pondering his seemingly contradictory attachment to social media on the one hand and mountain wilderness on the other:

Our need for experiencing both the rawest nature and the most instantaneous social technologies may seem contradictory but the root cause of these peculiar rituals stems from a deep and basic desire. We want to be connected, to be a part of something bigger than our individual selves.

In *The Art of Loving,* Erich Fromm writes, "The human race in its infancy still feels one with nature. The soil, the animals, the plants are still man's world. He identifies himself with animals. . . . But the more the human race emerges from these primary bonds, the more it separates itself from the natural world, the more intense becomes the need to find new ways of escaping separateness."

Fromm further believed that this devastating departure from nature is the root cause of all human suffering: "The experience of separation arouses anxiety. It is indeed the source of all anxiety. Being separate means being cut off, without any capacity to use my human powers. Hence, to be separate means to be helpless, unable to grasp the world, things and people actively. It means that the world can invade me without my ability to react."

And so this idea begins with nature and our need for connection with nature, as we have argued, because of its indifference. But the flip side of this is just as interesting and is implicit in our need for connection. In a perfect world, we face nature's indifference by connecting and drawing support from people who are not indifferent.

8

Tribe

The Molecule That Binds Us to One Another

We have been saving this story, one of our favorites, until now. It is odd that the research behind this story existed at all. It was examining a truly weird question about the safety of mothers sleeping with infants—weird because, through most of human history and in most contemporary societies, even, no one would question the safety of mothers sleeping with infants. There was, however, a particular focus of this experiment having to do with the relative positions of the two bodies being studied. Science has determined that there is a specific arrangement that does indeed optimize safety, a way for mother to curl around baby that makes the whole situation pretty bombproof, so that mother won't roll onto baby and hurt her. This was the fear that originally prompted the research.

Remember the example we cited early in this book about a dog having a litter of pups? The dog seemed to know all the proper steps of the process without instruction. Same deal with mothers sleeping with infants, or at least some mothers. The researchers found that mothers who were breastfeeding their infants assumed the prescribed position of maximum safety without instruction—even first-time mothers. Mothers who were not breastfeeding did not.

The dominant hormones of childbirth and lactation are prolactin and oxytocin, and it is this latter thread we pick up now. No better place to begin than at the very beginning, each of our literal beginnings, because this is the core relationship of human society and behavior, the one that explains who we are. True enough, oxytocin figures prominently in childbirth and lactation, but it continues to exert profound influences throughout our lives.

MOVING WITH OTHERS

At one point in thinking about this book, it occurred to us we were missing an important piece of our story, and we realized that Eva Selhub might be able to tell us what that was. The hunch came from a personal observation. We had followed Selhub's work and had spoken with her and her coauthor, Alan C. Logan, about their book, *Your Brain on Nature,* which provided a great deal of the information about biophilia in our last chapter. Beyond this, though, Selhub is a conventionally trained medical doctor who quickly moved beyond that training to study the healing power of nature, nutrition, and exercise, as well as meditation and traditional practices of healing, such as qigong. Her practice has followed many of the paths we have traced in this book, yet during our initial meeting with her, we couldn't help but notice that she was onto something new, that personally she had hit a stride that had pumped a fresh level of physical and mental vitality into her life. We wanted to know what it was.

And so we sat for a pleasant hour's conversation one sunny afternoon in Boston, and Selhub began by confirming our observations that in recent months she had in fact become a "very different person." She told us that the proximate cause of this was simple enough—deceptively so. She had joined a CrossFit gym, the regimen of physical exercise we spoke about earlier, with movements designed to provide a wide variety of challenges and ranges of motion that the human body probably encountered throughout evolutionary time. Yet this new variety of movement was not the whole story. It was certainly part of the explanation, but something else was at work, and that's mostly what Selhub wanted to talk about during our conversation.

Selhub admitted up front to a deep-seated loathing of gyms and the conditioned flee response to competitive athletics that's adopted by too many kids thanks to ill-conceived physical education programs. In her telling, the real attraction in her Cross-Fit practice was community.

"It feels good to have the rewards, to not only be able to excel and do something you've never been able to do but to compete with other people and have them be excited for you. For me, if it was just the competition, it wouldn't work, but it's the community. It's the camaraderie," she told us. "It's really a community.... It's kids running around, seeing parents and adults exercise and do crazy things, hugging, laughing, talking. It feels like the way it is supposed to be."

Feels like it is supposed to be.

Return for a second to the record compiled by Elizabeth

Marshall Thomas of her family's experience living among the Ju/wasi people of the Kalahari Desert in the 1950s. She quotes her mother, who wrote extensively about the experience:

> The [Ju/wasi] are extremely dependent emotionally on the sense of belonging and companionship. . . . Separation and loneliness are unendurable to them. I believe their wanting to belong and be near is actually visible in the way families cluster together in an encampment and in the way they sit huddled together, often touching someone, shoulder against shoulder, ankle across ankle. Security and comfort for them lie in their belonging to their group free from the threat of rejection and hostility.

Tribalism is a cultural universal, so identified by paleoanthropologists as one of the salient characteristics that has defined humanity since the beginning. The intense bonding of *Homo sapiens* was likely a major factor, if not *the* major factor, in giving us the edge that made us the lone survivor in our line of upright bipedal apes. Literally, we can trace our bonds in our bones, but better still to trace it in oxytocin, a chemical that's not just about nursing mothers. All women have it. So do all men. It holds us together. We're using oxytocin here to build the case that your well-being depends on solid relationships with other people.

THE BONDING AGENT

Sue Carter is at sea for a few minutes trying to decide where to begin, an excusable bit of indecision. How does one begin to summarize forty years of research into the effects of a single molecule, let alone one that's front and center at the core of human behavior (and the behavior of other species)? Evolution has been leaning on oxytocin and its close chemical relatives, especially vasopressin, to perform a variety of vital functions for a very long time, predating even humans but also predating mammals—even stretching back to the unimaginably distant and dank recesses of the evolutionary tunnel when vertebrates first split from the simpler creatures without spines. Vasopressin is an ancient chemical that likely appeared when all of life was contained in a water world, making it necessary to regulate the flow of water from inside to out of the organisms. It still does that job, even among the terrestrials, including humans.

Carter was also jet-lagged, having flown home the day before from Morocco, but she nonetheless had agreed to a conversation in her new town house just outside Chapel Hill, North Carolina, where she recently moved her work after spending most of her career as a neurobiologist at the University of Chicago. She takes a spot on a comfortable couch and is quickly joined by her Chin, a Japanese spaniel lapdog. And then she decides to begin where her work began in the 1970s: with prairie voles, an innocuous and silent mouselike species that navigates the tangled plant world of North American grassland ecosystems, mostly unseen by all except owls and biologists.

She began working in association with the field biologists who were asking the questions common in that discipline in the 1970s, questions that mostly had to do with survival and crashing population—and, when evolutionary ideas came into the picture, with the physical makeup of the beast in question, because then the emphasis was on finding those physical attributes that conferred fitness. At that time, prairie voles were undergoing boom-and-bust cycles—population explosions followed by crashes; it's the sort of phenomenon that alarmed biologists then but is now better understood as the normal course of events, especially among ground-level rodents. But the researchers quickly came to understand that there was something truly odd about this obscure little species of rodent. They were social. There was a vibrant vole society, and holding it together was monogamy (or at least that's how it looked from a hawk's-eye view), strong pair bonds between a single male and a single female, which is an uncommon practice among mammals.

What is most curious about this is that meadow voles—a closely related but separate species, the same genus in the same habitat—are not monogamous. All but a trained biologist—even owls—would be hard-pressed to spot the difference between a prairie vole and a meadow vole, yet prairie voles go in for lifelong bonding to a single mate and meadow voles do not. In the '70s monogamy was thought to be a complex, evolved behavior like bipedalism or omnivory, and so followed an evolutionary line and logic in a predictable progression. But here it was, a distinctive behavior dropped into a single species without warning, like a plug-in option in a new model year of a car.

Back then, though, evolutionary biologists had a ready explanation for monogamy, rare as it was in mammals—an explanation based in sexual selection. That is, a male bonds to a given female and invests his energy in raising the young because they are his genetic issue. This in turn is rooted in the idea of what is famously labeled the "selfish gene," meaning that evolution selects for genes that perpetuate themselves and so selects for individuals that ensure perpetuation of their own genes over those of others. This, for instance, is the common explanation for the widespread practice of infanticide in the animal world, including among human animals: males, on encountering a new female, often kill her young so that they might replace them with their own genetic issue. In most cultures, including ours, death rates among children with stepfathers are about equal to those among other mammals.

Even in her early work, though, Carter was skeptical of this explanation for monogamy in prairie voles. "I had been exposed to enough sociobiology and evolutionary biology to assume that reproduction was the core of evolutionary theory. I don't think it is true. I think it is actually social interactions that are driving many aspects of behavior," she told us.

She was right, but it was not until the 1980s and the availability of certain tools for analyzing DNA that the fuller story emerged. Monogamous in outward appearances these prairie voles might be, but the undeniable evidence of the genes of vole pups demonstrated that these loyal males laboring their lives away raising pups were in fact cuckolds. About half of the pups were not their genetic issue. What's more, this rough ratio held up across the animal kingdom, especially among birds, for which monogamy is far more common. Depending on whom you ask and when, you will likely as not be told that humans are monogamous, but if you ask DNA about this, the story is much the same as for other animals. Sexually monogamous? Well, no. Voles and all the rest of the animals prefer marriage of convenience, which does not mean that the concept of monogamy is irrelevant, but it does need refining. It does not describe a sexual behavior, an adaptation based in reproduction. Rather, it describes a social adaptation that is indeed useful in ensuring a next generation, even a selfish gene generation. Half of the kids might not be the kin of papa vole, but half of them are, and stable social arrangements make everybody better off.

Yet this realization meant that the inquiry had wandered into what was then shaky ground for biologists, who were used to considering issues like prey base, carrying capacity, length of stride, and length of fang. Monogamy was not a physical attribute; it was a behavior. But the evidence was saying that the behavior was innate, not learned. But more to the point, vole society started to uncannily resemble that of humans, and no one really had any idea where that came from.

"They have a social system that looks like humans': long-lasting pair bonds, two parents taking care of young, incest avoidance, extended families—just about everything that is cardinal to human society," Carter said.

But not all of them, and not all of their lives. There are a couple of modes of prairie vole living, and all of this talk of sex completely ignores something important: those voles that ignore sex. This is a common thread in all social animals, even termites and ants. We have long wondered why so many members of, say, a bee colony are simply not players in reproduction, that task being relegated to the few fertile: a queen and the several drones who are her mates. Most bees go through life oblivious to mating, and it is not that different with voles. Most of these rodents spend life in what Carter labeled a "prepubertal" stage. But biologists soon discovered what flipped that switch: a simple matter of a timely meeting with an appropriate mate. Each half of the budding couple discovers the other by chance while they are still in that prepubertal state, but the encounter itself triggers a response in each that looks very much like going through puberty. The male especially is completely transformed in a matter of hours from a clueless, sexless naïf to a rather fiercely attached partner, and the partnership lasts for life. At the root of this transformation, Carter figured out, was oxytocin and, especially in the male, vasopressin. These are two closely related biochemicals, technically neuropeptides (brain chemicals). This discovery alone ratchets up the relevance of the finding to the human condition: oxytocin is the most common gene-generated molecule in the human brain. In voles, it is the transformative switch.

And not just in prairie voles, it turns out, and this is in many ways the finding that nailed the centrality of this single molecule in the foundational behavior of a whole series of widely unrelated species. That initial work with prairie voles has spawned what Carter characterizes today as a "tsunami" of research. Literally hundreds of labs worldwide are working on this single molecule, but one of the early eureka experiments involved giving oxytocin to species such as rats. Males of this species are not given to hanging around rearing young and helping out with the housework. These males are by nature more inclined to be, well, rats—but oxytocin-dosed rats adopted monogamous habits, including attentive pup rearing. Even in the close relative of prairie voles, the meadow voles, tweaking their brains to enhance their ability to feel the effects of oxytocin caused exactly the same behavioral shift.

The initial research about oxytocin predated the work on voles. As early as the 1950s, the neuropeptide had been identified and cited for its role in birth, lactation, and even sexual attraction. Further work in sheep and rats in the 1970s showed oxytocin's role in bonding between mothers and young rats and sheep. Yet demonstrating oxytocin's ability to organize the social system of prairie voles has tipped off scientists to roles for this single molecule far beyond the fundamentals of intercourse and reproduction.

It is the social molecule, and interest in it has built to something of a fever pitch with the realization that, although the molecule is manufactured deep in the brain and has its most profound effects there, it need not be injected directly into the brain, as was painstakingly done in the early research. It works its magic administered as a simple nasal spray, which is by far the most direct route to the brain, as cocaine users know. Some substances that we inhale quickly enter the brain, as we talked about with the aromas of nature in the last chapter.

As a practical matter, this has made the experiment with human subjects easier and a lot less invasive, ramping up this line of inquiry. Notably, experiments using standard tests for altruism, exactly like those we saw with meditation and exposure to nature, have delivered clear demonstrations that oxytocin enhances empathy and altruism. Oxytocin made subjects more likely to part with their money to offset what they saw as unfairness to another person. Oxytocin also enhances what psychologists call social cognition—that is, social skills. For instance, we can easily see how—and research has demonstrated this—our social bonds are dependent on our brain's ability to recognize faces, and oxytocin enhances that ability. It also enhances the ability to identify emotional states as they are displayed on faces, meaning the ability to read emotions in others. A whole series of experiments has shown the molecule's ability to enhance trust in others, and this idea expands how we might think about the importance of social relationships.

Research has also shown that oxytocin plays a key role in business transactions, especially in establishing trust. This is not as squishy as it might sound. Economists will tell you that the workings of the marketplace depend on a foundation of trust, that the glue of our economic lives rests on our ability to trust one another well enough to do deals. Follow this idea backward now through evolutionary time, and you can begin to see where this winds through the human condition, and how this group cohesion is part of our evolutionary success, our ability to adapt and prosper. Trust enables economy, a rule best demonstrated in negative examples, in places where anarchy and chaos have undermined all trust. Those places have little hope of economic development.

There are a couple of interesting asides in this same line of research. People engaged in business transactions produce a spurt of oxytocin. If one person gives another person ten dollars, the recipient's oxytocin levels spike a bit. But here's the kicker: if a computer gives that same person ten dollars, his levels of oxytocin do not increase. And there's a bit of intraspecific research that is our personal favorite: if you engage your dog, your oxytocin level increases, as you might expect — but your dog's oxytocin level increases even more.

Take these realizations together, and it's easy to see how some of them might provoke a scientific feeding frenzy. You can get a hint of this in the appearance of a recent popular book about oxytocin that's gushing with promise and titled *The Moral Molecule*. This chemical begins to look like a magic bullet, especially to people with autism. Remember, autism is characterized by that very lack of social ability that seems at the center of oxytocin's field of expertise. Things like enhancing the ability to recognize facial cues and other such social skills can seem like exactly what the doctor might order, and, in fact, some work has been done with autistic people that encourages this conclusion. So here appears an inviting target right up the center of the medical model's line of thinking: an easily synthesized molecule that can be administered in a simple nasal spray, is already the most common molecule in the human brain, and deals straight on with one of modern medicine's most intractable maladies— and at the same time spins off into trust, empathy, love, and understanding. What's not to love? What's not to love for Big Pharma?

Science magazine caught this drift in an article in January 2013 that began as follows:

> Few substances produced by the human body have inspired as much hoopla as oxytocin. Recent newspaper articles have credited this hormone with promoting the kind of teamwork that wins World Cup soccer championships and suggested that supplements of the peptide could have prevented the dalliances and subsequent downfall of a certain high ranking U.S. intelligence official. Although the breathless media coverage often goes too far, it reflects a genuine and infectious excitement among many scientists about the hormone's role in social behavior.

Well, maybe, but haven't we been down this road before, seen the allure of magic-bullet, single-pathway solutions?

Or as Carter put it: "The public wants a fast answer. If we know it works, why don't we make a drug out of it [oxytocin]?"

She added that such a solution "seems a bit arrogant and stupid."

To begin with, we've known from the very beginning of the work on voles that if you focus on the yin of oxytocin and ignore the yang of vasopressin, you are going to miss some key elements. And, in fact, yin-yang probably overstates the separation, because both neuropeptides are very closely related in function, chemical structure, and evolutionary history. Both are important to both genders, but vasopressin has a decidedly male skew.

This is probably more than an interesting aside because everything in the human body is connected, but vasopressin research also appears in a very different arena, one that explores its function as a regulator for water. In its finer points, however, this regulation by vasopressin (which is in its chemical structure almost identical to oxytocin) turns out to be far more interesting and, in fact, seminal to some of our earlier discussions about exercise. Vasopressin is what gave us the ability to practice the form of persistence hunting that David Carrier (the mountain runner–researcher at the University of Utah) talked about and what helped him begin to understand why humans were born to run. We developed this skill in an arid landscape, after all. Modern bushmen still do persistence hunting in the desert, and observers have noticed that they do it without drinking water. Thomas, in fact, noted that groups of men who hunt and women who go on daylong forays of gathering food take nothing more than an ostrich eggshell full of water to last the whole day under a desert sun. That is to say, these bushmen could run full days in scorching heat on an amount of water that some people advise modern runners to drink every half hour.

The South African researcher Tim Noakes has done an

extensive study of this matter and has shown pretty clearly that the more excessive modern advice on runners and water is, in fact, just that: excessive. The data show that the advice to drink lots of water (actually to "hydrate," and that's part of the problem — that we no longer drink water; we "hydrate") is simply wrong. Noakes's analysis showed that runners who were the most dehydrated after marathon-length races actually tended to win. More to the point, no one suffered medical problems from dehydration, while those who drank the recommended amount of water or sports drinks often suffered severe consequences from *too much* water. Some even died.

The deal is, exercise, especially running in hot conditions, triggers a cascade of vasopressin, which causes the runner's body to conserve water. That's the very trick that allowed the bushmen to succeed in the desert, and the deaths in modern-day marathons are the result of our thinking that we need a solution like "hydration" to overrule evolution's design. One more example.

But the more telling bit of information in this aside is evidence that both vasopressin, as we have shown, and oxytocin, the "social molecule" we are trying to bottle in nasal sprayers, are triggered by exercise. Chalk up one more brain benefit from exercise. And by now, it should be no surprise that running, movement, social bonding, and emotional well-being have a common chemical pathway. Chemically, these seemingly disparate topics hang together, and we ought to pay attention to that as a big signpost of evolution's design.

But back to the social side of this chemistry. Many of the effects that produce monogamy in voles are triggered not just by oxytocin but by the right balance of oxytocin and vasopressin. In all of this, there is not a straightforward, dose-dependent response to oxytocin, no rule that says more oxytocin yields more warm and fuzzy behavior. Rather, these adaptive social traits emerge from a complex dance between the two neuropeptides—at least these two—and then play into a cascade of hormones. And all is gender-dependent.

But a second element of this discussion looms even larger. Oxytocin and vasopressin are molecules that carry a signal of sorts, and there need to be receptors in the brain specific to each molecule. The number and efficacy of these receptors have much to do with how the brain reads and accomplishes the effects called for in the cascade of these molecules and all the other neuropeptides that the body uses to regulate the mind. Indeed, the research has targeted these very receptors from the beginning. For instance, researchers, as we said, were able to make the normally inattentive and philandering male meadow voles behave like the monogamous and responsible prairie voles. But they did so not by amping up oxytocin levels but by genetically engineering vole brains for better receptors. Oxytocin is a universal chemical in vertebrate life, but the differences among the various species' behaviors are due in part to variations in receptors, not levels of oxytocin. This also explains why the trait of monogamy is not a neat, linear progression through evolutionary family trees, but rather pops up here and there. Genes that build the receptors kick in and out, like toggle switches.

Researchers also believe that the variability in receptors helps explain differences within species, why one individual is more touchy-feely than another. This is not the sole explanation. As we have seen, exercise or encountering the right mate triggers spikes in oxytocin, but genes play a role as well. Genes control, at least in part, the number of receptors, and that very idea is why Carter bristles at the current simplistic line of research that says all we need to do is spritz a bit of oxytocin up one's nose to provoke a lifetime of sweetness and light. Her caution is based on some hard research and some personal experience.

A postdoc working with Carter, Karen Bales recently completed work in voles meant to mimic the effect of giving autistic children a few squirts of oxytocin while they were young — and while the animals were young, the treatment worked as expected, making for warmer and fuzzier adolescent prairie voles. But as they aged, their behavior began to deviate from the norms of polite prairie vole society. That is, these same males had a hard time partnering up. Those early doses made them less, not more, social as adults.

Carter told us she thinks those early doses of oxytocin are, in effect, "downregulating" — that is, desensitizing — the normal receptors of those young voles. As they age, then, the receptors are less able to read normal levels of oxytocin.

And this is where her line of logic becomes at once deeply personal and near universal. Despite being the world's go-to expert on oxytocin, Carter was treated pretty much like any other delivering mother in a hospital in Germany a generation ago. Back then, she told us, it was relatively rare for doctors to inject mothers in labor with the synthetic form of oxytocin, Pitocin — it happened in maybe 10 percent of deliveries. But she was injected.

"This concerns me a great deal, and it concerned me right from the start," she said. "As a scientist, I wanted to know what I did to my baby by letting the doctor give me that, but I really didn't have a choice."

True, the doctors did not give the drug to the baby, but now we know that this same molecule shows up in the brain seconds after a mere mist of it is in the air, and a baby in utero is far more intimately connected to the source. Carter must think about this now, knowing as she does the results that showed up in those prairie voles only when they became adults. A very recent paper correlates an increase in the incidence of autism with receiving Pitocin during delivery. Carter says that Pitocin is routinely administered to delivering mothers in, she estimates, 90 percent of cases, although there are some signs that this practice is waning.

At the same time, the current spate of research has turned up some other drawbacks to this simplistic, medical-model approach to oxytocin and vasopressin — but these are as intriguing as they are cautionary. These findings open a window to some sobering realizations about evolution itself and our ability to comprehend its wisdom. They make us confront violence.

What one tends to remember and report from those early prairie vole experiments is that the neuropeptides in question provoked monogamy, bonding, and solid parenting — true enough. But Carter says it was also true from the beginning that once the adolescent male crossed the line of puberty in a chemical rush, he ceased to be a meek little field mouse. "He becomes a lethal weapon," she said. "He fights off any and all intruders and will fight to the death at the same time he is the nurturing father and devoted mate."

In its summary of research on oxytocin, *Science* magazine reported on a study in Amsterdam headed by Cartsen De Dreu that used a nasal dose of oxytocin and assessed the effects with a standard game that subjects played for money:

Compared with men who got a saline spray, those who sniffed oxytocin behaved more altruistically to members of their own team—but at the same time, they were more likely to preemptively punish competitors.... In a 2011 study in the Proceedings of the National Academy of Sciences, De Dreu's team found that oxytocin increased favoritism toward subjects' own ethnic group (native Dutch men) on a series of tasks and thought experiments done on a computer, and in some situations the treated men exhibited more prejudice against other groups (Germans and Middle Easterners, in this case).

This is a double-edged sword.

One goal of oxytocin research has been to promote desirable characteristics like trust, empathy, and loyalty, traits in short supply among us today. Yet we may want to place our assessment of "desirable" in context with a question that Carter put to us: if science could indeed deliver a pill that would make you a paragon of these very traits, would you take it?

And you need not think long to answer in the negative. That distrust of outsiders often leads to violence against those same people, and in evolutionary terms, violence is not necessarily a problem. Violence is useful and therefore adaptive; we need it to survive and always have. Even today, in situations where violence seems to be counteradaptive, it persists because in so many other situations it was critical to survival.

We did not get our first hint of this conclusion from biochemistry or even from evolutionary history. John Ratey has a long history of treating some exceedingly violent people, and a clear theme emerged in his practice, especially in dealing with domestic violence. The blowup and the violence in those situations (and this is not a trivial matter at all; by far, domestic violence is our most widespread form of violence in modern society) often come at a critical and common point: when the victim, the female, takes steps to leave an abusive partner. That threat triggers an irrational rage that quickly explodes—and it took time to see it, but it became clear to John that this explosion was defensive. The partner's threat to leave was a threat to the home, and the violence—no matter how irrational or misplaced—was a defense of the home.

We are not arguing that this sort of violence is justified or even adaptive. It is, in fact, a failure of the brain's coping mechanisms when faced with threat. The executive function of the brain in the frontal cortex gets hijacked in these situations, and violence ensues. It is irrational and pathological—but the wiring for it, the tendency, was put in place by evolution as an adaption. It is precisely the same impulse that sorts us into tribes, that causes us to feel best when in the circle of like-minded people we were born into and feel ill at ease when we are among others, maybe Ju/wasi, Masai, Apache, and Sarmatian once, now maybe Christians or Muslims, Republicans or Democrats, immigrants, operagoers, gardeners, bluegrass musicians, or the folks we know at the CrossFit gym. Distrust of outsiders is the flip side of the social bonding that allows us to trust those closest to us.

THE CORE HUMAN TRAIT

We deliberately entered this broader discussion of tribalism and violence through oxytocin because childbirth, nurturing, and bonding lie at the center of the human experience. Early in this book, we outlined the broad markers of human evolution and introduced this key point. Now it is time to revisit it in this new context.

We need only consider the cartoon image of cavemen in modern imagination to begin to understand our long-blinkered perception of the nature of our ancestors: in the cartoons, the caveman always carries a club. This is nothing more than an extension of the Hobbesian notion of nastiness, meanness, brutishness, et cetera, yet the notion is not limited to cartoons. Throughout paleoanthropology, there has been a persistent strain of imagining our species' development as governed by violence. Much of this has been rooted in the study of bones, skeletal remains that show signs of breaks and stabs and beatings, and so people reading these bones from time to time interpreted this as a sign of constant warfare.

At the same time, our closest living relatives—even the comparably peaceful bonobo, but especially chimpanzees—show plenty of ability when it comes to violence, even warfare, and so this, too, is part of the state of nature. Further, we have seen it emerge in the inquiries of people like Carrier, who began by looking at our body's adaptation for running but wound up concluding that we are equally adapted for and well suited to punching and throwing spears. Truly, violence is in our bones and muscle. This conclusion will not go away, evident also in the headlines of the day, the confirmation of hatred and carnage in our times and in all times. Indeed, the evolutionary psychologist Steven Pinker has argued that we in fact live in relatively peaceful times, and that the record shows the past has been characterized by stunning degrees of aggression toward one another far worse than today. He argues that a decline in violence is a benefit of civilization and that slowly humanity is learning to put this aside. We can only hope. Yet there are some lessons from evolution that may help us think about this most vexing of human dilemmas.

Pinker's argument is data-based, and he argues that it holds through all of human history — yet there is good reason to make the distinction that we have throughout this book: that the best evidence for our violent past comes from the past ten thousand years, a time when territory and ownership of land became vital, when farms supported cities, when monarchs could raise armies, and when we developed the tools for mass warfare. Much of the case that hunter-gatherers spent a great deal of time and energy killing one another is circumstantial at best. For instance, one analysis of the bumps and breaks on ancient skeletons — evidence earlier interpreted as resulting from warfare — got another look from researchers who found a close modern analogue to skeletons in this condition, and these were not the skeletons of warriors. The closest match to injuries like these in modern times were in rodeo cowboys, people who mix it up with big unruly animals for sport.

Some distinctions need to be drawn, and saying that primitive life was rough-and-tumble is not the same as saying it was violent.

It may help to be a bit more precise in our definitions. First, we would argue that hunting is not violence. It is killing, true enough. There will be blood. But the brain of the hunter is in a very different mode than the brain of a murderer or warrior. This is pretty clear-cut and demonstrable in measurable phenomena like brain waves. The hunter generally faces no threat that triggers a response of terror or aggression. Just the opposite, as we have seen on so many levels. The hunter is engaged, even empathetic. Indeed, through every bit of knowledge we have of hunting peoples—from the cave paintings in southern France to the rituals of plains bison hunters—comes evidence that these people regarded their prey with respect and awe.

Beyond, there seems to be a good case for separating out defensive violence against predators. Beating off lions and bears is not what we think about today when we discuss violence, yet fighting off predators probably was the form of fighting we knew best in evolutionary times. The threat of predation shaped us, and it had to, particularly the threat to our helpless infants. When we speak of violence as adaptive in evolutionary terms, this is the best example. This is why aggression is the flip side of the bonding powers of oxytocin; it is adaptive not only to cooperate and bond with our fellows but to protect and defend.

Yet none of this gets at aggression against other humans, and it should. Why does aggression persist beyond reasons for it? Why are we so riven with senseless killing and warfare? Is this simply who we are, as Pinker argues, and does this require the cultural evolution of civilization to gradually wear it away, wall it off to a silent corner of our gene pool?

Part of our thinking about human evolution has missed a great deal because we see what we want to see, and the caveman with the club is something of an icon in this regard. We are indeed fascinated by broken bones, spear points, and stacks of mutilated skeletons, yet much has been gained in reexamining the evidence from a different perspective. Put another way, the history of trying to understand human evolution has been beset with all sorts of debates about what defined us, what came first, and what is most important. Big brain? Opposable thumbs and use of tools? Fire? Fishing? In all of this there is an obvious bias toward things men do.

Yet one of the more thoughtful and interesting students of human evolution, the anthropologist Sarah Blaffer Hrdy, has told us much by reexamining the evidence in light of the things women do. In terms of evolution, her approach represents far more than correcting a gender bias. In evolutionary terms, the success of a species is completely dependent on reproduction— whether it goes on, and whether it fields a set of genes for the next generation. As we have said, *Homo sapiens* are unique in all the animal world, completely without precedent in one regard. No other species must spend as much time and energy rearing and protecting infants as we do. To Hrdy, this is the defining fact of our existence, and the term she uses is "cooperative breeding." That is, we come together as a species to raise children: "What I want to stress here, however, is that cooperative breeding was the *preexisting condition* [emphasis hers] that permitted the evolution of these traits in the hominin line. Creatures may not need big brains to evolve cooperative breeding, but hominins needed shared care and provisioning to evolve big brains. Cooperative breeding had to come first."

She is saying our cooperation and ability to bond to one another is primal, foundational, the bedrock. In her book *Mothers and Others*, she hits on the essence of this idea: "Brains require care more than caring requires brains."

Still, the persistence of violence seems to contradict the importance of bonding, but then humans are nothing if not contradictions. And this contradiction teases out an even more basic issue of evolution—one that today's evolutionary biologists debate at great length, but which has in recent years produced all sorts of insights into the forces that drive us. Much of evolutionary thought has rested on discussions of individual fitness, with an individual being a discrete unit of genes, and therefore the only unit on which evolution can act. Yet as studies of social animals (ants, termites, prairie voles, and humans) came to the fore, it occurred to thinkers that there was such a thing as group fitness. That is, the degree to which we were able to successfully cooperate and cohere as groups yielded clear advantages to our survival. This raised the idea of group rather than individual selection, a notion still hotly debated. And whether we know it or not, it is still hotly debated every day and every second in each of our brains. That's because it is sometimes to our advantage to do what is good for us as individuals and other times to do what is best for the group—selfish behavior versus altruistic behavior. Both confer advantages in evolutionary terms, and we are wired to heed both sets of messages.

It's best at this point to return to the evolutionary biologist E. O. Wilson: "The human condition is an endemic turmoil rooted in the evolution processes that created us. The worst in our nature coexists with the best, and so it will ever be. To scrub it out, if such were possible, would make us less than human."

9

Central Nerves

How the Body Wires Together
Health and Happiness

Let's go back to the town house near Chapel Hill, North Carolina. Sue Carter's husband, an intense-looking fellow, had met us at the door, introduced himself in a businesslike way, and retreated so we could talk with Carter. Later, there was a break in our conversation, and he was rummaging around in the kitchen, opening drawer after drawer, searching for the tamper for his espresso machine, a clear case of partner-based misplacement of crucial accessories.

"Sue puts things away, and I look for things," he announces without preamble. "I've decided it's all about the other person thinking you know exactly what they are doing. The problem is the interpretation of intent and whether the feedback from it modifies behavior."

It's not apparent that an espresso tamper merits this depth of analysis, but then this guy is Stephen Porges. His career has been nothing so much as tracing a vital thread, a literal twisting, winding cord that can tie together the ideas we have been tracking in these pages. Carter studies social bonding chemistry and oxytocin. Porges studies the neural structure of social bonding, especially the vagus nerve. Think of it as Carter knowing the software and Porges specializing in the hardware. But this nerve is also where all the topics we've been thinking about seem to converge, in signals along the vagus and the central nervous system, in which it is a key player. Remember that when we considered the sweep of evolution and its intention for our well-being, it brought us ultimately to social bonding; the whole business—the brain, exercise, eating, minding, and sleeping—traced in the end to our need to deal with one another, to empathy and altruism. More than any of our other signature traits, these two require the most brain power and allow us to be who we are, the most social of social animals. These are the capstones. And when we parse that out, especially when considering the evolutionary context—our deep history as pieces of meat for predators—then all of this must have something to do with stress, fear, terror, and dealing with these matters in order to survive.

Elizabeth Marshall Thomas, the writer who spent her formative years with African hunter-gatherers, writes a great deal about lions in her account of the San people of the Kalahari. The San people she knew did indeed face lions as predators, as all people have for almost all of time. Yet these people seemed to have a finely wrought and intricate relationship with lions, the animals that owned the night. "Among the people we knew, only lions generated profound respect," she wrote.

"Respect." Not "terror," but "respect."

Thomas witnessed a number of confrontations between lions and the San people and describes nowhere any reaction that looks the slightest bit like panic. No one ran from lions. No one froze in fear. No one, certainly, engaged in fight. So here it is, the fundamental, raw, tooth-and-bone confrontation with the barest facts of biology, and yet there's no evidence whatsoever of resorting to the basic biological mechanisms for terror: fight, flight, or freeze. Instead, there is respect.

But there is more in the specifics of what is really going on. Far from fleeing a lion, San people had a "protocol" (Thomas's word) — and it involved walking. Walking calmly, unhurriedly, and not directly, as fleeing prey might, but obliquely at an angle, away from the lion. At the same time, they spoke to the lion, in well-modulated tones of respect, addressing it as "old lion."

Richard Manning has had a direct and similar personal experience with a grizzly bear in the wild and observed exactly the same protocol, accepted by bear biologists as the way to deal with these big predators. The protocol is ancient and endures and has much to say about meeting not just predators but the challenges of modern life. Porges thinks he can trace the development of that protocol in the body's most ancient and tortuous nerve, the vagus nerve — it gets its very name from the same word as "vagabond," a wanderer, a traveler, a time traveler.

THE ANCIENT NERVE

Porges is a rare bird among scientists, a guy who has spawned his very own theory of human behavior, an idea that has acolytes and practitioners and real-world, on-the-ground applications. For instance, at the Center for Discovery in New York, we met a young, bright guy from MIT, Matthew Goodwin, who had used Porges's ideas to incorporate the same sort of telemetry that lurks in the guts of an iPhone to track and predict disruptive out-breaks in autistic people. This is the sort of application that started Porges thinking about all of this decades ago—the idea of measurable, readable physical manifestations of our state of mind, a literal pulse of our psychological well-being.

The vagus nerve is the only one that attaches to the most primitive, lower part of our brain, and from there it winds the unique and circuitous course that earns it its name. Unlike most other nerves in the body, it wanders, not straight from eyeball to brain like the optic nerve but downward along the neck and then branching and twisting through the core of our body, our guts, our gonads, our viscera, and if you hear in this the word "visceral" you are hearing right. But then, oddly, parts of it twist back up through the throat to take in larynx, ears, facial muscles. Why this odd assortment of disparate organs and functions? What does our heart—just a pump, really—have to do with the crinkle in the corners of our eyes?

This tortuous path, starting as it does in the most primitive part of our brain, is first an evolutionary trail, and it clearly marks the vagus as ancient. It makes its straight march to the chest and heartbeat but also back upward to innervate structures that had their origins in the gills of our very distant ancestors. It is an integral part of a network known as the autonomic nervous system, which regulates automatic responses in our organs—but not only automatic responses. Among the system's key tasks is regulation of our body's response to threat, terror, and lions, the center of control for fight, flight, or freeze.

When presented with a threat, each of these strategies requires regulation throughout the territory covered by the vagus nerve and the rest of the autonomic nervous system. For instance, heart rate and respiration increase, both effects that supply extra energy for fight or flight. The digestive system shuts down to save energy. Same with the gonads. Same with immune response. Facial muscles contract and contort to the fierce presentation of rage. The larynx tightens to pitch urgent vocalizations. This is your body at DEFCON 1. And then the threat passes, and the vagus nerve reverses all of this. The whole cycle, arousal and relaxation, is an oscillation that is adaptive and serves as the successful response to danger.

In all of this, the shutdown sometimes gets taken for granted, but it is not a given. The terror response doesn't just stop on its own; it requires a whole separate set of signals to shut it down. Over time, people who are repeatedly abused or terrorized, especially as children, lose the ability to return to normal, almost as if a switch got stuck. They literally live in terror. Further, tracing the course of the autonomic nervous system shows quickly why so many issues deemed psychological play out in the body: digestive issues, impotence, poor immune response, high blood pressure, elevated heart rate, tense faces.

A curiosity about the physical manifestations of a psychological state is what brought Porges to the vagus nerve in the first place. What kept him there was the realization that the vagus nerve runs both ways. It is mostly a control nerve, signaling organs to relax, but it also sends information back up to the brain on the state of the organs.

Begin, though, by understanding that social engagement, the ability to deal with another of our species on the basis of trust and understanding, is, in terms of all animals, truly bizarre behavior. Almost no other species can do it as well as we do, and those that can, like dogs, tend to hang around with us. Porges says the reason this is so in evolutionary terms is that very few species have the ability to apply the vagal brake. The ability to calmly speak with one's spouse as to the whereabouts of the espresso tamper means asking the autonomic nervous system to perform two contradictory goals at the same time—and the key to that, says Porges, is the vagal brake. The vagus nerve links up all the tools we need to respond to an existential threat, and so the vagal brake is a signal sent through the system for everything to stand down and engage—at ease.

And it turns out there is a simple measure of this. It can be read in the tension or lack of tension in facial muscles, heard in voice timbre and edge, and counted in rate of respiration. But at the heart of the matter is the heart itself and a subtle little signal called the respiratory sinus arrhythmia. When the vagal brake is applied, it calms the heart as it does everything else, and the unequal pressures of breathing (the increase with inhalation and decrease with exhalation) actually syncopate the heartbeat with a little asymmetry in rhythm, a slight difference between contraction and expansion. This is a respiratory arrhythmia and the syncopation can be read on a graph, plain as day. Further, says Porges, there is such a thing as vagal tone, completely analogous to muscle tone—and the tone shows how clear and distinct a given individual's ability to apply the brake is. That tone can be read in the amplitude of the arrhythmia. People who are comfortable engaging other people have strong vagal tone.

For openers, this realization revitalizes a whole collection of metaphors in our language and most others by suggesting that they are more than metaphors. A strict rationalist's reading of statements like "I know it in my heart" or "My heart is not in this" sees them as a cover for mushy thinking. In strict, reductionist, mechanistic thinking, the heart is just a pump, not so different from the circulating pump in the boiler in the basement. (Likewise, science has begun talking about a "second brain" in your body: the enteric nervous system. We have long known that the digestive system has a robust set of nerves of its own, but research is finding out that this system does far more than regulate digestion. It is a full complement of neurotransmitters and, in fact, seems to play a key role in regulating your sense of well-being, both physical and mental. It plays a role in your decision process, hence "second brain." Now metaphors like "gut instinct" get some real-world traction.)

Yet it now seems as if there was an instinctive understanding in the evolution of our language that recognized what we can now measure in graphs and blips and charts: that the heart and gut are deeply engaged in our emotional lives. But this might seem a bit much on the evidence we've delivered so far. It's cool that the heartbeat gives us a measure, but so what? It's only a slightly more sophisticated measure than, say, rate of respiration, galvanic skin response, or a twitch in our facial muscles that any dog can read.

To which Porges replies, no, no. The vagal brake can be driven by breath, a clear connection readable as blips on a chart. You are in control of your breath, to some degree. Thus, this is not simply a point for measuring or sensing arousal; it is a point for controlling arousal and, downstream, the health problems that stem from lack of control.

We have long had intriguing clues as to how our body might participate in psychological health. For instance, it is a no-brainer that if you feel better, you are more likely to smile. But people studying depression figured out long ago that if you force yourself to smile, the specific spots in the brain that register depression suddenly say your depression is better. Nothing else changed in your life, so why should this be? Through the years, neuroscience has produced a refinement of this intriguing little bit of information. It turns out that a halfway, forced smile won't do the trick because it won't light up the neurons of increased happiness in your brain. But if that forced smile goes so far as to engage the little muscles in the corners of your eyes — that is, if you do what socially adept people understand instinctively — these neurons do indeed light up. And the muscles at the corners of your eyes are within the reach of the vagus nerve.

Yet where this idea really hits home is with the breath, the one response over which we have control and which, in turn, exerts control through the alarm system that is the autonomic nervous system. Porges says he realized a long time ago — because he is a musician, specifically a horn player — that the act of controlling the breath to control the rhythm of music and at the same time engaging the brain to execute the mechanics of music works like a mental therapy. To his mind, it has all the elements of pranayama yoga, a form of yoga that stresses breath control.

Breath control is common in most of yoga but also in meditation, and even in modern-day "evidence-based practices" like cognitive behavioral therapy. Relax. Take a deep breath. This act of controlling the breath has a parallel brain response of calming our instincts for fear and danger. It's easy enough to see this in deliberate practices like yoga, but the same idea applies in many more time-honored practices: choral singing, Gregorian chants, even social music like bluegrass or blues derived from the chants and work songs that African slaves developed to help them tolerate oppression.

There is, in fact, a musical thread throughout this idea.

There is a bias in the system to detect what Porges calls prosody, the rhythm and lilt we associate with music, singing, poetry, and chants. It is the form that becomes immediately apparent in our voices when we talk to animals or babies and is the language of our foundational relationships with our mothers. Prosody is the form of speech the San people used to engage lions.

All of this begins to explain a curious finding among the bones and ruins of our ancestors, such as flutes carved from the leg bones of cranes. Recall that music or evidence of music appeared fifty thousand years ago in that sudden flourish of evidence of cultural evolution that defined humans as humans— and ever since, music has loomed as a cultural universal. All known cultures and peoples make music. Yet all of this also suggests that we lose something when the crane's leg bone gets replaced by an iPod. We lose the benefits of sitting in a circle of fellow humans and driving the breath and beat that drives the music.

The psychiatrist and neuroscientist Iain McGilchrist argues that music predated language in human development, simply because it was more important, more necessary, and already developed by evolution in other animals like birds and whales. Language merely allowed communication. Music and components of music like lilt and prosody facilitated engagement, even with other animals, even with predators. It engaged the breath in its making.

CONNECTIONS TO PHYSICAL WELL-BEING

The vagus linkage suggests that these sorts of activities might well extend beyond emotional well-being simply because so many of the physical maladies of modern times play out in the territory of the vagus nerve and the enteric nervous system. Your yoga practice or your choral group may well have some leverage on your irritable bowel syndrome or the persistent pain in your neck for no apparent reason, because both of these are wired to the signal path of breath.

But what of exercise — pumping lungs and heart in exertion? Porges says it depends. Done wrong, exercise can drive the emotional response in the wrong direction because it relies on arousal — the physical arousal that is the opposite of relaxation. But this is not the contradiction it seems to be. In much of the animal world, the choice is either fully aroused or fully shut down, but the sophisticated autonomic nervous system of humans allows us to accomplish both at once. The most profound statement of our ability to deal with contradiction is sexual congress, the state that demands arousal in the most basic and heart-thumping sense, and at the same time requires maximal emotional openness and engagement — that is, trust. The standout ability of a well-adjusted human is to handle both arousal and engagement at once in this and all other forms of social intercourse.

Which turns out, in Porges's view, to be terribly relevant to that workout of yours at the gym. Simply plunking yourself on a treadmill or stationary bicycle, armoring with earbuds to shut out auditory signals from the real world, and then watching cable news loop the litany of the day's lurid images — he argues that this speaks straight to the reptilian reaches of the nerves. Remember, you are running, as in "flee." Running is a setup for working the grooves of panic. The alternative, though, is group activity, group play and exercise, the very sort of activity that humans seem to have preferred through the ages. Done right, this does indeed involve the arousal of the flee response, but also the social engagement of teammates and competitors and the rich sensory messages from nature and the outdoors. Now both arousal and engagement are activated, meaning your heart, body, and mind are fully involved in the most elaborate of social exercises. All of this puts a new layer of foundation beneath developments like Eva Selhub's and Matt O'Toole's enthusiasm for the CrossFit gym. Even more deeply, it helps us see further significance in ancient activities such as persistence hunting, always done in groups with sublime levels of engagement and communication among members. Persistence hunting also required an almost instinctive level of understanding and predicting the movements of the animal being tracked, a skill that observers recorded as based in empathy.

TRAUMA

One of the best windows into the relevance of all of this frames a view most of us would prefer to avoid, filled as it is with nightmarish visions. Because while the vagus nerve is central to our trust and social connection, it is also central to terror, and too many of us live at the reptilian level of this response.

The guy generally credited with having done more thinking about this than anyone else is trauma researcher Bessel van der Kolk. Porges talked much about trauma during our interview and at least part of the credit for that, he acknowledges, goes to his association with van der Kolk.

Van der Kolk grew up in the Netherlands, but as a young

man he came to Boston and trained as a psychiatrist and then became involved in treating veterans of the Vietnam War who were plagued with psychological difficulties as a result of their experiences. At that time, there was a vague notion of the source of those troubles, labeled in earlier wars as "shell shock" or "battle fatigue." But as a result of work during the Vietnam era, psychiatry gave this problem a formal diagnosis of post-traumatic stress disorder, or PTSD, a diagnosis that van der Kolk helped formulate.

Shortly thereafter, though, he became interested in the problem as it plagued children, and he has founded a national network sanctioned by Congress to research what he calls "developmental trauma." The difference between the problem in children and in adults is critical and serves as the main finding of the whole area of research. Child abuse occurs while a helpless brain is still physically forming, and so it locks in patterns of neural response largely through the mechanisms of fight, flight, or freeze. This means that the effects of childhood traumatic events linger, in fact dominate, well into adulthood, and in some surprising ways that speaks directly to what ails us.

The pivot point in this thinking was a landmark study taken on by the Centers for Disease Control and Prevention. It looked at seventeen thousand middle-class employed adults in California and assessed their history of childhood abuse against the primary causes of premature death in the United Sates, like heart disease, diabetes, stroke, and liver disease—our nation's most expensive public health problems. The results are head-turning. The researchers found, first, that there is a surprising amount of abuse in most people's lives—physical, mental, and sexual abuse as well as the experience of growing up with violent or alcoholic parents. More important, though, the researchers found that not only did abuse serve to predict poor health later in life, but the amount of abuse was directly related to the severity of the later health problems; it was, in the language of epidemiology, "dose-dependent."

Some of this can be explained by the usual routes. People abused as children tended to self-medicate as adults with alcohol, drugs, and cigarettes, and those behaviors in turn sponsored some of the later health problems. But the researchers performed statistical techniques to account for this and still showed a straightforward physical response to child abuse. This may seem a strange connection, unless one realizes that the diseases in question affect organs like the heart and lungs and processes like digestion and immune response, all of which falls into the territory of the vagus nerve.

"Trauma lives in the body," van der Kolk says often, an aphorism that tracks the vagus nerve but also the path of his own career. He has been known to state bluntly that despite his training and lifetime of experience in psychiatry, what he has learned through trauma has caused him to stop practicing psychotherapy. He is openly and frankly dismissive of talk therapy, labeling it "yakking."

And so one cold, gray afternoon in Boston, we found him holed up in a modest little ground-floor office in a brick town house, where we'd come to ask him what works — what makes people better.

"Trauma is about immobilization," he says. "What works is people moving together in time, rhythmically." Through the decades of his dealing with this problem, he's gotten results by making people move.

People who have been abused, especially as children, are often simply practicing the normal and adaptive response of freezing. That's the tool that evolution gave us. The trauma response is not a mental disease or failure of the genes and neurons; rather, it is a normal response to an abnormal situation. And at the same time, we are evolved and adapted to return to normal, to begin motion again, once the danger passes. The problem, especially with children but also with warriors who suffer PTSD, is that the danger and terror happen again and again and again; they become a way of life, and over time the biochemical and neurological systems for returning to normal, for modulating, for shutting down the alarm, just lock in place instead. And the body seizes up in the bargain. Maybe not in complete paralysis, but parts of the body do freeze, terrified to move.

"Immobilization without fear, which is really what society is all about, as opposed to immobilization with fear, which is what trauma is about," was the way Porges expressed this to us.

This is where van der Kolk slides from the biological evolution that has dominated our discussion so far to the idea of cultural evolution. His reasoning is this: Humans have dealt with terror and psychic injury for as long as there have been humans, and certainly as long as there have been lions, and more certainly as long as there have been wars. So we have developed time-tested—no, deep-time-tested—methods of coping. Van der Kolk looks for these methods, and he finds them in places you might expect, all in line with his foundation tenets of moving rhythmically together, controlling breath, and feeling the vibrations of voice. He practices yoga himself and prescribes it for others. He likes the ancient Chinese practice of qigong, a form of ritualized movement. Meditation, certainly. Many forms of dance, and chanting. He pays particular attention to theater, citing examples such as successful projects in troubled high schools, where students—many of them the victims of violence—write, rehearse, and stage musical theater as a means of recovering from the damage. One such project, called Shakespeare in the Courts and headed by the actor Tina Packer, specializes in Shakespearean theater, summoning as it does the primal cadence and earthiness of Anglo-Saxon words like "murder," "father," and "blood" to tap and relate emotional content in public.

There's nothing new about any of this. Van der Kolk points to the roots of Western theater in Greek tragedy, performances of which were filled with more public venting of emotion than modern theater is today. He believes that these rituals developed in what were then unarguably violent societies for many of the same reasons this sort of thing works in a modern context. The elements align nicely with what we are learning about emotional trauma and the intricacies of our visceral nervous system. Breath control, rhythm, whole-body movement, narrative, social ties and cues—all of these are physical impulses that travel at the literal core of our being.

Besides, he says, "people cannot rhythmically move together without beginning to giggle." Laughter trumps trauma.

BEYOND STRESS

There is a word, an overused, worn-out, imprecise, deflated word, that comes up when we talk about danger and challenge. "Stress? We shouldn't use the word," says Porges. "I think it's a bad word."

And now we've gone and done it, opened a can of worms that is in fact going to cause us to backtrack on another word, one that has served us well in our discussion so far. But once you deflate the idea of stress, then you also begin to undermine the notion of homeostasis, which is precisely what we need to do now. Homeostasis? Old hat. Last week's news. Think, instead, allostasis.

The fact that some enterprising folks in the tech world began marketing a new sort of household thermostat makes this distinction easy to analogize. Homeostasis is like a thermostat — in some cases, it behaves exactly like one. Exert yourself on a hot day and your body temperature rises above its set point of 98.6; you begin to sweat so that evaporation and cooling return you to your set point. This is homeostasis, the body's mechanism for maintaining stability at set points, such as heart rate, respiration, blood pressure, hunger, thirst, and on and on. And it's just like the sort of thermostat that hangs on the wall. Set a temperature and a furnace or an air conditioner kicks in appropriately to maintain it. Or at least that's how it worked for a hundred or so years.

But the newer, high-tech thermostats actually remember changes you make in room temperature according to conditions, not through a simple memory and program. They actually learn, remember, and predict your behavior. So they know when you get up on a cold day, and they turn up the heat in advance, just as you would do.

This, argues the new thinking, is more in line with how your body works, only your body is even more sophisticated — because unlike the thermostat on your wall, humans have big brains. The neuroscientist Peter Sterling laid out the difference in the introduction to a key paper on the topic, offering the beginnings of an idea that is providing some needed traction for our thinking:

> The premise of the standard regulatory model, "homeostasis," is flawed: the goal of regulation is *not* to preserve constancy of the internal milieu. Rather, it is to continually *adjust* the milieu to promote survival and reproduction. Regulatory mechanisms need to be efficient, but homeostasis (error-correction by feedback) is inherently *in*efficient. Thus, although feedbacks are certainly ubiquitous, they could not possibly serve as the primary regulatory mechanism.
>
> A newer model, "allostasis," proposes that efficient regulation requires *anticipating* needs and preparing to satisfy them *before* they arise.

Put another way, homeostasis can deliver only stability, and in life, stability is literally a dead-end strategy. The only stable condition of a biological organism is dead. Your body's systems must allow for growth, which means more than simply adjusting for existing conditions. Your vital systems must roll with the punches today and build capacity to absorb future punches.

We have already seen the fundamental design feature of this at work, and it goes beyond the example of the high-tech thermostat. A thermostat controls one system in your home, but your body is made up of a series of interlocking systems: circulation, digestion, immune, nervous, endocrine, and so forth. Sterling points out what any designer of an efficient car already knows. If each of those systems needed its own energy reserves and capacity to meet all needs at all times independently, the whole system would be inherently overdesigned and inefficient. Better, then, to allow energy borrowing between the systems, just as we have seen. Fight, flight, or freeze shuts down the digestive and immune systems simply to allow the muscles to use that energy instead.

Yet that same principle explains exactly why it makes no sense to treat a particular malfunction or disease by considering only one system. The overload that is producing the problem may be in another part of the body altogether, which is why "psychological" problems like PTSD show up as digestive issues and can be treated in the body. Or why, for that matter, Carol Worthman's contention that we pay for sleep deprivation in the currency of stress is true. The body is making adjustments throughout the system to meet immediate needs, and all of this is checked and balanced by the brain. At the same time, though, this system is looking to the future, both short-term, in seasonal cycles, and long-term, in changes in the conditions of life.

One example of a short-term systemic change comes as days lengthen in the spring. At this time of year, we react to increasing sunlight by producing skin pigment that protects us from increasing sunlight later in the year. Another example is that most mammals store fat as winter approaches.

But long-term regulation seems even more critical in light of the issues that have concerned us throughout this book, and we have already seen examples of just how long-term we might mean by this. Remember the research that concluded that the best predictor of obesity in children was low birth weight. The fetus senses the conditions that produce low birth weight in utero as a predictor of a lifetime of scarce resources, and so his body adjusts by becoming good at storing fat. This is not a disease or a malfunction, really, but an adaptation. But remember, too, that an important predictor of an infant's low birth weight is his mother's low birth weight, meaning the body is setting in those adaptive processes across generations.

We always assume that the method for transmitting traits across generations is genetic. For a long time, science has made much of genetic predisposition, and certainly genes play a role in governing our lives. But it is also true that much was made of genes because at the time we happened to know a lot about genes; that is, we were looking for the car keys where the light was best. In recent years, though, a whole new field has exploded on the scene: epigenetics, which is the study of gene regulation, how it is influenced by environment, and how it is inherited across generations. Much will be illuminated by this line of inquiry, but it has already pointed to one key mechanism, and, in fact, we have already seen it in action in a couple of areas we have talked about.

Remember Sue Carter's worries about oxytocin doses to infants based on the research that showed how young voles given nasal doses of oxytocin had weird relationships as adults? Her explanation was a "downregulation" of receptors. That is, the voles' bodies still produced the oxytocin, but the brain had adjusted to the excess by turning down the sensitivity of special cells that detect the signals — thus, downregulation. Sterling identifies this as a key mechanism in allostasis: the body's ability to adjust to variations in the environment, a recalibration of its instruments.

His paper on this says: "Thus, when blood glucose is persistently elevated and triggers persistent secretion of insulin, insulin receptors eventually anticipate high insulin and down-regulate. The system learns that blood glucose is *supposed* to be high." This is the smoking gun for insulin resistance, the very issue that lies at the heart of our worst health problems, like obesity, diabetes, and heart disease. It is our bodies' collective response to a long-term change in the conditions of life wrought by industrial agriculture and processed food.

Yet wrapped in this sort of adaptation for change is the mechanism for growth, and it, too, is rooted in what we might call stress. This is the process at work in every long run uphill or in every set of bench presses that reaches for a new personal record. We build muscles by tearing them down, stressing them beyond their limits. The body reads this as a need for more muscle to meet these new conditions of your life, and so the body builds it. And this works the same way in the brain: brain-building chemicals build new cells and make existing cells stronger.

Yet Sterling's paper refines this line of thought by pointing out that the brain is not simply executing all of these controls on autopilot, but is in fact engaging our consciousness and sense of well-being in the entire process. The brain is wired with what he labels a set of carrots and sticks that move each of us to adapt and respond along with the rest of the body. Pain is a part of this—surely a big stick—but more intriguing is the degree to which all of these circuits for adaptation are tied directly to our brain's dopamine circuits, the pleasure circuits and the brain's reward system. Sterling makes the same argument we heard from Robert Sapolsky when we talked about meditation. That is, we get the greatest pleasure not out of a predictable reward but out of an unexpected one. We take pleasure in challenge and get more mindful and focused at the same time by dopamine, which is the carrot pulling us along to overcome the challenges of survival, short- and long-term.

The flip side of this is anxiety, the stick that pushes us in elemental fears, the most common and elemental fear being, at least in evolutionary times, concern over where your next meal is coming from. The relief arrives in a squirt of dopamine that is the result of answering that concern every day. Sterling writes this: "*Sensitivity* to dopamine also declines because dopamine receptors, anticipating high levels, have down-regulated. This may explain Goethe's famous remark, '*Nothing is harder to bear than a succession of fair days.*' "

Yet in engineering a society that is nothing so much as a succession of fair days, we have removed the dopamine reward, and so we go mindlessly looking for ways to replace it. Some of us climb mountains or ride roller coasters. More commonly, though, the void gets filled with a suite of addictions, especially to drugs and alcohol, which play to the dopamine circuits, now governed by downregulated receptors that leave us asking for more.

All of this suggests that the strategy for coping is not removing stress, or what we call stress, from our lives. Rather, as we have argued throughout, the real problem, the killer, is the chronic, unrelenting, unremitting series of regular events that wears us down. You can skip a night's sleep now and again. It may, in fact, even be good for you to do so. But not day after day. You can tolerate and even thrive on astounding variety and variability in your diet, even enjoying an occasional slice of chocolate cake, but the daily, unrelenting dose of Big Gulp Cokes will kill you. Every runner knows you build strength on rest days. Dealing with a lion every now and again makes you better at dealing with lions. Allowing your life to surmount occasional challenges is inoculation—almost literally—against future stress.

This brings us back to a central point in this book: variety. Remember, we argued from the beginning that the hallmark of the human condition is our ability to tolerate and thrive and in a wide variety of conditions—the Swiss Army knife model. So if our tolerance for variety is so great, how can we argue that modern life, with all its apparent variety—wheat, sugar, agriculture, iPads, noise, and the rest—is killing us? Much of that answer lies in deciding who each of us is.

The neuroendocrinologist Bruce S. McEwen and the researcher Linn Getz build on Sterling's idea of allostasis by using it to form a strategy of personalized medicine that involves employing specific and complex information about each individual to decide on interventions for problems. This idea has some currency in mainstream, medical-model medicine, but usually it is couched in terms of genetics. An individual's course of treatment would depend on sequencing his genome to decide his genetic predisposition to disease and its cures.

Yet McEwen and Getz argue that this ignores epigenetics and life history and that those influences are if anything more important. Specifically, they argue that there is such a thing as "orchid" children and "dandelion" children, individuals sorted by their specific tolerance for variability and challenge as shaped by the events in their lives. Dandelion children thrive anywhere; orchids are hothouse flowers. How far one goes in the direction of novel challenge and how attentive one needs to be to a safe, familiar base is a matter of where one falls on the orchid-dandelion continuum, and this is true for adults as well as children. But over time, with effort, one can move toward the dandelion end of the scale. This is growth. This is building resilience by inoculation against stress. This is re-wilding.

The idea summons an image we used to introduce this book, the common scene employed in teaching students of child development: mother and toddler alone in a room, toddler clinging to mother to draw strength and foundation and courage, and then using that base to leave mother to explore, to be challenged, and then being surprised in fear and retreating to mother for reassurance. And then, if mother is good and does her job well, toddler explores again and grows.

This is not just for toddlers. The evolutionary conditions that shaped us are that base of comfort and strength, the mother. Gather that strength and then venture forth to explore the variety and wonder of the world, the wild. And when it jolts you, pull back, rest, and grow among people you love and trust. Whether you're stressed or relaxed, well-being is not about always being safe or fed or comfortable. Rather, it is learning to walk the line between the two, to balance, to move back and forth between them with ease and grace. Well-being comes from learning to talk to the lions.

10

Personal Implications

What We Did and What You Can Do

Indeed, the sources of our happiness are complicated, rooted as they are in the complexity of our bodies, but also, as we have argued, in the complexities of the twists and turns of our individual life stories, all of which forces the conclusion that there is no single prescription for well-being. Given this, the temptation is to paraphrase our favorite advice on writing from the great journalist A. J. Liebling: The only way to live is well, and how you do that is your own damned business.

But this is a cop-out of sorts. There is a better way to deal with this matter of personal prescription: Our bodies and minds are endowed by evolution with marvelous systems tuned to attend to our happiness. Our task is to learn to listen to those systems and stay out of their way. As we argued in the beginning: if this grail of well-being is so elusive, so unattainable, then why can hunter-gatherers who have never heard of the scientific marvels that we have cited here achieve what we are after without even really trying?

Yes, living organisms are complex, but now it's time to shift gears and deliver, as we promised, some synthesis of all of this that you might use in your own life. Both authors have learned through years of public appearances that audiences will often ask a pointed question that eliminates the cop-out of not offering a prescription: "Yeah, but what do *you* do?"

There are a lot of scientific uncertainties and dueling studies that plague this issue. But the simple and necessary realization is that in all really interesting questions of science, there is no such thing as certainty. And yet there is a certainty that each of us must live a life, and each of us must make the choices that guide that process.

We—each of the authors—did not hatch and assemble the ideas that brought us to this point solely from within the confines of research, inquiry, conversation, and logic. These notions came to us like most: after years of living. This book is not an academic exercise for either of us, but rather a product of living our real and textured lives. So, each in his turn, we are now going to give you some parts of our personal stories, especially recent parts, when we used our own bodies as laboratories for exploring these ideas. The truth is, our lives changed greatly during the process of writing this book—changed for the better. And we think that our experiences might offer some guideposts for your own explorations.

JOHN RATEY

Probably like many of you reading this, my life can be described as hectic, overscheduled, too much to do with too little time. In addition to running a psychiatric practice in Cambridge, Massachusetts, I teach, lecture around the world, write books and papers—and if that isn't enough, I have a bicoastal relationship with my wife, Alicia, a television producer in Los Angeles, which sends me on planes back and forth between the coasts.

Over the years, I have certainly been guilty of getting too little sleep, grabbing a hot dog and a soda on the run, being too wired after spending hours at the computer returning email, checking the news, the latest science reports, and even the New England Patriots scores. In the city jungles of Boston and L.A., "nature" is not readily available, and certainly finding quality time to spend with my tribe, recently made bigger by the important addition of my very first grandchild, hasn't always been easy.

But change can happen. If I can incorporate the concepts laid out in this book in my own hectic life, thereby creating a healthier physical self along with a greater sense of emotional well-being, so can you. Of course, my life didn't start out in so many directions, at a frenzied and sometimes unhealthy pace. When I look back on my childhood, I see how "wild" I really was without even knowing it. I grew up in Beaver, Pennsylvania, a small town outside Pittsburgh, where we lived in a real old-style neighborhood. "Tribe" was important. Beaver was a place where everybody knew and cared for one another, with the usual crabs and discontented folks, but mainly people who were strivers of Tom Brokaw's greatest generation. Our food was natural and home-cooked. My mother always had a garden, and we delighted in the fresh summer tastes of tomatoes, onions, leaf lettuce, and carrots. Sleep was regimented, and when the day ended, there was little TV, let alone the digital life that wires us now. Rather than playing video games or texting friends, my job was to play vigorously with my close band of buddies, Fred and Joe, and we were always on the move. From almost the time we could walk, it seemed that every kid in town was playing Little League on the field or touch football on a neighbor's front lawn. We were frequently in the elements, running through the nearby woods playing cowboys and Indians, putting our architectural prowess to the test as we built forts in the backyard with giant piles of leaves, or just doing nothing as we sat on the banks of the Ohio River fishing for carp and catfish.

As I grew up, my understanding of sleep, diet, movement, nature, meditation, and the importance of connection also grew. Over the years, I've been fortunate to delve into these areas, taught by some of the most impressive academic and professional minds out there. Looking back, I now see where, even as lessons were being firmly implanted into my intellectual self, in my personal life, I frequently moved farther and farther away from my wild child days and my inherent genetic roots.

Upon moving away from Beaver and on to medical school, sleep was one of the first things to go. I was surviving on fumes, burning the candle at both ends as a medical student and resident at Massachusetts Mental Health Center. If I could have, I would have stayed awake 24-7, because this was the mecca of psychiatric training. There I met with the world famous sleep researcher Dr. Allan Hobson. The irony is, although I was sleep-deprived then, he would become a good friend, guide, and mentor. We spent our days and nights in a lab, observing animal behavior in studies of sleep onset and trying to unpack what sleep was. This was the beginning of neuroscience; sleep was a subject of great interest, and it seemed as though we would discover what it was for. But as we said in our sleep chapter, we still do not know that answer. We just know we need sleep.

I knew that eight hours was necessary for a good night's sleep, but in my whole life I had never gotten close to this regimen. I was the wellness revolutionary who was proud of how little sleep he needed and even bragged about it. I realize now how wrong this was, and today I see that the more sleep I get, the better.

The head and emotional leader of the department was Elvin Semrad. He was all about connecting with your patients and their bodies, how they felt, and how you could empathize with them. He shooed us away from constructs and reading, and instead got us to observe ourselves in the moment. We needed to be present with our patients to deeply understand how they felt, both in their body and at an unconscious level. This wasn't about a symptom checklist but about being mindful and getting them to be mindful of how and where they were in pain.

Connection is one of the most important tenets of my personal life as well. I do not work or live well alone, and so family, friends, and coworkers are a constant support. My good friend and collaborator Ned Hallowell is a champion at emphasizing the need to work at this, to create the time and rituals to connect regularly with friends. But the power of this was quite evident. We needed to ritualize it with ironclad times, or it would go away. I always created or joined groups that interested me and kept me going professionally. Bessel van der Kolk and others started a group focused on trauma, attention, and neuroscience, and we have met every second Monday of the month for more than twenty years, with frequent guest speakers on a wide variety of subjects. I have never written alone and have a new tribe formed with Dick Manning.

Along with appreciating the power of connection, I have

had a profound respect for the effect of movement on our brains and psyches. Exercise is deeply ingrained in my DNA and I feel it. From my early days in medical school, I saw the power of movement and its ability to regulate emotional well-being. In medical school, I saw an article about a hospital in Norway that was admitting depressed patients and offering our then brand-new miracle drugs (the antidepressants that effected norepinephrine) or an exercise program three times a day. The hospital claimed that each treatment had the same results. This stuck with me during my residency, when the Boston Marathon was just booming—everyone, or almost everyone, was training for the marathon, or at least running.

In the '70s we had just discovered endorphins, and everyone was talking about the endorphin rush and its power to stave off depression (simplistic causality was the rule). Then I learned that drugs that approximated the effects of chronic exercise and meditation—the beta-blockers, which act to tamp down the drive of the sympathetic nervous system and allow the parasympathetic to take over—were useful for aggression, violence, autistic disruptive behaviors, self-abuse, anxiety, social anxiety, stress-related disorders in general, and certainly attention deficit disorder. The magical effect of exercise on my own and others' attention systems led to a whole career of writing about ADHD, then to the brain itself, and finally to exercise, in my most recent book, *Spark: The Revolutionary New Science of Exercise and the Brain*. After reviewing more than a thousand papers for this book, I redoubled my efforts to exercise daily despite my overly jammed schedule. I run, use the gym frequently to provide the scaffolding for other activities, and love hiking, and a big part of most vacations is physical activity in the mountains or near the water.

With all my training and access to the greatest minds at Harvard and MIT, the interconnectedness of concepts in this book never really hit me until a chance encounter at a gym in a small town on the eastern coast of northern Michigan. It was here that I met Casey Stutzman, who would send me on a journey I never anticipated.

It was here, while on vacation with my wife, that I put the final pieces of the puzzle together. Alicia's family cottage is fairly "wild." We were surrounded by nature, with the beauty of Lake Huron at our doorstep. We relished sleeping in until we were no longer tired, and it was the perfect environment to connect with each other and disconnect from the world. The only Internet connection involved a drive to the local library.

Of course, exercise is always a must, and wherever we are in the world, Alicia and I seek out a gym or a hike. Being in Harrisville, Michigan, was no exception. It meant a forty-five-minute drive to the biggest city in the area, Alpena, a town of thirteen thousand, in what some would consider the middle of nowhere. By the oddest of coincidences, though, it is the town where Dick was raised, leading me to believe there's something special in the waters of the Great Lakes. It was at the gym connected to the regional hospital rehab center that we met an enthusiastic, cutting-edge trainer, Casey Stutzman. Always expanding his knowledge and introducing the community to the latest development, he was offering Tabata and TRX training well before our fancy Los Angeles and Boston health clubs did. Casey incorporates fun and challenge into each hour, and every year since that first we've looked forward to our week away from the madding crowd in part because it means working with him. After one very challenging class, I told him we had just signed on to write this book, and he immediately piped up about his wife Mary Beth's life-changing experience when she began a new diet—how bad she had been feeling, and how it had saved her life. He had also changed his diet and found that he had a lot more energy, focus, and joy in his life. This inspired me, and I began to both change my diet and make sure I got outside more.

Like many of my colleagues, I had been lowering my carbohydrate and trans fat intake for years, but now I approached this with new vigor and commitment. I concentrated on eliminating all grains from my diet. That meant no more pizzas, crackers, rice, or pasta. Finally, I gave up breads, which I had previously devoured. I added more vegetables and fruits to my usual fare and began to appreciate nuts as an easy, delicious, and filling snack. Also, I started to notice that the cream in my coffee led to a GI reaction, so I stopped that ritual and found that I actually enjoyed black coffee.

In about six weeks, I lost ten pounds; I was close to my weight in high school. I was never overweight but had gotten a little soft around the middle like most people my age.

Now Alicia calls me "faux paleo" because I still have Manhattans when I am in a bar or a restaurant. I'm fanatical about the diet—and it's difficult to be, given my travel schedule, but I do notice that in restaurants and even in airports things are changing a bit, with low-carb options and farm-to-table offerings becoming more prevalent.

I have to watch myself, as I can tend to drop below my high school weight; then I have to splurge on a pasta dinner or take a break from my usual diet for a day or two. I've found that I am now more "mindful" of my food and more open to new tastes and textures; I enjoy greater variety.

I want to emphasize that I am not a paleo zealot, and I am never hungry. I have seen a great change in my energy and mood, and I no longer have the midafternoon slump I used to have before I adopted this extraordinary low-carb diet. I sleep better and have more exercise stamina, and even with my hectic schedule, my energy remains. I am hooked.

At about the same time that my "re-wilding" was taking place, I joined an extraordinary group of researchers and caregivers on a massive project to investigate the effects of "smart living" on 360 adolescents with autism at the Center for Discovery in Harris, New York. There, on a hundred-acre farm in the middle of the Catskills, an amazing program was set up that turned the lives of many of these troubled adolescents around.

Most of the students had been at other programs and arrived on a load of medication, or they'd been in programs that used M&M's as a reward for good behaviors. So they came in overweight for different reasons and experienced a radical change in diet, with much of the food grown on the farm and a total elimination of sugar drinks, trans fat, and treats. They spent as much time outside as possible and spent up to 65 percent of the day moving. Their sleep was closely monitored and the intrusion of the virtual world limited as much as possible. The treatment worked magic, fairly quickly for some and more gradually for others. Disruptive behaviors diminished, weight dropped, on-task time went way up, and socialization improved.

I am lucky enough to have the chance to re-wild at a health spa at the home of Deborah Szekely. She and her husband created Rancho La Puerta about seventy years ago, and it serves as a re-wilding paradise that people flock to from all over the world. It has exercise at the core, followed by diet—mostly grown on the land here, surrounded by beautiful mountains and flowers, where ever-present bunnies play with the many cats. It is nature in all its glory. Most of the one hundred to two hundred guests spend a large chunk of time sleeping, because there is little to do after dark—no phones, no TV, no Internet except in one small area. You can almost feel the oxytocin flowing while you drop stress by letting yourself down, down, down. There's a three-and-a-half-mile hike up Mount Kuchumaa in the morning, followed by a day chock-full of hourly boot camps, circuit training, African dance, Zumba, yoga, Pilates, tai chi, and more. Here, we are members of a new tribe that sometimes lasts beyond the week.

One of the things that has helped me in my own life is having the ever-present awareness of what happens to my body and mind when I don't incorporate the principles of going wild on a daily basis. I look for ways to fit them in, whether I'm on the road or in the middle of city life in Los Angeles or Boston. I always look for a chance to run or walk outside before my day begins. And after a day with patients in Boston, I jog along the Charles River. When in L.A. with Alicia, I take a ten-minute drive to Franklin Canyon for a hike, surrounded by trees, leaving city life behind, or we head to the infamous Santa Monica Stairs, where the faithful climb up and down a set of stairs while taking in the ocean views. I monitor my sleep much more than before, shutting off the digital world early to try to get enough sleep. I keep taking on new challenges: new playful activities, new projects, new ideas to follow. All of this keeps me mindful just as walking in the woods, sorting through the novel environments, demands that I be present.

RICHARD MANNING

I have been instinctively drawn to wilderness my entire life, so you might think I would have figured out its benefits a long time ago and would not have waited until my sixtieth year to realize the potential of living wild to effect my own well-being. And yet here I am, for the first time in my life, fit, reasonably happy, wholly unmedicated, and optimistic. I weigh less than I did in high school, had to buy all new clothes last year, and run marathon trail races in rocks-and-ice terrain. I am sober. All of this is new.

In truth, this turnaround was a long time coming, a product of a lifetime of thinking and living, and yet the process that led to this book, the thinking and living of these ideas, intensely built a critical mass that can be easily read today in my body and bearing. A long-held tenet of my writing life has been that there is no reason to write a book unless the process of doing so irrevocably changes your life. This book exceeded those expectations.

It's difficult to mark the exact moment, the single thread I pulled to begin unraveling it all, but then it is not altogether arbitrary to say it began in earnest with a fifty-dollar heart monitor. The whole process came together in a flash of realization: I was no longer taking steps to solve a problem. Instead, each new step was directed at exploring how much better life could be. I was no longer salving wounds; I was exploring a potential that seemed limitless.

The heart monitor I owe to John. We met in the summer of 2010, by coincidence, introduced by a mutual friend, Bessel van der Kolk. I read *Spark*, which recommended the heart monitor but also introduced many more important matters. At about the same time, I had admitted to myself that I had become fat and sedentary, and so I would resurrect my long-standing, off-again, on-again relationship with running to get back in shape. I did that but was plagued by injuries and meager results, forcing myself into the daily slog as one would swallow a bitter pill. The heart monitor turned out to be the first step in making the pill less bitter. Inexperienced runners try to run too fast, which is torture while you are doing it but especially in the periods between runs. Too much speed too early makes the activity anaerobic, and this heady level of exertion takes a heavy toll, especially on a fat, old body. I was feeling worse, not better, but a heart monitor slows down those of us who push too hard. It governs a sustained aerobic pace, and then you start to feel better.

I was still fat and depressed, clinically so, but I was moving. Then I happened to read Christopher McDougall's *Born to Run*, and it struck a deep and resonant chord in the wild side of my nature. It said nothing so much as this thing, this running I was somehow driven to do, was driven by evolution. Evolution I knew. What's more, the book argued that I didn't need to pound pavement negotiating a roar of ill-mannered traffic. Running could in fact be done on mountain trails, places I know and love. I live in Montana, and wild is all around, a simple fact that has more to do with my well-being than any other.

But there were deeper tones in the chord. I had long thought and written about environmental well-being, especially about the role of agriculture in reshaping the natural world and our bodies. All of this was summarized in my 2005 book *Against the Grain: How Agriculture Has Hijacked Civilization*. This was more than environmental theory for me. I had adopted a low-carbohydrate diet in the midnineties and have all my life been a hunter. The red meat supply in my house has been dominated by venison and, in Montana, elk and the occasional pronghorn antelope since I was a child. Yet, like John, I was not fanatical about my diet, occasionally lapsing into plates of pasta and, probably much more critically, drinking too much wine and beer.

The ideas about evolution and running in McDougall's book were an exact parallel to the arguments I had long made about food and agriculture: that we were damaging our planet and our lives by ignoring the conditions that shaped us through deep human time. Recognizing that parallel almost instantly, it seems in retrospect, brought me to two thunderbolt realizations: if this was true for food and motion, it must be true for other topics, like sleep and state of mind. But more to the point, if these matters were so fundamental and important to our well-being, they were worth more than intellectual investigation and thought: they were worth living.

Now I play a wild card in the story: neurofeedback, which is becoming an accepted method for treating depression, among other things.

Before I knew depression's proper name, I had my own term, even as a kid: the black hand. I saw it settle periodically on my father, that he would for no reason retreat into brooding silence and anger, it seemed for weeks on end. Soon enough, those habits became my own, and I eventually learned to call this state depression. It is often called "the sadness for no reason," which is true enough, but it also thrives well if you give it a reason to do so. I had spent a couple of decades leading up to this book writing especially about global environmental degradation, poverty, and government collapse, but not just writing about them. I am a meat-and-potatoes journalist and so researched these matters by traveling and reporting in some of the more desperate corners of the globe.

All of this made me a solid citizen of the Prozac nation, medicated like many for years at a stretch and advised by physicians that these pills would be a condition of the rest of my life. Then I heard about neurofeedback. This technique is a modification of neuroscience's EEG, but it is not simply a passive measure of brain activity. A therapist designates desired areas of the brain and levels of activity that will open up underused neural pathways. The patient watches a display that looks like a video game and that rewards him for using these neural pathways — simple rewards like brighter colors or richer, louder music. No one knows why the patient is able to, almost at will, activate those pathways to achieve the reward, but he does. And because depression, like many other problems, stems from locking into old pathways, using new ones helps make it abate.

I got better, but the technique here is not the point. Plenty of evidence says there are other ways to get a bit better when you have depression, and Prozac is one of them. In retrospect now, though, three years later and unmedicated all that time, I think the real point is how I treated that improvement, not as a cure but as an opportunity, a bit of breathing room, a platform of strength that could be the basis of what else needed to be done.

I have since come to categorize neurofeedback or medication

or tricks like heart monitors and treadmills as essentially the same: they are not solutions. I am not opposed to using them, but they must be used in the right, limited way, the way a builder might use scaffolding as a necessary support to allow the foundation to be built, but then remove it once the project is on more solid ground. If I had stopped with neurofeedback, I would be stuck inhabiting the scaffolding of a life, not a real life.

I began to think very differently about the whole business, and this was the key shift in attitude, the foundation, the core idea that I hope you can take from this book. I abandoned the notion that I was correcting a deficit or fixing a fault. Take the pill and good to go. It occurred to me that I had taken a small step and felt better, so how much "better" was there, how much better could I feel? Were there limits on this? At the outside, what are the limits on human potential for happiness?

July 25, 2011. Unmedicated. Two hundred and ten pounds. A knee sprain has healed to the point of allowing running. This is the day I have chosen to begin, and I quit drinking. I put on a heart monitor. I have selected a marathon, 26.2 miles, and it is five months hence, on New Year's Eve, in Bellingham, Washington, called Last Chance Marathon. Training begins. This is an easy step to plan. Enough people have done this, and enough research has been done that the prescription for a guy in my position — old, fat, and somewhat out of shape — is a matter of consensus. Stay aerobic. Establish a base mileage you can run comfortably and then increase it by no more than 10 percent a week. One long run a week, long and slow. A couple of rest days each week, with no running at all. Maybe a rest week every three weeks or so. There are apps for this. The process is dialed in, and it works pretty well. I finished the marathon. Slow, but finished. I weighed then 185 pounds—25 pounds lighter than when I had begun training five months before.

But what's next? More races out there. I signed up for a thirty-mile trail run, an ultramarathon, in April 2012. I finished, but I was a wreck, crashed into "the wall," not once but at least twice during that run. The wall is that horrible state of fatigue, disorientation, and confusion that strikes distance runners when they have depleted glucose to below the point that the brain needs. The deal was, I was following the standard advice on nutrition, which included heavy doses of carbohydrates and sugar gels administered during long runs. This remains the boilerplate advice of the sport, and I should have known better, understanding well by then the dangers of a high-carb diet. But I figured athletics were the exception, so I took the standard advice. My experience in that first ultra sent me back to the drawing board and resulted in a happenstance change in direction that I now think was my most important discovery.

The reasoning that fronted my doubts about sugar gels and carb-fueled marathons paralleled that found in *Born to Run*: that we'd evolved running without shoes so didn't need them, and in fact probably did damage by running in heavily padded, stiff, heeled shoes. I had taken that advice from the beginning, trained from the start in minimalist "barefoot" shoes, and it had paid off. It allowed me to gear up for ultramarathons without injury. I am a minimalist runner to this day, and it pleases me simply because I have learned that running with unrestricted feet is more fun. No other way to put it. More giggles and smiles in it.

So what about the sugar gels? Hunter-gatherers didn't suck on foil pouches of corn syrup every half hour or so, just as they didn't have foot coffins. Had anyone thought about this? It turns out that people had, especially a guy named Peter Defty and the researchers Steve Phinney and Jeff Volek. They have developed and advocate an ultra-low-carbohydrate school of nutrition called ketogenic, named for the forms of fat that become your fuel. You limit your body to about fifty grams of carbohydrates a day, the total from maybe an apple and turnips at dinner. Fat is your fuel, and in a matter of a couple of weeks, the body adapts. The brain gets the glucose it needs by making it from spare molecular parts, and the metabolic cycle runs on fat. This is probably a reasonable approximation of the way our ancestors ate most of the time, before agriculture. It is of the same order as other low-carbohydrate diets, such as the paleo diet or the Zone, although it's set off from the former by including dairy products. Dairy and lactose are indeed important considerations in finding your particular path, but I seem to have no lactose issues and I like yogurt and cheese, so this is mine.

My goal in this was to run long races without resorting to sucking on sugar water and without crashing with wild undulations of hyper- and hypoglycemia. It worked. Simply and quickly. I can now run as long as seven hours without any food whatsoever, and I never think twice about it. I have since gone for many runs of four hours or more and have never once crashed into a wall. The conventional nutritional wisdom of the sport says this is not supposed to be, but it is, and it's easy.

Almost immediately after changing the way I ate, weight began to fall off my body, although I was not trying to lose weight, nor did I change my running routine, not a bit. I was then and still am running about forty miles a week. But from day one of my ketogenic diet, I began losing about a pound or two a week, step, step, step, in a straight uninterrupted curve until I hit 160 pounds, and then it plateaued and my weight has not varied by more than a pound or two in a year or so since. I pay no attention whatever to total calorie intake, mileage, or the amount of food I eat. Just no sugars. No grains. No processed foods. Lots of nuts, cheese — fat, runny cheeses — bacon, eggs, sausages, sour cream, and vegetables. No high-glycemic fruits like bananas, but apples, pears, and berries, fresh and simple. Lots of venison. Salmon at least once a week. Grass-finished beef. Not a diet. Just the way I eat, and it makes me happy. I repeat, I do not count calories. I am never, ever hungry.

My new eating habits had another unexpected brain benefit, but there is no way I can say for sure that the sum total of my better life stemmed from food choices. Maybe that was just the last piece, the keystone of the arch. Remember, I'd already made the changes with exercise and was at a point in training when I could expect to see some real benefits from running alone. Truly, I had. But remember, too, that this is not about a single intervention; it's more about building a foundation for life.

Still, it was clear that something had worked: my head was getting better. The depression was gone. These changes were no longer an intervention or therapy or cure. They had become my life.

Indeed, I am giving you the barest of outlines of my life during the period, and much that I have left out may in fact be relevant: my solid marriage; the fact that I live in Montana, a wild place; that my work schedule is my own; that I have a dog who runs with me; and that I play music with friends. All of this is relevant, too, and maybe even more so. This is why we can't serve up recipes for others or even research these matters in epidemiological precision. Lives vary, and through time.

OUR PRESCRIPTION FOR YOU

So now it all comes down to the ultimate question: what do you do about all of this? We hope by now it's clear that only you can answer that question fully. But it should also be just as clear that the weight of the evidence offers some sound advice on how one goes about getting better.

First, find your lever. Remember the lever? Beverly Tatum introduced the concept when she told her story about how correcting her sleep deprivation meant she was soon thinking about her nutrition and exercise; the simple act of shutting off her computer at ten each night led to better health on a number of fronts. For Mary Beth Stutzman, the lever was food, specifically carbohydrates. One thing leads to another, and the lever is the key change in your life that triggers others. The first step. Food, microbiome, movement, sleep, mindfulness, tribe, biophilia— all are pieces of the whole.

We don't know what your lever is, but from our own experience, we'd suggest you begin by looking at food or movement or both. We have talked about many issues here, but food and nutrition have been researched the most, are best understood, are profoundly different today from the food and nutrition that formed us as a species, and are so basic to the human condition that it would be hard to imagine anyone getting better without getting these on the right track.

The good news, though, is that it's pretty easy and straightforward to get them on the right track. Here are the basics, and they are simple enough:

Food. Eat no refined sugar in any form. Fructose contained in fresh fruit is okay if not excessive. But no fruit juices. And pay special attention to avoiding sugar dissolved in water: soft drinks but also energy drinks and juices that contain sugar in any form. Don't eat grain. Don't eat anything made from grain. Get your calories from fat, but avoid manufactured fats, otherwise called trans fats. Don't eat processed food. Don't eat fast food. Look for foods high in omega-3 fats, like eggs, grass-finished beef, cold-water fish like salmon, and nuts. Go for simple fresh fruits and vegetables. Go for variety. Eat as much as you like. Enjoy what you eat.

Movement. Look for a form of exercise you like. That comes first. Something you can do easily and as part of your daily routine. Look for forms that involve a variety of movements, full body, with lots of variability, as in both trail running and CrossFit workouts. The gym is okay in a pinch, but look for ways to get outside. Exercise in nature is exercise squared. Feel the sun but also the wind and the rain in your face. Slog through the snow. Get cold. Get hot. Get thirsty. Gear up and go. And especially look for exercise that involves other people. Move with your tribe. Look also to time-honored forms of movement, like dance, qigong, or tai chi. Buy a heart monitor and know your heart. Begin slowly and carefully. Schedule rest days and even rest weeks. And don't stop experimenting and trying new things until you are having fun, until you look forward to each day's run or dance.

If you do these things, you probably will find a lever. Now follow that process as it leads to other steps. Remember, you are no longer checking boxes or putting out fires or whacking moles; you are exploring potential. This process is iterative. Take a step. Assess. Then take another. This whole business becomes not an assignment or duty—rather, an exploration, a process of discovery. It's guided by rewards. So you've been doing this for a couple of weeks. Do you feel better? Want to feel better still? What else is out there? Does the lever lead to better sleep? Awareness? Better engagement with your tribe? Better brain? It should. In time, and not much time, it should.

There is a frustrating irony buried in this whole topic: The more you understand about what needs to be done, the less you are inclined to write about it. Someone once said (the real source is a matter of some debate) that writing about music is a bit like dancing about architecture. The Zen Buddhists have another way of saying pretty much the same thing: meditation is not something you think about; meditation is something you do. Same with well-being. No matter what ails you, you are not going to think your way out of it or read your way out of it. Living well is something you do.

So then it's not something we can do for you as authors, and this realization, too, is informed by our own experience with wilderness. All our lives, we have hiked trails and learned much about life from the experience. Part of the learning comes with finding one's way. This is the lesson of the wild, and to fully realize it, you need to go to the woods and get lost and find your own way, find a trail that suits you.

But we can take you to the trailhead. That's what we have tried to do here, to reveal that there is a series of pathways leading up the mountain and point you to the trailhead. After that, you are on your own.

Acknowledgments

This book was a true collaboration throughout, so the authors accrued common debts to people who helped that process.

We are, of course, grateful to the people we depended on to share information that helped shape and develop our ideas. We identified a number of those when we introduced and quoted them in the text. We have cited key sources and pivotal books. In addition, a number of other people were generous enough with their time and ideas to grant us interviews and give us information and ideas that we used on background but that were still crucial to this work. They include Jennifer Sacheck, a nutritionist at Tufts University; Frank Forencich, who lives in Portland, Oregon, and writes and thinks about the role of movement and play in people's lives; Daniel Lieberman, who is at Harvard and is famous for his ideas on running and evolution; Dennis Bramble, now retired from the University of Utah, who collaborated on a series of pivotal papers with Lieberman; Bryon Powell, editor of the iRunFar website, which covers the world of trail running; Nikki Kimball, a world-class competitive trail runner and a hunter; Martha Herbert, the researcher at Massachusetts

General Hospital known for establishing connections between nutrition and autism; Richard Deth, a researcher in autism at Northeastern University; and Alan Logan, who, with Eva Selhub, wrote *Your Brain on Nature*.

We also got particular help, support, and access from the staff at the Center for Discovery, the forward-looking autism treatment center in New York. We especially thank Terry Hamlin, Matthew Goodwin, and Jenny Foster.

As is the case with most books, this one was borne along to publication by people in the business. Our agent, Peter Matson of Sterling Lord Literistic, served us well in finding a home for these ideas. Tracy Behar, our editor at Little, Brown, was bold enough to take a chance on a big, unruly idea and helped us develop and refine it into what we present here.

In addition to these debts accrued jointly, we also made some severally.

JOHN RATEY

My debt extends to many people who have contributed to my always asking *why* and *why not!* It began as an undergraduate when I was a philosophy major at Colgate and was pushed to think critically of all that I read or thought I knew. It was the late '60s, and exploration of the self and striving for change was the norm. While there, I also lived as a Zen monk for a month and experienced the benefits of meditation, nature, and being in the present.

Then, in medical school at the University of Pittsburgh, I gravitated to some of the best doctors in the land, who seemed to know everything but were secure enough to say they did not. Their honesty was very apparent despite the orthodoxy of medicine. This learned background of uncertainty grew tenfold at the Massachusetts Mental Health Center, were I was guided by my mentors Les Havens, George Vaillant, Richard Shader, and Allan Hobson, who were giants in their fields yet challenged themselves constantly and were never satisfied with the party line. There I began my lifelong association and great friendship with Edward Hallowell, who has been a source of courage and challenge — which has kept me moving toward this end. This determination allowed me to follow the serendipitous leads to develop my work with aggression, then ADHD, and now Go Wild.

This "go for it" attitude to pursue the new or unpopular allowed me to concentrate on the benefits of exercise for the brain. Here I was backed by the science emanating from people such as Carl Cotman, James Blumenthal, Ken Cooper, and Mark Mattson. This eventually led me to what is now a more global appreciation of the brain, mood, and cognition benefits of good living, when most of my tribe were counting on the next drug to come along to push the field forward. I witnessed firsthand the squabbles over the first "scientific" DSM-III, which reinforced the fact that science was unduly influenced by economic and political issues.

I owe much to Phil Lawler and Paul Zientarski, true pioneers who revolutionized their school's physical education program at District 203 in Naperville. In addition, they enlisted me to try to lead their whole profession to change into a more health-and-wellness-oriented discipline. This mission led me to travel the United States, Canada, and around the world to meet many scholars, educators, and movers and shakers who were aware of the problems of the present and wanted to do something about it. The growing awareness that something was not right with our world and the way we were living led me to challenge my own habits.

Finally, I owe a great deal to Richard Manning, a true iconoclast who is a brilliant and tireless intellectual. He is a throwback to the truth-seeking reporter, and our time spent together continues to guide my thinking and sharpen my constructs. Also I am truly grateful to my dear wife, Alicia Ulrich, who continues to share the ideas and ideals we portray in the book.

RICHARD MANNING

My largest debt in any book is usually on the ledger even before I begin, with the help I get leading up to the genesis of an idea. This one is no exception, and goes way back to the 1980s, when I read a profile of Wes Jackson in *Atlantic* magazine. Jackson, the great agronomist and MacArthur genius, had the idea of reinventing agriculture to make it wild, "farming in nature's image," he called it. This revolutionary notion led me to years of thinking about wildness, food, and the essence of who we are.

In recent years, though, I have been oddly steered through the last of those—human essence—through a chance encounter with Rick van den Pol, who runs the Institute for Educational Research and Service at the University of Montana. My work with Rick soon steered me to the seminal ideas of Bessel van der Kolk and then a chance meeting with John Ratey, van der Kolk's good friend. I am indebted to all of these people, but especially to John, whose vast knowledge of the human brain and groundbreaking ideas on the importance of exercise and movement helped close the circle almost thirty years in the making. Throughout this process, he was inspirational and thoroughly patient with my meanderings and quixotic tendencies, not to mention he deftly corrected some of my more boneheaded and embarrassing errors of fact. He was broad-minded enough to partner with an unrepentant journalist, an ink-stained wretch, and I thank him for it.

My other major debt piled up during every day of the writing of this book and is really owed to a place, not some people — or, more to the point, to the people who preserve the place. During part — the most important part — of almost every day for the months of writing, I ran on a remarkable series of mountain trails that weaves the rim of the valley that holds Helena, Montana. This setting was crucial to the writing process, provided some scenes that appear in this book, and anchored the project in the wilds of the Northern Rockies. During a week John and I spent hammering through the edits on a first draft, we both hit these same trails every day together. The debt here accrues to the Prickly Pear Land Trust, a nonprofit in Helena that has taken it upon itself to acquire the land and easements and do the literal pick-and-shovel work that allows this system to exist and, in the process, makes Helena a biophilic city. Bless them.

This, however, is only a short chunk of trail compared to the long, twisted, and far more treacherous path stretching back to the point where I met a young woman named Tracy Stone, now my wife. Only she knows the full difficulty of the terrain leading to this point, because she has been with me every step of the way, and I couldn't have done it without her. The true paradox here is that all of my other debts are trivial in comparison, yet this one is the easiest to bear.

Index

Index

cardiovascular diseases. *See* heart disease

Carrier, David, 22, 24–27, 121, 205, 212

Carter, Sue, 196–97, 199–201, 204–5, 208–10, 217–18, 235

case study (Mary Beth Stutzman), 65–73, 95–97

cave paintings (Lascaux and Chauvet), 147, 214

Center for Discovery (Harris, New York), 13–15, 219, 249

Center for Investigating Healthy Minds, 155

Centers for Disease Control and Prevention, 228

Chabris, Christopher, 170

children: bad dreams of, 135–36, 137, 143–44

childhood abuse, 221, 228–30; sleeping alone seen as, 144

child-rearing ("cooperative breeding"), 215

detached from nature, 178, 186; and vitamin D deficiency, 185

empathy for helpless young, 36–37

health problems of, 40; autism, 208; obesity, 79, 88, 234–35; type 2 diabetes, 46

lactose tolerance of, 89

mother-child relationship, 12–13, 37, 239; mothers sleeping with infants, 193–94

"orchid" and "dandelion," 238–39

physical education programs for, 195

raising intelligence of, 87

sleep patterns, 141, 143; sleep-deprived, 129

See also teenage

cholesterol, 58, 81–86, 93

chronic obstructive pulmonary (lung) disease (COPD), 40, 104–5

circadian rhythms, 141, 148–49

Cisco Systems, 129

civilization, agriculture and, 73. *See also* agriculture; "disease of civilization"

cognitive psychology, 153

cognitive behavior therapy, 161, 224

cognitive skills: exercise and, 93, 105–7; among young people, 108–11

impairment of, in aging, 106–7

IQ, 109

sleep and, 129–31

See also brain, the; memory

Cohen, Mark Nathan, 64

conditioning, 176–77

"cooperative breeding," 215. *See also* children

Copernicus, Nicolaus, vii–viii

Cordain, Loren, 64

corn (maize), 50. *See also* grains

corn syrup. *See* fructose

cortisol: increased by sleep deprivation, 146

stress and, 146, 161–62, 164, 165, 179

cost of transport. *See* energy efficiency

"Counterclockwise" experiment, 169–70

Crisco, 84

Crohn's disease, 54, 71–72

CrossFit exercise. *See* exercise

dairy products, 88–90, 257

Dalai Lama (Tenzin Gyatso), 155

dance, 37, 231, 250, 260

Darwin, Charles, 18

Davidson, Richard, 153–60, 167–68

Dawkins, Richard, 188

De Dreu, Cartsen, 209–10

Defty, Peter, 257

dehydration, 206

dementia, 106–7

Denisovan man, 31

dental cavities, 44, 48

depression, 4, 5, 40, 179, 256

artificial light and, 149

clinical, omega-3 shortage, and trans fats and, 85–86

exercise and, 103–4, 109–10, 246

meditation and, 157, 161

neurofeedback as treatment, 253

sleep deprivation and, 131

smiling and, 223–24

urban vs. natural settings and, 183

De Revolutionibus (Copernicus), vii–viii

diabetes, 149, 236

type 1, 54, 77

type 2, 44, 51, 73, 80, 104; among children, 45–46

Index

Index

Judeo-Christian tradition, 6
junk food, 57–58
Ju/wasi. *See* !Kung or San people

Kabat-Zinn, Jon, 160
Kalahari Desert, 44, 92, 125, 196, 218
Kepler space observatory, vii–viii
ketogenic (low-carb) diet. *See* nutrition
Keys, Ancel, 81–82, 84, 85–86
koala bears, 97
Konner, Melvin, 64
Korean research, 181, 183
Koyukon people (Alaska), 151–53, 184
!Kung or San people (Ju/wasi, Kalahari
　　Desert), 12, 15, 44, 92–93, 125, 196
　　as prey, 138, 141, 218–19, 225

lactose tolerance/intolerance, 21, 89–90
Lancet, The (medical journal), 40
Langer, Ellen, 169–71
Last Chance Marathon, 255–56
leaky gut, 95–96
Leary, Timothy, 154
"lever effect," 134, 187, 259
Lieberman, Daniel, 22–25
Liebling, A. J., 241
life expectancy, 47. *See also* aging
light: artificial, 150; and diseases, 149
　　and sleep, 147–50, 178
　　sunlight, 149
　　ultraviolet, 184
lipoproteins (LDL and HDL), 82–84
Llinás, Rodolfo, 100
locomotion. *See* movement
Logan, Alan C., 179, 183, 187, 194
longevity. *See* aging
Louv, Richard, 178
low birth weight. *See* obesity
low carbohydrate (ketogenic) diet. *See*
　　nutrition
lying, 34–35

malaria, 21, 40, 41, 55–56
manic-depressive disorder, 160. *See also*
　　depression
Manning, Richard, 15, 152, 219, 245,
　　247, 251–59
marathons, 190, 206, 246, 255–56

margarine, 84, 85
Masai people (Kenya), 8
Massachusetts Mental Health
　　Center, 244
Mayberg, Helen, 161
Mayo Clinic, 105, 107, 108
McBride, Willie, 190
McClelland, David, 154
McDougall, Christopher, 25, 114–15,
　　252–53
McEwen, Bruce S., 238
McGilchrist, Iain, 225
measles, 54
meat-eating. *See* nutrition
meditation, 153–60, 165–66, 231, 261
　　and anxiety, 157
　　and the brain, 167–68; brain-body
　　　connection, 157
　　and depression, 157, 161
　　and empathy, 156, 168
　　endocrine analogue for, 164
　　and immune response, 157, 166
　　See also mindfulness
melatonin, 148, 178
memory: improvement of, 106–7
　　PTSD a disease of, 132
　　See also cognitive skills
menarche, age of, 52–53
mental retardation, 160
metabolism, 50, 68, 73, 257
　　metabolic syndrome, 51, 73, 80, 81
microbes, 56–57, 186. *See also* bacteria
Micronesian aborigines, 44
mindfulness, 15, 152, 161, 169–71, 245.
　　See also meditation
Mind's Own Physician, The (Kabat-Zinn
　　and Davidson), 160–61
mirror neurons, 34, 35, 113
"missing link," 18–19. *See also* evolution
MIT (Massachusetts Institute of
　　Technology), 219, 247
monogamy. *See* bonding, social
Moral Molecule, The (Zak), 203
morphine, 183
mortality rate, 47
mother-child relationship. *See* children
Mothers and Others (Hrdy), 215
Mount Kilimanjaro, 122

273

About the Authors

JOHN J. RATEY, MD, is a clinical associate professor of psychiatry at Harvard Medical School. He is the author or coauthor of numerous bestselling and groundbreaking books, including *Spark, Driven to Distraction,* and *A User's Guide to the Brain.* He lives in Cambridge, Massachusetts, and Los Angeles.

RICHARD MANNING is an award-winning journalist. He is the author of nine books, including *Against the Grain* and *One Round River.* His work has appeared in *The Best American Science and Nature Writing 2010, Harper's,* the *New York Times,* the *Los Angeles Times,* and other publications. He lives in Helena, Montana.